UNITED NATIONS CONFERENCE ON TRADE

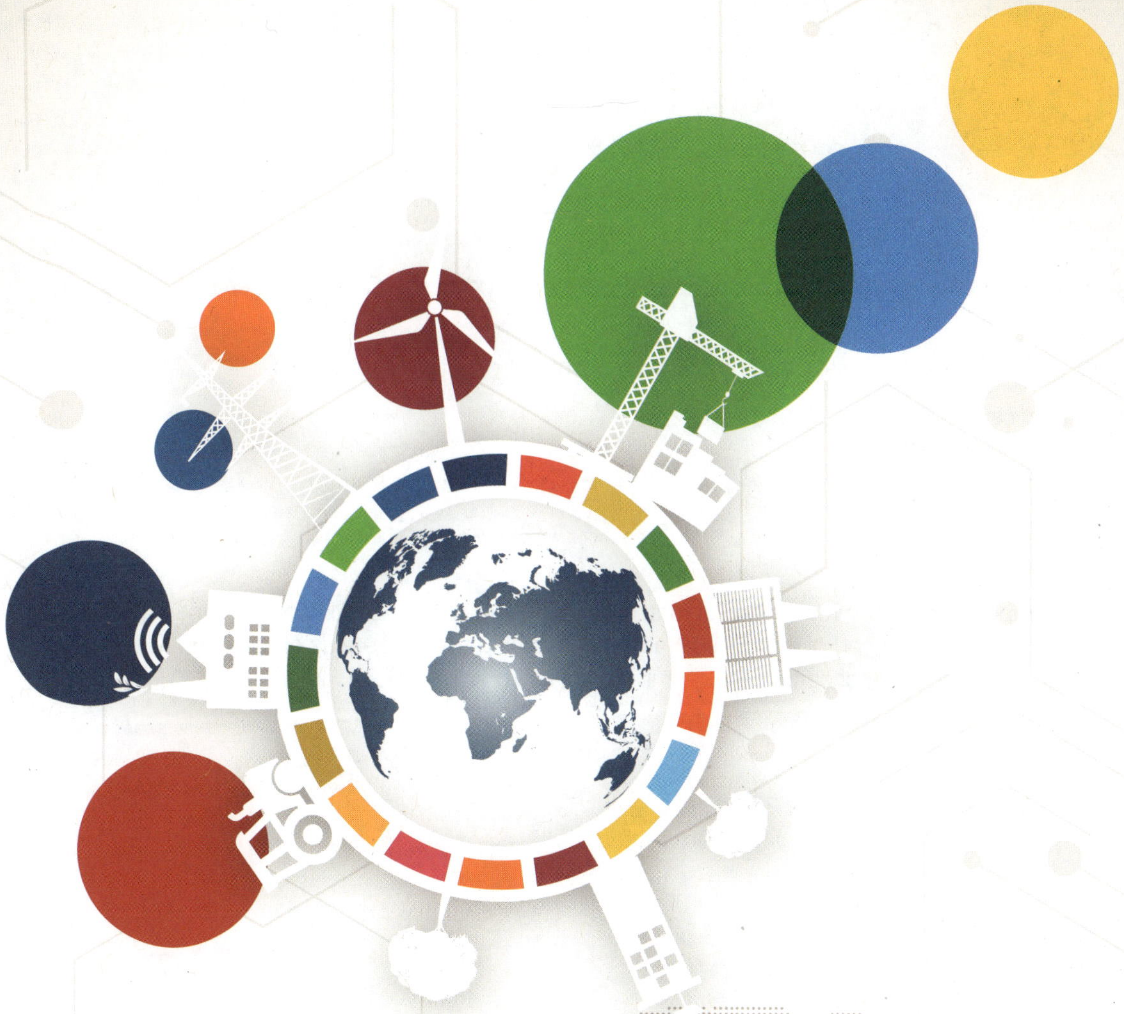

THE LEAST DEVELOPED COUNTRIES REPORT 2020

Productive capacities for the new decade

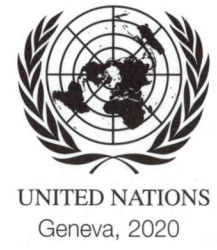

UNITED NATIONS
Geneva, 2020

The Least Developed Countries Report **2020**

© 2020, United Nations
All rights reserved worldwide

Requests to reproduce excerpts or to photocopy should be addressed to the Copyright Clearance Center at copyright.com.

All other queries on rights and licences, including subsidiary rights, should be addressed to:

United Nations Publications, 300 East 42nd Street,
New York, New York 10017,
United States of America

Email: publications@un.org
Website: un.org/publications

The designations employed and the presentation of material on any map in this work do not imply the expression of any opinion whatsoever on the part of the United Nations concerning the legal status of any country, territory, city or area or of its authorities, or concerning the delimitation of its frontiers or boundaries.

United Nations publication issued by the United Nations Conference on Trade and Development.

UNCTAD/LDC/2020

ISBN: 978-92-1-112998-4

eISBN: 978-92-1-005384-6

ISSN: 0257-7550

eISSN: 2225-1723

Sales No. E.21.II.D.2

Acknowledgements

The Least Developed Countries Report 2020 was prepared by UNCTAD. The report was written by Rolf Traeger (team leader), Benjamin Mattondo Banda, Matfobhi Riba and Giovanni Valensisi, with the assistance of Kyeonghun Joo, Tobias Lechner, Anja Slany, Carlotta Schuster and Komi Tsowou. The work was carried out under the overall supervision of Paul Akiwumi, Director of the UNCTAD Division for Africa, Least Developed Countries and Special Programmes, and Junior Roy Davis, Head of the Policy Analysis and Research Branch.

A virtual meeting was held 24–25 June 2020 to conduct a peer review of the report, chapter by chapter and as a whole. It brought together specialists in the fields of development policies and strategies, agriculture and rural development, industrial development, science, technology and innovation, labour market and policies, entrepreneurship and human rights. The participants were: Martin Bell (University of Sussex), Andrzej Bolesta (United Nations Economic and Social Commission for Asia and the Pacific), Mafa Evaristus Chipeta (independent expert in agricultural development), Michael Danquah (United Nations University – World Institute for Development Economics), Charles Gore (United Nations Research Institute for Social Development), Noelia Gracia Nebra (International Organization for Standardization), Nobuya Haraguchi (United Nations Industrial Development Organization), Poorva Karkare (European Centre of Development), Jodie Keane (Overseas Development Institute), Haile Kibret (United Nations Development Programme), Massimiliano La Marca (International Labour Organization), Oliver Morrisey (University of Nottingham), Ahmad Mukhtar (Food and Agriculture Organization of the United Nations), Viviana Muñoz Tellez (South Centre), Arsène Nkama (University of Yaoundé II), Irmgard Nübler (International Labour Organization), Chukwuka Onyekwena (Centre for the Study of the Economies of Africa), Naylin Oo (United Nations Economic and Social Commission for Asia and the Pacific), Oliver Paddison (United Nations Economic and Social Commission for Asia and the Pacific), Martin Phangaphanga (University of Malawi), Annalisa Primi (Organisation for Economic Co-operation and Development), Raymond Saner (Centre for Socio-Eco-Nomic Development), Yusuke Tateno (United Nations Economic and Social Commission for Asia and the Pacific), Dirk Willem Te Velde (Overseas Development Institute), Taffere Tesfachew (Committee for Development Policy), Diego Valadares Vasconcelos Neto (Office of the United Nations High Commissioner for Human Rights), Rolph van der Hoeven (International Institute of Social Studies), Franck Van Rompaey (United Nations Industrial Development Organization), Kwami Ossadzifo Wonyra (University of Kara), as well as the members of the report team and the following UNCTAD colleagues: Lisa Borgatti, Olivier Combe, Mussie Delelegn, Piergiuseppe Fortunato, Stefanie Garry, Kamlman Kalotay, Malou Le Gaet, Jörg Mayer, Moritz Meier-Ewert, Kuena Molapo, Alberto Munisso, Rostand Ngadjie-Siani, Patrick Osakwe, Dan Teng'O and Anida Yupari Aguado.

Matthias Brückner and Márcia Tavares (CDP Secretariat, United Nations Department of Economic and Social Affairs) provided comments on the "What are the least developed countries" section (pp.x–xii).

Constantine Obura Bartel prepared a background paper for the report. Mark Bloch edited the text.

Nadège Hadjemian designed the cover and the infographics, with the assistance of Antoine Andary. Juan Carlos Korol did the overall layout, graphics and desktop publishing.

The Least Developed Countries Report **2020**

Note

Material in this publication may be freely quoted or reprinted, but full acknowledgement is requested. A copy of the publication containing the quotation or reprint should be sent to the UNCTAD secretariat at:

Palais des Nations, CH-1211 Geneva 10, Switzerland.

The overview of this report can also be found on the Internet as a separate document, in all six official languages of the United Nations, at: www.unctad.org/ldcr

Main text

The term "dollars" ($) refers to United States dollars unless otherwise specified.

The term "billion" signifies 1,000 million.

Annual rates of growth and changes refer to compound rates.

Exports are valued "free on board" and imports, on a "cost, insurance, freight" basis, unless otherwise specified.

Use of a dash (–) between dates representing years, e.g. 1981–1990, signifies the full period involved, including the initial and final years. A slash (/) between two years, e.g. 1991/92, signifies a fiscal or crop year.

Throughout the report, the term "least developed country" refers to a country included in the United Nations list of least developed countries.

The terms "country" and "economy", as appropriate, also refer to territories or areas.

Tables

Two dots (..) indicate that the data are not available or are not separately reported.

One dot (.) indicates that the data are not applicable.

A dash (–) indicates that the amount is nil or negligible.

Details and percentages do not necessarily add up to totals, because of rounding.

Figures

Some figures contain country names abbreviated using ISO (International Organization for Standardization) alpha-3 codes, which can be consulted at: https://www.iso.org/obp/ui/#search.

Contents

Note iv
Classifications ix
What are the least developed countries? x
Abbreviations xiii
Foreword xv
Overview I

CHAPTER 1   The COVID-19 crisis in LDCs 1

    A. Introduction 3
    B. Impacts of COVID-19 on LDCs 3
    C. LDC vulnerabilities 14
    D. The continued relevance of the LDC category 17
    E. Objectives and structure of this report 22

CHAPTER 2   Productive capacities and structural transformation: Giving concrete form to concepts 25

    A. Introduction 27
    B. The concept of productive capacities 27
    C. Structural transformation 30
    D. Recent patterns of structural transformation in LDCs 33
    E. LDCs' productive capacities in the new decade 47

CHAPTER 3   Measuring productive capacities: LDCs' progress towards sustainable development 51

    A. Introduction 53
    B. The UNCTAD productive capacities index 54
    C. Assessing the progress of LDCs towards IPoA goals 61
    D. Conclusion 86
    ANNEX: A technical introduction to the UNCTAD Productive Capacities Index 89

CHAPTER 4   Transition to the digital economy: technological capabilities as drivers of productivity 93

    A. Introduction 95
    B. Agriculture 101
    C. Manufacturing and services 109
    D. Case study synthesis 118
    E. Conclusions 119

CHAPTER 5   Policies to develop productive capacities in the new decade 123

    A. Introduction 125
    B. Putting productive capacities at the core 126
    C. What can the international community do? 138

References 147

Figures

1.1	Impact of COVID-19, by country group	5
1.2	LDC export vulnerabilities	9
1.3	Remittances as a share of GDP, selected LDCs	11
1.4	LDC poverty estimates in 2020, pre- and post- COVID-19, by poverty line	14
1.5	Economic Vulnerability Index, by country group, 2000–2020, selected years	16
1.6	LDC share of world merchandise exports, total and by product group, 2000–2019	18
1.7	LDC population and share of world total, 2000–2020	19
1.8	LDC population structure by age class	20
1.10	LDC share of world population and of world poor, by international poverty line	21
1.9	Average expansion in LDC labour force, 2011–2030	21
2.1	Productive capacities and structural transformation	28
2.2	Internet user gender gap, 2013 and 2019	37
2.3	Distribution of labour by major category of service sectors, by country groups, 2019	41
2.4	Growth of labour productivity, 2001–2017	43
2.5	Labour productivity growth and pace of structural transformation	44
2.6	Sectoral dispersion of labour productivity by contry groups, 2001–2017, selected years	44
2.7	LDCs / ODCs labour productivity ratio by country groups, 2000–2017	45
3.1	The PCI thematic structure	54
3.2	Clustering of LDC productive capacities, ranked by cluster-medians, 2001, 2011, 2018	57
3.3	Economic development (per capita income) and Productive Capacities Index, 2018	59
3.4	PCI of selected economies by income group and LDC average, 2000–2018	60
3.5	GDP growth rates for developing economies	61
3.6	GNI per capita gap of least developed countries in comparison to other developing countries, average in current US dollars	62
3.7	Hodrick-Prescott filter trend growth rates of GDP per capita and real GDP	63
3.8	Stochastic production frontier 2018	65
3.9	Marginal change in per capita income, per unit of productive capacity utilization	66
3.10	Change in employment and agriculture value added, per cent: 2000–2008	67
3.11	Prevalence of moderate or severe food insecurity in the adult population, 2015–2018	68
3.12	Agriculture value added per worker in dollars, at 2010 prices	69
3.13	Gross fixed capital investment and value added in agriculture	70
3.14	LDC exports as a share of world exports	71
3.15	LDC export concentration and Productive Capacities Index, 2000 and 2018	72
3.16	Commodity export growth rates for LDCs: 2000–2018	73
3.17	Children out of school	75
3.18	Gross secondary enrollment and productive capacities	76
3.19	Proportion of the urban population living in slums	78
3.20	Human capital component of the Productive Capacities Index, LDCs and ODCs	79
3.21	Economic and environmental vulnerability index, 2011 and 2019	81
3.22	Liberia: Economic vulnerability and subindices, 2011–2020	82

3.23	Savings, investment and external resource gaps	83
3.24	External resource gaps as a percentage of GDP, 2011–2014 and 2015–2018	84
3.25	Population of displaced people in least developed countries, 2018	85
3.26	Worldwide governance index rankings and the UNCTAD PCI	87
4.1	Production technologies: From the first industrial revolution to the fourth	96
4.2	A representation of the digital economy	97
4.3	The capabilities escalator	98
4.4	Agriculture Total Factor Productivity index	102
4.5	Agriculture orientation index on government expenditure in agriculture	104
4.6	Agriculture 4.0 technology map	105
4.7	Digital agriculture use cases in Myanmar	106
4.8	Key M2M applications	107
4.9	Mobile-data-and-voice basket in PPP$, 2019	110
4.10	Industry 4.0 technologies by most profound impact	111
4.11	Regional trade facilitation scores by dimension	117
5.1	Summary of fiscal measures in response to COVID-19 (selected countries)	129

Tables

1.1	Health system indicators, per country group	4
2.1	Indicators of digital infrastructure and internet use by country groups, 2000–2018, selected years	35
2.3	Sectoral composition of output and employment by country groups, 2001–2017, selected years	39
2.2	Pace of structural change by country groups, 2001–2017	39
2.4	Average annual growth of labour productivity, 2001–2017	42
2.5	Frontier technologies	48
3.1	Productive capacities index scores of individual least developed countries and other country groups, average, 2011–2018	56
3.2	Productive capacities by country group, medians 2011 and 2018	58
3.3	Partial elasticities of GDP per capita to productive capacity components based on the stochastic frontier estimates	66
3.4	Pairwise correlations between components of the productive capacities index and major export commodities	74
3.5	Country groups by graduation status and criteria	80
3.6	Correlation between economic vulnerability and productive capacities	81
4.1	Business model features and barriers	109
4.2	Pervasive technologies and likely future impacts	112

Annex Tables

3.1	Indicators used in constructing the PCI and its subindices	90

Boxes

2.1 Measuring the pace of structural transformation 38
3.1 Stochastic frontier analysis at a glance.. 64
3.1 Digital technologies and the gender gap in agricultural productivity 103
4.2 3D Printing and manufacturing in LDCs 113
5.1 Using the PCI to identify common challenges in productive capacity development..................................... 137

Box figures

5.1 Visualization of LDC clustering according to PCI dimensions, 2018... 137

Box Tables

5.1 Mean values of Productive Capacity Index dimensions, within-cluster 137

Productive Capacities for the New Decade

Classifications

▶ LEAST DEVELOPED COUNTRIES

Unless otherwise specified, in this report, the least developed countries are classified according to a combination of geographical and structural criteria. The small island least developed countries that are geographically in Africa or Asia are thus grouped with Pacific islands to form the island least developed countries group, due to their structural similarities. Haiti and Madagascar, which are regarded as large island States, are grouped together with the African least developed countries.

The resulting groups are as follows:

African least developed countries and Haiti:

Angola, Benin, Burkina Faso, Burundi, Central African Republic, Chad, Democratic Republic of the Congo, Djibouti, Eritrea, Ethiopia, Gambia, Guinea, Guinea-Bissau, Haiti, Lesotho, Liberia, Madagascar, Malawi, Mali, Mauritania, Mozambique, Niger, Rwanda, Senegal, Sierra Leone, Somalia, South Sudan, Sudan, Togo, Uganda, United Republic of Tanzania, Zambia.

Asian least developed countries:

Afghanistan, Bangladesh, Bhutan, Cambodia, Lao People's Democratic Republic, Myanmar, Nepal, Yemen.

Island least developed countries:

Comoros, Kiribati, Sao Tome and Principe, Solomon Islands, Timor-Leste, Tuvalu, Vanuatu.

▶ OTHER GROUPS OF COUNTRIES AND TERRITORIES

Developed countries:

Andorra, Australia, Austria, Belgium, Bermuda, Bulgaria, Canada, Croatia, Cyprus, Czechia, Denmark, Estonia, Finland, France, Germany, Greece, Greenland, Hungary, Iceland, Ireland, Israel, Italy, Japan, Latvia, Lithuania, Luxembourg, Malta, Netherlands, New Zealand, Norway, Poland, Portugal, Romania, San Marino, Slovakia, Slovenia, Spain, Sweden, Switzerland, United Kingdom of Great Britain and Northern Ireland, United States of America, Holy See, Faroe Islands, Gibraltar, Saint Pierre and Miquelon.

Other developing countries:

All developing countries (according to UNCTAD) that are not least developed countries:

Algeria, American Samoa, Anguilla, Antigua and Barbuda, Argentina, Aruba, Bahamas, Bahrain, Barbados, Belize, Plurinational State of Bolivia, Bonaire, Sint Eustatius and Saba, Botswana, Bouvet Island, Brazil, British Indian Ocean Territory, British Virgin Islands, Brunei Darussalam, Cabo Verde, Cameroon, Cayman Islands, Chile, China, Hong Kong SAR, Macao SAR, Taiwan Province of China , Colombia, Congo, Cook Islands, Costa Rica, Côte d'Ivoire, Cuba, Curaçao, Dominica, Dominican Republic, Ecuador, Egypt, El Salvador, Equatorial Guinea, Eswatini, Falkland Islands (Malvinas), Fiji, French Polynesia, French Southern Territories, Gabon, Ghana, Grenada, Guam, Guatemala, Guyana, Honduras, India, Indonesia, Islamic Republic of Iran, Iraq, Jamaica, Jordan, Kenya, Democratic People's Republic of Korea , Republic of Korea , Kuwait, Lebanon, Libya, Malaysia, Maldives, Marshall Islands, Mauritius, Mexico, Federated States of Micronesia, Mongolia, Montserrat, Morocco, Namibia, Nauru, Netherlands Antilles, New Caledonia, Nicaragua, Nigeria, Niue, Northern Mariana Islands, Oman, Pacific Islands, Trust Territory, Pakistan, Palau, Panama, Papua New Guinea, Paraguay, Peru, Philippines, Pitcairn, Qatar, Saint Barthélemy, Saint Helena, Saint Kitts and Nevis, Saint Lucia, Saint Martin (French part), Saint Vincent and the Grenadines, Samoa, Saudi Arabia, Seychelles, Singapore, Sint Maarten (Dutch part), South Africa, South Georgia and South Sandwich Islands, Sri Lanka, State of Palestine, Suriname, Syrian Arab Republic, Thailand, Tokelau, Tonga, Trinidad and Tobago, Tunisia, Turkey, Turks and Caicos Islands, United Arab Emirates, United States Minor Outlying Islands, Uruguay, Bolivarian Republic of Venezuela, Viet Nam, Wallis and Futuna Islands, Western Sahara, Zimbabwe.

What are the least developed countries?

▶ 47 countries

As of 2020, forty-seven countries are designated by the United Nations as least developed countries (LDCs). These are: Afghanistan, Angola, Bangladesh, Benin, Bhutan, Burkina Faso, Burundi, Cambodia, the Central African Republic, Chad, the Comoros, the Democratic Republic of the Congo, Djibouti, Eritrea, Ethiopia, the Gambia, Guinea, Guinea-Bissau, Haiti, Kiribati, the Lao People's Democratic Republic, Lesotho, Liberia, Madagascar, Malawi, Mali, Mauritania, Mozambique, Myanmar, Nepal, the Niger, Rwanda, Sao Tome and Principe, Senegal, Sierra Leone, Solomon Islands, Somalia, South Sudan, the Sudan, Timor-Leste, Togo, Tuvalu, Uganda, the United Republic of Tanzania, Vanuatu, Yemen and Zambia..

▶ Every 3 years

The list of LDCs is reviewed every three years by the Committee for Development Policy, a group of independent experts that report to the Economic and Social Council of the United Nations. Following a triennial review of the list, the Committee may recommend, in its report to the Economic and Social Council, countries for addition to the list or graduation from LDC status.

Between 2017 and 2020 the Committee for Development Policy undertook a comprehensive review of the LDC criteria and established the following three criteria, starting with the triennial review scheduled for February 2021:

(a) A **per capita income** criterion, based on a three-year average estimate of the gross national income (GNI) per capita, with a lower threshold of $1,018 for identifying possible cases of addition to the list and a higher threshold of $1,222 for possible cases of graduation;

(b) A **human assets index (HAI)**, consisting of two sub-indices: a health sub-index and an education sub-index. The health sub-index contains three indicators: (i) under-five mortality rate; (ii) maternal mortality ratio; (iii) and prevalence of stunting. The education sub-index contains three indicators: (i) gross secondary school enrolment ratio; (ii) adult literacy rate; and (iii) gender parity index for gross secondary school enrolment.

(c) The **economic and environmental vulnerability index**, consisting of two sub-indices: an economic vulnerability sub-index and an environmental vulnerability sub-index. The economic vulnerability sub-index contains four indicators: (i) share of agriculture, hunting forestry and fishing in GDP; (ii) remoteness and landlockedness; (iii) merchandise export concentration; and (iv) instability of exports of goods and services. The environmental vulnerability sub-index contains four indicators: (i) share of population in low elevated coastal zones; (ii) share of the population living in drylands; (iii) instability of agricultural production; and (iv) victims of disasters.

For all three criteria, different thresholds are used to identify additions to the list of LDCs and graduations from LDC status. A country qualifies to be added to the list if it meets the addition thresholds on all three criteria, and does not have a population greater than 75 million. Qualification for addition to the list effectively leads to LDC status only if the government of the country in question accepts this status. A country normally qualifies for graduation from LDC status if it has met graduation thresholds under at least two of the three criteria in at least two consecutive triennial reviews of the LDC list. However, if the three-year average per capita GNI of an LDC has risen to a level at least double the graduation threshold ($2,444), and if this performance is considered durable, the country will be deemed eligible for graduation, regardless of its score under the other two criteria. This rule is commonly referred to as the "income-only" graduation rule.

▶ Five countries have graduated from least developed country status:

- **Botswana** in December 1994;
- **Cabo Verde** in December 2007;
- **Maldives** in January 2011;
- **Samoa** in January 2014; and
- **Equatorial Guinea** in June 2017.

In a resolution adopted in December 2013, the General Assembly of the United Nations endorsed the 2012 recommendation of the Committee for Development Policy to graduate **Vanuatu** by December 2017. In December 2015, the General Assembly decided, on an exceptional basis, to delay to December 2020 the graduation of Vanuatu from LDC status due to the setback for the country triggered by Tropical Cyclone Pam in March 2015.

The 2015 recommendation of the Committee for Development Policy to graduate **Angola** was endorsed by the General Assembly in February 2016 through a resolution which set February 2021 as the date of the country's graduation from LDC status. This decision was an exceptional measure which took into account the high vulnerability of the commodity-dependent Angolan economy to price fluctuations.

In a June 2018 resolution, the Economic and Social Council recalled the Committee's 2012 recommendation to graduate **Tuvalu** from LDC status and deferred, to "no later than" 2021, the Economic and Social Council's consideration of the question of the country's graduation, after having previously deferred the consideration in 2012, 2013 and 2015. In the same resolution, the Council also deferred its consideration of the graduation of **Kiribati** to "no later than" 2021, after the Committee for Development Policy recommended the reclassification of Kiribati, to graduate from least developed country status, in its March 2018 review of the list of the least developed countries.

Also recommended for graduation in the 2018 review of the LDC category were **Bhutan**, **Sao Tome and Principe** and **Solomon Islands**. The General Assembly endorsed these three recommendations in December 2018. Bhutan is scheduled to graduate in 2023, while Sao Tome and Principe and Solomon Islands are scheduled to graduate in 2024. At the same time, two LDCs (**Nepal** and **Timor-Leste**), which the Committee for Development Policy found to have met the graduation criteria for the second time in 2018, were not recommended for graduation owing to concerns about the sustainability of their development progress. The Committee deferred its decision on recommendations for the graduation of these two countries to the 2021 triennial review.

Lastly, in the 2018 review of the list of LDCs, three Asian countries were found pre-eligible for graduation from this status: **Bangladesh**, the **Lao People's Democratic Republic** and **Myanmar**. While the pre-eligibility for reclassification of the Lao People's Democratic Republic is grounded in improved performance exceeding two of the three graduation thresholds, as in most previous graduation cases (per capita income and human assets), Bangladesh and Myanmar are the first historical cases of pre-qualification for graduation through heightened performance under all three graduation criteria (per capita income, human assets and economic vulnerability).

The Least Developed Countries Report **2020**

▶ The COVID-19 crisis and graduation

The world economic crisis brought by the COVID-19 pandemic may affect the above-mentioned graduation schedule.

For those LDCs whose case will be examined in the triennial review of 2021 for possible graduation (Bangladesh, Lao People's Democratic Republic, Myanmar, Nepal and Timor-Leste) the Committee for Development Policy will, in line with established procedures, take into account not only the LDC criteria (which will be based on data until 2019), but also other indicators, analyses and views of the country concerned (which reflect the impacts of the crisis). The Committee will adopt the same approach in its consideration of other countries which may pre-qualify for graduation in 2021 and may be recommended for graduation in 2024.

The Committee will consider the adverse impacts of the world economic crisis brought on by the COVID-19 pandemic on the countries with an already agreed date for graduation (Angola, Bhutan, Sao Tome and Principe, Solomon Islands and Vanuatu) during its annual monitoring of graduated and graduating countries.

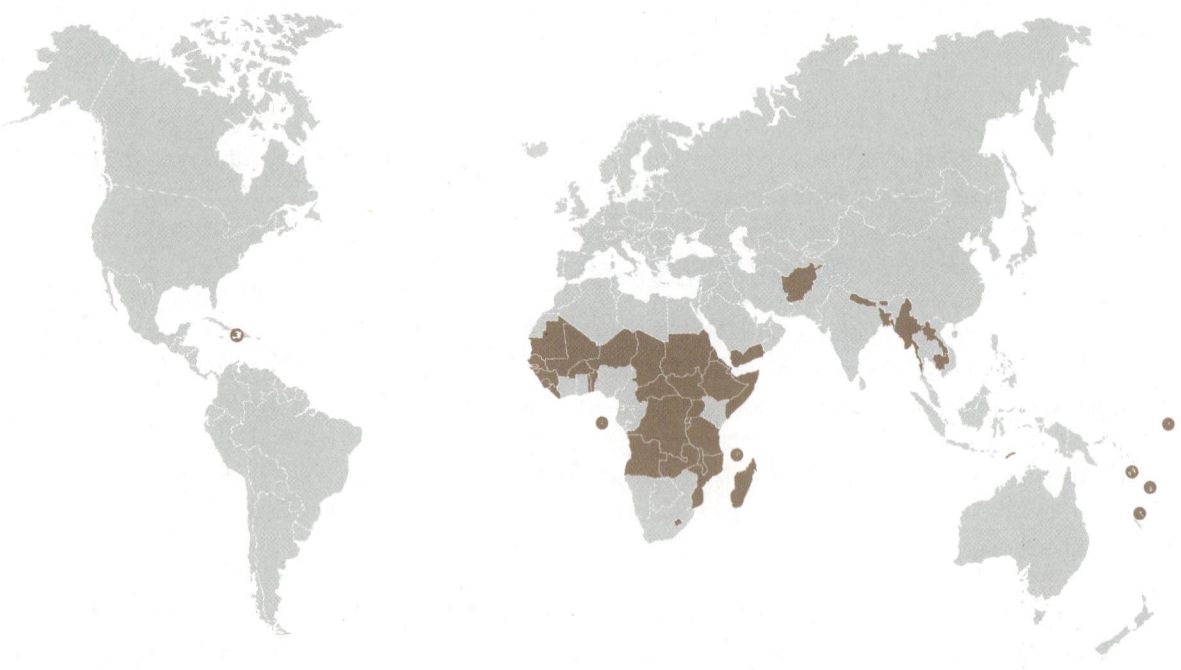

Abbreviations

4IR	Fourth Industrial Revolution
AfCFTA	African Continental Free Trade Area
AfDB	African Development Bank
AGOA	African Growth and Opportunity Act
Agri VAS	agricultural value-added service
ASEAN	Association of Southeast Asian Nations (ASEAN)
AUC	African Union Commission
B2B	business to business
B2C	business to consumer
BPoA	Brussels Programme of Action
CDC	Centre for Disease Control and Prevention
CDP	Committee for Development Policy
CSR	corporate social responsibility
D4Ag	digitalization for agriculture
DAC	Development Assistance Committee
EAC	East African Community
EVI	Economic and Environmental Vulnerability Index
FAO	Food and Agriculture Organization of the United Nations
FDI	foreign direct investment
GDP	gross domestic product
GNI	gross national income
GSMA	Global System for Mobile Communications
GVC	global value chain
HALE	health-adjusted life expectancy
HIV/AIDS	human immunodeficiency virus and acquired immune deficiency syndrome
ICTs	information and communication technologies
IDA	International Development Association
ILO	International Labour Organization
IMF	International Monetary Fund
IPoA	Istanbul Programme of Action
IPR	intellectual property right
ISM	international support measure
LDC	least developed country
LMICs	low- and middle-income countries
MFN	most-favoured nation
MSEs	micro- and small-enterprises
MSMEs	micro, small and medium-sized enterprises
MVA	manufacturing value added
NTM	non-tariff measure
ODA	official development assistance
ODCs	other developing countries
OECD	Organisation for Economic Co-operation and Development
PCI	Productive Capacities Index
PPP	public-private partnership
PwC	PricewaterhouseCoopers
R&D	research and development
SAFTA	South Asian Free Trade Area
SDGs	Sustainable Development Goals
SDT	special and differential treatment
SEZ	special economic zone
SIDS	small island developing States
SMEs	small- and medium-sized enterprises
SPS	sanitary and phytosanitary
STEM	science, technology, engineering and mathematics
STI	science, technology and innovation
TFP	total factor productivity
TRIPS	Agreement on Trade-Related Aspects of Intellectual Property Rights
UAV	unmanned aerial vehicle
UN DESA	United Nations Department of Economic and Social Affairs
UNECA	United Nations Economic Commission for Africa
UNFCCC	United Nations Framework Convention on Climate Change
UNHCR	United Nations High Commissioner for Refugees
UNIDO	United Nations Industrial Development Organization
UNLDC-V	Fifth United Nations Conference on the Least Developed Countries
UN-OHRLLS	United Nations Office of the High Representative for the Least Developed Countries, Landlocked Developing Countries and Small Island Developing States
WEF	World Economic Forum
WTO	World Trade Organization
WTTC	World Travel & Tourism Council

Foreword

The least developed countries are suffering the ruinous economic consequences of the coronavirus disease of 2019 (COVID-19) pandemic. As a result of the global economic downturn and the restrictive measures adopted, the least developed countries today are undergoing the worst recession in 30 years. Their already low standards of living are falling. Their stubbornly high poverty rates are rising further, reversing the slow improvement they had achieved prior to the pandemic. Progress towards achievements on nutrition, health and education are being undone by the onslaught of the crisis.

The least developed countries have deployed their limited means to counter the recession, but they find themselves the countries the worst hit by a crisis for which they are not responsible, similar to their situation vis-à-vis climate change. This is an injustice which needs to be redressed. The international community needs to show its resolve to assist its weakest members by giving them the tools to tackle the root causes of the vulnerabilities that have left them so exposed to the economic impacts of the pandemic.

The time to act is now. The international community has started discussing and negotiating a new plan of action for the least developed countries for the new decade. To treat the "pre-existing economic conditions" that have left them disproportionately vulnerable to the effects of the global pandemic, the least developed countries deserve a plan of action focused on developing productive capacities for their successful structural transformation. This is the only way to ensure sustainable development and overcome the long-term development challenges of the least developed countries.

UNCTAD analysis and empirical work offers a major contribution towards tackling the root causes of weak productive capacities. We have developed the Productive Capacities Index, which is an innovative tool to measure and benchmark not only the overall level of productive capacities, but also their underlying determinants. The Productive Capacities Index offers a powerful tool to policymakers for identifying bottlenecks and benchmarking progress on building productive capacities.

The international community needs to show its support to the least developed countries, through a holistic view of their development, which includes decisive and effective support measures that address the root causes of weak productive capacities. Putting productive capacity development at the heart of the forthcoming Fifth United Nations Conference on the Least Developed Countries is the right way to do so.

Mukhisa Kituyi
Secretary-General of the United Nations
Conference on Trade and Development

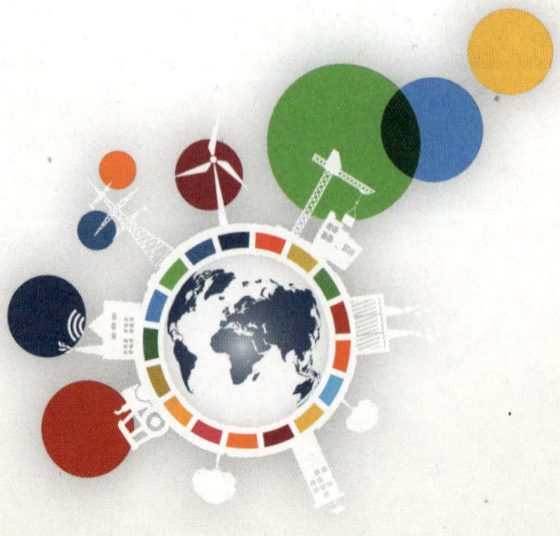

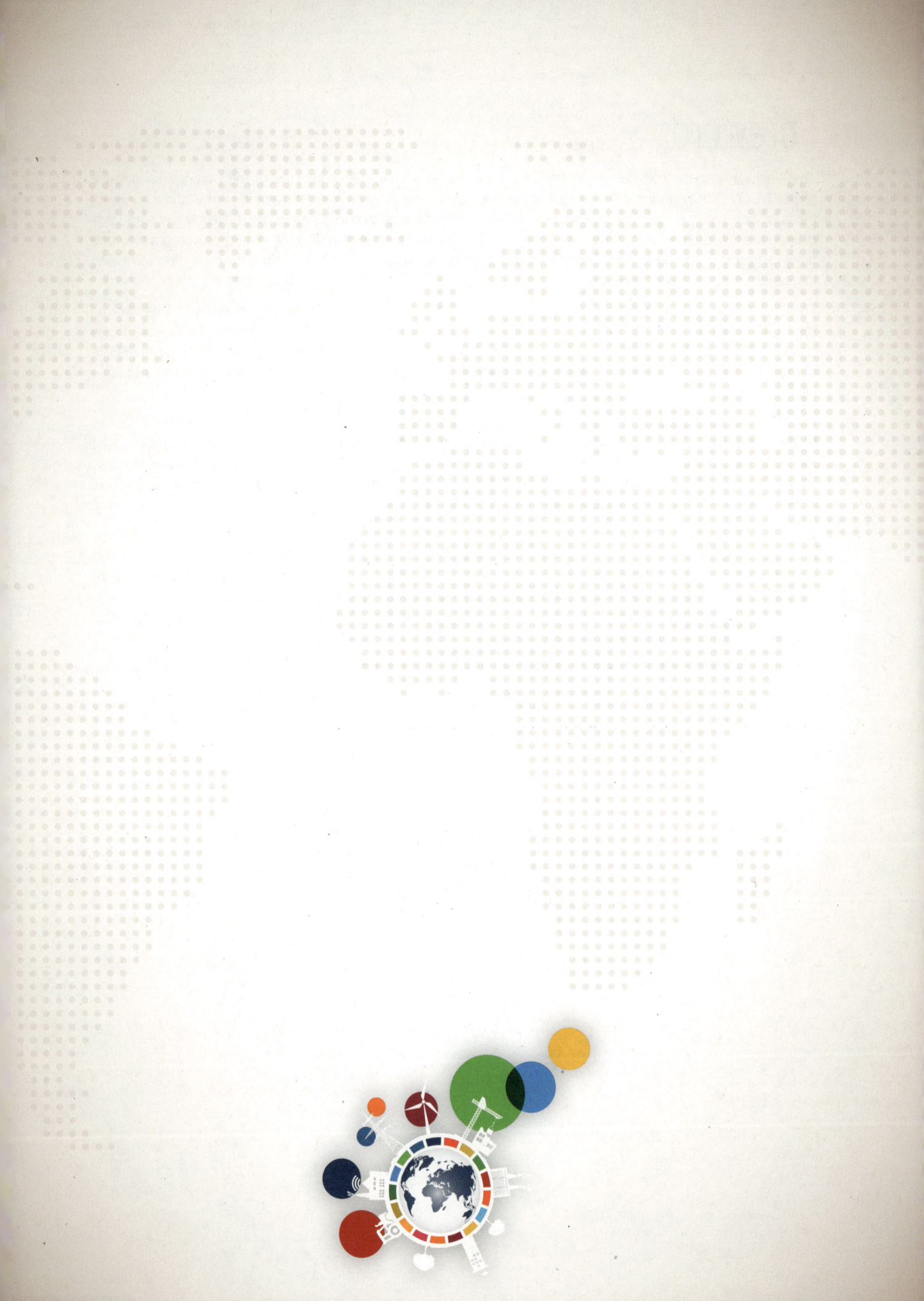

Overview

The Least Developed Countries Report **2020**

The COVID-19 crisis in the LDCs

Initial fears that the global coronavirus disease (COVID-19) pandemic would have catastrophic *health* impacts on the least developed countries (LDCs) have not materialized; however, some LDCs (e.g. Sao Tome and Principe, Djibouti, Gambia, Afghanistan and Nepal) have experienced more wide-ranging and stronger health impacts from the pandemic. A further significant expansion of the pandemic in some LDCs in the closing months of 2020 cannot be excluded, and would have dire consequences for these countries, due to the weak health systems of most LDCs.

LDCs were able to weather the health aspects of the pandemic better than initially predicted due to country-specific factors, including: previous experience with epidemics; the policy and technological innovations adopted in reaction to COVID-19; and favourable demographics, e.g. young populations and, in most cases, low population density.

The LDCs that have better weathered the COVID-19 pandemic from a health policy perspective are those with a broader and more sophisticated base of productive capacities in their economy. More generally, the same reasoning also applies to their capacity to respond to other shocks (e.g. medical, economic or natural disasters). Countries that have been able to develop a denser and more diversified fabric of productive capacities have shown greater resilience and have been better prepared to weather different types of shocks.

While the pandemic had (at least initially) a less than catastrophic *health* impact, its *economic* repercussions have been ruinous. In 2020, the COVID-19 pandemic led to LDC economies experiencing their strongest economic shock in several decades; this, in turn, resulted in a sharp economic downturn, brought about by the combined effects of a deep world economic recession, and the consequences of the domestic containment measures adopted by LDC governments. Worse still, these consequences are likely to linger in the medium term.

Between October 2019 and October 2020, the economic growth forecast for LDCs was revised sharply downwards from 5 to -0.4 per cent. This revision is expected to lead to a 2.6 per cent reduction in per capita income in LDCs in 2020, with 43 out of 47 LDCs experiencing a fall in their average income levels. This is the worst economic outcome in 30 years for this group of countries, and represents a significant reversal of the economic and social progress achieved in recent years, including in terms of poverty and social outcomes. It also makes reaching the Sustainable Development Goals by 2030 a more distant prospect.

A protracted recession could lead to permanent job destruction, threaten enterprise survival – with related losses in terms of productive capacities and tacit knowledge – and could have a long-term effect on potential output. Avoiding this dramatic outcome will be particularly crucial in LDCs because of the structural characteristics of the entrepreneurship that are prevalent in these countries. A prolonged crisis would further deteriorate an already weak LDC entrepreneurial landscape as currently characterized by a plethora of mainly informal traditional and non-innovative businesses; a structure of firms largely skewed towards micro, small and medium-sized enterprises (MSMEs); and a private sector with limited access to credit.

The impact of the world economic recession on LDC economies has probably been stronger than the domestic demand shock. This, in turn, brought about a sharp downturn in the external demand for LDC goods and services; depressed the prices of their main exports; and caused a slump in inflows of external resources (e.g. remittances, capital). The LDCs most dependent on the export of a few products are the most vulnerable to foreign trade shocks, and were strongly affected by the sharp fall in the volume and prices of exported products on which their economies are most reliant. This pertains especially to exporters of fuels (e.g. Angola, Chad, Timor-Leste, Mozambique and Yemen); minerals and metals (e.g. Democratic Republic of the Congo, Zambia, Guinea, Sierra Leone, Eritrea and Mauritania); garments (e.g. Bangladesh, Haiti, Cambodia, Nepal and Lesotho); and tourism services (e.g. Vanuatu, Cambodia, Sao Tome and Principe and the Gambia).

The combined merchandise trade deficit of LDCs in 2020 is forecast to exceed the record level reached in 2019 ($91 billion). Similarly, LDC exports of services have suffered a sharp blow from the virtual standstill of their main export sector – tourism. The countries hardest hit by the severe downturn in world tourism are small island States (e.g. Vanuatu, Sao Tome and Principe), but also Cambodia, the Gambia and Madagascar. It is therefore likely that the combined deficit in trade in goods and services of LDCs will widen further in 2020, thus extending the trend that started with the global financial crisis of 2008–2009. In the context of these falling volumes of world trade and plummeting LDC exports, it is unlikely that this group of countries will meet their long-standing goal on trade enshrined in Sustainable Development Goals Target 17.11, i.e. that of doubling their share of world exports of goods and services between 2011 and 2020.

International migration and remittances flows have also suffered a major blow from the lockdowns that were introduced, and the ensuing worldwide recession. Total remittances to low- and middle-income countries (LMICs) are forecast to fall by one fifth in 2020, with an even sharper contraction expected in South Asian and sub-Saharan African countries. The LDCs most vulnerable to falling remittances are those that rely the most on them as a source of external financing, and include: Haiti, South Sudan, Nepal, Lesotho, Gambia, Yemen, Comoros, Kiribati and Senegal.

The widening trade deficit in goods and services and the contraction in remittance receipts in 2020 are expected to lead to a further expansion of the total current account deficit of LDCs as a group; this is forecast to deepen sharply from 4.6 per cent of their combined GDP in 2019 to 6.8 per cent of GDP in 2020. This will be the highest ever (or second highest) collective current account deficit for LDCs, and will continue the sequence of swelling current account deficits experienced by the LDCs since the last global financial crisis.

Widening current account deficits represent a major challenge for LDCs, as they will need to be financed by higher capital inflows. However, increasing financing needs come at a time when LDCs are seeing diminished levels of capital inflows. LDCs are the most aid-dependent economies in the world, with official development assistance (ODA) representing the most prominent type of capital inflow into these countries. This heightened need for ODA is taking place in a context in which the volume of ODA has been stagnating since 2013. Donor countries have not been respecting their long-standing commitment to deliver to LDCs ODA levels of 0.15–0.20 per cent of their gross national income (GNI). In addition, access to private financing has become even more difficult in a context of diminishing worldwide private capital flows, thereby compounding the difficulties that LDCs face in closing their external financing gap amidst the recession.

The global downturn is also expected to have a dramatic negative impact on global poverty and food insecurity. This may give rise to path-dependency and turn transient forms of poverty into chronic poverty. The COVID-19 outbreak led to a very bleak economic growth outlook for countries across the world; however, the impact on the LDCs will be even worse, as the pandemic is expected to lead to an increase of 3 percentage points – from 32.2 to 35.2 per cent – in their average poverty headcount ratio according to the $1.90 per day poverty line. This is equivalent to a rise of over 32 million people living in extreme poverty in the LDCs, and is expected to have the deepest impact on African and island LDCs.

While this situation represents a setback for attaining Goal 1 of the Sustainable Development Goals, it also could mean that a number of other Goals, notably those related to health and education, will not be reached, as populations adopt adverse coping strategies, such as reducing their intake of healthy and nutritious food, or taking children out of school.

The downturn is likely to further undermine gender equality, as the gender dimension intersects with other axes of structural marginalization, including economic status, membership to minority groups, disability, human immunodeficiency virus (HIV) status and the like. In LDCs and elsewhere, women tend to be over-represented in vulnerable occupational categories (from health personnel to informal own-account workers), as well as in value chains that have been the hardest hit by the crisis, e.g. tourism or the textile and apparel sector.

LDC economies are beset by vulnerability, understood as the exposure of a national economy to exogenous events (shocks and instabilities) that are largely beyond domestic control, and which negatively affect their capacity to grow and develop. These economies are highly exposed to economic, environmental and health shocks. The LDCs are among the world's most vulnerable economies, as reflected in the Economic and Environmental Vulnerability Index (EVI), which indicates that they are 30 per cent more vulnerable than other developing countries (ODCs – developing countries that are not LDCs).

Under present circumstances, the major economic priorities of LDCs could fall into two time horizons. In the short term, the priority of governments should be to do "whatever it takes" to counter the present recession, support the livelihoods of their citizens, the perennity of their firms and farms, and buttress the activity level of their economy. These short-term priorities are equally valid for LDCs, ODCs and developed countries. Second, LDCs need to build resilience, which is understood as the ability of an economy to withstand exogenous shocks and/or their capacity to recover from them. Resilience is the result of a successful development process, following which economies are able to overcome the major structural features of underdevelopment, such as: concentration of output and exports; widespread poverty; over-dependence on imports of critical goods and services; and chronic current account deficits. Building resilience therefore entails tackling the underlying structural causes of their vulnerability, underdevelopment and ingrained poverty.

The long-standing development challenges faced by LDCs predate the COVID-19 crisis. While the economic, social and political context which gives rise to extreme forms of vulnerability and poverty are complex, these phenomena have a common underlying factor, namely the low level of development of LDC productive capacities. Expanding, upgrading and better utilizing productive capacities result in overcoming the structural features which are at the origin of vulnerability. These imperatives have only been strengthened by the COVID-19 pandemic.

Against this background, it is all the more vital to highlight the continued relevance of the LDC category, not only during the "great lockdown" and its immediate aftermath, but also importantly for the new decade, which will witness the overlap between the remaining horizon of the 2030 Agenda for Sustainable Development and the next programme of action for LDCs.

In the context of the 2030 Agenda for Sustainable Development, the importance of the LDCs is even starker in relation to the objectives of shared prosperity and the eradication of extreme poverty. From the point of view of the international community, the development challenges faced by LDCs deserve particular attention, not least because low socioeconomic development is typically regarded as an influential driver of instability, conflict and migration, particularly when coupled with increasing pressure on natural resources, the intensifying adverse impacts of climate change, and limited institutional capabilities.

The reasons for reiterating that the LDCs are the battleground on which the 2030 Agenda for Sustainable Development will be won or lost go beyond the moral commitment to "leave no one behind", and reflect long-term considerations with respect to global public goods and the potential for positive and negative spillovers across nations in an increasingly interconnected world.

Productive capacities and structural transformation: Giving concrete form to concepts to meet the needs of LDCs

Productive capacities are defined as "the productive resources, entrepreneurial capabilities and production linkages which together determine the capacity of a country to produce goods and services and enable it to grow and develop". Sustained economic growth can only be made possible through the expansion, development and full utilization of productive capacities. Hence, the central role that productive capacities need to have in national and international development strategies.

The development of productive capacities operates, first, within firms/sectors as the profit-investment nexus fosters capital deepening and productivity gains. Second, it also takes place across sectors through, as the acquisition of productive capabilities – itself contingent on the existing pattern of production – paves the way for the emergence of new products and higher value-added activities. The process of productive capacity development hinges on a mutually reinforcing dynamic relationship between the supply- and demand-side of the economy, in so far as the expansion of aggregate demand creates the scope for denser intersectoral linkages, factor reallocation and pecuniary externalities, which collectively sustain the financial viability of investments, including in "social overhead capital".

Productive resources develop though three processes: (i) capital or resource accumulation; (ii) technological learning and innovation; and (iii) deepening of division of labour and increasing specialization of sectors, firms and farms. Together, these three processes lead to the structural transformation of the economy. This complex process is multi-dimensional and comprises the movement of a country's productive resources (e.g. natural resources, land, capital, labour and know-how) from low-productivity to high-productivity economic activities (typically gauged by the level of labour productivity, i.e. the value added generated during a certain period of work). Alternatively, structural transformation is understood as the ability of an economy to constantly generate new dynamic activities characterized by higher productivity and increasing returns to scale.

The process of structural transformation takes diverse forms at different income levels. At low-income levels, it is mainly the result of the transfer of resources from one sector to another. This is the case of LDCs, many of whom are at the initial stages of structural transformation. At high-income levels, by contrast, the intersectoral transfer of resources has largely been accomplished and structural transformation mainly takes the form of the transfer of resources within sectors.

Structural transformation of the productive sphere of the economy takes place within a specific economic, social and institutional context, and there is a mutual interaction and influence between structural transformation and this environment.

Productive resources comprise physical infrastructure, which enables the supply of, among others, energy, transport, communications, irrigation, and water and sanitation services. The availability and affordability of these services is crucial for the development of productive units, as they enable the supply of inputs essential to the operation of firms and farms, and affect the costs that firms pay to access resources and markets for inputs and outputs. They are also crucial to improving living standards and the wellbeing of citizens and households.

Another type of infrastructure which has become increasingly critical is that of information and communication technologies (ICTs). They are the backbone of the digital economy and the so-called Fourth Industrial Revolution (4IR). As these technologies are increasingly critical infrastructure, they have generated increasing interest among policymakers focusing on issues related to the digital divide among and within countries. In the meantime, ICTs have expanded in several developed countries, to the point of reaching maturity (in terms of technology diffusion). The pace of diffusion of these technologies has also been accelerating in ODCs and LDCs at a quicker pace than in developed countries. This has given rise to high hopes that the international digital divide was narrowing.

However, these hopes have not been borne out by evidence. In spite of the rapid diffusion of mobile telephony and mobile-broadband access in LDCs since the beginning of the century, the digital divide remains very wide between LDCs on the one hand, and ODCs and developed countries on the other. Access to the Internet remains restricted to a minority of the population in LDCs and gender divides in Internet access are wide. Moreover, the uptake by individuals and households of mobile voice and data technologies has been larger than the uptake by productive units (e.g. firms and farms). This remains a major hindrance to the development of productive capacities in these countries, as well as to the adoption of other more modern technologies and, more broadly, the acceleration of their structural transformation.

The pace of structural transformation of output declined worldwide between the periods of 2001–2011 and 2011–2017, due to the general deceleration of worldwide economic growth in the aftermath of the global financial crisis of 2008–2009 and its lingering consequences.

The process of structural transformation in LDCs indicates that over the long run most of them have experienced a falling share of agriculture in both output and employment. The transfer of resources has been mostly in favour of the tertiary sector (i.e. services), especially in the case of African LDCs. Most of these countries have experienced the reallocation of labour from low-productivity agriculture to low-productivity urban activities, mostly occurring in the informal service sector.

Growth in the share of services in output and employment is generally seen as a sign of economic modernization. However, this overlooks the strong heterogeneity among different service subsectors. To more closely examine the composition of the service sector in LDCs, as compared to that of other country groups, service sectors are classified according to whether they are: (i) knowledge-intensive; (ii) less knowledge-intensive; and (iii) non-market.

In developed countries, the share of the three types of service activities are more or less equal. In LDCs, by contrast, the bulk of tertiary employment is concentrated in less knowledge-intensive services, e.g. retail trade, repair of motor vehicles, and accommodation and food. These are typically low-productivity and low value-added activities, and often carried out in the informal sector. These service sectors are especially important for African and island LDCs, and account for some two-thirds of employment in the service sector in these countries; however, in Asian LDCs, knowledge-intensive services account for one-fourth of services employment – a higher level than in other LDC groups.

LDCs achieved a healthy pace of labour productivity gains in the 2001–2011 period, following annual growth of 3.9 per cent, a slightly lower level than in ODCs which recorded an annual expansion of 4.6 per cent. During the following period, however, these two groups of countries diverged. Labour productivity growth decelerated in both sets of countries, but much more in LDCs, where it declined to 1.9 per cent annually, whereas in ODCs it decelerated more moderately to 3.7 per cent per annum.

The highest pace of productivity growth took place in the Asian LDCs, largely as a result of relatively faster productivity growth in manufacturing and services in countries, e.g. Bangladesh, Cambodia, Lao People's Democratic Republic and Myanmar. The deceleration in labour productivity in African LDCs during the 2011–2017 period was largely driven by the actual decline in productivity in services and other industries (especially in the mining sector). The adverse performance of productivity in services is due to two factors: (i) the continuous influx of labour not being matched by commensurate output growth in the tertiary sector; and (ii) the concentration of tertiary employment in less knowledge-intensive services, and their typically lower productivity growth potential. The share of employment in these services in LDCs is the highest among major country groups.

The overall labour productivity level of LDCs as a group has been diverging from that of ODCs as a group over the long term, as has the strength and direction of their structural transformation. In 1991 the LDC/ODC ratio was at 25 per cent, while at the beginning of the new millennium it was down to 21 per cent, finally reaching 18 per cent in 2017. The process of divergence was somewhat interrupted in the 2000s, largely as a result of the long commodities cycle, but has resumed since the global financial crisis of 2008–2009. If this divergent trend is not reversed, LDCs as a group will not be able to escape from their long-term marginalization in the world economy.

There is, however, a strong contrast between the three groups of LDCs in their structural transformation. Asian LDCs as a group are undergoing what most resembles a classical process of industrialization. Several of the countries in this group have a rising share of manufacturing in output and employment, specialization in manufacturing exports, and have experienced the strongest performance in terms of labour productivity growth, together with the attendant reduction of poverty levels and stronger progress in social outcomes. However, in order to maintain the process of growth-enhancing structural transformation, even Asian LDCs need to deepen and broaden their structural transformation, and further build their entrepreneurial and technological capabilities, in anticipation for the loss of LDC-specific trade preferences once they graduate from LDC status.

African LDCs continue to face the challenge of diversifying their economies and developing high-productivity economic activities. Given the still very significant share of employment in agriculture, these countries have a very high potential for further structural transformation. African LDCs face two contemporaneous challenges: they must strongly accelerate the rhythm of agricultural labour productivity growth; and, substantially generate employment in other sectors for their rapidly growing populations. Moreover, these new jobs need to be of a considerably higher productivity level than those found in their respective agricultural sectors.

In the 2020s the development of productive capacities in LDCs will be strongly influenced by developments in the global environment (as these are typically small open economies), as well as by policies they and their development partners will adopt. Overall, this global environment will inevitably be characterized by the lingering effects of the COVID-19 health and economic crises, and by how international economic and political relations will evolve thereafter. Some broad trends will exert a particularly marked influence on the development of productive capacities of LDCs and the broader development prospects of these countries. These trends include the reorientation of international economic and political relations in the post-COVID-19 context, the future of globalization, global value chains and regional integration, progression in climate change and policies to tackle it, demographic trends and the unfolding technological revolution (including especially digital technologies). These new technologies can potentially have a very strong impact on the development of productive capacities in LDCs in the new decade.

Measuring productive capacities: LDCs' progress towards sustainable development

The UNCTAD Productive Capacities Index. Assisting LDCs to develop their productive capacities could enhance the social development returns of economic growth and accelerate structural transformation. This is critical in the decade left to implement the 2030 Agenda for Sustainable Development. Productive capacities could help LDCs to ramp up progress on reducing extreme poverty (Sustainable Development Goal 1), bolstering agricultural productivity (Goal 2), and industrial growth (Goal 8). Achieving these goals hinges on improvements to labour productivity; however, labour productivity gains alone will not be enough to reset the course of economic development among LDCs. Improvements in human capacity should concurrently be implemented with surges in other productive capacities, e.g. energy (Goal 7), investment in infrastructure, and market interlinkages (Goal 8) and private sector development (Goal 9). Progress on these different lines is complementary and mutually supportive.

UNCTAD has developed an aggregate measure representing the endowments of productive factors, their management and transformation, and the effectiveness of market interlinkages. The Productive Capacities Index (PCI) is the most extensive analytical work done to date in terms of scope and technical effort. It encompasses eight broad categories defined over many indicators representing the main channels through which productive capacities of a country develop, namely: energy; human capital; ICTs; natural resources; transport infrastructure; institutions; the private sector; and structural change. Each category has a dedicated sub-index.

The PCI adds a crucial dimension in the assessment of the progress made by LDCs to reach internationally agreed objectives. This is demonstrated in the context of the thematic priorities of the Programme of Action for the Least Developed Countries for the Decade 2011–2020 (otherwise known as the Istanbul Programme of Action – IPoA).

The PCI scale ranges from 0 to 100, with 100 being the best score. The aggregate PCI is an average of its eight sub-indices. The PCI can be used to benchmark differences among LDCs and between LDCs and other country groups. In 2011–2018, the PCI scores in LDCs ranged from 9 to 36, with the average at 17. The median productive capacity climbed from 14.9 to 17.2 during that period, while for ODCs it rose from 27.3 to 28. Countries with a relatively high PCI have also been successful at fostering structural transformation, and have used their productive capacities to diversify their economies and exports. In 2018, the PCI of the top two developed countries ranged from 48 (Luxembourg) to 53 (United States of America), while the top two LDCs scored 28 (Bhutan) and 35 (Tuvalu) on the PCI scale.

An interactive clustering of best, least and average performers among the LDCs shows that for the years 2001, 2011 and 2018, productive capacities had improved slightly among the least performing LDCs, with the subgroup median PCI rising from 18 to 22 in 2000–2018. Overall, the rate of change in productive capacities is low for all countries, and individual LDC performances have been lacklustre. Of note is that the number of countries in the high-productive group fell from eleven countries in 2001 to only six in 2018. Meanwhile, the number of countries in the least productive group rose from 18 countries to 25 over the same period, while the number of countries in the average group ranged from 16 to 18 in 2001–2018. In addition, the composition of countries in the lower two clusters changed significantly over the years. Only two countries, Rwanda and Myanmar, climbed up the clusters in 2001–2018, moving from the low-capacity group into the average group.

LDCs posted major improvements with respect to ICTs, transport infrastructure and the structural change categories of productive capacities although, in absolute terms, their scores in 2000 and in 2018 on the bounded PCI scale (0–100) are too low compared to the scores of other country groups. LDCs lag behind ODCs in all PCI categories – with the exception of natural resources – and more particularly in ICTs, human capital and institutions. There are also significant differences among countries in energy, the private sector and structural change factors. Although the rankings by PCI scores show significant challenges among the LDCs, the performances of several LDCs, e.g. Bangladesh, Bhutan and Cambodia, prove that LDCs can reach the productive capacities level of other country groups. However, their performance is contingent on several regional factors, including a diversified economy, along with strong value chains among contiguous countries.

Progress made by LDCs towards attaining the IPoA goals. UNCTAD has carried out a comprehensive assessment of the IPoA using PCI as an added dimension. Only 13 LDCs have ever attained the 7-per-cent growth target during 2015–2018, and fewer still have managed to maintain that pace in consecutive years. The extent of the fallout from the COVID-19 pandemic is uncertain as the situation is still evolving. However, what emerged as a public health crisis has exposed the weak structures of LDC economies, their vulnerability to economic shocks, and their inability to mobilize productive capacities to adapt to changing market conditions.

The low efficiency in productive capacities utilization cannot be generalized across all LDCs. A given level of productive capacities may be associated with numerous output levels, as countries differ in their utilization of productive capacities. The per capita incomes of some LDCs, e.g. Bhutan, Sudan and Tuvalu, grew significantly in 2011–2018.

The priority sectors for economic development need to be chosen carefully. The IPoA identified the critical productive capacities as; infrastructure; energy; science, technology and innovation (STI); and private sector development. The assessment of productive capacity utilization suggests that a 1 per cent increase in energy infrastructure leads to an increase of only 0.12 per cent in per capita income. The blending of unproductive agriculture with a high share of employment in the sector, and an uncompetitive service sector with low productivity, high levels of informality and weak integration into global value chains (in terms of intensity of integration and position achieved within the value chains) reduces the impact of structural change on real GDP per capita.

During the IPoA (2011–2020), the long-standing marginalization of LDCs in international trade continued as the trade in commodities faltered because of unfavourable commodity market conditions. The clustering of LDCs around various sub-components of UNCTAD's PCI confirms the existence of specialization enclaves, which determine the level of export diversification and sophistication. Relative cost advantages and geographical advantages offering better linkages to global value chains have continued to play a critical role in boosting exports, particularly among Asian LDCs, African LDCs have, however, continued to be heavily reliant on abundant natural resources.

Human development is often a neglected agenda in LDCs, despite the fact that the objective of economic development is human development through the reduction of inequalities, the building resilient communities, and the eradication of all forms of poverty. An uneducated and untrained labour force remains an unproductive and underutilized resource. Hence, the key to reaping the demographic dividend and bridging the technology gap between LDCs and ODCs is to ensure that public investments in education and training bring skills development and knowledge to the centre of their policies. Ultimately, human beings determine investments in technology and knowledge, including with respect to how existing production systems are utilized, and the structural changes needed to improve the production systems.

Skills acquired through education and work determine the utilization of all other productive capacities, including hard and soft assets (e.g. infrastructure, institutions and policies). If LDCs are to catch up with the level of ODCs, they must at least attain the same level of human capacity development as these countries; if this is to be achieved, it will require tangible investments in education and training and targeting the right age groups. If artificial intelligence is a major component of 4IR and the heartbeat of the digital economy, LDCs should not underrate the value of innovation, knowledge and the linkages created through innovation.

The IPoA assessment also revealed the extent to which factors, such as conflict and weak institutional and governance systems, heighten the risk exposure to specific shocks. The correlation between economic vulnerability and the productive capacity categories shows that structural change is associated with lower economic vulnerabilities for all LDCs, except those that in 2018 met two of the three criteria for graduation from the LDC category. Natural resources are also associated with lower economic vulnerability for countries that graduated, and for LDCs with a high GNI in 2018. By contrast, human capital, ICTs and institutions are associated with lower economic vulnerability among countries scheduled to graduate. The countries that met the EVI and income criteria registered more vulnerability in the natural resources dimension, which they compensated with higher GNI, a vibrant private sector, or better transport infrastructure.

An important asymmetry is also observed between the countries that graduated from the LDC category and the entire set of ODCs. Energy, human capacity, the private sector and structural diversity components are associated with lower economic vulnerability among ODCs, but institutional quality and transport infrastructure have the opposite effect. For countries that graduated from the category, energy, transport infrastructure and human capital are significantly associated with higher economic vulnerability. This confirms the observation that LDCs that graduated, or those scheduled to graduate (based on the income criterion), do so because of the wealth of their natural resources. If LDCs aspire to reach the level of ODCs, the weaknesses exposed by their low score in other productive capacity components should be the focus of their policies. This is clear from the productive capacity components that are associated with lower economic vulnerability scores among ODCs.

The IPoA assessment confirms that productive capacities are key building blocks for structural transformation and trade, but their dynamic impacts on the economy will not take a concrete form until they are activated by government policy. The state of productive capacities in LDC economies limits the extent to which public policies can influence development; in some cases, countries face additional challenges because of their geographical location and subregional dynamics. The analysis of these categories suggests a trade-off among the building blocks, with most of the productive capacity categories having complementarity impacts; however, the existence of non-conventional negative correlations among the categories suggests low synergy. LDCs should exploit complementary trade structures offered by their subregional markets, for example, the Asian LDCs should make best use of their neighbours, both for providing the necessary inputs, including the technology they need, and as a market for the goods and services they export. African and island LDCs equally need to exploit their subregional markets, but they will have to intensify their investments in interlinkages, institutions and infrastructure.

It is getting harder for LDCs to graduate from the category in which they find themselves. The few countries that have graduated have often done so based on their large natural resource capacity. However, natural resources also pose the greatest source of instability to exports and raise the vulnerability of countries. The result is that economic vulnerability persists even after countries have graduated from the LDC category. The international community may need to agree on specific support measures for the countries in the graduation pipeline, as well to others that have recently graduated, to ensure the sustainability of their respective development momentum. A differentiated support structure seems inevitable given the low graduation rates, and the slow progress towards graduation among LDCs.

Transition to the digital economy: technological capabilities as drivers of productivity

As the digital economy becomes increasingly inseparable from the functioning of modern economies, concerns about the supposed potential of digital technologies in LDCs have been heightened. LDCs are increasingly advised to rapidly design and implement development policies that support and incentivize investments in the acquisition of the technological capabilities that are needed to enable them to ride the wave of digital innovation. LDCs are falling behind in the global digital transformation race, as evidenced by the already apparent trend of a widening digital divide between and within countries. UNCTAD research confirms that traditional support programmes to small- and medium-sized enterprises (SMEs) are unlikely to be effective in addressing technological capabilities gaps.

Compelling claims about the unprecedented opportunities presented by digital technologies currently dominate the normative discourse on sustainable development. Two central predictions on the impact of 4IR in the context of LDCs exert an influence on policymaking, namely: (i) their predicted ability to induce the creation of new business models and value propositions that stimulate inclusive growth; and (ii) the potential of latecomer countries to leapfrog development. Policymakers are faced with the task of transforming such predictions into strategies that prioritize active problem-solving. This will require deep insights and understanding of digital technologies and their application across different sectors, and will only be possible by ensuring that policy responses avoid the dilution of focus from causes to symptoms. The risks associated with the latter are high because the emphasis of much of the available literature is on showcasing examples of the digital presence in LDCs, or the specific attributes of 4IR technologies that are perceived to demonstrate the predicted superior ability of these technologies to address intractable developmental problems. However, there is little concrete evidence on how these predictions could be realized in the context of LDCs, nor the policy lessons that can be learnt from this, particularly as the existing body of literature is weighted with symbolism and aspiration, but falls short of providing a detailed picture of the technological capabilities needed by firms to unlock the latent potential of 4IR technologies in LDCs.

In the context of the central aims of fostering competitive productive activities and structural economic transformation in LDCs, economic theory and emerging evidence from UNCTAD research suggests that policy responses will need to descend from the macro to the meso and micro levels in order to address the challenges of the digital era, particularly as technological capabilities are vested in economic actors at the level of the firm, or in other productive units, e.g. farms. Hence, while the critical role of ICTs as an obligatory gateway to the digital economy is undisputed, access to ICTs and other economic infrastructure needs to be complemented by investments in technological capabilities to fulfil the promise of enhanced productivity, given that 4IR technologies embody complex technological capabilities. Technological capabilities are fundamental elements of productive capacities and critical to increased productivity, competitiveness and profitability. These capabilities transform assets or resources, e.g. ICTs, into tangible, physical or intangible outputs of greater value.

LDCs face the risk of being left further behind as the technological gap vis-à-vis more technologically advanced countries widens. Industrial policy has become even more relevant than before to ensure that LDCs are not further marginalized. This need became evident with the emergence of the digital economy, and has become even more relevant in the wake of the COVID-19 pandemic. In this context, policymakers need to refocus on the role of industrial policy and its interaction and interdependence with a range of other sectoral policies, including the gendered dimensions of the digital divide, and the changing nature of production and sectoral interdependencies. For example, evidence at the global level points to the increasing servicification of manufacturing and the industrialization of agriculture. To adopt technology and invest in technological capabilities, firms need to be confident that the right policies are in place before they adopt technology and invest in new technological capabilities. This implies that targeted and coherent policy packages will be needed to support national-level investments in institutional and regulatory capacity as these will be vital to building digital policymaking capacity and the maintenance of policy coherence. Moreover, maximizing the return on investments in complementary economic infrastructure will require LDC governments to pay closer attention to the impact of market concentration on the affordability of access to critical digital services, and the ability of LDC firms to gain entry and compete in global and national digital markets. Policymakers will also need to address the security and privacy concerns of productive actors and consumers. Global consensus has not yet been reached on the appropriate policy responses to competition issues in digital markets. Notwithstanding this, the enforcement of these responses needs to be bolder, quicker and context-specific, given the tendency for "winner-take-all markets" to generate near-monopolies.

Firms typically face internal and external barriers that disincentivize technological upgrading and the adoption of new business models. The first barrier for LDCs is that the process of unlocking the potential of ICTs and 4IR technologies is an incremental transition that engenders costs for firms. Digital transformation and leapfrogging draw disproportionately on the tacit knowledge component of technological capability, which is neither easily aggregated nor disseminated. Thus, 4IR technologies increase the cost and associated risks of acquiring technological capabilities for firms. This major market failure justifies policy action to address this problem. A second and related barrier for LDCs is that the overwhelming majority of their productive actors are resource- and talent-poor MSMEs. A third compounding factor is that the dynamic and continuous changes in production systems that are expected to be at the centre of the digital transformation give rise to a lagged emergence of productivity impacts. A further crippling factor is that digital transformation at the firm level is dependent on technological capabilities which have accrued in preceding iterations of the industrial revolution (i.e. it is path-dependent). While the world is said to be in the midst of a fourth industrial revolution, most LDCs are languishing in the first and second industrial revolutions, thereby underlining the severity of the challenge of technology absorption in LDCs. All these factors lie at the heart of the truism that firms do not naturally upgrade themselves, despite proven high returns or operating in an environment that is increasingly characterized by the presence of digital technologies.

The universe of technological capabilities that will be important for the transition of firms to acquire a digital status is likely to be as vast as the number of processes, procedures, product lines, business models and strategies that firms can adopt to set themselves apart from their competitors. Capabilities are also likely to vary by sector, the production network segment that firms are active in, as well as the nature of the interactions they may have with other firms in this network. They are also likely to differ by orientation, e.g. in the case of a firm pursuing an export-led strategy.

Key sectors of strategic interest in LDCs, such as agriculture, manufacturing and services, are in urgent need of a reset and 4IR technologies represent an unrealized opportunity. At least three prospects, which will require to be pursued concurrently, are available to LDCs. The first lies in the need to continue to consolidate the gains that have been achieved in raising productivity and fostering structural transformation through the strategic use of industrial policies. Studies suggest that some LDCs have the necessary, but nonetheless time-bound, breathing space for traditional business models to continue to be successful. The second opportunity lies in the use of digital technologies, especially ICTs, to accelerate and further strengthen the latter process of consolidation – e-commerce being an obvious example. The third opportunity is to actively pursue the digital transformation of firms in the economy as this process is path-dependent and takes time. The size of the investments and the breadth of the public policy reconfigurations that are needed to support this digital transformation are likely to be substantial. Going forward, strategic choices focused on long-term gains will be crucial in the current climate of habitually constrained LDC budgets, which have been further constricted by the impacts of the COVID-19 crisis and its repercussions on ODA flows.

Policies to develop productive capacities in the new decade

With the IPoA set to remain largely unfinished business by 2021, and the fallout from COVID-19 laying bare once again the structural vulnerabilities of LDCs, the centrality of productive capacities for sustainable development prospects is increasingly apparent. This calls for policies at all levels aimed at setting in motion the process of structural transformation through the gradual broadening, deepening and full utilization of LDC productive capacities.

Bold countercyclical policies are sorely needed to cushion the impact of the downturn and avert longer-term damage to the already-weak productive fabric of LDCs, particularly as the global recession threatens to roll back the clock on the encouraging signs of progress made by LDCs in recent years. However, this will not, in itself, foster a broad-based sustainable recovery. This will require marrying stable fundamentals with a sustained and concerted investment push to narrow the infrastructural and technological gaps of LDCs. This requires, to the extent possible, an expansionary fiscal policy, buttressed by accommodating monetary and exchange rate policies to support domestic resource mobilization and private sector development. In this context, the role of public investment remains particularly critical for LDCs, both in the short term – to contain job losses – and over the longer term – to redress supply-side bottlenecks related to infrastructures and basic services provision, thus crowding in private investments.

Beyond the pure macroeconomic realm, industrial policies – including actions geared towards strengthening STI ecosystems – are back to the fore of the political debate. The policy experimentation ushered in in response to the pandemic has demonstrated that – when coordination problems are addressed – significant achievements can be made even in LDCs, as shown by the rapid development of testing kits in countries, such as Bangladesh, Senegal and Uganda. Interestingly, the COVID-19 pandemic has brought about a renewed debate on the pivotal role of the state not only as a "rule setter", but also as a "coordinator" and "investor", which calls for renewed emphasis on institutional capacities to steer development strategies and mobilize a wide range of stakeholders.

Two key priorities emerge from an LDC perspective. First, with LDC labour supply expected to increase by 13.2 million workers per year in the 2020s, the challenge of employment creation cannot be overemphasized. This will require a multipronged approach which simultaneously supports labour demand in higher-productivity labour-intensive sectors, and enhances the employability of new entrants into the labour market. Second, the role of technologies for sustainable development has become all the more pivotal in the post-COVID-19 scenario, as the fallout from the pandemic is likely to accelerate some facets of the ongoing process of industrial digitalization and servicification. The position of LDCs in the global division of labour could be further marginalized if their distance from the technological frontier lengthens and the digital divide persists or widens further. Hence, the long-standing challenges in upgrading their technological base and setting in motion meaningful technology transfer will likely become even more vital. Emerging evidence points to the serious risk of a widening divide as a result of the sharp concentration in the production and deployment of advanced technologies, the marginal engagement of LDCs in their adoption, as well as the prevailing shortages of complementary skills.

With respect to sectoral policies, if agricultural development cannot be disregarded, in view of its importance for job creation, inter-sectoral linkages and the imperative of closing long-standing productivity gaps, the creation of a viable manufacturing basis remains fundamental for LDCs, in line with Goal 9 of the 2030 Agenda for Sustainable Development. The advent of digitalization and servicification imply that some features traditionally ascribed to manufacturing – notably the scope for productivity growth and increasing returns – might also potentially apply to some services, especially in knowledge-intensive services. However, the opportunity to engage in the adaptation and production of advanced technologies and weather future external shocks largely depends on the presence of a certain manufacturing base and the acquisition of complementary skills. One of the key lessons of the COVID-19 pandemic is that resilience requires adaptability and the capacity to innovate, e.g. repurposing the production of textiles to that of personal protective equipment, or that of alcoholic beverages into disinfectants. These features are inevitably contingent on pre-existing capabilities. From a policymaking perspective, rather than framing the discussion as a dichotomy between manufacturing-led versus a services-led model, the advent of new technologies puts a premium on systemic coherence. This entails designing policies to strategically target synergies and complementarities across sectors, with a view to gradually enhance the sophistication of the economy. It also involves an awareness of the political economy dimensions underlying technological change and its potential distributional effects.

The on-going global response to the COVID-19 pandemic has provided numerous concrete examples of industrial policy measures which could be considered to redress this situation. These range from the strategic use of public procurement to advanced market commitments (which lower risks and entice investment in research and development – R&D), and from swift legal action to ensure that intellectual property rights flexibilities are actionable to proactive efforts aimed at facilitating coordination across stakeholders. More broadly, numerous developing countries have recently deployed other policy tools, including local content requirements or targeted special economic zones (SEZs). The success record of these measures remains somewhat mixed, as upgrading opportunities and spillovers to the rest of the economy have not always materialized, or have not been commensurate with the related costs. Nevertheless, industrial policies have been instrumental to industrial upgrading when designed in a balanced pragmatic manner, and within a holistic policy framework incorporating a macroeconomic framework and STI policies.

Beyond the domestic border, it remains crucial to enhance the strategic coherence of trade and investment policies with industrial policy objectives. Harnessing international trade strategically to achieve structural transformation is part and parcel of this effort. Regional integration, in particular, can give a significant boost to attaining greater economies of scale, harness trade complementarities, and gradually enhance the competitiveness and sophistication of the economy. It can also prove instrumental to attracting foreign direct investment (FDI), and enhancing the scope for integration into regional and global value chains. Hence, in the case of African LDCs, the importance of moving forward with the implementation of the Africa Continental Free Trade Area.

It remains clear, however, that there is no "one size fits all" approach, nor a single pattern of structural transformation. The mainstream prescription of pursuing export-led growth risks falling victim to a fallacy of composition, especially in the current depressed context, as it is not possible for all countries to simultaneously export their way out of recession. Hence, to be successful, strategies geared towards productive capacity development must address the context-specific realities of each individual LDC, as well as harness their own set of comparative advantages, and account for local political economy dynamics and structural characteristics.

The accumulation of productive capacities largely occurs within the domestic economy, but is very strongly influenced by the interactions between the domestic economy and the international environment. The forms and conditions under which LDCs integrate into the global market inevitably exert a far-reaching influence on their needs, policy space, available means, and the effectiveness of different policy measures. The international community therefore has an important role to play to support the LDC quest to achieve sustainable development. These considerations are all the more relevant at the current juncture, when humanity just experienced a shock of unprecedented magnitude and is entering a decade that simultaneously marks the remaining horizon of 2030 Agenda for Sustainable Development and the new programme of action for the LDCs. In a context of intensifying global interdependence, calls for a global partnership in support of LDCs reflect the need to "build back better" and enhance the world's systemic resilience.

The fallout from the COVID-19 pandemic has once again exposed the long-standing flaws and asymmetries inherent to the prevailing multilateral trade and financial architecture. In this context, LDCs cannot but be among the most fervent supporters of a revamped, more effective and inclusive multilateralism, capable of addressing today's challenges and creating a more conducive international environment. They also have a large stake in the solution of long-standing systemic issues, notably in securing an adequate provision of international liquidity and of sufficient long-term development finance (including climate finance) which is compatible with their development goals. Equally, the worsening debt sustainability situation and outlook of LDCs, as well as that of many ODCs, calls for the adoption of measures that go well beyond the debt service standstill agreed by the G-20 in April 2020. Broader and more effective initiatives include: (i) renewed debt cancellation and relief programmes; (ii) the creation of an effective, comprehensive and transparent framework for sovereign debt workout; and (iii) the strengthening of the use of state-contingent debt instruments.

The limited progress against the IPoA targets also warrants an overhaul of existing international support measures (ISMs) in favour of LDCs, along five main axes. First, if trade preferences and other ISMs rooted in some forms of trade liberalization are to succeed, stronger support through the Aid for Trade initiative is needed. Second, broad capacity development efforts are necessary to improve the quality of LDC institutions and their ability to harness existing ISMs, particularly in areas related to non-tariff measures (NTMs), digital trade and trade in services, where issues of measurement, transparency and predictability are more challenging. Third, adequate policy space continues to be vital for LDCs. This calls for a strengthening of special and differential treatment, and at the very minimum for the renewal beyond 2021 of existing flexibilities under the Agreement on Trade-Related Aspects of Intellectual Property Rights (TRIPS). It is also imperative that LDCs be reassured that they will not be subjected to litigation, under the WTO or other regional or bilateral trade and investment agreements, for policies adopted to counter the damage resulting from the COVID-19 pandemic. This can be done through a "peace clause", or long-term standstill, that would protect LDC governments from litigation on issues of intellectual property, data and information.

Fourth, stronger mechanisms to foster meaningful technology transfer by private firms are critically needed. This theme should feature prominently in the formulation of investment promotion regimes for LDCs (Sustainable Development Goal Target 17.5). Equally, the use of public development finance through private sector instruments should be explicitly linked to genuine and documentable practices fostering technology transfer. Fifth, without dismissing the urgent need for multilateral efforts to promote meaningful technology transfer to LDCs, there is an ample scope to strengthen regional and South-South mechanisms for technological cooperation, notably in areas such as green technologies, industrial and digital cooperation.

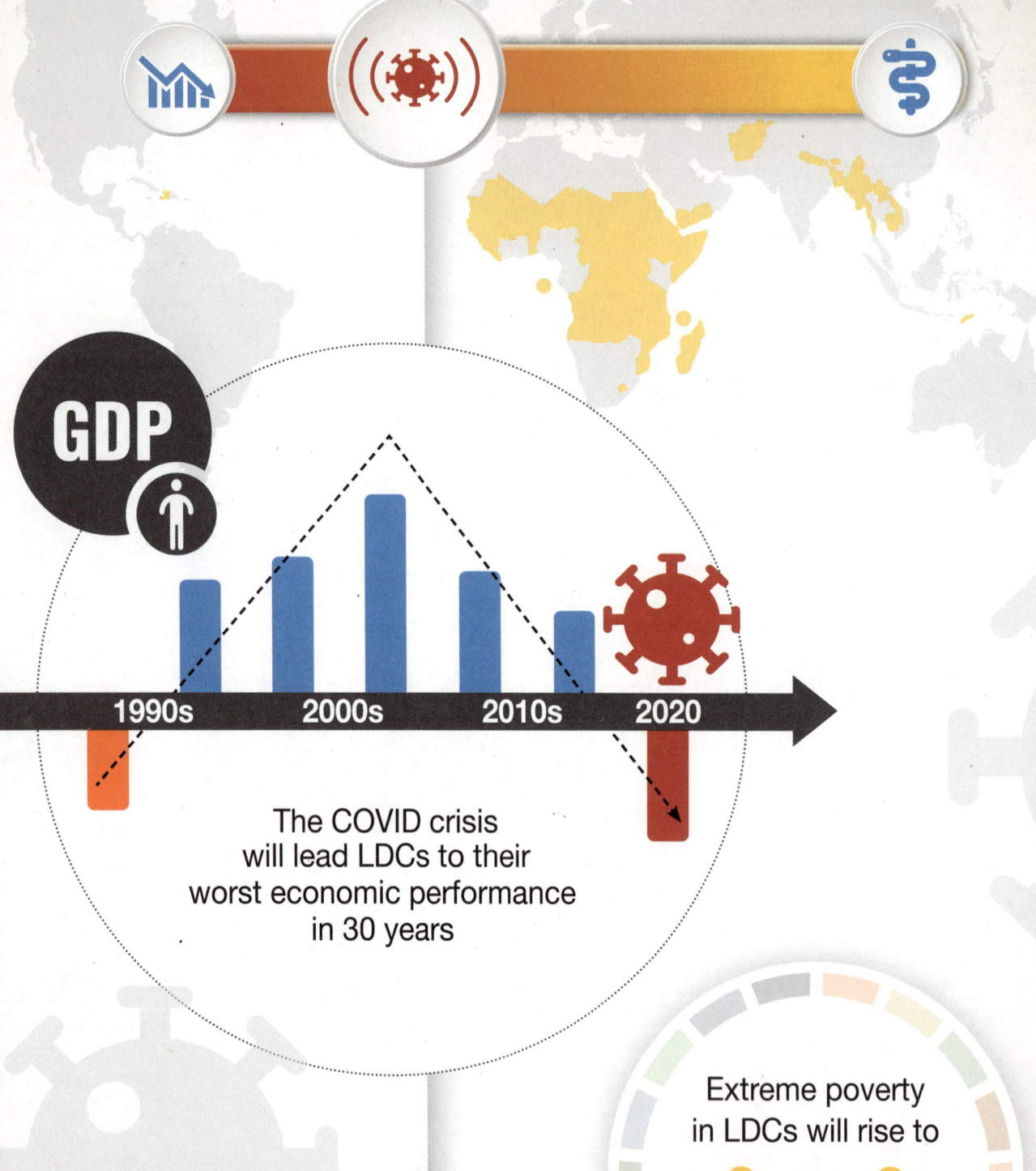

CHAPTER 1

The COVID-19 crisis in LDCs

CHAPTER 1
The COVID-19 crisis in LDCs

A. Introduction	**3**
B. Impacts of COVID-19 on LDCs	**3**
1. The health impact	3
2. The economic impact	7
a. Output and employment	*7*
b. Foreign trade	*8*
c. Migration and remittances	*10*
d. Current account and capital flows	*12*
3. Poverty and social impact	13
C. LDC vulnerabilities	**14**
1. What are vulnerabilities?	14
2. LDCs: the most vulnerable group of countries	15
3. Implications in the short and medium term	16
D. The continued relevance of the LDC category	**17**
E. Objectives and structure of this report	**22**

CHAPTER 1: The COVID-19 crisis in LDCs

A. Introduction

The world continues to confront the effects of the COVID-19 pandemic, including both its lingering health effects and, crucially, the deep economic recession caused by the so-called "Great Lockdown".

As the pandemic began to spread globally in the first quarter of 2020, concerns were expressed that it would have catastrophic *health* consequences on those countries with the least performant health system and/or the poorest countries. Most least developed countries (LDCs) typically fall in either category or both. Moreover, it was feared that the *economic* consequences of the pandemic would impact the world's most vulnerable and least resilient economies the hardest. Again, many LDC economies fit this depiction. In other words, it was feared that the LDCs would be the worst affected group of countries by the pandemic, across both the health and economic/social dimensions.

In order to assess the extent to which these dire predictions have so far been borne out by actual developments on the ground, the present chapter undertakes an initial and still partial assessment of the impact of the COVID-19 pandemic on LDCs by first analysing its *health* impact and second, its *economic and social* effects. It shows that while the *health* effects of the pandemic have not been as serious as initially feared, its *economic and social* impacts have been grave. The research was undertaken with data and information available as of mid-September 2020. Still, while COVID-related statistics are updated on a daily basis, many of the related health, economic and social challenges faced by LDCs are structural, and have a lasting impact on the capacity of these countries to face external shocks originating in the health or economic spheres, or elsewhere.

B. Impacts of COVID-19 on LDCs

1. The health impact

The first LDC to declare a case of COVID-19 infection was Nepal, already in January 2020. By March 2020, the disease had spread widely throughout the LDC group, leading to a rapid increase – from three to 37 – in the number of LDCs reporting cases of COVID-19 infection between the beginning and the end of the month. By mid-May 2020 43 LDCs reported cases of infection.[1]

---

[1] The only LDCs that reported not having a single COVID-19 case by late August 2020 were Kiribati, Solomon Islands, Tuvalu and Vanuatu. Their geographic isolation together with international travel bans helped many small island developing States (SIDS) escape COVID-19 infection (at least initially). However, their location and economic structure make them more vulnerable to fluctuations in international tourism, the sector in which most of them are internationally specialized (see section B.2.b).

The LDC density of medical doctors corresponds to one tenth of that of developed countries

The rapid spread of the disease gave rise to catastrophic forecasts about the likely effects and consequences of the pandemic in LDCs, especially those in Africa (Okereke and Nielsen, 2020). These dire scenarios were based on the low level of development of most health system in LDCs, and their consequent incapacity to respond adequately to a possible sudden surge in infections if there had been a rapid spread among the population of these countries.

This weakness of most health systems in LDCs stems from the insufficient quantity and quality of personnel, infrastructure, equipment and medical supplies. Despite recent improvements, decades of under-investment have left many health care systems in LDCs severely under-resourced and constrained, including for surveillance, testing, contact tracing, and case management (treatment).[2] In terms of health personnel, the average density of medical doctors in LDCs corresponds to just one tenth of the level in developed countries and one fifth of the figure in other developing countries (ODCs – i.e. developing countries excluding LDCs) (Table 1.1). In 31 out of 46 LDCs where data are readily available, the density is two medical doctors per 10,000 inhabitants or lower, as opposed to an average of 14 in ODCs. The density of medical doctors is particularly low in African LDCs. Similarly, the average density of nurses in LDCs is less than one third the level to be found in ODCs; in only four LDCs (Tuvalu, Kiribati, Lesotho and Nepal – mostly countries with small populations) is it higher than the ODC average.

LDCs not only face a dearth of health professionals relative to the size of their populations but also inadequate health systems infrastructure. Their average density of hospital beds before the outbreak of the pandemic was one-fourth the level of ODCs, with only one LDC (Sao Tome and Principe) having a higher density than the ODC average. At the same time, the average density of hospital beds in LDCs corresponded to about 10 per cent of the level of developed countries. In terms of equipment,

---

[2] Domestic government health expenditure per capita in LDCs was $29 in 2017 in purchasing-power parity (PPP), one tenth of the level of ODCs ($315) and less than 1 per cent of the level of developed countries ($3,692) (Development Initiatives, 2020).

The Least Developed Countries Report 2020

Table 1.1

Health system indicators, per country group

(Per 10 000 population, 2010–2019, most recent data available)

Country group	Density of medical doctors	Density of nursing and midwifery personnel	Hospital beds
Developed countries	31	113	52
Other developing countries (ODCs)	14	26	22
LDCs	3	7	6
African LDCs and Haiti	1	7	4
Asian LDCs	5	8	8
Island LDCs	4	16	11
LDCs / ODCs ratio (%)	**20**	**28**	**25**

Source: UNCTAD Secretariat calculation, based on data from WHO, World Health Statistics 2020 and The Global Health Observatory database, and UNCTAD, UNCTADStat database [both databases accessed July 2020].

at the outbreak of the pandemic many LDCs were unprepared to provide intensive care to patients critically affected by COVID-19, due to the dearth of intensive care units (ICUs) and ventilators.[3] Overall, the Global Health Security Index classified (before the outbreak of COVID-19) two thirds of LDCs' health systems among the world's "least prepared" to effectively govern and coordinate a successful response to an epidemic, pandemic or other health risk.[4] This means that their health systems are very vulnerable to any health crisis or emergency.

In spite of the initial catastrophic forecasts, the *health* impact of the COVID-19 pandemic on LDCs during the first eight months of 2020 was considerably less severe than what had been initially feared.[5] Seventy-one ODCs and 42 developed countries had higher infection rates than the LDC average on 31 August 2020. Infection rates in the LDCs corresponded to one fifth of those prevalent in ODCs, and less than 10 per cent of those of developed countries. Among LDC of subgroups, the most affected were the Asian LDCs (Figure 1.1), especially Bangladesh and Nepal, which had more than 1,000 cases per million inhabitants as of 31 August 2020. On average, African LDCs and Haiti as a group had the lowest infection rate. Countries with small populations, e.g. Djibouti, Sao Tome and Principe, Mauritania, Gambia and Guinea-Bissau,

also had more than 1,000 infection cases per million inhabitants, but infection rates in other countries in the subgroup were significantly lower. The infection rate of the island LDCs stood somewhere in-between that of the other two subgroups (Figure 1.1).

Considering the deaths caused by COVID-19, the contrast is even sharper (Figure 1.1). Two LDCs, Sao Tome and Principe and Djibouti, reported slightly more than 50 deaths per million inhabitants. These high figures, however, are partly due to a basis effect because, as countries with small populations (less than 1 million), even a reduced number of deaths appears large in relative terms. The next four most affected were larger countries, which experienced between 20 and 40 deaths per million inhabitants: Gambia, Afghanistan, Mauritania and Bangladesh (in descending order of deaths relative to population). The other 37 LDCs reporting COVID data had experienced less than 20 COVID-related deaths per million inhabitants.

The health outcome of the pandemic in LDCs during the first eight months of 2020 contrasts with that of ODCs, 64 of whom had a higher COVID-19 mortality rate than the LDC average, as well as developed countries, 50 of whom had more deaths relative to the population than the LDC average. As of late August 2020 the COVID-19 mortality rate of LDCs corresponded to 13 per cent of that of ODCs and 3 per cent of that of developed countries (Figure 1.1).[6]

The fact that the health impact of the pandemic on LDCs was less severe than initially feared (at least during the first eight months of 2020) has to be

---

[3] In early 2020 South Sudan had only 24 ICUs to serve the whole population (International Rescue Committee, 2020). By mid-April 2020 ten African countries did not have ventilators and several LDCs (Central African Republic, Democratic Republic of the Congo, Liberia, Madagascar, Mali and South Sudan) had less than ten ventilators to serve the entire country (Maclean and Marks, 2020).

[4] One third of the world's countries fall into the "least prepared" category (Nuclear Threat Initiative et al., 2019).

[5] The cut-off date for pandemic statistics for this report is 2 September 2020.

[6] All of these figures were calculated by the UNCTAD secretariat based on data from the WHO Coronavirus Disease (COVID-19) Dashboard and the UNCTADStat database [both accessed in September 2020].

Figure 1.1
Impact of COVID-19, by country group
(As of 31 August 2020)

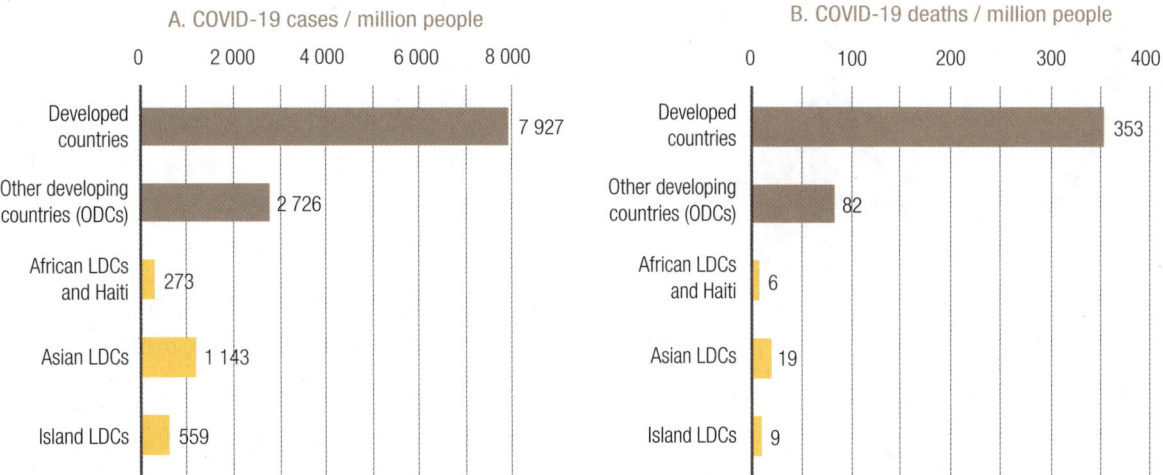

Source: UNCTAD secretariat calculations, based on data from the WHO Coronavirus Disease (COVID-19) Dashboard and UNCTAD, UNCTADStat database [accessed September 2020].

regarded with caution. It is possible that the picture of the less serious health impact of COVID-19 in LDCs than in other country groups is influenced by spurious factors. First, it is likely that under-reporting of COVID-19 cases has occurred in some LDCs due to their lower COVID-19 testing capacities, as well as less efficient casualty counting and reporting systems, as compared to other country groups. Second, there may be a timing issue: typically, LDCs were affected by the pandemic later than other countries, and it cannot be excluded that they will experience a broader spread of the pandemic in the final months of 2020 or later. This could be the consequence of different developments, such as: (i) a possible acceleration of domestic spread; (ii) further infection brought about by higher international traffic of people, goods and services as lockdown measures and travel bans are eased or lifted; or (iii) worsening infection rates in other countries having an indirect effect on LDCs. Such an acceleration of the spread of the pandemic in LDCs would further lay bare the high vulnerability of these countries and the limited preparedness of their health system to deal with a major surge in infections.

Nevertheless, the fact that LDCs were (at least initially) less impacted than other countries by the pandemic has been attributed to different reasons, including policy action and demographic factors. As most LDCs were affected by the pandemic later than countries in East Asia and Western Europe, they had the time to adopt containment and mitigation measures, such as confinement, quarantine, social distancing and travel bans, which prevented the pandemic from spreading further. As of mid-May 2020 the average stringency of measures adopted by LDCs – as measured by the Stringency Index – stood at 79, similar to the other developing countries (80), but higher than developed countries (74).[7] The most stringent measures were adopted by the Asian LDCs (with a Stringency Index of 85), which were the subgroup of LDCs most affected by the pandemic (Figure 1.1). Moreover, LDCs with experience of previous epidemics (e.g. Ebola, Lassa fever, polio and human immunodeficiency virus and acquired immune deficiency syndrome – HIV/AIDS) had already developed some institutional and health policy capacity to respond to new epidemic outbreaks, which facilitated their reaction to COVID-19 (Massinga Loembé et al., 2020).

The outbreak of the pandemic spurred health sector innovations – in both the institutional and technological spheres – by domestic agents and institutions. These innovations helped address the consequences of the pandemic and/or limit its spread. Innovative mechanisms adapted to local conditions were adopted by different LDC governments,

---

[7] The Stringency Index calculated by Oxford University's Blavatnik School of Government records the strictness of 'lockdown style' policies which restrict people's behaviour [https://www.bsg.ox.ac.uk/research/research-projects/coronavirus-government-response-tracker#data, accessed July 2020]. The Index ranges from 1 to 100. The data mentioned in the text are population-weighted and were calculated by the UNCTAD secretariat. The date quoted was selected because it marked the moment when the stringency measures were at their peak around the world.

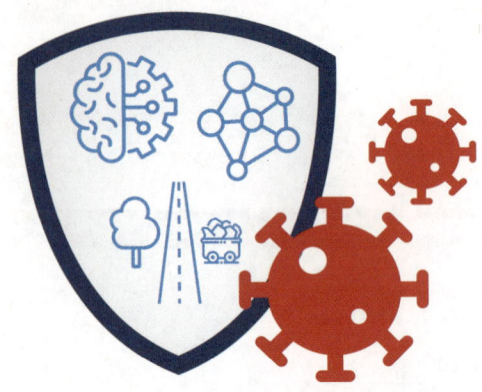

LDCs with more developed productive capacities have been better equipped to withstand COVID-19

e.g. by having traditional chieftains transmit health information and advice on COVID-19 to the local population, as in the case of Sierra Leone; using locally assembled drones to increase awareness through in-flight public broadcasts, as Rwanda did; or making available public mobile handwashing facilities in city centres and transportation nodes like bus stations (e.g. Rwanda). In terms of medical technologies, researchers in Senegal developed an immune-based diagnostic test for COVID-19 available for only $1. Rwanda adopted innovative measures, such as deploying robots to screen and monitor COVID-19 patients, mathematical modelling to forecast the spread of the pandemic, and using drones to rapidly deliver medicines throughout the country. In terms of manufacturing medical equipment and supplies, some LDCs with manufacturing capacity (e.g. Senegal, Bangladesh) repurposed industrial facilities to produce low-tech medical goods such as face masks, hand sanitizers and personal protective equipment (PPE). In some cases, more sophisticated equipment such as innovative and less-technology-intensive ventilators were produced, as happened in Uganda thanks to the collaboration between Makarere University and a local car manufacturer (Nebe and Jalloh, 2020). In Senegal, engineering students built a multifunctional medical robot to lessen the load on healthcare workers (Travaly et al., 2020).

LDCs with a pre-existing manufacturing capacity have been the most capable of formulating innovative local manufacturing solutions in response to the pandemic. Therefore, those LDCs which had a relatively broader industrial base (such as those mentioned above) were better prepared to confront the medical emergency and implement innovative solutions based on local conditions. This indicates that a link exists between the preparedness of countries to face an epidemic and the level of development of their productive capacities. The same reasoning applies to other shocks (medical, natural or economic): the countries which have a broader and more sophisticated base of productive capacities are better prepared to weather different types of shocks, i.e. they are more resilient (see section B). This is one of the leitmotivs of the present report.

The demographic factors explaining why COVID-19 had a lesser impact on LDCs is that the proportion of young population – known to be more resilient in case of infection – in these countries is much larger than in the most affected countries. Another demographic factor favouring a weaker impact in LDCs is lower population density, which reduces the likelihood of contagion. This is particularly true in rural areas, where two thirds of the population of LDCs currently live (the highest share of rural population among major country groups).[8] This effect was likely strengthened to some extent by the fact that a large number of people originating from rural areas but living in cities reacted to government containment measures by returning to their areas of origin, thus somewhat and temporarily reducing the urban population. Asian LDCs typically have higher population density than African LDCs, which translated into the pandemic spreading more extensively in the former than in the latter countries (Figure 1.1). Small island LDCs, by contrast, were also favoured by their natural isolation, which was further accentuated by the implementation of travel bans.[9]

Moreover, the COVID-19 indicators analysed above do not take into account the indirect health effects of the pandemic, which comprise among others: (i) the impact of the economic slowdown/recession on social outcomes, including poverty, nutrition and health outcomes not directly stemming from the pandemic; and (ii) the impact of falling government revenues and household incomes on health spending. Apart from its properly economic aspects in terms of employment, personal income and macroeconomic performance, it also has an indirect negative effect on the health of LDC citizens. These indirect effects may be as serious, or even more acute, than the direct effects of the pandemic. The next section analyses some of these major indirect effects.

---

[8] Data from the UNCTADStat database [accessed July 2020].
[9] The only LDCs that had not declared COVID-19 infection cases by late June 2020 were all small island developing states (SIDS).

2. The economic impact

Even if the pandemic does not spread in the LDCs to the same extent as other countries (both ODCs and developed countries), they are nonetheless being severely hit by its economic, social and environmental consequences. In 2020 LDC economies suffered the strongest economic shock in several decades due to the consequences of the COVID-19 pandemic. This, in turn, has led to a sharp economic downturn due to the combined effects of a deep world economic recession and the consequences of the domestic containment measures taken by LDC governments. Worse still, these consequences are likely to linger in the medium term.

The severe economic impact on LDCs is explained by their structural economic shortcomings and by their not having fully recovered from the shock of the 2008–2009 global financial crisis (UNCTAD, 2019a). Since then the economic performance of LDCs has been adversely affected by the "new normal" of sluggish growth in the global economy, persistently low international commodity prices, growing trade and current account deficits leading to rising external debt, and an exhaustion of the fiscal space available before the outbreak of the global financial crisis (UNCTAD, 2019b). Therefore, LDC economies started the current economic slump from a situation of heightened economic vulnerability.

The economic situation of LDCs was clearly different when the global financial crisis of 2008–2009 broke out as they had weathered the international turbulence relatively better than initially expected. They were able to do so thanks to a combination of some degree of isolation from major international financial flows and the availability of policy space accumulated during the years of strong economic growth of the early 2000s.

The adverse economic impacts of the present COVID-19 crisis has severely affected the process of growth and development of LDCs, including a setback or reversal in their progress towards reaching their development goals, starting with poverty (see subsection 3 below). It is also likely to delay or extend the graduation process of several LDCs that had been scheduled to graduate as of December 2020 (page xi).

a. Output and employment

The measures adopted by most LDCs, e.g. lockdown, movement restriction and travel ban measures, caused a sharp downturn in economic activity, and created a shock in both demand and supply, similarly to what also occurred in other economies. Between October 2019 and October 2020, the economic

43 out of 47 LDCs are forecast to experience a fall in their average income levels in 2020

growth forecast for LDCs was revised sharply downwards from 5 to -0.4 per cent. This revision is expected to lead to a 2.6 per cent reduction in per capita income in LDCs in 2020,[10] with 43 out of 47 LDCs experiencing a fall in their average income levels. This represents the worst economic outcome in 30 years for this group of countries. It has not only led to a reversal in the economic and social progress achieved over recent years, including in terms of poverty and social outcomes (see section 3), but also makes reaching the Sustainable Developed Goals a more distant prospect.

The International Labour Organization (ILO) stated that working-hours losses in the first half of 2020 could be equivalent to over 400 million full-time jobs worldwide, while 1.6 billion workers in the informal economy were at immediate risk of seeing their livelihoods reduced (ILO, 2020a). Other studies have raised profound concerns about the challenges faced by enterprises and small businesses simultaneously facing the dire consequences of the recession, and the disruptions caused by lockdowns and related measures to respond to the health emergency (UNECA, 2020; Le Nestour and Moscoviz, 2020; Aung, et al., 2020; Bosio et al., 2020).

A protracted recession could cause permanent job destruction, threaten enterprise survival – with related losses in terms of tacit knowledge and productive capabilities – and potentially have a long-term effect on potential output. Avoiding this dramatic outcome will be particularly crucial in LDCs, because of the structural characteristics of their forms of entrepreneurship (UNCTAD, 2018a). With a plethora of mainly informal "me-too businesses",[11] a predominance of small firms, and limited access to credit for the private sector, a prolonged crisis would further damage the already weak entrepreneurial landscape of LDCs. According to early surveys carried out by the United Nations Economic Commission for Africa (UNECA), African firms were operating at 43 per cent of their capacities by mid-2020, with labour-intensive

---

[10] UNCTAD secretariat calculations based on data from IMF, World Economic Outlook database [accessed October 2020].
[11] "Me-too business" are firms producing mostly well-established goods and services using well established technologies, and which tend innovate very little, if at all.

LDC inflows of external resources shrank sharply in 2020

sectors, e.g. manufacturing, transport, trade, tourism and restoration services, as the hardest hit sectors (UNECA, 2020). Similar difficulties were reported in relation to the garment industry in Asia, as supply chain disruptions were compounded with a deep recession in key export markets (Aung, et al., 2020). In this context, the deeper or longer the crisis the higher the risk of exacerbating the LDCs' "missing middle", as the downturn threatens hard-gained entrepreneurial capabilities and ultimately jeopardizes a broad-based recovery.

The restrictive measures adopted by LDCs caused a shrinking of economic activity especially in wholesale and retail trade (including in the informal sector), transport and manufacturing.[12] The information and communication technologies (ICTs) sector expanded its activities (as happened worldwide) and e-commerce grew as new firms and services were established or existing ones expanded their activities (as occured in Senegal and Rwanda). Still, given the small weight of these activities and sectors in LDC economies, their expansion was more than compensated by the contraction taking place elsewhere. Agriculture was considered an essential sector in LDCs and therefore exempted from most restrictive measures. However, it could face challenges if continued restrictive measures were to jeopardize the mobility of labour, the availability of inputs (seeds, fertilizers, agro-chemicals, agricultural equipment), or access to finance (see below). This could negatively affect the new planting season.

Moreover, agricultural production in East African countries and the southern Arabian Peninsula was affected by huge swarms of desert locusts during the first half of 2020, which destroyed crops in Djibouti, Eritrea, Ethiopia, Somalia, South Sudan, United Republic of Tanzania and Yemen.

The delay of fixed investment (including infrastructure) projects not only compounds the fall in domestic demand, but also has a negative impact on medium-term economic growth (see chapter 2). Micro-finance institutions in many LDCs have ground to a halt following a sharp drop in their revenues due to plummeting savings and loan repayments, thereby impairing their capacity to give out loans. Fiscal accounts were directly impacted by the slump in economic activities, which led to shrinking revenues at a time when expenditure had to expand due to rising health spending, personal and firms' income support schemes and other forms of expenditures deriving from the existing limited social protection schemes. The latest deterioration of the fiscal situation comes on top of a trend of rising fiscal deficits in LDCs during the 2010s (UNCTAD, 2019b). The fiscal situation prevailing prior to the outbreak of the pandemic prevented LDCs from taking more decisive fiscal measures to prop up their economies in response to the COVID-19 shock. The median additional spending/foregone revenues implemented by LDCs amounted to just $17.8 per capita, less than one fourth of the corresponding figure for ODCs ($76), and just 1 per cent of the amount mobilized by developed countries ($1,365).[13]

b. Foreign trade

Likely stronger than the domestic demand shock was the impact of the world economic recession on the LDC economies. This is the deepest downturn the world is undergoing since the Great Depression of the 1930s, with per capita output contracting in the largest fraction of countries since 1870 (World Bank, 2020c). The downturn also brought about a sharp shrinking in the external demand for LDC goods and services, depressed the prices of their main exports, and caused a slump in inflows of external resources (remittances, capital).

The most deeply affected export commodities of LDCs during the first half of 2020 were fuels, which accounted for over one fourth of the group's merchandise exports before the outbreak of the pandemic. Fuel prices slumped by 36 per cent in

---

[12] The manufacturing activity of LDCs was further depressed by disruption in global supply chains, which caused the suspension or delay of imports of critical industrial inputs (e.g. intermediate goods).

[13] UNCTAD secretariat calculations, based on data from IMF (2020b) and UNCTAD, UNCTADStat database [accessed June 2020].

CHAPTER 1: The COVID-19 crisis in LDCs

January-July 2020, as compared to the corresponding period in 2019.[14] Quantities exported also declined sharply following a worldwide shrinking of transport, travel and manufacturing-related activities. The LDCs expected to be the most affected were those for which these products accounted for the highest share of their merchandise exports prior to the pandemic; this particularly affected Angola, Chad, Timor-Leste, Mozambique and Yemen, where fuels contributed more than 40 per cent of their merchandise exports (Figure 1.2 A).

World demand for minerals and metals also shrank during the first half of 2020 due to plummeting manufacturing and building activity across the world. This depressed worldwide demand for these products and strongly contributed to a 7-per-cent decline in prices during the first seven months of the year. The LDCs which suffered the most from these developments were likely to be countries, such as the Democratic Republic of the Congo, Zambia, Guinea, Sierra Leone and Eritrea, where minerals and metals accounted for over 40 per cent of merchandise exports before the outbreak of the COVID-19 crisis (Figure 1.2 B).

Manufactured goods exports accounted for 37 per cent of total LDC merchandise exports (before the pandemic). The bulk of their merchandise exports consist of garments (and, to a lesser extent, textiles). The effects of the lockdown on retail trade and the massive global job losses that occurred as a consequence of the pandemic, together with the fact that spending on these items can typically be delayed by consumers, has led to an especially acute slump in worldwide demand for garments. Orders from developed countries to LDC producers were therefore cut back sharply and LDC exports of garments are forecast to shrink by 20 per cent in 2020 (UN DESA, 2020). This caused a deep fall in exports of LDCs, such as Bangladesh, Cambodia, Haiti, Nepal and Lesotho, for which manufactures account for over 50 per cent of merchandise exports (Figure 1.2 C).[15]

Tourism and travel were among the industries most sharply affected by the restrictive measures adopted to contain the spread of the pandemic, including both the direct effects (travel bans and movement restrictions) and indirect effects (the worldwide

[14] According to the UNCTAD Free-Market Commodity Price Index. This index is also used for price variations mentioned further down in the text.

[15] Figure 1.2 C also indicates that more than half of Bhutan's merchandise exports are made up of manufactures, but this figure must be interpreted with caution and may be due to misclassification of exported goods.

Figure 1.2
LDC export vulnerabilities

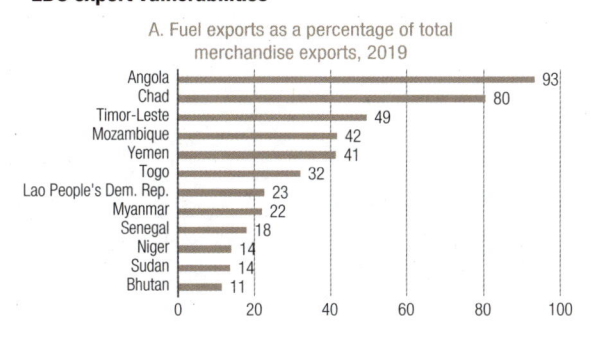

A. Fuel exports as a percentage of total merchandise exports, 2019

Country	%
Angola	93
Chad	80
Timor-Leste	49
Mozambique	42
Yemen	41
Togo	32
Lao People's Dem. Rep.	23
Myanmar	22
Senegal	18
Niger	14
Sudan	14
Bhutan	11

B. Ores and metals exports as a percentage of total merchandise exports, 2019

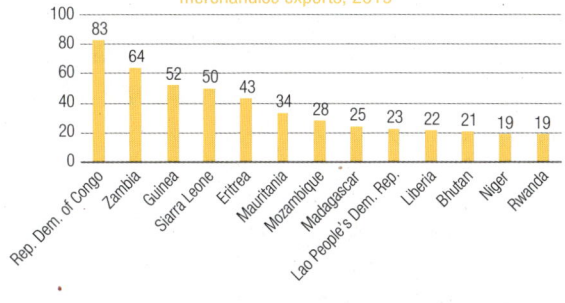

Country	%
Rep. Dem. of Congo	83
Zambia	64
Guinea	52
Sierra Leone	50
Eritrea	43
Mauritania	34
Mozambique	28
Madagascar	25
Lao People's Dem. Rep.	23
Liberia	22
Bhutan	21
Niger	19
Rwanda	19

C. Manufactures exports as a percentage of total merchandise exports (2019)

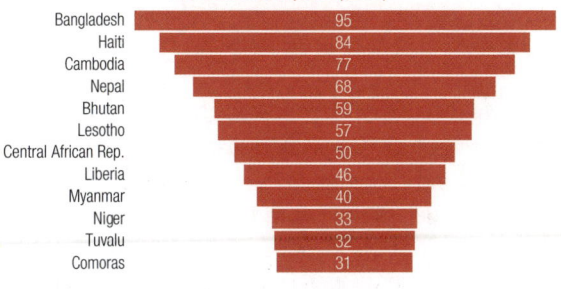

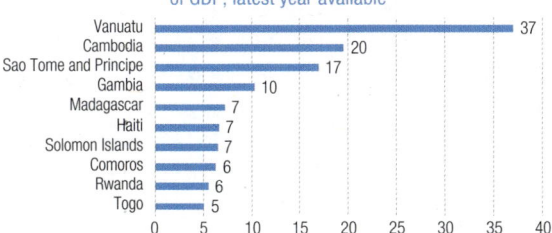

Country	%
Bangladesh	95
Haiti	84
Cambodia	77
Nepal	68
Bhutan	59
Lesotho	57
Central African Rep.	50
Liberia	46
Myanmar	40
Niger	33
Tuvalu	32
Comoros	31

D. Inbound tourism expeditures as a percentage of GDP, latest year available

Country	%
Vanuatu	37
Cambodia	20
Sao Tome and Principe	17
Gambia	10
Madagascar	7
Haiti	7
Solomon Islands	7
Comoros	6
Rwanda	6
Togo	5

Source: UNCTAD secretariat calculations based on data from UNCTAD, UNCTADStat database and UNWTO, Compendium of Tourism Statistics dataset [Electronic] [both accessed September 2020].

slump in business activities, household earnings and employment). The worldwide tourism sector is forecast to shrink by between 30 and 62 per cent in 2020 (WTTC, 2020). LDC tourism and travel exports were initially strongly hit by COVID-19 lockdowns and multiple travel bans. Thereafter, even with the relaxation of these restrictive measures, LDC tourism receipts continued to be jeopardized by the

LDCs will not meet the goal of doubling their share of world trade by 2020

fact that they depend strongly on personal and leisure demand, which can easily be delayed and cut back in view of shrinking household income in the main countries of origin of tourists, as well as lingering concerns relating to the spread of the pandemic in the different origin and destination countries of tourists. The adverse development in tourism will likely hit Vanuatu, Cambodia, Sao Tome and Principe and the Gambia particularly hard, as inbound tourism expenditures in these countries accounted for more than 10 per cent of gross domestic product (GDP) (Figure 1.2 D).

In the context of this shrinking of world trade and plummeting LDC exports, it unlikely that LDCs will meet their long-standing goal on trade, i.e. that of doubling their share of world exports of goods and services in 2020. This goal was expressed initially in the Programme of Action for the Least Developed Countries for the Decade 2011–2020 (commonly referred to as the Istanbul Programme of Action – IPoA) (United Nations, 2011), and later reaffirmed in the 2030 Agenda for Sustainable Development (2015) (United Nations, 2015c). There had been no progress towards that goal before the present crisis, as the group's share of world exports had hovered around 1 per cent since the objective of doubling the share was adopted (UNCTAD, 2019a). Moreover, it is unlikely that demand for LDC main export products (e.g. garments, fuels, tourism) will pick up faster than other types of goods and services when world trade recovers from the COVID-19 slump. Rather, economic stimulus packages adopted in the major economies are expected to focus on products and sectors, such high-tech services, green energy and construction. Long-distance tourism is also not expected to recover quickly (IMF, 2020c).

LDC imports are likely to have contracted less than their exports, in spite of the fall in domestic demand. The reason for the likely asymmetric developments in exports and imports is their composition and their respective elasticity to foreign and domestic demand. Typically, LDC merchandise exports are very sensitive of cyclical developments in the world economy (including both developed countries and ODCs), especially trends relating to industrial production, construction and household income. By contrast, LDC imports of goods are dominated by essential products, such as food, fuel, capital equipment and intermediate goods, several of which are more difficult to cut back on even during a cyclical downturn. Thirty-nine of the 46 LDCs for which data are available[16] are net food importing countries. Contrary to the fall in prices of energy, and minerals and metals exported by LDCs, world food prices in January-July 2020 were actually 3.5 per cent higher than in the corresponding period in 2019, thereby generating a higher food import bill. By contrast, the fuel import bill of the 39 net fuel-importing LDCs will benefit from lower import prices and the contraction of domestic activity level.

The benign effect for fuel-importing countries is expected to be overwhelmed by the adverse export developments mentioned above. Therefore, the merchandise trade deficit of LDCs in 2020 is forecast to exceed the record level reached in 2019: $86 billion. This means that LDCs will extend the trend towards widening merchandise trade deficits which started with the global financial crisis of 2008–2009 (UNCTAD, 2019b).

Concerning services trade, a similar asymmetry exists between the composition of exports and imports, leading to similarly divergent paths in the context of both a worldwide and domestic recession. While most of their services exports stem from activities that can easily be delayed and cut back during a world recession (especially leisure tourism), LDC imports consist more of business and professional services which continue to be required by domestic economies even during an economic downturn. Although services import demand shrank, it occurred at a slower pace than exports. Overall, it is likely that the combined deficit in trade in goods and services of LDCs will expand further in 2020, thus extending the trend that began with the global financial crisis of 2008–2009 (UNCTAD, 2019b), similar to that of merchandise trade. Moreover, widening trade deficits are expected to be compounded by adverse developments in other current account components, as analysed hereafter.

c. Migration and remittances

International migration and the remittances flows it generates were severely affected by the "Great Lockdown" and the ensuing worldwide recession. Thousands of immigrants originating in LDCs lost their jobs, had their working hours reduced and/or suffered wages cuts or even non-payment of wages in their host countries (ILO, 2020b). Many of these foreign workers were expelled by host countries and had to return to their country of origin. Total remittances to

---

[16] Trade data for South Sudan are not available.

Figure 1.3
Remittances as a share of GDP, selected LDCs
(2019, %)

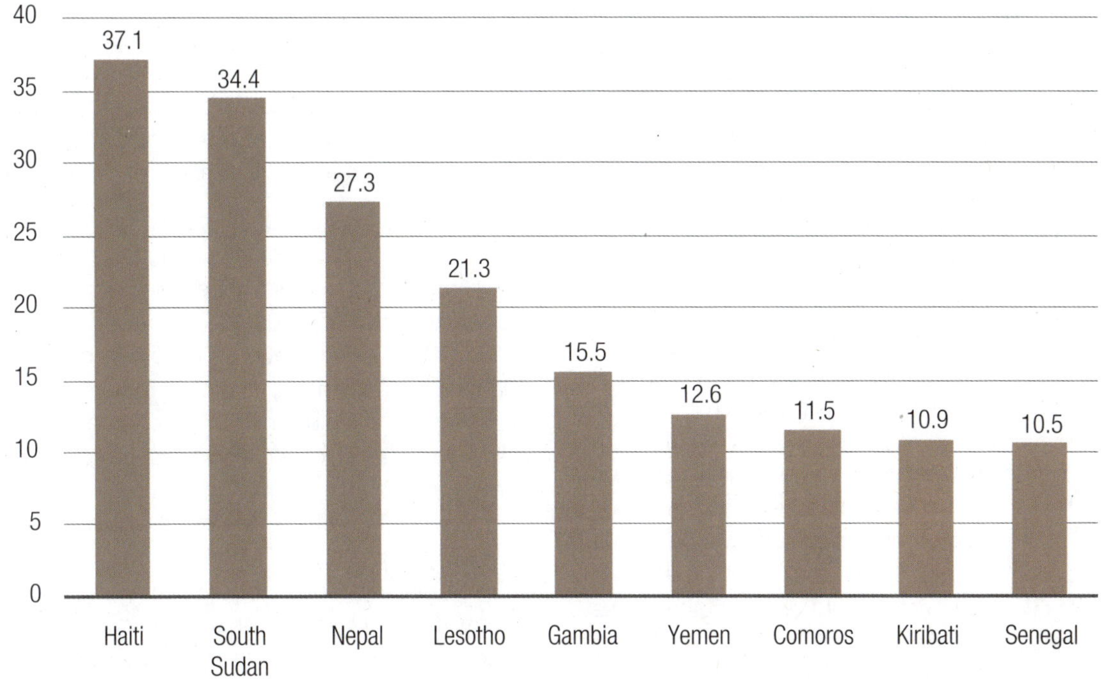

Country	%
Haiti	37.1
South Sudan	34.4
Nepal	27.3
Lesotho	21.3
Gambia	15.5
Yemen	12.6
Comoros	11.5
Kiribati	10.9
Senegal	10.5

Source: UNCTAD elaboration based on data from World Bank, Remittances Inflows dataset [www.knomad.org, accessed June 2020].

low and middle-income countries are forecast to fall by one fifth in 2020 (World Bank, 2020b).

The major destination countries of LDC emigration before the pandemic were hardly hit by the COVID-19 crisis, including both its health and economic aspects. India, Saudi Arabia, Thailand, United States, Islamic Republic of Iran and Côte d'Ivoire (in descending order) each hosted more than 20 million immigrants from LDCs before the outbreak of the pandemic. An estimated 3 million foreign workers were expected to leave Saudi Arabia between 2019 and 2020 as a result of the local economic downturn exacerbated by the pandemic (Kerr and England, 2020). With 30 per cent of the country's immigrants originating from LDCs, Saudi Arabia is the world's second largest host country for LDC immigrants.[17] In 2020, 1 million Bangladeshis, 200,000 Ethiopians and 100,000 nationals from Afghanistan and Myanmar returned home (Kerr and England, 2020; Aung, 2020).

In 2020 remittances to the regions of origin of most LDC emigrants are expected to decrease by more than the world average. Those to South Asia are projected to decline sharply by 22 per cent and those to sub-Saharan Africa by 23.1 per cent (World Bank, 2020b). The impact of these developments on remittances' levels is strongly contingent on labour market developments and immigration policy changes adopted by host country authorities in reaction to the COVID-19 pandemic. The repercussion will therefore be very country-specific. Before the outbreak of the pandemic, remittances' receipts corresponded to more than one third of the GDP of Haiti and South Sudan GDP, and one fifth to one fourth of the GDP of Nepal and Lesotho. For the following countries they amounted more than 10 per cent of GDP: Gambia, Yemen, Comoros, Kiribati and Senegal (Figure 1.3). This means that these foreign inflows are important for a wide range of LDCs, including countries from all regions, size of economy and type of export specialization.[18] Therefore, the forecast shrinking of worldwide remittances flows in 2020 is expected to have a negative impact on a large number of LDCs.

---

[17] UNCTAD secretariat calculations, based on data from World Bank, Migration and Remittances Data [https://www.worldbank.org/en/topic/migrationremittancesdiasporaissues/brief/migration-remittances-data, accessed July 2020].

[18] Apart from the countries shown in Figure 1.3, remittances accounted for over 5 per cent of GDP in another seven LDCs, including the largest LDC economy, Bangladesh.

The LDC current account deficit will deepen from 3.8% of GDP in 2019 to 5.6% of GDP in 2020

Falling remittances receipts will further depress domestic consumption in LDCs, since remittances are an important source of income, especially for rural (and often poor) households. Rural households that are dependent on remittance inflows rely on this source of income to finance consumption of goods and services such as food, health and education. Therefore, reduced remittances inflows (both from abroad and from inside the country) will negatively impact their living conditions and cause a deterioration of LDC's social outcomes. Moreover, some rural households rely on foreign remittances to finance hiring agricultural workers. Therefore, a fall in these inflows will further depress labour demand and employment levels, in a context of rising unemployment. Taken together, these developments will strongly contribute to a worsening of poverty in LDCs (section 3 below).

Returnees need to be reabsorbed in the domestic and local economic and social tissue. This may prove challenging, especially in rural areas, where the majority of returned emigrants are likely to originate. They will be looking for jobs and/or other sources of earning and will raise the demand for social services (e.g. health) at a time when the national public sector is already stretched to its limits due to the surge in demand for public health services brought about by the pandemic. The population in certain villages could suddenly grow disproportionally and could actually increase the pressure on local natural resources. This could result in more disorderly small-scale land clearing and shifting cultivation for food production, and an increase of fuelwood harvest from forests (Aung, 2020).

d. Current account and capital flows

The widening trade deficit and contraction in remittances receipts in 2020 are expected to lead to a further expansion of the total current account deficit of LDCs as a group. It is forecast to deepen sharply from 3.8 per cent of GDP in 2019 to 5.6 per cent of GDP in 2020.[19] This will be the highest collective current account deficit of the LDCs, and it will exacerbate the trend towards widening current account deficits since the global financial crisis of 2009–2009 (UNCTAD, 2019b).

Widening current account deficits need to be financed by higher capital inflows and this will represent a major challenge for LDCs. This heightened financing need comes at a time when the major forms of capital inflows of LDCs are also shrinking.

The foremost type of capital inflow into LDCs as a group is official development assistance (ODA), as LDCs are the most aid-dependent economies in the world (UNCTAD, 2019b). It could therefore be expected that ODA inflows rise in order to cover the rising external financing needs of LDCs. However, this heightened need for ODA arises in a context in which the volume of the flows disbursed to LDCs has been roughly stagnating since 2013. Donor countries are far from respecting their long-standing commitment to deliver ODA to LDCs at the height of 0.15–0.20 per cent of donor country gross national income (GNI). Moreover, this heightened need for additional ODA comes at a time when the national budgets of donor countries are themselves under pressure due to sharply higher fiscal deficits. If donor countries were to maintain their ODA as a share of their own GNI constant, total ODA to developing countries (including LDCs) could decline by as much as 10 per cent in 2020, as compared with 2019 (Development Initiatives, 2020). On the other side, the resources required for donor countries to honour their aid commitments are but a fraction of the value of stimulus packages they adopted in response to the COVID-19 crisis.

A statement by the Development Assistance Committee (DAC) of the Organisation for Economic Co-operation and Development (OECD) acknowledges the pressure on the official finances of its members and calls on them to "protect ODA budgets" and pledges "to support Least Developed Countries […] via a coherent and coordinated humanitarian-development-peace response" (OECD-DAC, 2020). At the time of writing, there were no signs of a coordinated response by donor countries to the economic crisis in LDCs, but there have been several indications of rising levels of ODA to the health sector in these countries, as well increasing levels of multilateral aid, especially for the health sector. However, it is unlikely that the effort being made will meet the acutely heightened needs of LDCs (Djankov and Kiechel, 2020).

After ODA and remittances, the next most important source of external development finance for LDCs is

---

[19] Similarly, the median current account deficit of LDCs is forecast to expand from 4.9 per cent of GDP to 6.5 per cent of GDP between 2019 and 2020. These figures and those in the text are estimated by the UNCTAD secretariat based on data from IMF, World Economic Outlook database [accessed October 2020].

foreign direct investment (FDI). However, this form of capital is among the most directly hit by the global recession, both on a worldwide scale and in terms of FDI flows to LDCs. Shrinking new investments, a slowdown of FDI from existing investors and possible divestments has slowed FDI inflows into these countries; these inflows had already shrunk by 5.7 per cent in 2019 and are forecast to fall further in 2020. Several investment projects in LDCs were cancelled in 2020, leading to a 20 per cent fall in FDI inflow value during the first quarter of the year. The natural resources and tourism sectors were among the most affected sectors (UNCTAD, 2020a).

The above developments are making it even harder than usual for LDCs to close their external financing gap. This difficulty has been further aggravated by reduced access to private financing, which has become even more difficult in a context of diminished worldwide private capital flows. Yields on LDCs bonds rose sharply in 2020 and bond issuance plans had to be postponed (as in the case of Burkina Faso). The cost of servicing their external debt increased during the great recession, due to rising yields and, in many cases, the depreciation of national currencies. Additionally, there are indications that other capital outflows have accelerated at a faster pace than after the global financial crisis of 2008–2009 (UNCTAD, 2020b).

3. Poverty and social impact

The global downturn is expected to have a dramatic negative impact on global poverty and food insecurity, as indicated by a host of studies (Gerszon Mahler et al., 2020a; Sumner, Hoy, et al., 2020; Sumner, Ortiz-Juarez, et al., 2020; Valensisi, 2020; UN, 2020; Laborde et al., 2020; Vos et al., 2020). This may give rise to path-dependency and turn transient forms of poverty into chronic forms of poverty.

Historically, the incidence of extreme poverty in the LDCs had remained stubbornly high even prior to the coronavirus pandemic, and the pace of poverty reduction, which was moderately encouraging in the early and mid-2000s, has slowed down markedly in the aftermath of the global financial and economic crisis. As a result, the share of people living in extreme poverty has virtually stalled at about 35 per cent of the population for most of the past decade. Due to the combined effect of persistently widespread poverty and rapid demographic growth, this implies that the number of LDC inhabitants living in extreme poverty had been rising prior to the pandemic, and the LDCs were already accounting for a rising proportion of the world's extreme poor (UNCTAD, 2010, 2014).

> **The crisis will drive an additional 32 million people into absolute poverty in LDCs**

There are growing concerns that the crisis may be deeper or linger on beyond the end of 2020, especially if a balance of payments and/or debt crisis occurs in the developing world. Moreover, the negative impact of the pandemic on households' welfare may be felt through other transmission channels than the pure income dimension, and some of the non-monetary channels may trigger adverse long-term effects, creating path-dependency from "transient" into "chronic poverty" (Valensisi, 2020).

The immediate impact of the COVID-19 pandemic on poverty rates in LDCs is assessed according to different poverty lines and is depicted in Figure 1.4, displaying pre- and post-COVID 19 poverty estimates for the year 2020.[20] The estimates reveal that the downward growth revision in the wake of coronavirus outbreak will lead to a three percentage points' increase – from 32.2 to 35.2 per cent – in the headcount ratio against the $1.90 per day poverty line. This is equivalent to a rise of over 32 million people living in extreme poverty in the LDCs. When measured against the $3.20 per day poverty line, the incidence of poverty will rise by 3.6 percentage points (corresponding to 38 million additional poor), while the impact is smaller when assessed against the $5.50 per day poverty line, as the overwhelming majority of the population in LDCs fell below this threshold even before the pandemic.

A few considerations are warranted on the above figures. First, should the crisis turn out to be deeper than expected – as many indeed fear – the impact on poverty measures would be even higher. It is estimated that if growth in 2020 were two percentage points lower than what the IMF initially forecast (IMF, 2020a), poverty headcounts could rise further by more than one percentage point (Valensisi, 2020). Second, taking IMF forecasts at face value, it is important to highlight the broad difference between the situation faced by about ten LDCs (especially in South East Asia and

---

[20] This methodology assumes that the shock leaves the distribution of income unchanged; however, it is reasonable to expect that some of the poorer segments of the population will be the hardest hit, at least within urban areas.

The Least Developed Countries Report **2020**

Figure 1.4
LDC poverty estimates in 2020, pre- and post- COVID-19, by poverty line

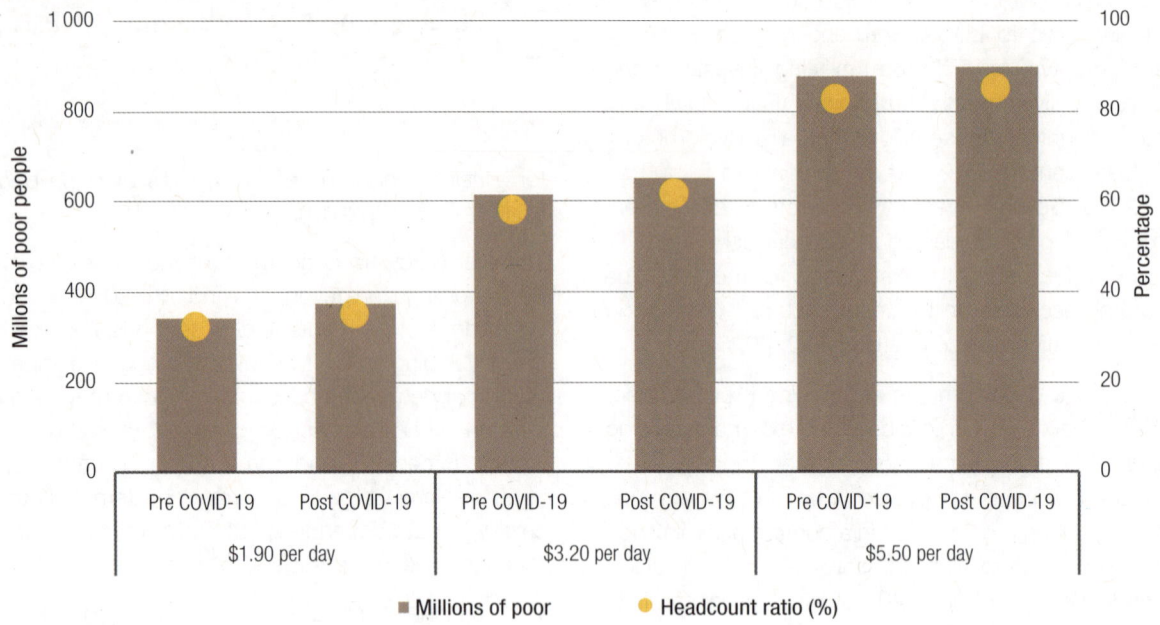

Source: UNCTAD Secretariat calculation based on Valensisi (2020).

East Africa) – where the shock is expected to entail a sharp slowdown of growth but not an outright decline in per capita income – from the situation of many more of them, which are expected to experience a full-fledged reduction in per capita GDP. In the former case, the likely (net) impact of the pandemic will be a sharp deceleration in poverty reduction, whereas in the latter case it will cause a net increase in the incidence of poverty. Third, the COVID-19 outbreak will reinforce the geographic polarization of extreme poverty in Africa and South Asia.

Beyond Sustainable Development Goal 1, this situation represents a significant setback for a number of other Goals, notably those related to health and education, as adverse coping strategies might entail reducing food intake or taking children out of school. Moreover, at a macroeconomic level, the crisis may lead to a reallocation of scarce public resources away from education or general health support. In the same vein, the downturn is likely to further undermine gender equality, as the gender dimension intersects with other axes of structural marginalization, including economic status, membership to minority groups, disability, HIV/AIDS status and the like. In LDCs and in the rest of the world alike, women indeed tend to be over-represented in vulnerable occupational categories (from health personnel to informal own-account workers), as well as in some of the value chains hardest-hit by the crisis, such as tourism or textile and apparel. Moreover, women tend to disproportionately shoulder the burden of care-related tasks and are exposed to heightened risks of gender-based violence in the context of strict lockdowns (UN Women, 2020). The conjunction of these factors is likely to further widen gender gaps and inequalities.

C. LDC vulnerabilities

LDCs have so far been spared from the most severe health impacts of the COVID-19 pandemic, they have nonetheless been among the worst hit by the economic and social consequences of this multidimensional crisis. This apparent contradiction stems from the acute vulnerability of LDC economies and societies to shocks that are out of their control. The pandemic outbreak has exacerbated pre-existing LDC vulnerabilities. The limited capacity of LDC policymakers to react to the shocks originating abroad, regardless of whether they are related to health, the economy or the environment, dramatically highlights the low level of resilience of LDC economies. Since vulnerability and resilience have been brought to the fore by the current crisis and will be central to the post-crisis recovery and (re)construction, they are analysed hereafter in more detail.

1. What are vulnerabilities?

Vulnerability is understood as the exposure of a national economy to exogenous events (shocks and instabilities) that are largely beyond domestic control and that negatively affect its capacity to grow and develop (Guillaumont, 2009). It is considered as structural when it is independent of current or recent domestic policies, but is the result of persistent factors (Guillaumont, 2011). Therefore, it cannot be changed in the short term.[21] Traditionally, the major types of exogenous shocks to which national economies may be exposed to are two-fold.

The first type is made up of economic shocks, such as adverse terms of trade shocks (e.g. due to strong commodity price volatility), or international economic and/or financial crises causing sharp slumps in global demand (or supply). Exposure to these shocks is likely to be higher in countries with one or more of the following characteristics: (i) small countries with very open economies; (ii) countries where national production and/or exports are highly concentrated in a few sectors/products (e.g. in commodities or tourism services); (iii) economies dependent on critical imports (e.g. food, fuel, medical supplies and capital goods), thereby incurring chronic current account deficits; and (iv) countries remote from major world markets. These are typically structural features of economies at low levels of development. Still, they can be changed over the medium to long term as a result of the interaction of effective growth and development processes and under the aegis of appropriate development policies.

The second type of shocks are natural shocks, including natural disasters, e.g. earthquakes or tsunamis, and climatic shocks, e.g. droughts, floods, or typhoons (Feindouno and Goujon, 2016). Risk of exposure to these shocks is mainly determined by geographic features.

Facing obstacles to development has traditionally been recognized as a common feature of LDC economies, and as part of the definition of the LDC category since its establishment in 1971. In 1999 the category's concept was changed to "low-income countries suffering from low levels of human resources and a high degree of economic vulnerability". The Economic Vulnerability Index (EVI) was adopted as one of the LDC criteria used for both inclusion in, and exclusion from, the group. Initially, the EVI measured just economic vulnerability but has gradually come to incorporate natural shocks variables as well (UNCTAD, 2016a: 29). The comprehensive review of the LDC criteria adopted by the Committee

The present crisis dramatically highlights the vulnerability of LDCs to shocks beyond their control

for Development Policy in 2020 strengthened the recognition of the importance of environmental shocks, and renamed the EVI as the Economic and Environmental Vulnerability Index, which now comprises an economic and environmental subindex, each carrying equal weight (CDP, 2020).

The COVID-19 pandemic has starkly demonstrated that national economies are not just vulnerable to the economic and environmental shocks which are traditionally considered in development analysis and policymaking but also to shocks originating in the health sphere. As mentioned above (section B.1), the poor state of development of health systems in LDCs renders them especially vulnerable to a health-related exogenous shock, so that in spite of the relatively moderate *health* impact of the first eight months of 2020, these countries remained vulnerable to a possible pickup of COVID-19 infections.

In sum, the combination of the health, human, economic and social aspects of the present crisis dramatically highlight the vulnerability of LDC economies to shocks beyond their control. They will result in a sharp setback in the process of growth and development of LDCs, including an impediment or reversal in their progress towards their development goals, starting with poverty (section B.3 above).

2. LDCs: the most vulnerable group of countries

Consistent with the definition of the category, the LDCs are among the world's most vulnerable economies as they are the most exposed to shocks and events outside their control. In 2020 their average EVI – 39.3 – is 27 per cent higher than that of ODCs and currently stands at 30.9.[22] The mean vulnerability of the LDCs has declined only marginally since the early 2000s, from 41.3 in 2000 to 39.3 in 2020. The gap between the level of vulnerability of the LDCs and that of the ODCs has remained approximately constant over that period (Figure 1.5).

Among LDC subgroups, the most vulnerable are the island LDCs, which is to be expected given the

---

[21] Domestic shocks, such as civil wars and political and social instability, are not considered as either structural or exogenous, although they also are likely to adversely affect national growth and development.

[22] The higher the EVI, the more vulnerable the country's economy. Therefore, economic progress is reflected in a *reduction* of the EVI.

Figure 1.5
Economic Vulnerability Index, by country group, 2000–2020, selected years

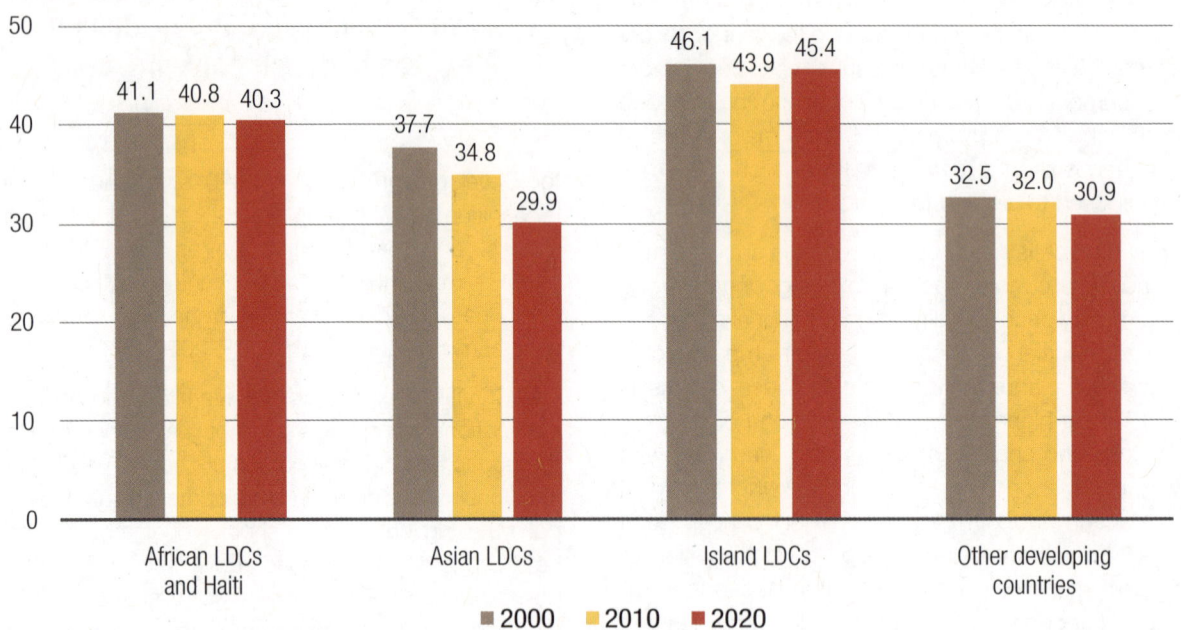

Country group	2000	2010	2020
African LDCs and Haiti	41.1	40.8	40.3
Asian LDCs	37.7	34.8	29.9
Island LDCs	46.1	43.9	45.4
Other developing countries	32.5	32.0	30.9

Source: UNCTAD secretariat calculations, based on data from the United Nations Committee for Development Policy Secretariat, time series estimates of the LDC criteria [accessed April 2020].
Notes: 1. Unweighted average of country indices. 2. Data reflect the composition of the EVI as decided during the last revision of the index, adopted in 2020.

geographical situation of these countries, which entails large distance from major economic centres, difficulties in diversifying the economy and high exposure to natural disasters. The second most vulnerable LDC subgroup is that of African LDCs and Haiti. The level of vulnerability of these two subgroups of LDCs has remained virtually unchanged since 2000.

The situation of Asian LDCs is markedly different from that of other LDC subgroups. First, their level of vulnerability is considerably lower than that of other subgroups. Second, they achieved a 21-per-cent reduction in their level of vulnerability since 2000, ultimately bringing it to a lower level than that of ODCs (Figure 1.5). The attenuation in their vulnerability was achieved thanks to the structural changes undergone by those economies (further analysed in chapter 2), which brought down the share of the primary sector in total economic activity, and reduced the exposure of these economies to export and agricultural instability. All Asian LDCs experienced a fall in their level of vulnerability since the early 2000s, with the strongest falls occurring in Cambodia, Lao People's Democratic Republic, Nepal and Bhutan. By contrast, other LDC subgroups include countries which experienced increased or decreased levels of vulnerability.

3. Implications in the short and medium term

The adverse health, economic and social impacts of the COVID-19 crises currently faced by LDCs and their long-standing development deficits call for urgent policy action by policymakers of these countries and their development partners. The major economic priorities of LDCs fall into two time horizons. First, in the short term, these countries need to do "whatever it takes" to counter the present recession, support the incomes of their citizens, firms and farms, and buttress the activity level of their economy. These short-term priorities are shared among LDCs, ODCs and developed countries (UNCTAD, 2020c; Baldwin and Weder di Mauro, 2020a).

Any short-term measures to be taken should have the medium-to-long term economic outlook for LDC economies in its sight and be coherent with the development policies implemented for longer time horizons.[23] This entails addressing the enduring structural challenges of LDC economies, including their vulnerabilities, which can be overcome or compensated by building resilience.

Resilience is understood as the ability of an economy to withstand exogenous shocks or to recover from

---
[23] This point is analysed in further detail in chapter 5.

them or, alternatively, as "the capacity of a system to anticipate, adapt, and reorganize itself under conditions of adversity in ways that promote and sustain its successful functioning" (Ungar, 2018: 1). In developed or mature economies, it is the result of prudent macroeconomic policies (Briguglio et al., 2008). In the case of developing countries, resilience can only be built over the medium-to-long term, and is the result of a successful development process which enables economies to overcome the major structural features of underdevelopment, such as concentration of output and exports, over-dependence on imports of critical goods and services, chronic current account deficits, etc. While some forms of vulnerability (e.g. openness and small size) may remain in some countries, even after a sustained period of economic growth, the development process results in an economy being much better able to withstand exogenous shocks and recover from them. This is illustrated by the so-called Singapore paradox (Briguglio et al., 2008), which refers to the fact that this country was able to grow, develop and build resilience, in spite of its geographical features (smallness, (originally) distance from major economic centres), which should have represented an obstacle to its growth and development but was eventually overcome.

Building resilience in LDCs therefore entails tackling the underlying structural causes of their vulnerability, underdevelopment and ingrained poverty. These long-standing development challenges of LDCs predate the COVID-19 crisis. While the economic, social and political context which gives rise to extreme forms of vulnerability and poverty are complex, these phenomena have a common underlying factor: the low level of development of their productive capacities (the concept is extensively developed in chapter 2). The expansion, upgrading and utilization of productive capacities results in overcoming the structural features leading to vulnerabilities. In fact, the reduction in the level of vulnerability achieved by some LDC economies since the beginning of the century (Figure 1.5) is largely explained by the progress these countries have achieved in developing their productive capacities and thereby achieving structural transformation (these processes are analysed in chapters 2 and 3).

Nevertheless, there is a serious risk of a widening gap between LDCs and other developing and developed countries. Such a divergence might be further accentuated in the future, considering that, broadly speaking, the best performing LDCs are those in the process of graduation, or close to that milestone. Once this process is achieved, the LDC category will be composed of the most vulnerable countries. However, it is worth stressing that an analysis of the EVI suggests that even graduating LDCs or recent graduates remain exceedingly vulnerable to exogenous shocks. Lacking a sustained process of structural transformation of these economies, vulnerability factors, e.g. export concentration, limited domestic value addition, dependence on sensitive imports and foreign financial resources will likely linger on, making them more liable to fall prey of the so-called middle-income trap (UNCTAD, 2016a).

D. The continued relevance of the LDC category

As the world scrambles to cope with the fallout from COVID-19 and the ensuing global recession, there is an understandable temptation to prioritize in the policy discourse either domestic concerns or issues that are relevant to the global economic, social and political system as a whole. This entails a concrete risk that LDC-specific issues will be largely treated by the international community as a second-order priority.

However, rather than face such an outcome, LDCs need to receive special attention from the international community when addressing both their short-term priorities and their medium-to-long term challenges, not only because of the severity of the current crises and their continuing vulnerability but also because these developments come at a time when LDCs and their development partners are discussing a plan of action to guide domestic and international policymaking for LDCs in the decade 2021–2030, to follow the Istanbul Programme of Action (IPoA) and expected to be adopted during the Fifth United Nations Conference on the Least Developed Countries (UNLDC-V).

Both the international community and LDCs themselves are advised to concentrate their future actions and policies for LDCs on the expansion, strengthening and utilization of productive capacities in these countries, particularly as their deficit is at the root of their vulnerability. This response will bring about the structural transformation of the LDC economies, which they will need to achieve if they are to reach their development goals. This refers to the Sustainable Development Goals (UNCTAD, 2014), as well as the goals to be adopted in the context of UNLDC-V.

Against this background, it is all the more vital to highlight the continued relevance of the LDC category, not only during the "Great Lockdown" and its

Figure 1.6
LDC share of world merchandise exports, total and by product group, 2000–2019

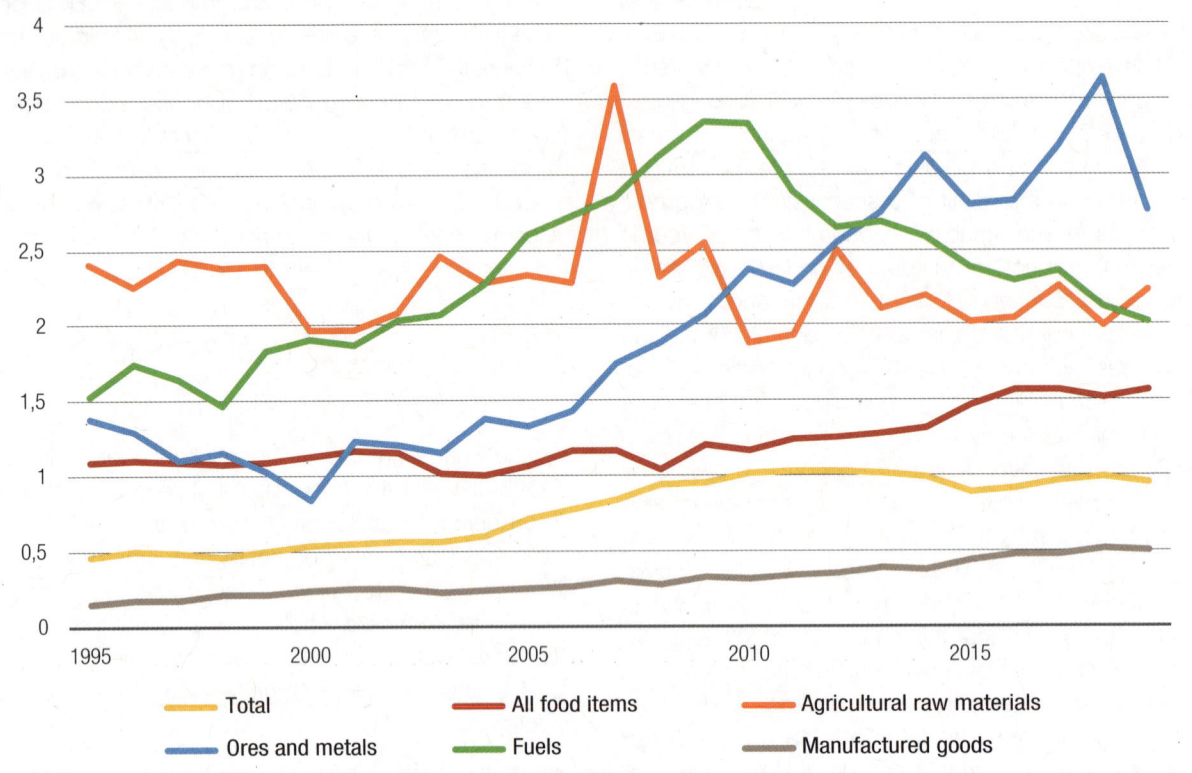

Legend: Total — All food items — Agricultural raw materials — Ores and metals — Fuels — Manufactured goods

Source: UNCTAD secretariat calculations based on data from UNCTAD, UNCTADStat databased [accessed September 2020].
Note: For the sake of comparability over time, the figure refers to 46 current LDCs throughout the period (trade data for South Sudan are not available).

immediate aftermath but, equally importantly, over the course of the decade, which will witness the overlap between the remaining horizon of Agenda 2030 for Sustainable Development and the next Programme of Action for LDCs. In this respect, the reasons for reiterating that the LDCs are "the battleground on which the 2030 Agenda for Sustainable Development will be won or lost" (UNCTAD, 2015a: 14) go beyond the moral commitment to "leave no one behind", and reflect long-term considerations related to the notions of global public goods and the potential for positive and negative spillovers across nations in an increasingly interconnected world.

Even before the current crisis there were few indications that the LDCs were on track to meet the targets set in the IPoA. Over the last few years the number of LDCs able to meet the 7 per cent growth target has been steadily declining (UNCTAD, 2018b, 2019a). Meanwhile, the LDC share of global output has remained stubbornly low at below 1.5 per cent, thereby further highlighting their economic marginalization and the persistent gaps vis-à-vis other developing and developed countries. In the same vein, the LDC share of global exports has hovered around 1 per cent since 2008, notwithstanding the IPoA target (subsequently reiterated in the Sustainable Development Goals) of doubling that proportion. As a matter of fact, LDC export shares are relatively small (at below 3.5 per cent), even for those primary commodities that constitute the backbone of their export revenues, namely fuels and to a lesser extent ores and metals, as well as agricultural raw material (Figure 1.6). What is most striking, however, is the persistently low market share in global manufacturing exports, reaching barely 0.5 per cent of the world total and mainly accounted for by garments and textiles. This is mirrored in the relatively limited contribution (12 per cent) of the manufacturing sector to total value added, marginally higher than in 2011 but roughly at the same level as in the early 1980s. Against this background, it is evident that much of the IPoA will remain unfinished business by 2021; nor it is plausible to expect significant improvements in the short term, considering that COVID-19 is expected to trigger "the worst recession since the Great Depression" (IMF, 2020a: v).

Regardless of their small economic weight, part of the relevance of the LDC category stems from the fact that these 47 countries account for a significant and rising share of the world population. It is estimated that

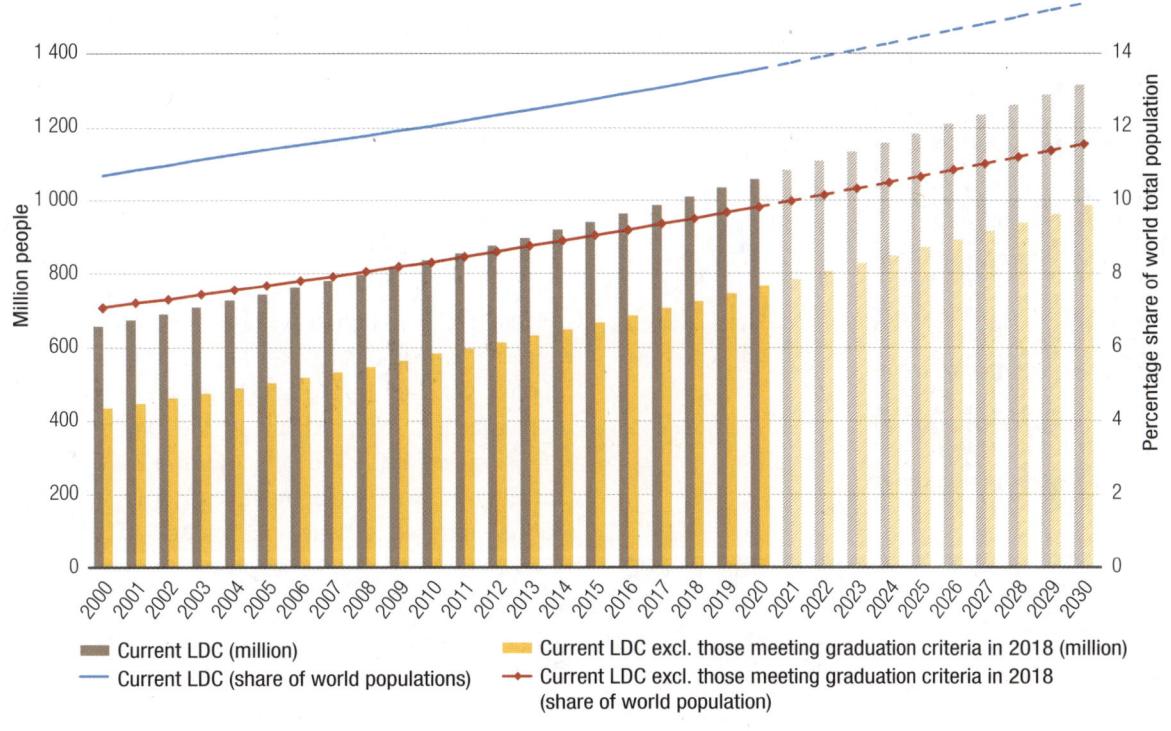

Figure 1.7
LDC population and share of world total, 2000–2020

■ Current LDC (million)
— Current LDC (share of world populations)
■ Current LDC excl. those meeting graduation criteria in 2018 (million)
◆ Current LDC excl. those meeting graduation criteria in 2018 (share of world population)

Source: UNCTAD Secretariat calculation, based on data from UN DESA (2019).

1.06 billion people currently live in LDCs, and that the population of these countries will expand to 1.31 billion by 2030, which will see them hosting 15 per cent of humanity (Figure 1.7). Nor are foreseeable cases of graduation from the LDC category likely to radically alter this picture. Even excluding the countries meeting the criteria for LDC graduation in 2018, i.e. Angola, Bangladesh, Bhutan, Kiribati, Lao People's Democratic Republic, Myanmar, Nepal, Sao Tome and Principe, Solomon Islands, Timor-Leste and Vanuatu, the remaining LDCs account for 766 million people (10 per cent of the world's total), and this is expected to increase to nearly 1 billion people in 2030.

Moreover, as demographic transition continues to progress at a sluggish pace, the population structure in the LDCs continues to be characterized by a high proportion of younger age cohorts – a trend which is expected to continue in the new decade (Figure 1.8). As of 2020, 39 per cent of the population of LDCs was less than 15 years old, while the dependency ratio is forecast to decline from the current 74 per cent to 67 per cent in 2030.[24] In a global perspective, this implies that LDCs currently account for 20 per cent of the world's youth, and their weight is set to increase by four percentage points by 2030. These long-term tendencies have wide-ranging implications in terms of potential market size and dynamism, and challenges in labour markets, education and health, but also with respect to prospects for urbanization, migration, and potential socioeconomic tensions. All of which adds further emphasis to the importance of fostering a sustainable and broad-based recovery in the LDCs – a recovery underpinned by the development of their productive capacities and the resulting structural transformation of their economy, as well as the generation of sufficient employment opportunities to accommodate the growing number of new entrants into labour markets.

With demographic growth reaching 2.3 per cent per year, and as much as 39 per cent of the population aged less than 15 years old, and rising female labour participation, the labour supply in LDCs is expected to continue expanding rapidly. In the period 2021–2030 the LDC labour force will increase by an average 13.2 million workers per year – or as much as 46 per cent of the global labour force expansion – up from 10.1 million under the IPoA period, according to ILO estimates (Figure 1.9). History suggests that harnessing such a rapid expansion of the labour

---

[24] The dependency ratio is a measure of the number of dependents aged zero to 14 and over the age of 65, compared with the total population aged 15 to 64. It is used to measure the pressure on the productive population.

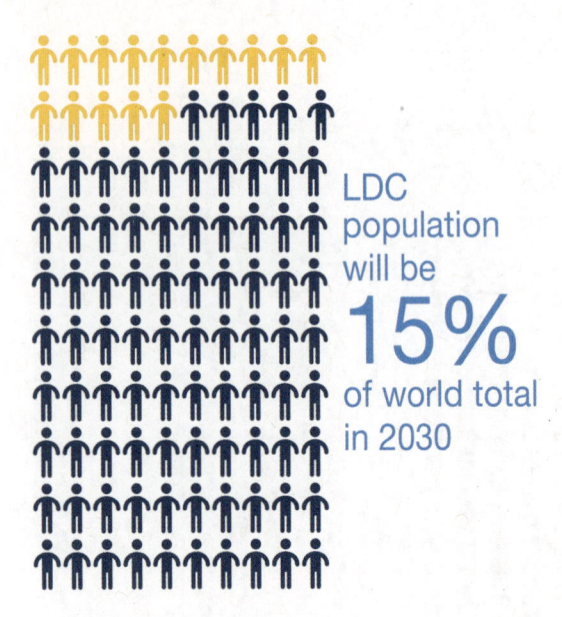

The Least Developed Countries Report **2020**

LDC population will be 15% of world total in 2030

force will inevitably hinge on the capacity of LDC economies to generate sufficient opportunities for productive employment outside the agricultural sector, thus ultimately setting the direction and pace of their structural transformation process.

Consequently, as preparations for the UNLDC-V Conferences accelerate, LDCs have come to represent the main locus of extreme poverty worldwide (Valensisi, 2020). With barely 14 per cent of the world population, they are estimated to account for over 50 per cent of the people living with less than $1.90 per day at a global level, and about 34 per cent of those with less than $3.20 per day (Figure 1.10). Evidence of this nature points to the ongoing geographic polarization of poverty and speaks volumes to the sheer magnitude of global inequalities. It also vindicates the argument that LDCs represent the litmus test for the 2030 Agenda for Sustainable Development, especially in relation to the promises to "leave no one behind", reducing global inequalities and eradicating extreme poverty (UNCTAD, 2015a).

Figure 1.8
LDC population structure by age class
(2020 and 2030; 47 current LDCs)

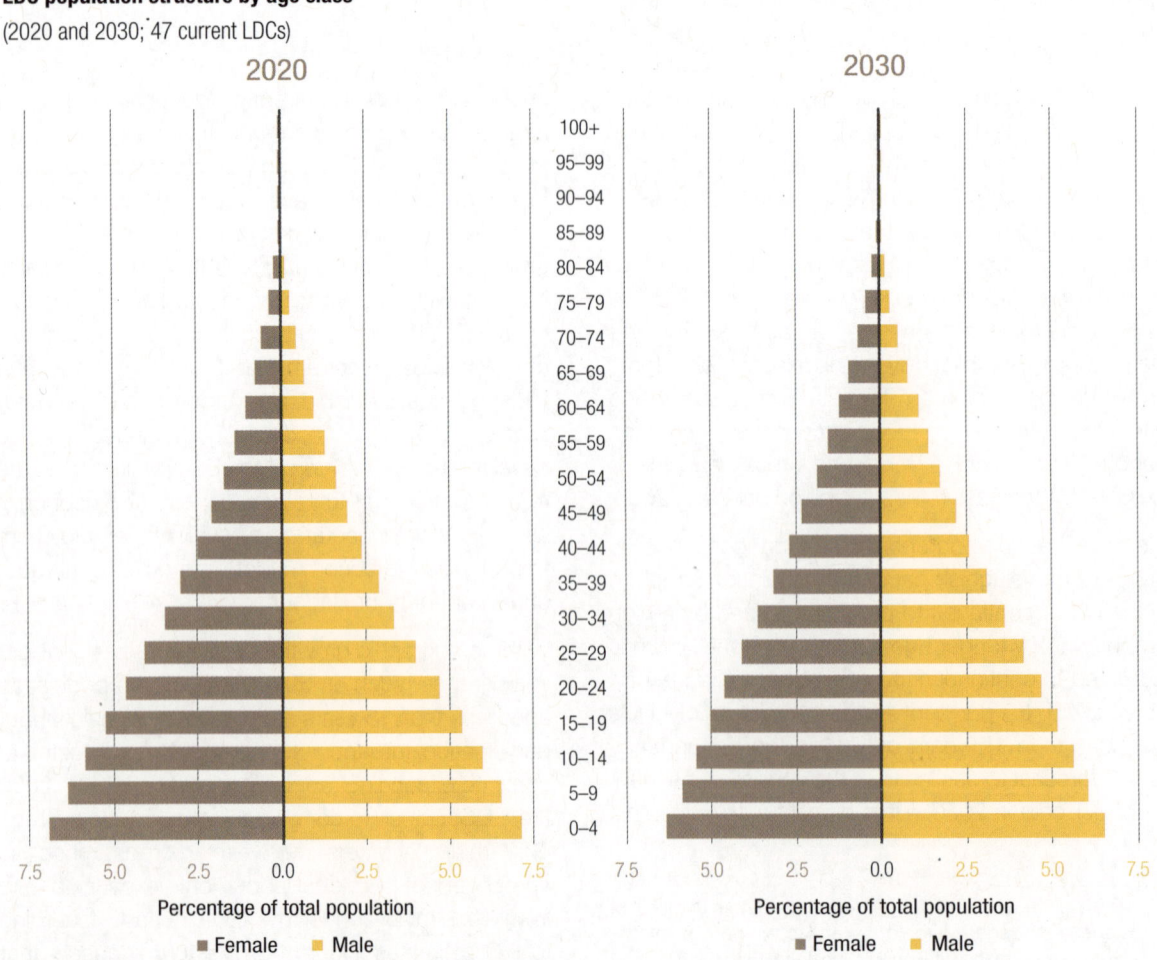

Source: UNCTAD Secretariat calculation based on data from UN DESA (2019).

CHAPTER 1: The COVID-19 crisis in LDCs

Perhaps more fundamentally, these trends underscore the challenges faced by many LDCs as they seek to escape potential poverty traps, which are situations where their limited purchasing power constrains their domestic market size, and potentially hampers the viability of much-needed investments (notably in "social overhead capital", where fixed costs and locally increasing returns are pervasive). Figure 1.10 also serves as a reminder of the concrete risk that many LDCs will lag further behind in poverty eradication efforts, as compared to other developing and developed countries; this will become more likely if the current downturn turns out to be deeper and/or longer than expected, or if it weighs down LDC debt sustainability and triggers balance of payment crises. This is a source of concern especially for African LDCs, many of which have displayed relatively sluggish progress in their efforts to reduce poverty.

From the point of view of the international community, the above evidence deserves particular attention, not least because low socioeconomic development is typically regarded as an influential driver of instability, conflict and migration, particularly when coupled with increasing pressure on natural resources, the intensifying adverse impacts of climate change, and limited institutional capabilities (Hendrix and Salehyan, 2012; Mach et al., 2019; United Nations, 2019; Peters et al., 2020). Although the literature is far from unanimous on the relationship between these elements, there is little doubt that poor socioeconomic outcomes in LDCs risk undermining the very enablers of sustainable development, potentially exerting negative spillovers on neighbouring countries and beyond. Equally, poverty inequalities and power asymmetries critically shape the political economy context in which concrete international cooperation projects take place, and therefore have a large bearing on their overall outcomes and effectiveness (UNCTAD, 2017a, 2019b; Sovacool et al., 2017).

The above considerations suggest that the relevance of sustainable development in the LDCs goes well beyond their marginal role in the world economy and deserve adequate attention and commensurate support from an international standpoint. This argument acquires further strength in the light of the COVID-19

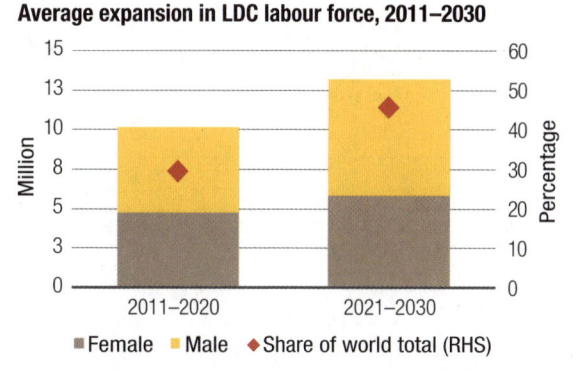

Figure 1.9
Average expansion in LDC labour force, 2011–2030

Source: UNCTAD secretariat calculation based on data from ILO, ILOStat database [accessed June 2020].

Figure 1.10
LDC share of world population and of world poor, by international poverty line

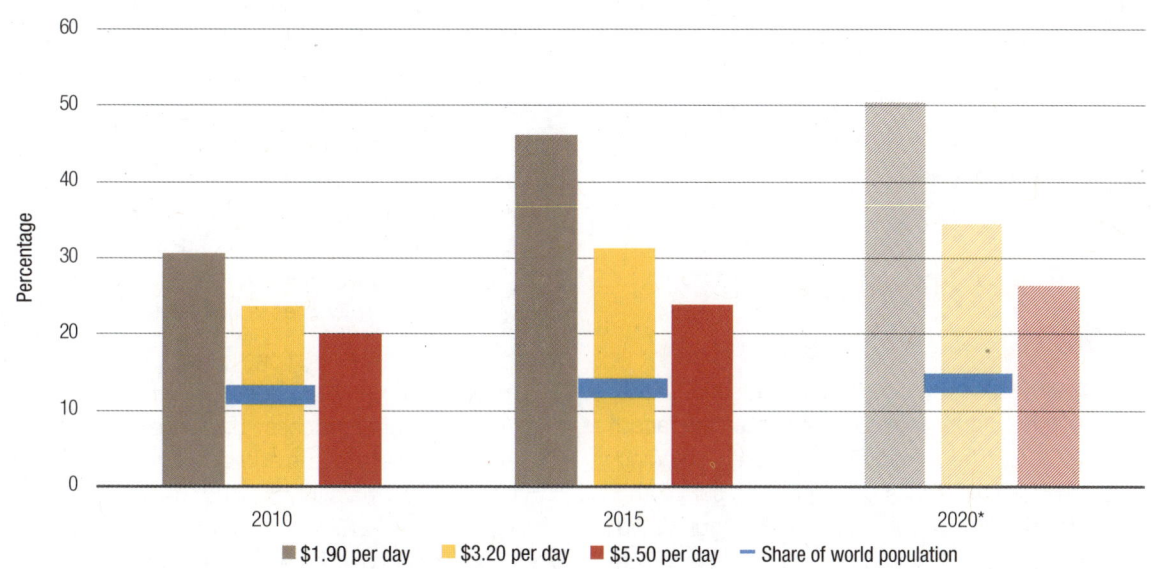

Source: UNCTAD secretariat calculations, based on Valensisi (2020).
Note: For the sake of comparability over time, the figure refers to the 47 current LDCs even for 2010 and 2015.

> **The relevance of development in the LDCs goes beyond their marginal role in the world economy**

pandemic, which has brought to the fore the notion that was until then mainly used in the engineering and ecological/environmental sphere, namely that of system resilience. In this context, the rapid cascading of a health shock on many other dimensions, ranging from the socioeconomic sphere to mobility and the environment, has underscored critical elements of systemic interdependence that can no longer be disregarded. Potential tensions between the (over) emphasis on efficiency and specialization, as opposed to redundancy and connectivity have also surfaced (OECD, 2020b; Ungar, 2018). In the framework of complex patterns of global interdependence, the emerging debate on resilience puts renewed emphasis on inclusivity/universality and on the fundamental role of international cooperation, adding a new strategic dimension to the call for ensuring that LDCs do not fall behind in their quest for sustainable development.

One final reason for the continued relevance of the LDC category stems from the emerging international context. After years of eroding support for multilateralism and as the world struggles to cope with the most consequential global downturn since the Great Depression, there is a growing realization that the multilateral system needs to be revamped and updated to match the challenges of the 21st century, sustainable development being a particularly critical case in point. There are, however, also mounting concerns that the international order may become increasingly fragmented and politicized. At this time of heightened uncertainties and disenchantment, it is remarkable that the notion of LDCs remains a meaningful and universally agreed category to identify countries in need of special support.

E. Objectives and structure of this report

The previous sections have highlighted the seriousness and magnitude of the development challenges faced by the LDCs. The structural and long-standing nature of these challenges were present before the COVID-19 pandemic but have been aggravated by the subsequent outbreak of multiple crises. The present report aims to provide a contribution to the discussion and planning of the economic orientation of LDCs and their development partners' actions in support of LDC development in the new decade. It is focused on the productive capacities that LDCs will need for the 2020s to achieve the Sustainable Development Goals and other development goals that will likely be formulated at UNLDC-V.

The remainder of the report is structured as follows. The second chapter provides a framework which guides the subsequent presentation of UNCTAD's research and analysis on LDCs, as well as the ensuing policy discussions. It starts with a discussion of the concept of productive capacities, which includes UNCTAD's contribution to their conceptualization and measurement, and then adopts a dynamic approach to the development of the core elements of productive capacities. The chapter shows how their progression results in the structural transformation of economies and how the process has played out in LDCs so far, and discusses some of the main factors conditioning the development of LDCs' productive capacities in in the next decade, especially the technological revolution which the world is currently undergoing.

Chapter 3 undertakes an empirical analysis of the development of productive capacities in the LDCs, and draws comparisons between individual LDCs and other developing countries. It makes use of UNCTAD's Productive Capacities Index (PCI) and its subcomponents, and showcases their use for empirical research and policy analysis, including an evaluation of the performance of LDCs during the period of implementation of the IPoA. It shows that most LDCs have been left behind vis-à-vis other developing countries, and typically operate below efficiency frontiers.

Given the sobering analysis of the development of productive capacities during the IPoA period, it is important to look for alternatives and take pro-active measures to reverse the past trend of LDCs being left behind. Chapter 4 analyses the uptake of digital technologies in LDCs and enquires whether this technological uptake is limited to a few cases, or whether it is bound to have a transformative impact. The importance of policy approaches in influencing these alternative outcomes is highlighted.

Chapter 5 outlines options that LDCs and the international community have in order to strengthen the development process of these countries in the 2020s. The analysis is addressed to policymakers in the LDCs themselves and the international community. The COVID-19 crises have shed new light on the linkages between productive capacities and resilience, and on the deficits that LDCs have in both accounts. These shortcomings need to be tackled by the combination of a strong investment push at the macro level and meso-level industrial and STI policies focused on accelerating the structural transformation of LDC economies. Public policies need to be pro-active and play a coordinating role. Externally, they should strategically harness foreign trade and regional integration initiatives at several levels, including infrastructure and research and development (R&D).

Internationally, there is a risk that LDC issues are marginalized in view of current global developments. This report reaffirms the importance of the LDC category and the need for the international community to renew its commitment to these countries through a new generation of international support mechanisms. Initiatives need to be strengthened or established, especially in the fields of trade support and technology transfer.

Productive capacities are

the productive resources

entrepreneurial capabilities

and production linkages...

...whose dynamic development results in the

structural transformation of economies

Digital technologies will strongly influence the development of future productive capacities

PRODUCTIVE CAPACITIES

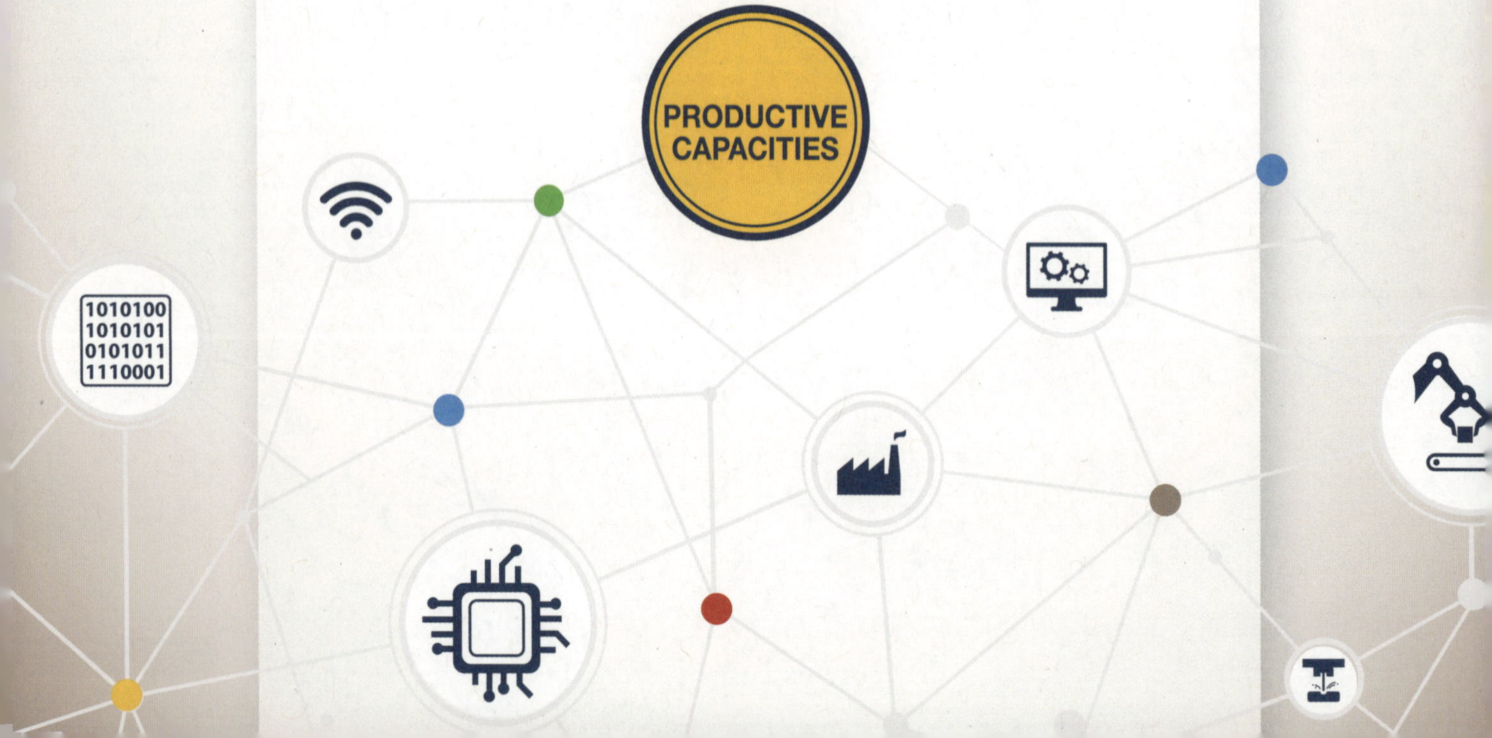

CHAPTER 2

Productive capacities
and structural transformation:
Giving concrete form
to concepts

CHAPTER 2

Productive capacities and structural transformation: Giving concrete form to concepts

A. Introduction	**27**
B. The concept of productive capacities	**27**
1. Components	27
2. Policymaking	29
3. Measurement	30
C. Structural transformation	**30**
1. Processes and outcomes	30
2. The context of structural transformation processes	32
D. Recent patterns of structural transformation in LDCs	**33**
1. The critical role of infrastructure	33
a. *The multifunctionality of infrastructure*	*33*
b. *ICT infrastructure and digital divides*	*35*
2. The pace and direction of structural transformation	37
a. *Output*	*38*
b. *Employment*	*39*
c. *Productivity*	*41*
d. *Are the LDCs converging or diverging?*	*44*
3. Implications	45
E. LDCs' productive capacities in the new decade	**47**
1. Trends affecting the future development of productive capacities	47
2. The technological revolution	48

A. Introduction

As chapter 1 has shown, the main priority for the least developed countries (LDCs) in the present context is to recover from the COVID recession, and regain the ground lost during the current crisis in terms of output, employment and social conditions, but also to set the conditions for a more resilient future. This can only be achieved by building, accumulating and upgrading productive capacities in a way that leads to the structural transformation of their economies, with the accompanying social change. Before the policy implications of such a strategy and course of action can be formulated (see chapter 5), it is necessary to define precisely the concepts of productive capacities and structural transformation. Beyond grasping the conceptual formulation, policymakers need to understand the dynamics of productive capacity development and structural transformation. By knowing these processes, it is possible to devise strategies and policies that lead to economically and socially desirable outcomes. Moreover, it is crucial to place these processes in the context of their current manifestations, especially with respect to broad current international trends and developments that condition the development of productive capacities and structural transformation. This will allow them to face the challenges of the new decade, which is the final timeframe for the world to reach the Sustainable Development Goals and for the LDCs to implement the new plan of action expected to be agreed during the Fifth United Nations Conference on the Least Developed Countries (UNLDC-V).

The present chapter presents the conceptual framework on which the remainder of the report is organized. Section B discusses the concept of productive capacities and its components. Section C examines the concept of structural transformation and explains why it is a *sine qua non* for LDCs to attain their development goals. Section D assesses the patterns of structural transformation that LDCs have experienced in the new Millennium, and compares the progress achieved towards goals and objectives of the Brussels Programme of Action (BPoA) and the Istanbul Programme of Action (IPoA). The final section (E) is forward-looking. It considers the productive capacities which LDCs will need in the new decade in order to reach their development goals, highlighting the main factors that will shape the development of productive capacities in the 2020s, especially frontier technologies.

B. The concept of productive capacities

UNCTAD has played a major role in raising the profile of productive capacities in its analysis and policymaking

Productive capacities enable countries to grow and develop

for sustainable development, especially with respect to the LDCs. Its contributions have been in terms of conceptualization, measurement and advocacy for their mainstreaming in development policymaking. These different contributions are reviewed hereafter.

1. Components

The notion of productive capacities was first systematically presented by UNCTAD in *The Least Developed Countries Report 2006: Developing Productive Capacities* (UNCTAD, 2006). This report conceptualized productive capacities and drew the attention on how focusing development strategies on them provided a new foundation for development policies for LDCs. While focusing on LDCs, this approach was also pertinent in the case of other developing countries (ODCs).[1] The 2006 report proposed a broad concept, based on different theoretical traditions relevant to the understanding of economic growth and development.

The conceptualization presented in this report remains valid to this day. The concrete manifestations of productive capacities and the actual processes influencing their development have evolved considerably since then. UNCTAD has revisited and deepened its conceptual work on productive on several occasions, most recently in UNCTAD (2020d). The concept is presented below to show its continued theoretical validity and the lasting policy relevance of its approach to development policymaking.

Productive capacities are defined as "the productive resources, entrepreneurial capabilities and production linkages which together determine the capacity of a country to produce goods and services and enable it to grow and develop" (UNCTAD, 2006: 61).[2] Its basic elements are productive resources, entrepreneurial

---

[1] The report acknowledged that productive capacities had also been conceptualized in different manners by other international organizations and bodies, which had highlighted some specific aspects of productive capacities, such as the industrial, trade or human capacity facets (UNCTAD, 2006: 62–63).

[2] An alternative definition of productive capacities is: "a set of different types of productive, organizational, technological and innovation capabilities embedded in organizations, institutions and infrastructures whose integration determines the capacity of a country to produce goods and services in a competitive global market" (UNCTAD, 2020d: 29).

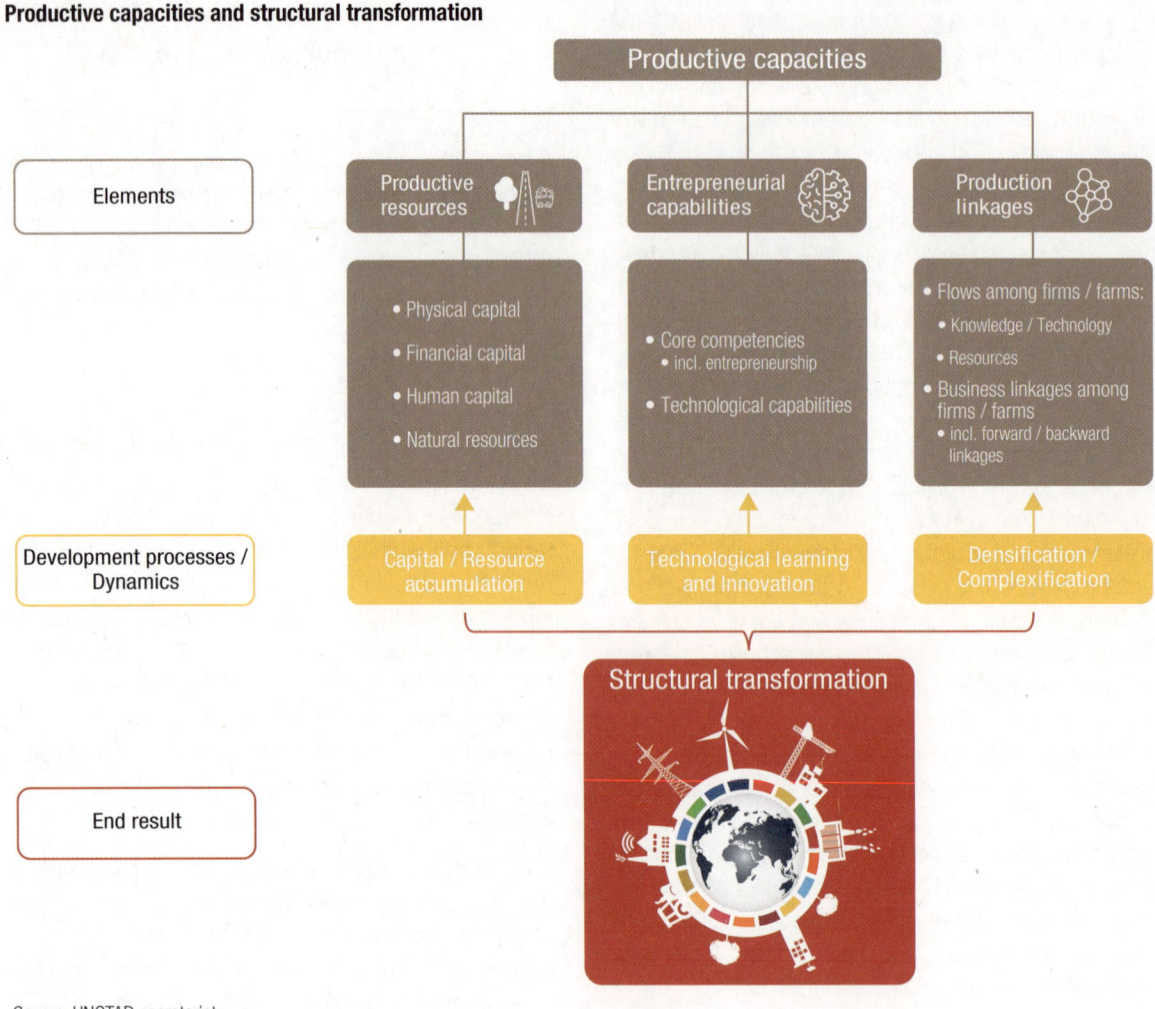

The Least Developed Countries Report 2020

Figure 2.1
Productive capacities and structural transformation

```
                              Productive capacities
                                      │
          ┌───────────────────────────┼───────────────────────────┐
Elements  │    Productive             │   Entrepreneurial         │   Production
          │    resources              │   capabilities            │   linkages
          │                           │                           │
          │  • Physical capital       │  • Core competencies      │  • Flows among firms / farms:
          │  • Financial capital      │    incl. entrepreneurship │      • Knowledge / Technology
          │  • Human capital          │                           │      • Resources
          │  • Natural resources      │  • Technological          │  • Business linkages among
          │                           │    capabilities           │    firms / farms
          │                           │                           │      incl. forward / backward
          │                           │                           │      linkages
                   ▲                           ▲                           ▲
Development      Capital / Resource     Technological learning       Densification /
processes /      accumulation           and Innovation               Complexification
Dynamics

End result                      Structural transformation
```

Source: UNCTAD secretariat.

capabilities and production linkages, each one understood as comprising the components indicated in Figure 2.1.

Productive resources are factors of production, including different types of productive resources and capital. They include financial capital and physical capital, the latter comprising both machinery and equipment (typically operating at the firm / farm level) and infrastructure. Physical infrastructure is one type of productive resources where LDCs have especially wide gaps vis-à-vis other countries and these shortcomings tend to hamper the development of other components of productive capacities (Section D.1). Natural resources, in contrast, are one of the few areas where LDCs tend to perform better than other countries, whether developing or developed (chapter 3).

Entrepreneurial capabilities are the "skills, knowledge and information which enterprises have, firstly to mobilize productive resources in order to transform inputs into outputs which can competitively meet present and future demand, and, secondly, to invest, to innovate, to upgrade products and their quality, and even to create markets" (UNCTAD, 2006: 64). They comprise, critically, entrepreneurship, whose crucial contribution to the development of LDCs is extensively discussed in *The Least Developed Countries Report 2018: Entrepreneurship for Structural Transformation: Beyond Business as Usual* (UNCTAD, 2018a).

Entrepreneurial capabilities also include technological capabilities, which comprise skills required for investment, production and establishing linkages at the firm / farm level. These include the skills needed to determine the appropriate technology and scale of investment projects, as well as the efficiency with which productive units operate. Nationally, these capabilities are not just the aggregation of individual firms / farm capabilities, but also the complex interaction of individual units with the macroeconomic environment

(Lall, 1992). The technological capabilities required by the latest major wave of technological innovation (i.e. digital technologies) are discussed in detail in chapter 4.

Production linkages are flows among productive units (firms / farms) of goods and services, knowledge, technology and information, and productive resources (including human resources). They include exchanges among productive units of different sizes (micro, small and medium-sized enterprises, MSMEs, and large ones), ownership (domestic / foreign, public / private), and operating in different sectors.

Sustained economic growth is only possible through the expansion and development and full utilization of productive capacities. Hence, the central role that productive capacities need to play in national and international development strategies. The processes of development of productive capacities and outcomes are discussed in section C below.

The objective of UNCTAD's conceptualization of productive capacities was to provide policymakers with a better understanding of the dynamics of growth, development and structural transformation, as well as highlight the obstacles jeopardizing these processes. It challenged several commonly made assumptions and (mis-)conceptions (UNCTAD, 2006). Its main advantages to policymakers are threefold. First, the concept points to the importance of both supply and demand factors for economic growth, rather than focusing just on the supply side.

Second, UNCTAD's approach highlights the feature that most productive capacities are not generic but rather activity-specific and enterprise-specific. Different sectors / activities have a distinct potential to contribute to economic growth, development, diversification and productivity improvement. This potential varies according to their knowledge intensity, capital intensity and type of returns to scale. Hence, the importance of the structure and distribution of economic activities, and their contribution to structural transformation (section C).

Third, the concept of productive capacities points out to the possibility that productive capacities may be underutilized. An economy would be producing at its maximum potential only when its productive capacities are fully utilized. However, this is generally not the case in LDCs. These countries have tended to have chronically under-utilized their human resources, which manifests itself in very high rates of underemployment (UNCTAD, 2013a). Additionally, one of the major economic consequences of the COVID-19 crisis has been the massive underutilization

> **Both supply and demand factors are important for sustainable economic growth**

of productive capacities (including both human and physical resources).

A growing consensus is emerging that developing productive capacities, as conceptualized above, play a central role in setting in motion the long-term process of transformation, which lies at the heart of sustainable development (UNCTAD, 2006, 2010, 2014, 2018c, 2019b).

Productive capacity development operates both within firms / sectors, as the profit-investment nexus fosters capital deepening and productivity gains, as well as across sectors, as the acquisition of productive capabilities, itself contingent on the existing pattern of production, paves the way for the emergence of new products and higher value-added activities. The process of productive capacity development hinges on a mutually reinforcing dynamic relationship between the supply and demand-side of the economy, in so far as the expansion of aggregate demand creates the scope for intersectoral linkages, factor reallocation and pecuniary externalities that sustains the financial viability of investments, including in "social overhead capital".[3] In so doing, productive capacity development fosters structural transformation and economic diversification, with knock-on effect on employment opportunities, inclusive growth and, potentially, also resource efficiency and environmental sustainability.[4]

2. Policymaking

Since the publication of *The Least Developed Countries Report 2006*, UNCTAD's work on productive capacities has been well received and taken up by the development policy community. The Istanbul Programme of Action (IPoA) mentions the term "productive capacities" 20 times and designates them as a priority area for action. Still, it can hardly be said that productive capacities occupy a central position in this plan of action: in the IPoA, they are

---

[3] "Social overhead capital" refers to the source of certain basic services required in the production of virtually all commodities. In its most narrow sense, the term refers to transportation, communication, and power facilities.
[4] This argument follows from the discussion of "relative decoupling" and "weak sustainability" (Cabeza Gutés, 1996; UNCTAD, 2012; Lange et al., 2018).

> **LDC governments spend more on productive capacities than donors**

one of eight priority areas, although two other priority areas refer more or less directly to productive sectors: Agriculture, food security and rural development, and Commodities.[5] In terms of allocation of official development assistance (ODA) to LDCs by traditional donor countries, two types of sectors more directly associated with productive capacities – economic infrastructure and services on one side, and production sectors on the other – accounted for just 14 per cent and 8 per cent, respectively, of ODA disbursements to LDC in 2015–2017, compared to 45 per cent of ODA directed to social infrastructure and services (UNCTAD, 2019b). In 2020 (and possibly beyond) this prioritization of social sectors is expected to be strengthened, in view of the surge in health expenditures related to the COVID-19 pandemic. In fact, donor countries have already launched initiatives to finance new or urgent types of health programmes and interventions in response to the pandemic.

In contrast, LDC governments have been intensifying their efforts of spending relatively more on productive capacities. Public spending on capital formation rose seven-fold between 2003 and 2017, and capital expenditures averaged 21 per cent of total government spending in the period 2012–2016. However, additional capital spending (or other types of expenditures on productive capacities) by LDC governments is hampered by their limited fiscal policy space, by the volume of current expenditures obligations and – often – by the need to match sectoral allocation of ODA to donors' priority sectors through national budgets. This forces national governments to align parts of their total spending to donor priorities (UNCTAD, 2019b).

3. Measurement

The widespread understanding and acceptance of the central place of productive capacities in the development process has led many developing countries and development stakeholders to call on UNCTAD to develop a measurement instrument to gauge the state of development of productive capacities in individual countries and groups of countries, to track their evolution in time, and to benchmark domestic productive capacities vis-à-vis other countries.[6] Following these requests, UNCTAD developed the Productive Capacities Index (PCI). The PCI is analyzed in chapter 3, which showcases the use of the Index for analytical and policymaking purposes.

C. Structural transformation

1. Processes and outcomes

Having established the concept of productive capacities in the previous section, it is important to understand the processes through which such capacities develop and the consequence of these processes. A key process is associated with each of the three core components of productive capacities (Figure 2.1).

Productive resources develop though **capital accumulation or resource accumulation**. This is the result, first, of investment in physical capital (including infrastructure), which keeps / renews / expands / upgrades the production capacity of productive units (firms and farms) and, ultimately, of the whole economy. Fixed investment is required to achieve the technological upgrading of (parts of) the capital stock of productive units or physical infrastructure. Resource accumulation also includes investment in the expansion and upgrading of human capital. This is achieved by means of spending on education, training and capacity-building, as well as on health. The importance of solid health systems has been dramatically highlighted by the COVID-19 health crisis, as well as the dramatic adverse consequences of weak health systems.

Entrepreneurial capabilities evolve basically through **technological learning and innovation**, the latter being understood as the introduction of novelties in the production process. These novelties refer classically to innovation, as identified by Schumpeter (1926), with respect to the introduction of new products, processes, input sources, markets and business models in the productive sphere. In the context of developing countries, innovation is typically

---

[5] The progress achieved by the LDCs in implementing the IPoA is analyzed in chapter 3.

[6] The latest ministerial declaration of UNCTAD – the Nairobi Maafikiano – mandated UNCTAD to "Provide an operational methodology for, and policy guidelines on, mainstreaming productive capacities in national development policies and strategies, including through the development of productive capacity indices, so that productive capacities are placed at the centre of national and international efforts to address the specific needs and challenges of the least developed countries, landlocked developing countries, small island developing States and Africa" (UNCTAD, 2016e: para.60(k)).

understood in a broad sense, i.e. referring to what is new to the local or national market or context, rather than new to the world (UNCTAD, 2007).

Production linkages develop through the **deepening of division of labour and increasing specialization of firms and farms**. These productive units develop a wider, thicker and deeper web of productive linkages with a much larger number of suppliers and clients – i.e. they evolve broader and deeper backward and forward linkages. In this process the economic tissue becomes denser and more complex – hence the processes of densification and complexification (Figure 2.1) and the economy becomes more integrated domestically.[7]

Capital accumulation, innovation and densification together result in the **structural transformation** of the economy. This is a complex process with several dimensions. A "positive" perspective highlights long-term changes in the composition of an aggregate (UNIDO, 2013). Specifically, the process of economic development leads to changes in the composition (structure) of output (production), employment, exports and aggregate demand (Hagemann et al., 2003). Structural transformation is path-dependent, which means that the present state of development of an economy is largely a function of the processes through which its productive capacities have evolved. Hence, strategies of transformation need to take into consideration the sequencing of changes, reforms, policies and strategies.

It is important to be careful, however, when gauging structural transformation only through compositional changes. Beyond these compositional changes, it is important to analyze whether these processes of transition are sustainable, and whether they are accompanied by other important features of structural transformation, especially: (i) diversification of output and exports; (ii) rising labour productivity; (iii) convergence of the level of labour productivity of different economic sectors (McMillan and Rodrik, 2011); (iv) higher income per capita; and (v) substantive poverty reduction. These are all features of traditional development process which make it economically and socially desirable and sustainable. However, these outcomes do not always occur because these desirable features to not necessarily accompany changes in the composition of output, employment, exports and demand. Under some circumstances, such compositional changes can occur, although they are not a consequence of traditional development patterns and do not point to

Compositional changes do not always signal sustainable development

the sustainable development of a country's economy, as shown hereafter.[8]

Examples of this occur in cases of premature deindustrialization or reprimarization. The former happens when the share of industry (and especially manufacturing) in output and employment declines before countries have reached relatively high income levels (as happened historically in most present-day developed countries). Premature deindustrialization has typically followed a shock, such as rapid and widespread trade liberalization, or the introduction of labour-saving technologies in manufacturing (Tregenna, 2015; Rodrik, 2016). Reprimarization is the rise in the share of commodities in gross domestic product (GDP) and/or exports, e.g. during a higher phase of a commodity prices cycle. It took place in many LDCs during the so-called commodity super-cycle of the 2000s. In both cases, these forms of structural change lead to challenges for the sustainability of the growth and development process in the medium term (UNCTAD, 2016b).

Given the limitations of the "positive" perspective on structural transformation, a "normative" perspective has been formulated. This perspective extends the compositional changes highlighted in the "positive" view mentioned above to emphasize the results of the changes undergone by the economy and evaluate their social desirability. In this sense, it has been defined as "the movement of a country's productive resources (natural resources, land, capital labour, and know-how) from low-productivity to high-productivity economic activities" (Monga and Lin, 2019: 1), or also "the ability of an economy to constantly generate new dynamic activities characterized by higher productivity and increasing returns to scale" (UNIDO, 2013: 16).

The process of structural transformation takes diverse forms at different income levels. At low income levels, it is mainly the result of the transfer of resources from one sector to another (UNIDO, 2013). This is the case of LDCs, many of which are at the initial stages of structural transformation. Therefore,

---

[7] See also footnote 11 of chapter 5.

[8] An analysis of the pace and direction of structural transformation in the case of LDCs is undertaken in section D.

> **Manufacturing is historically the engine of progress (and structural transformation)**

the analysis of structural transformation undertaken in section D focuses on intersectoral dynamics. At high income levels, by contrast, the intersectoral transfer of resources has largely been accomplished and structural transformation is mainly taking the form of a transfer of resources within sectors.

Historically, the main form of structural transformation has been industrialization, achieved by the transfer of resources from agriculture to manufacturing. Manufacturing has been a driver of economic growth for centuries because it has several specific features, especially the following ones. First, it has traditionally had the capacity to absorb large quantities of labour freed from agriculture. Second, the more advanced segments of manufacturing have increasing returns to scale.

Third, the capacity to generate technological innovation for itself and for other sectors. In the first case, this derives from manufacturing's strong propensity to invest in research and development (both in developed and developing countries). Moreover, manufacturing has the capacity to generate spillover effects to other sectors, thanks to its forward and backward linkages. This occurs by demanding inputs of higher quality from other sectors, e.g. agriculture and services, thereby inducing innovation in these upstream sectors. Conversely, the output of manufacturing serves as input to other sectors (agriculture, industry and services); the innovations generated by manufacturing are incorporated by these downstream activities, contributing to their own technological upgrading and productivity rise.

Thanks to these properties, manufacturing has historically served as an engine of technological progress, economic growth and rising income levels.

In many countries the process of structural transformation has successively meant industrialization and later (at much higher levels of income) to de-industrialization and tertiarization. These processes are typically the result of the transfer of resources (labour, capital) from agriculture to industry, and from industry to the services sector, respectively. These long-run macro processes have been driven to differing degrees by the changing composition of output, employment, exports and demand.

2. The context of structural transformation processes

The structural transformation of the productive sphere of an economy takes place within an economic, social and institutional context, and there is a mutual interaction and influence between structural transformation and this context.

The economic sphere is where supply–demand interactions occur. Hence, for the productive structure of a country to undergo transformation, it needs to be underpinned by growing demand. In turn, the expansion of productive capacities generates growing incomes to economic agents (firms, farms households), which bring about the expansion of demand. Structural transformation requires therefore a dynamic interaction between aggregated supply and demand.

Demand for the output produced is not just domestic but also international. The process of structural transformation is, therefore, conditioned by the way a national economy interacts with its international environment. These interactions take the forms of different types of flows, especially goods and services (i.e. foreign trade), capital (public, private, foreign direct investment, official development assistance, private financing), technology and knowledge, and human resources.

Institutions are non-market entities which allow the functioning of market economies (Rodrik, 2011). These include the state, which should take the form of a developmental state in order to support the structural transformation of the economy (UNCTAD, 2009). Technological change also interacts dynamically with institutional change. Technological innovation is typically accompanied by organizational innovation and by institutional innovation, as successive generations of technological revolution require, and are made possible by institutional changes in regulatory frameworks, administrative structures in the public and private sectors, etc. (Edquist and Johnson, 1997). More broadly, these forms of innovation tend to co-evolve with social innovation.

As part of the social setting in which productive transformation takes place, social development needs to accompany structural transformation. Social development comprises proper healthcare, education, gender equity and equality, peace and social stability, human rights, public participation and rule of law. It has as its ultimate goal fostering the development of people, communities and cultures to help achieve a meaningful life (Mensah, 2019). Economic development makes possible social development, but also requires it. These two pillars of sustainable development are mutually supportive and synergistic.

D. Recent patterns of structural transformation in LDCs

The previous sections have presented the concept of productive capacities and the theory of the processes through which they evolve and lead to structural transformation, given a certain type of interaction with the context in which this transformation takes place. The present section analyzes empirically how the process of structural transformation has been taking place in the specific case of the LDCs. It starts by considering the critical role of infrastructure in constraining or leveraging structural transformation, and the state of development of some critical types of infrastructures in the LDCs. It then examines the pace and direction of structural transformation in the LDCs in the new Millennium. It concludes by drawing the implication of this analysis for future development outlook and policymaking in the LDCs, which sets the framework for the remaining chapters of this report.

1. The critical role of infrastructure

The first pillar of productive capacities – productive resources – covers physical infrastructure, which enables the provision of services of energy, transport, communications, irrigation, water, sanitation, etc., to productive units and households. The availability and affordability of these services are crucial for the development of productive units, as they are responsible for the supply of inputs essential to the operation of firms and farms, and affect the costs that firms pay to access resources and markets for both inputs and outputs. Thereby, availability and conditions of infrastructure services affect firms' incentives to invest. They are also crucial to improving the standards of living and wellbeing of individuals and households.

The availability, quality and cost of infrastructure services are a necessary precondition for the development of other productive capacities, and for the rollout of the process of structural transformation. They can be a binding constraint on these processes, which is often the case in many LDCs. Alternatively, if used strategically, infrastructure can leverage the development of other forms of productive capacities and contribute to structural transformation. This occurs thanks to the property of multifunctionality of infrastructure.

a. The multifunctionality of infrastructure

Infrastructure is multifunctional and contributes through different channels to economic growth,

> **Availability, quality and cost of infrastructure (services) is a binding constraint**

innovation, structural transformation and human wellbeing. The main ways in which this takes places are mentioned hereafter.

Economic growth. Investment in infrastructure has both a direct and indirect impact on economic growth. First, investment in infrastructure is part of gross fixed capital formation, one of the demand factors contributing to GDP growth. Second, infrastructure provides services (whether energy, water, transport, communication, etc.), which are critical inputs to the production of all other sectors of economic activity, enabling the operation of firms and farms. A ten-per-cent increase in infrastructure development contributes to one-per-cent growth in the long term (Vandycke, 2012). Investments in infrastructure can thus favour the expansion and upgrading of firms and farms, which allows for growing economic specialization and, therefore, for the processes of densification and complexification through which production linkages develop (Figure 2.1). It can also contribute to specialization within rural areas and between cities and rural areas (UNCTAD, 2015b), as well as internationally.

Human capital and skills. Infrastructure services contribute to the formation of human capital and skills, thanks to the services they supply to households and institutions, for example those dedicated to the provision of education and health services. The adequate supply of energy services, for instance, is crucial in modern health systems. Energy access deficits have been highlighted as major obstacles to an adequate response to the COVID-19 pandemic, due to the number of medical equipment, exams, operations, treatments, therapies, machinery, etc. which depend on continuous and reliable electricity to function properly (including lighting), as well as the need for cooling devices to conserve vaccines and medicines (Fetter et al., 2020). Through its contribution to the building of human capital and skills, investment in infrastructure helps narrow income disparities (Calderón and Servén, 2010), and thereby contribute to reaching Goal 10 of the Sustainable Development Goals.

Technological capabilities and innovation. Infrastructure is a bundle of knowledge and technology, whether incorporated in infrastructural hardware or in the form of skills of the personnel that

> **Electricity is a precondition for technology adoption and diffusion**

are building, maintaining and operating infrastructure (engineers, technicians…). These persons need to have technological capabilities in engineering, logistics, mechanics, energy, transport, communication, water, etc. (UNCTAD, 2007; Juma, 2015). Beyond the technological capabilities of the infrastructure sectors themselves, these sectors have the potential to generate technological spillovers to all economic activity sectors to which they provide inputs (i.e. through the forward linkages of infrastructure). Most infrastructure technologies are general purpose technologies, meaning that they can establish interactive links with application sectors (i.e. other sectors of economic activity using these general purpose technologies as an input) which, in turn, spurs innovation on both sides (infrastructure and application sector), and generates increasing returns to innovation (Bresnahan, 2010). Therefore, the increased availability and affordability of infrastructure services is an enabler of innovation by firms and farms, and thereby contribute to the development of entrepreneurial capabilities (Figure 2.1).

Employment. Infrastructure sectors are also important employment generators, a feature especially important in developing countries (including LDCs). In these countries infrastructure deficits are much more acute than in developed countries and therefore, they have a more pressing need to build, maintain and renew infrastructure. If the necessary funds can be mobilized for the required investment in roads, bridges, ports, dams, power plants, buildings, etc, and if the tasks of building, maintaining and renewing infrastructure are carried out, this will have a positive impact on employment in the areas where these works are being carried out. The employment-generating potential of infrastructure works can be strengthened by the deliberate choice of labour-intensive techniques. Contrary to what may be thought, this does not compromise the quality of the hardware being built, (UNCTAD, 2013a).

Entrepreneurship. The use of local contractors and local inputs for infrastructure works, maintenance and operations – to the extent this is possible – can be a powerful stimulus for local entrepreneurship, especially if policymakers actively seek to create synergies between their infrastructure policies and their entrepreneurship policies (UNCTAD, 2013a, 2018a).

The multiple functions of infrastructure outlined above have been recognized in the "Principles for Recovery", issued by a group of international organizations, development agencies and academic institutions (Sustainable Infrastructure Partnership et al., 2020). These principles were developed to guide investment in infrastructure in the post-COVID recovery / reconstruction phase by catering to all dimensions of sustainable development and alignment with the Goals contained in the 2030 Agenda for Sustainable Development.

Deficiencies in access to infrastructure are especially strong in many LDCs (UNCTAD, 2006). While all forms of infrastructure are important, energy is especially critical as it is a key input in virtually all other sectors of economic activity, households, and other forms of infrastructure (e.g. transport, ICTs, irrigation). In recognition of this, Goal 7 of the Sustainable Development Goals is dedicated exclusively to energy.

Adequate and affordable access to modern energy is a condition for the development of productive capacities. At present, 42 per cent of LDC firms identify electricity as a major constraint to their activities, and three-fourths of them experience an average of ten outages per month, each lasting five hours (UNCTAD, 2017).

Deficient access to modern energy is a major obstacle to the adoption of other modern technologies, to enterprise development and to structural transformation. Upgrading and modernizing productive activities, and ensuring that they can function continuously depends on affordable, efficient, accessible, reliable, stable, at scale and economically viable, modern energy, especially electricity. This is what *The Least Developed Countries Report 2017* referred to as "transformational energy access" (UNCTAD, 2017a), which is an enabler of structural transformation, as understood in section C above.

Electricity is a precondition for the adoption and diffusion of other technologies. Beyond the direct applications of electricity in industry, lighting, heating / cooling, etc. mentioned above, modern energy services are crucial for the running of digital infrastructure. The infrastructure of information and communication technologies (ICTs) is indispensable for present frontier technologies, the emerging digital economy and future productive capacities which the LDC will need to build in the 2020s. Given their pivotal role for future development of productive capacities in LDCs, and for the prospects of their structural economic transformation, it is important to acknowledge the state of development of ICT infrastructures in the LDCs.

Table 2.1
Indicators of digital infrastructure and internet use by country groups, 2000–2018, selected years

	Telephony							Internet					
	Fixed-telephone subscriptions per 100 inhabitants			Mobile-cellular telephone subscriptions per 100 inhabitants			Fixed-broadband subscriptions per 100 inhabitants			Mobile-broadband subscriptions per 100 inhabitants			Percentage of individuals using the internet		
	2000–2001	2010–2011	2017–2018	2000–2001	2010–2011	2017–2018	2000–2001	2010–2011	2017–2018	2000–2001	2010–2011	2017–2018	2000–2001	2010–2011	2017–2018
Developed countries	55.2	46.9	39.1	52.7	107.1	123.3	2.0	27.4	34.0	n.a.	55.4	119.6	33.2	72.7	84.8
Other developing countries	9.6	13.4	9.3	7.6	78.3	104.7	0.3	5.5	12.0	n.a.	7.6	63.1	2.9	24.8	55.3
Least developed countries	0.6	1.0	0.8	0.4	39.9	72.5	0.0	0.1	1.3	n.a.	4.0	29.8	0.1	3.9	19.4
of which:															
African LDCs and Haiti	0.6	0.8	0.4	0.5	38.4	60.3	0.0	0.1	0.3	n.a.	1.4	20.8	0.1	3.4	15.5
Asian LDCs	0.0	1.4	1.5	0.0	42.5	93.8	0.0	0.2	3.1	n.a.	0.2	45.9	0.1	4.7	30.6
Island LDCs	0.0	2.0	1.0	0.0	41.9	87.8	0.0	0.2	0.3	n.a.	0.9	37.9	1.3	6.1	19.5
LDCs / ODCs ratio (%)	6.1	7.8	8.6	5.6	51.0	69.2	0.1	2.6	10.8	n.a.	12.7	47.2			

Source: UNCTAD sercetariat calculations, based on data from ITU, ITU Statistics database and UNCTAD, UNCTADStat databases [both accessed June 2020].

b. ICT infrastructure and digital divides

Information and communication technologies (ICTs) are the backbone of the digital economy and of the so-called Fourth Industrial Revolution (4IR). The increasingly critical role they play has rekindled international policy attention to the digital divide among countries, which was already a major theme of the World Summit on the Information Society in the early 2000s.[9] Since then, ICTs have expanded in developed countries, to the point of reaching maturity (in terms of technology diffusion) in several of these countries. At the same time, the pace of diffusion of these technologies has accelerated in developing countries, including LDCs, at a quicker pace than in developed countries. This gave rise to high hopes that the international digital divide was narrowing. This warrants a closer analysis of actual trends, as they have consequences for LDCs' possible participation in the digital economy.

Access to fixed telephony has traditionally been considerably lower in developing countries – and especially in LDCs – than in developed countries. However, this gap narrowed marginally until the mid-2000s, as this technology diffusion in both other developing countries (ODCs) and LDCs, but still leaving open very wide international gaps. In 2010–2011, LDCs had one fixed-telephony subscription per 100 inhabitants, as compared to 13.4 in ODCs and 46.9 in developed countries. This gap remained extremely wide. While the density of fixed telephony declined in all major country groups indicated in Table 2.1, it fell more sharply and from much lower levels in developing countries than in developed countries. Fixed mobile telephony density in LDCs never even reached the level of 10 per cent of that of ODCs. While to some extent this reflects the rise of mobile telephony, such lingering low density is also due to the low level of fixed telephony pick-up for productive uses in LDCs, i.e. the subdued adoption of this technology by their firms and farms.

Since the mid-2000s, telephony in developing countries started following a trend that had started earlier in developed countries, namely the sharp uptake and expansion of mobile telephony to the detriment of fixed telephony. This was especially the case in LDCs, where the adoption of this technology has accelerated significantly since the beginning of the century. The consequence was that this dimension of international digital divide has narrowed drastically. The number of mobile telephone subscriptions in LDCs reached 72.5 per 100 inhabitants in 2017–2018. While lower than the uptake of mobile telephony in ODCs, the LDC level of adoption amounts to some 70 per cent of the level of ODCs, as compared with less than 9 per cent in the case of fixed telephony (Table 2.1).

Many developing countries have witnessed the technological leapfrogging of fixed telephony in favour of mobile telephony, leading to this dimension of the digital divide narrowing to a much greater extent than in the case of traditional fixed telephony. Still, it begs the question whether the extent this narrowing is due to a very fast uptake of the new technology by individuals and households, rather than by firms and farms (i.e. for productive uses). An indication of this dynamic is given by the regional contrasts in the use

---

[9] The World Summit on the Information Society, convened by the United Nations, was held in two phases: this firs on 10–12 December 2003 in Geneva and the second on 16–18 November 2005 in Tunis.

The gender gap in Internet use is widest in LDCs

of telephony. The highest density is found in Asian LDCs, followed by island LDCs, while the lowest density is in African LDCs. Moreover, comparing the uptake in the two larger groups of LDCs, the gap between African and Asian LDCs is much higher in fixed telephony than in mobile telephony.[10] This likely reflects the stronger use of fixed telephony for productive uses by firms and farms in the Asian LDCs, which as a group have a higher level of development of productive capacities than African LDCs. Mobile telephony uptake, by contrast, is more strongly influenced by individuals and households, hence the lower gap among the two groups of LDCs in the uptake of this type of ICT.

The issue of technology adoption by firms and farms as opposed to individuals also arises in the case of the uptake of a newer type of ICT, namely the Internet. This aspect of ICT diffusion has become a much critical aspect of access to ICTs in the digital age. Since the mid-2000s the most widespread of use of fast access to the Internet worldwide has been through mobile broadband, as opposed to fixed broadband. The expansion of use in developing countries – including LDCs – in the mobile form has been faster than that of the fixed technology, similarly to what happened in telephony. Therefore, the digital divide has narrowed somewhat in mobile broadband subscriptions but remained very large in fixed broadband subscriptions. The density of the former in LDCs reached 47.2 per cent the level of that in ODCs, as compared to the much wider digital divide in fixed broadband subscriptions,

where the level of LDCs corresponds to just 10.8 per cent of the level of ODCs (Table 2.1).

The quality of Internet access in LDCs also lags wide behind that of other developing countries. International bandwith usage per Internet user in LDCs in 2019 was 21 kbits/s, while the average for all developing countries was 91 kbits/s and in developed countries it was 189 kbits/s (ITU, 2019).

While it may be argued that LDCs have leapfrogged fixed access to the Internet through mobile access, the contrast in both forms of access likely also reflects the type of agents adopting these technologies. The strongest form of narrowing the digital divide has taken place where use by individuals is strongest, i.e. mobile technologies. These can also be used by producers (firms and farms), but mostly by micro, small and medium-sized enterprises (MSMEs), including those operating in the informal sector. By contrast, larger firms and farms are more likely to use fixed forms of access to the internet than mobile ones.

While access to the Internet through mobile devices is important both for households and productive units, fixed access is even more important for firms in view of the increasing role that connectivity has come to play for their expansion and competitiveness. Therefore, the fact that the digital divide in this form of internet access is much wider reflects the lower level of development of productive capacities in LDCs, as compared to ODCs and developed countries.

The contrast among LDC groups confirms this, and in the same manner as with telephony. Internet uptake is much widespread in Asian LDCs than in island and African LDCs and Haiti. The gap between the last group and that of Asian LDCs is much wider in terms of fixed-broadband access (where the level of uptake of African LDCs and Haiti amounts to less than 9 per cent of the level of Asian LDCs) than in mobile-broadband subscriptions (where the corresponding ratio is a much higher 45 per cent). Again, these contrasts reflect the relative state of development of productive capacities in the major LDC groups. Moreover, the higher level of uptake of Internet access by productive units in Asian LDCs is an enabler of future development of their productive capacities.

While the vast majority of the population of developed countries use the Internet, ODCs crossed the mark of half of its population using it during the 2010s. In the LDCs, by contrast, the uptake of the Internet among the population has been much lower and only one fifth of the population currently uses the internet. Similar to other indicators, Internet use is more widespread in Asian LDCs, followed by island LDCs and African LDCs and Haiti (Table 2.1).

---

[10] The ratio of telephony density in African LDCs and Haiti / Asian LDCs is 29 per cent in fixed telephony and 64 per cent in the case of mobile telephony, indicating a wider gap in the former.

Access to the Internet in LDCs is plagued by deep gender divides. Unequal access to this technology is highly correlated with development levels. The share of women in developed countries accessing ICTs is approaching the same proportion as men using them, and some countries have reached gender parity in ICT access. By contrast, in LDCs women are the most disadvantaged in accessing Internet, as compared to men. In fact, the gender gap has been widening in recent years due to the quicker expansion in the number of men accessing the Internet than in that of women. In 2019 the percentage of women in LDCs using the Internet was less than half that of men (Figure 2.2). In 2019 only 13.9 per cent of LDC women used the Internet, as compared with 80.3 per cent in Europe (ITU, 2019).[11]

These trends show that in spite of the very quick diffusion of mobile telephony and mobile-broadband access in LDCs since the start of the new Millennium, digital divides continue to remain very wide between LDCs, on the one hand, and ODCs and developed countries, on the other. Access to the Internet remains restricted to a minority of the LDC population and gender divides are wide. Moreover, the expansion of uptake of mobile technologies for voice and data has more likely been achieved through the expansion of individual and household use rather than through the uptake by productive units (firms and farms). This remains a major hindrance in the development of productive capacities in these countries, the adoption of other more modern technologies and, more broadly, for the advancement of their structural transformation. The process of structural transformation that LDCs have been undergoing since the beginning of the century is analyzed hereafter.

2. The pace and direction of structural transformation

Previous analysis by UNCTAD of the process of structural transformation in LDCs in the early part of the 21st century indicated that, over the long run, most of them have experienced a falling share of agriculture, in both output and employment (UNCTAD, 2014). The transfer of resources has been mostly in favour of the tertiary sector, especially in the case of African LDCs. Some of these countries, especially African and Island LDCs, have undergone "pre-industrialisation deindustrialisation" (Tregenna, 2015). Many LDCs experienced the transfer of labour from low-productivity agriculture to low-productivity urban activities, basically in the services sector, often in informal activities.

Certain Asian LDCs lead advancement on structural transformation

In several Asian LDCs, by contrast, there has been some relative expansion of the share of manufacturing in output and employment since 2000. The industrialization process experienced by these LDCs was accompanied by the expected effects of labour productivity growth, poverty reduction and rising incomes (UNCTAD, 2014).

Figure 2.2

Internet user gender gap, 2013 and 2019

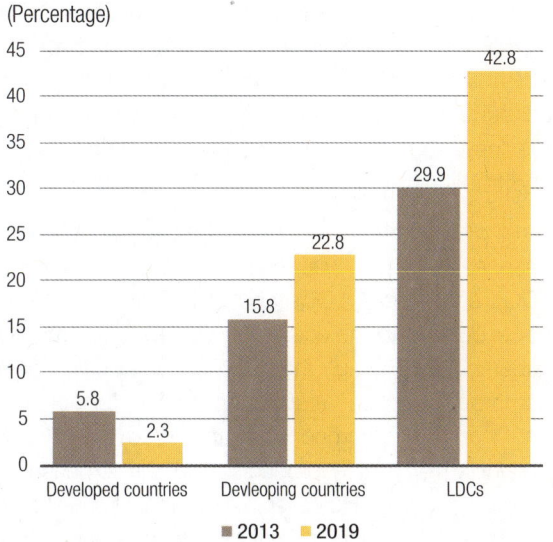

(Percentage)

	2013	2019
Developed countries	5.8	2.3
Developing countries	15.8	22.8
LDCs	29.9	42.8

Source: ITU (2019).
Note: The gender gap represents the difference between the Internet use penetration rates for males and females relative to the Internet user penetration rate for males, expressed as a percentage.

---

[11] The gender divide in access to ICTs has adverse consequences for the potential contribution of these technologies to raising productivity in agriculture in LDCs (Box 4.1 in chapter 4).

Box 2.1 Measuring the pace of structural transformation

In this report the pace of structural transformation is measured by the annual structural change index (ASCI), based on the structural change index (SCI, it is also known as Michaely index or Stoikov index), and calculated according to the formulae below:

$$ASCI = \frac{SCI}{t-x}, \text{ where:}$$

$$SCI = \frac{1}{2}\sum_{i-1}^{n}\left(|\varphi_{i,t} - \varphi_{i,t-x}|\right), \text{ where:}$$

$\varphi_{i,t}$ is the share of sector i in output / employment at time t
$\varphi_{i,t-x}$ is the share of sector i in output / employment at time t-x

Higher values indicate a greater intensity of change in the composition of a given whole. The index is applied to the composition of output and employment according to the following sectors: agriculture, manufacturing, other industries (mining, public utilities and construction) and services.

The index provides a measurement of the pace of structural transformation, but not of its direction. In other words, if the economy is experiencing growth-reducing forms of structural change (as can be re-primarization or premature deindustrialization), they will be reflected in higher ASCIs, but this does not mean that the economy is geared for higher long-term growth. This measure therefore needs to be complemented by other indicators of the direction of change, as is done in the text.

An update of the analysis of structural transformation in the LDCs was undertaken for the present report in order to ascertain whether trends have changed, and if there have been any marked differences between the period of implementation of the Brussels Programme of Action (BPoA) (2001–2011) (United Nations, 2001) and the IPoA (2011–2020).[12]

a. Output

The pace of structural transformation of output declined worldwide between the periods of 2001–2011 and 2011–2017. At varying degrees, this is also true for developed countries, ODCs and LDCs (Table 2.2). This slowdown is due to the general deceleration of worldwide economic growth in the aftermath of the global financial crisis of 2008–2009 and its lingering consequences. The ensuing period has been dubbed the "new normal" of slow expansion of world output and trade in the 2010s.

Among LDCs, the slowdown in the pace of structural change in output was especially strong in island LDCs and African LDCs and Haiti (Table 2.2). This corresponded to the end of the so-called commodity super-cycle. During the 2000s, historically high commodity prices (especially those for energy and industrial commodities) had led to the relative expansion of mining production, at the expense of that of agriculture. However, the reversal of price hikes and their stabilization at relatively low levels since 2011 stopped the expansion of investment and production in mining in African and island LDCs. In the case of the latter group, these dynamics are driven by the large swings caused by the oil cycle in Timor-Leste.

Asian LDCs, by contrast, experienced only a modest deceleration in the pace of change of output structure, in line with the fact that economic growth in these countries since 2011 has been more resilient than that of other LDCs. Both before and after 2011 the structural transformation of output has been dominated by the relative shrinking of agriculture and a corresponding expansion of manufacturing and, to a lesser extent, services.

Table 2.3 shows sectoral composition of output and employment for major groups of countries, and how they changed over 2001–2011 (the BPoA period) and 2011–2017 (the IPoA period). Overall, agriculture remains much more important for LDCs than for other country groups, reflecting the earlier phase of structural transformation in LDCs. Other industries (including mining), in contrast, contribute more the GDP in LDCs and in other country groups, mirroring LDCs' stronger reliance on natural resource extraction for the generation of economic activity, especially in African LDCs and Timor-Leste. Services still contribute to less than half of GDP in LDCs as a group, contrary to other country groups. Among LDCs the remarkable exception is island LDCs excluding Timor-Leste, for whom services contribute more than 60 per cent of their GDP. Since industry typically develops little in small island developing States (SIDS), the group

---

[12] Due to the availability of sectoral data on output and employment at the time of writing, the analysis of the IPoA period ends in 2017.

CHAPTER 2: Productive capacities and structural transformation: Giving concrete form to concepts

has also a stronger contribution of agriculture to GDP than other LDC subgroups (Table 2.3).

b. Employment

The pattern of structural change in employment has been quite different from that of structural change in output. First, the pace of intersectoral change in employment has been quicker than that of output for all major country groups (Table 2.2). Second, for most country (sub)groups the pace of intersectoral transfer of labour has been slower post-2011 than in the preceding period. This is related to the deceleration of economic activity during the period following the global financial crisis, which provided decreasing possibilities of labour reallocation.

Table 2.3 shows the sectoral shares of employment, and changes in those shares between 2001–2011 and 2011–2017. The overall pattern of change in employment in LDCs is a shift away from the agricultural sector towards services and, to a lesser degree, towards industry. Nevertheless, the overall level of employment in agricultural of these countries remains much higher than in other country groups. The sector still absorbs more than half of the labour force, as compared with 30 per cent in ODCs and just 3 per cent in developed countries. The importance of agriculture as a generator of employment is especially strong in African LDCs and Haiti, where agriculture generates as much as 62 per cent of jobs. It is likely that the agricultural labour force in LDCs rose somewhat as a consequence of the COVID health and economic crises. A large number of workers who lost their job in urban areas and of migrants who had to return from

Table 2.2
Pace of structural change by country groups, 2001–2017
(Annual structural change index – ASCI)

	Output		Employment	
	2001–2011	2011–2017	2001–2011	2011–2017
Developed countries	0,20	0,12	0,55	0,14
Other developing countries	0,86	0,24	1,09	1,02
Least developed countries	0,47	0,36	0,72	0,72
of which:				
African LDCs and Haiti	0,66	0,14	0,50	0,64
Asian LDCs	0,68	0,64	1,21	0,94
Island LDCs	4,91	2,88	0,59	0,56

Source: UNCTAD secretariat calculations, based on data from UNCTAD, UNCTADStat database, and ILO, Key Indicators of the Labour Market database [both accessedf May 2020].
Note: For an explanation of the index, see Box 2.1.

Table 2.3
Sectoral composition of output and employment by country groups, 2001–2017, selected years

	Agriculture					Manufacturing					Other industry					Services				
	2001	2011	2017	Change 2001–2011	Change 2011–2017	2001	2011	2017	Change 2001–2011	Change 2011–2017	2001	2011	2017	Change 2001–2011	Change 2011–2017	2001	2011	2017	Change 2001–2011	Change 2011–2017
	(Per cent)			(Percentage points)		(Per cent)			(Percentage points)		(Per cent)			(Percentage points)		(Per cent)			(Percentage points)	
Output
Developed countries	1	1	1	0	0	15	15	14	0	-1	11	9	9	-2	0	73	75	75	2	0
Other developing countries	11	9	8	-2	-1	16	24	23	8	-1	22	16	16	-6	0	51	52	53	1	1
Least developed countries	29	24	22	-5	-2	11	11	13	0	2	15	18	18	3	0	46	47	48	1	0
of which:
African LDCs and Haiti	30	24	23	-6	-1	10	9	9	-1	0	16	21	22	5	1	45	46	46	1	0
Asian LDCs	27	23	19	-4	-4	12	16	19	4	3	15	11	11	-4	0	48	50	50	2	1
Island LDCs	30	12	15	-18	3	6	2	3	-4	1	5	54	34	49	-20	60	32	42	-28	11
Island LDCs excl. Timor-Leste	*30*	*27*	*26*	*-3*	*-1*	*6*	*6*	*7*	*1*	*0*	*5*	*6*	*5*	*1*	*-1*	*60*	*61*	*62*	*1*	*2*
Employment
Developed countries	5	4	3	-1	-1	18	14	14	-4	0	9	9	9	0	0	68	73	75	6	1
Other developing countries	46	35	30	-11	-6	15	16	15	1	-1	5	9	9	4	0	34	40	46	6	6
Least developed countries	68	60	56	-7	-4	6	6	7	0	1	3	5	5	2	0	23	28	31	5	3
of which:
African LDCs and Haiti	71	65	62	-5	-4	5	5	5	0	0	3	4	5	1	1	22	26	29	4	3
Asian LDCs	64	52	46	-12	-6	8	11	12	3	1	4	6	6	2	0	25	32	36	7	4
Island LDCs	52	48	45	-4	-3	6	5	5	-1	0	9	6	6	-3	0	38	41	45	4	3
Island LDCs excl. Timor-Leste	*52*	*47*	*44*	*-5*	*-4*	*6*	*6*	*6*	*0*	*0*	*4*	*5*	*5*	*1*	*0*	*38*	*42*	*45*	*4*	*4*

Source: UNCTAD sercetariat calculations, based on data from ITU, ITU Statistics database and UNCTAD, UNCTADStat databases [both accessed June 2020].

Significant heterogeneity across services subsectors in skill-intensity and value-added contribution

their foreign host countries (as analyzed in chapter 1) transferred to rural areas, thereby increasing (at least temporarily) the agricultural labour force, given the predominance of agriculture in rural employment in LDCs (UNCTAD, 2015b).

The only exception among major country groups on the deceleration of inter-sectoral labour mobility between the BPoA and the IPoA periods were African LDCs and Haiti. There the pace of labour transfer among sectors rose somewhat after 2011. Qualitatively, this reflects the process of labour transfer out of agriculture mostly towards services (and largely in urban areas), which accelerated slightly between the two periods (Table 2.2). This is a somewhat troublesome feature. The direct transfer of labour from agriculture to services allows LDC economies to maintain economic growth in the short to medium term. However, the tertiary jobs generated are not necessarily sustainable (UNIDO, 2013). Moreover, given the heterogeneity of the tertiary (services) sector, the contribution of these jobs to overall productivity largely depends on the knowledge intensity of different services subsectors (see below). In other words, this type of labour transfer can be growth-reducing in the long term (de Vries et al., 2015).

Asian LDCs experienced some expansion of the manufacturing share of employment during the first period (BPoA), and a moderate expansion during the second period (IPoA). They were the only country group with an expanding manufacturing share of employment during the second period, thus confirming the industrialization-like pattern of structural transformation of Asian LDCs.

The services sector has increased in significance for all country groups since the early 2000s, but each has started from quite different levels (Table 2.3). At present the tertiary sector accounts for slightly less than one third of employment in LDCs, as compared with almost half in ODCs and three quarters in developed countries. Among LDCs, the largest increase in the services share of employment took place in the Asian subgroup.

The growth of the share of services in output and employment is usually taken as a sign of economic modernization. However, this ignores the strong heterogeneity among different services subsectors. These range from low-value-added, low-skill activities (e.g. informal retail trade) to high value-added, skill- and knowledge-intensive activities (e.g. business services such as engineering and information technology services). In order to examine in more detail the composition of the services sector in LDCs, as compared to that of other country groups, employment data has been classified according to three categories: (i) knowledge-intensive; (ii) less knowledge-intensive; and (iii) non-market.[13]

The relative importance of the different types of services sectors according to country groups is striking. In developed countries, there is an approximate balance between the three types of service activities. In LDCs, by contrast, the bulk of tertiary employment is concentrated in less knowledge-intensive services, which includes activities such as retail trade, repair of motor vehicles, accommodation and food. Often these are low-productivity and low-value-added activities, in many cases taking place in the informal sector. These service sectors are especially important for African LDCs and Haiti, and island LDCs, where they account for some two thirds of services employment (Figure 2.3).

Knowledge-intensive services, by contrast, generate less than one fifth of tertiary services in African LDCs and Haiti, and island LDCs. They include high-value-added and high-productivity activities, such as finance, business services and communications. They contribute to the performance of firms and farms by supplying specialized inputs to them. Their importance grows as the knowledge intensity of economic activities deepens and as the densification of economic activities intensifies (Figure 2.1). In Asian LDCs knowledge-intensive services account for one fourth of tertiary jobs, higher than in other LDC subgroups.

Another important contrast between LDCs concerns non-market services, which contribute directly to human capital formation and skills accumulation, such as education and health, thereby contributing to the development of productive capacities (Figure 2.1).

---

[13] The UNCTAD secretariat aggregated ILO data on employment in services based on the classification of Sorbe et al. (2018). The services categories are composed as follows (ISIC rev.4 sections indicated in parentheses): (i) Knowledge-intensive: Financial and insurance activities (K); Real estate, business and administrative activities (L, M, N); Transport, storage and communication (H, J); (ii) Less knowledge-intensive: Wholesale and retail trade, repair of motor vehicles and motorcycles (G); Accommodation and food service activities (I); Other services (R, S, T, U); (iii) Non-market: Public administration and defence, compulsory social security (O); Education (P); Human health and social work activities (Q).

CHAPTER 2: Productive capacities and structural transformation: Giving concrete form to concepts

Figure 2.3
Distribution of labour by major category of service sectors, by country groups, 2019
(Share of total employment in services)

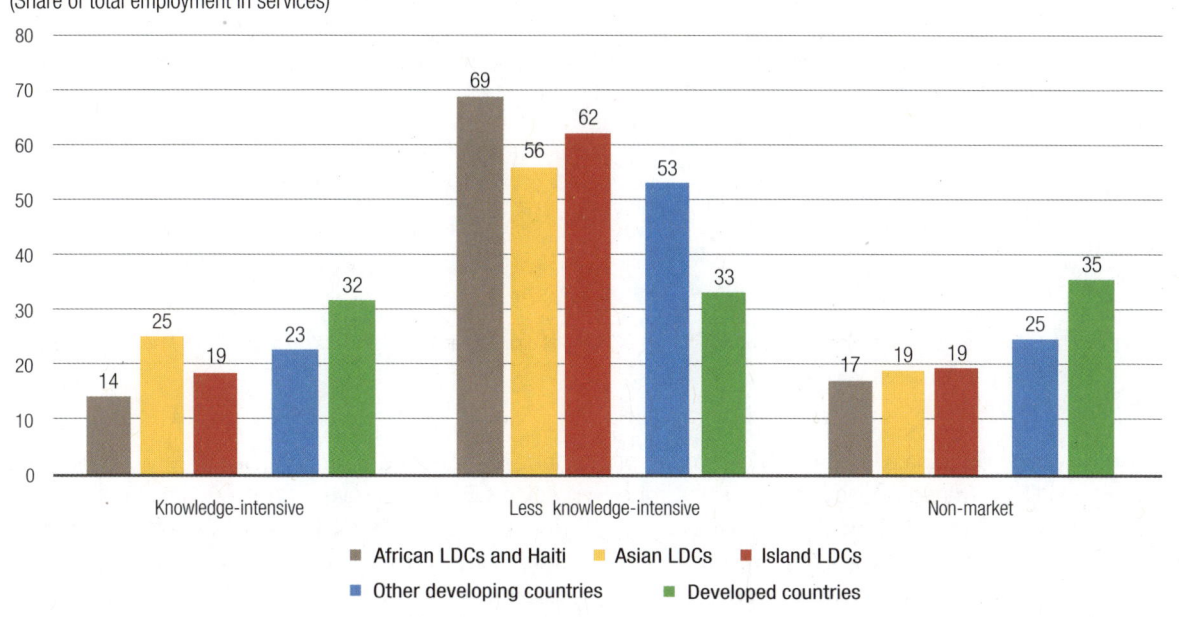

Category	African LDCs and Haiti	Asian LDCs	Island LDCs	Other developing countries	Developed countries
Knowledge-intensive	14	25	19	23	32
Less knowledge-intensive	69	56	62	53	33
Non-market	17	19	19	25	35

Source: UNCTAD secretariat calculations, based on data from ILO, Key Indicators of the Labour Market [accessed May 2020].
Note: For the explanation of the classification, see footnote 10 in the main text.

While they contribute less than one fifth of tertiary employment in LDCs, in developed countries they generate more than one third of services jobs. As a share of total employment, the contrast is even starker. Non-market services generate more than one fourth of total employment in developed countries, but just 6 per cent in LDCs. This reflects the reduced spending of LDC governments (and firms) in health and education, which contributed to the weaknesses of LDCs' health systems (chapter 1), and hence their limited preparedness to deal with the COVID-19 pandemic.

c. Productivity

This subsection compares trends in labour productivity in LDCs (and subgroups) with those in other major country groups, and among different LDCs. Labour productivity is a major source of rises in GDP per capita, and hence of improved standards of living. From the point of view of the structural analysis used in this report, changes in a country's overall labour productivity are determined by the sectoral composition of employment and output, and by productivity levels of different sectors. Therefore, trends in labour productivity are determined by the developments in the composition and growth of output and employment analyzed in the previous subsections. The analysis of labour productivity trends allows us to understand the extent to which LDCs are converging to or diverging from ODCs and developed countries.

LDCs achieved a healthy pace of labour productivity gains in the 2001–2011 period, when it grew at an annual pace of 3.9 per cent, slightly lower than in ODCs, which recorded an annual expansion of 4.6 per cent. During the following period (2011–2017), however, these two groups of countries diverged. Labour productivity growth decelerated in both, but much more in LDCs, where it declined to 1.9 per cent annually, whereas in ODCs it decelerated more moderately to 3.7 per cent per annum (Table 2.4).

Among LDC subgroups, the performance of Asian LDC outpaced that of the others. They experienced the fastest labour productivity growth in both periods, and their growth deceleration between 2001–2001 and 2011–2017 was milder. At 3.2 per cent per annum in the latter period, it was only slightly slower than in ODCs. In African LDCs and Haiti, by contrast, the pace of labour productivity growth decelerated more markedly to 1.3 per cent per annum in the second period (Table 2.3). Island LDCs excluding Timor-Leste experienced very low rate of labour productivity in both periods.[14]

---

[14] The strong fluctuation of the pace of labour productivity growth pf the island LDCs subgroup (including Timor-Leste) is explained by the impact of the oil price cycle on the economic performance of this country. Between the beginning and the end of the respective periods, international fuel commodity prices rose by 254 per cent in 2001–2011, but declined by 47 per cent in 2011–2017, according to UNCTAD's Free Market Commodity Price Index.

Table 2.4
Average annual growth of labour productivity, 2001–2017
(Per cent)

	Agriculture		Manufacturing		Other industry		Services		Total	
	2001–2011	2011–2017	2001–2011	2011–2017	2001–2011	2011–2017	2001–2011	2011–2017	2001–2011	2011–2017
Developed countries	3.8	2.5	3.5	1.0	-0.6	0.8	0.4	0.4	0.9	0.6
Other developing countries	5.0	5.1	8.6	3.6	-4.7	2.8	3.1	1.8	4.6	3.7
Least developed countries	3.0	1.8	2.6	3.4	1.6	-1.3	2.1	0.2	3.9	1.9
of which:										
African LDCs and Haiti	1.9	1.8	1.6	2.0	3.0	-2.1	2.0	-0.5	3.4	1.3
Asian LDCs	5.3	2.2	4.0	4.7	-2.7	0.3	2.4	1.3	4.7	3.2
Island LDCs	-2.5	0.8	-1.0	1.9	41.0	-11.6	-1.7	-0.5	5.6	-3.9
Island LDCs excl. Timor-Leste	0.4	1.6	1.8	1.2	1.1	-1.4	-0.2	-0.2	0.7	0.7

Source: UNCTAD secretariat calculations, based on data from UNCTAD, UNCTADStat database, and ILO, Key Indicators of the Labour Market database [both accessed May 2020].

Beyond group aggregates, the performance of individual LDCs varied considerably since the beginning of the Millennium. Ten LDCs achieved annual average labour productivity growth ranging between 4 to 10 per cent. Five of these countries are located in Asia: Myanmar, Lao People's Democratic Republic, Bhutan, Afghanistan and Cambodia; while the other five are in Africa: Ethiopia, Mali, Mozambique, Rwanda and Chad (Figure 2.4). This positive performance was achieved by a combination of structural transformation and diversification of their economies. Generally, there is a positive correlation between labour productivity growth in the LDCs, and the pace of structural transformation of output and employment (Figure 2.5). Still, the correlation is lower than 0.35 in both cases, indicating that structural change in LDCs in the new Millennium has not been productivity-propping (and growth-enhancing) in all cases.

At the other end of the performance range are LDCs that have experienced a contraction in labour productivity since 2001, they include: Burundi, Central African Republic, Comoros, Gambia, Haiti, Madagascar, Timor-Leste and Yemen. Their negative outcome was impacted by factors ranging from military and political conflicts to natural disasters and extreme levels of oil dependence.

The analysis of the sectoral patterns of labour productivity growth reveals what has been driving these contrasting trends between the LDC subgroups. The better performance of labour productivity growth in several Asian LDCs stemmed largely from the relatively faster productivity growth in manufacturing and services. These two sectors together accounted for almost half of total employment in 2017. As shown by Figure 2.3, the share of higher-productivity knowledge-intensive activities in total services employment is higher in Asian LDCs than in other LDC groups, which has contributed to stronger total labour productivity growth of the services sector in Asian LDCs. Moreover, these countries experienced the fastest rhythm of growth of labour productivity in manufacturing among all the major country groups shown in Table 2.4. Thereby, the sector contributed to overall productivity growth, in spite of its relatively small share of total employment (12 per cent in 2017). While agriculture remains the largest employer (even in Asian LDCs), their labour productivity growth (2.2 per cent per annum) was faster than in other LDC subgroups. In other words, the group's labour productivity was stronger than other LDC groups across all major sectors of economic activity, which reflects a growth-enhancing pattern of structural transformation.

The deceleration in labour productivity in African LDCs between 2011–2017 was largely driven by an actual decline in productivity in services and other industries, especially mining. The adverse performance of productivity in services is due to two factors: (i) the continuous influx of labour not being matched by commensurate output growth in the tertiary sector; (ii) the concentration of tertiary employment in less knowledge-intensive services (the highest among the major country groups analyzed here, as shown in Figure 2.3), and their typically lower productivity growth potential. The sharp reversal in labour productivity growth in other industries is associated with the reversal of the commodity cycle that occurred in the 2000s and 2010s, which led to a strong contraction in investment and low expansion of production of the mining sector. In agriculture, productivity between 2001–2001 and 2001–2017 continued rising at the same pace but was lower than the one for all other major country groups, except island LDCs (Table 2.4).

One of the features of structural transformation is the narrowing of intersectoral differences in levels

Figure 2.4
Growth of labour productivity, 2001–2017

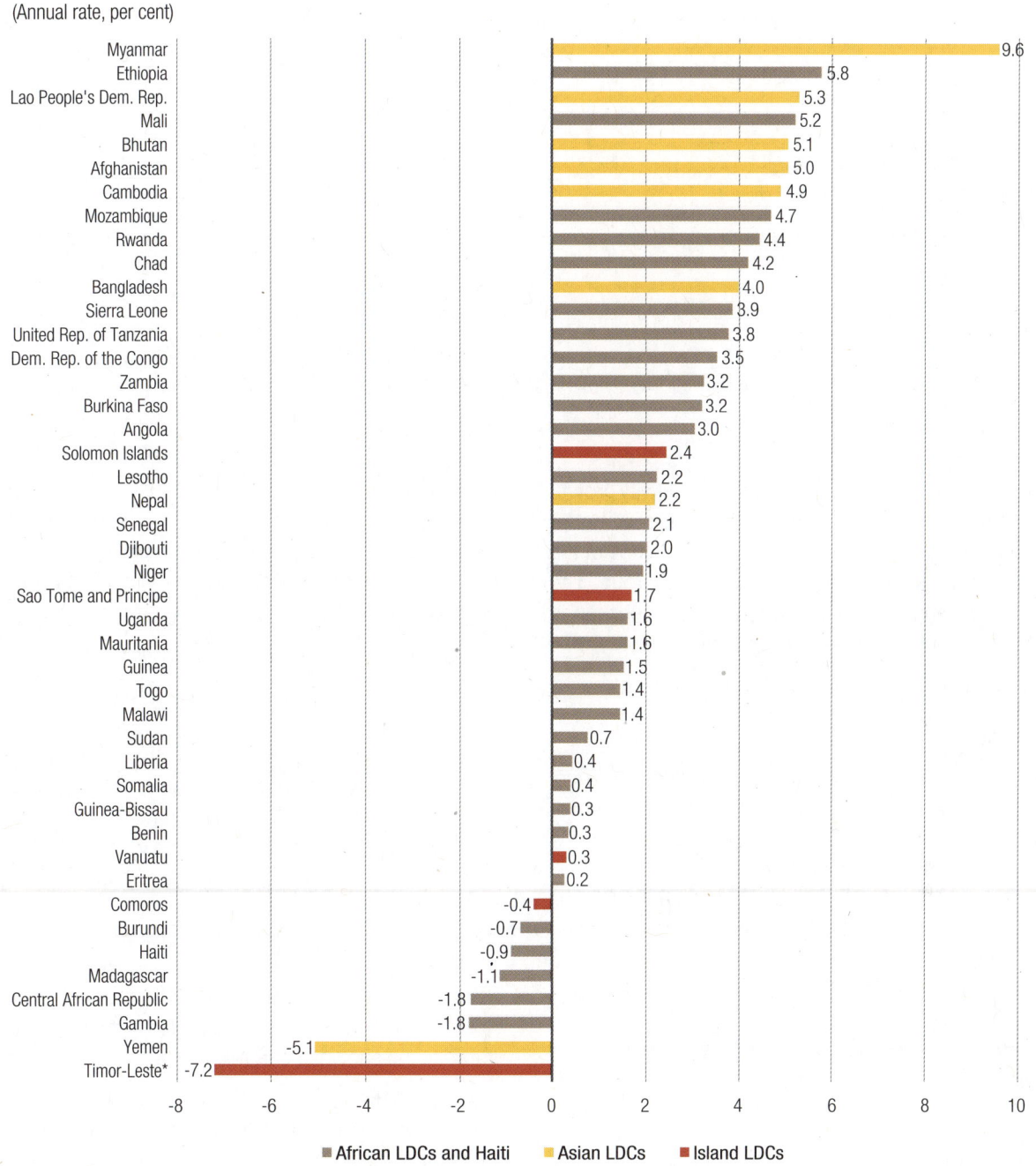

(Annual rate, per cent)

Myanmar	9.6
Ethiopia	5.8
Lao People's Dem. Rep.	5.3
Mali	5.2
Bhutan	5.1
Afghanistan	5.0
Cambodia	4.9
Mozambique	4.7
Rwanda	4.4
Chad	4.2
Bangladesh	4.0
Sierra Leone	3.9
United Rep. of Tanzania	3.8
Dem. Rep. of the Congo	3.5
Zambia	3.2
Burkina Faso	3.2
Angola	3.0
Solomon Islands	2.4
Lesotho	2.2
Nepal	2.2
Senegal	2.1
Djibouti	2.0
Niger	1.9
Sao Tome and Principe	1.7
Uganda	1.6
Mauritania	1.6
Guinea	1.5
Togo	1.4
Malawi	1.4
Sudan	0.7
Liberia	0.4
Somalia	0.4
Guinea-Bissau	0.3
Benin	0.3
Vanuatu	0.3
Eritrea	0.2
Comoros	-0.4
Burundi	-0.7
Haiti	-0.9
Madagascar	-1.1
Central African Republic	-1.8
Gambia	-1.8
Yemen	-5.1
Timor-Leste*	-7.2

■ African LDCs and Haiti   ■ Asian LDCs   ■ Island LDCs

Source: UNCTAD secretariat calculations, based on data from UNCTAD, UNCTADStat database, and ILO, Key Indicators of the Labour Market database [both accessed May 2020].

Note: * 2011–2017.

of productivity, as mentioned in section C.1. Since the beginning of new Millennium, the dispersion of labour productivity among major sectors in LDCs has declined, indicating some degree of domestic convergence. This was the consequences of continuous increase in the productivity of the lowest-productivity sector (agriculture), along with a decline in labour productivity in the "other industry" sector (driven by the contraction in mining since 2011), which is the highest-productivity sector. These processes are sobering. While rising labour productivity in agriculture is a central element of structural transformation, LDCs need to accelerate the pace further, especially African LDCs and Haiti, and island LDCs. At the same time, narrowing intersectoral differences in labour productivity should

The Least Developed Countries Report 2020

Figure 2.5
Labour productivity growth and pace of structural transformation

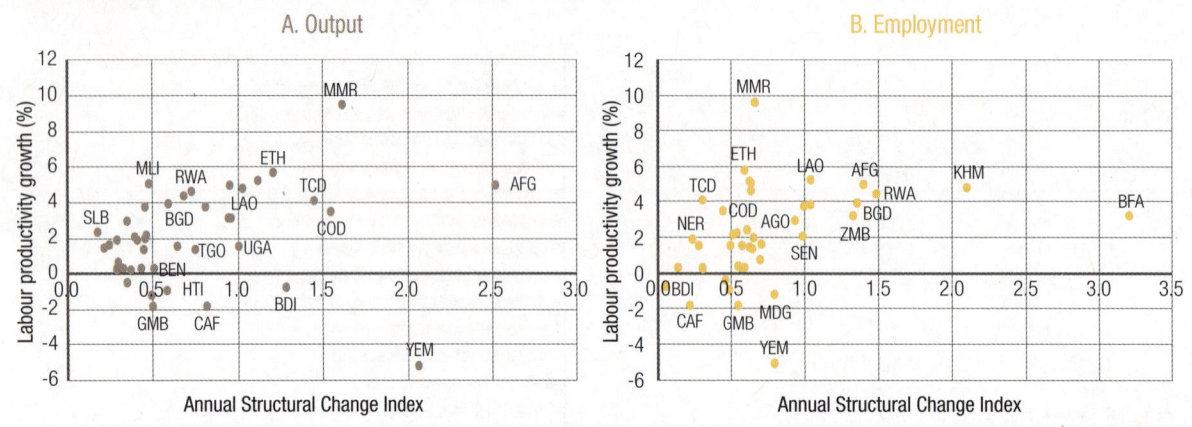

A. Output

B. Employment

Source: UNCTAD secretariat calculations, based on data from UNCTAD, UNCTADStat database, and ILO, Key Indicators of the Labour Market [both accessed May 2020].

be the result of differential rates of productivity growth combined with intersectoral transfer of labour, rather than of the actual decline in productivity in one of the sectors, as happened in the LDCs as a group. The sectoral dispersion of LDCs remains higher than in ODCs, as well as developed countries (Figure 2.6).

Once again, trends have been quite different among different LDC groups, which is partly correlated with the weight of the mining industry, which has a much higher labour productivity, thanks to its very high capital intensity. Thus, in African LDCs, where the mining sector is more important, the dispersion declined from 13.5 to 11.9 between 2001 and 2017. In Asian LDCs – where the mining share of GDP is half of that of African LDCs – the ratio of dispersion fell from an already lower level of 9.5 to 3.9 over the same period. Finally, in island LDCs, which have the highest share of mining in output among the LDC groups, the sectoral productivity dispersion has been erratic since the beginning of the new Millennium.

d. Are the LDCs converging or diverging?

Developments in labour productivity can converge or diverge internationally. The comparison is made between laggard countries and leading countries typically in overall productivity level, to determine whether there is a trend towards international income convergence or divergence. In the case of the former, international inequality is falling and the international community is advancing towards the achievement of Goal 10 of the Sustainable Development Goals. If divergence is occurring, however, international inequality is rising even further from already high levels, with all the destabilizing potential this brings in its wake (as shown in chapter 1).

The overall labour productivity level of LDCs as a group has been diverging from that of the group of ODCs. In 1991 the ratio LDCs/ODCs was at 25 per cent (UNCTAD, 2014), while at the beginning of the 21st century it was down to 21 per cent, finally reaching 18 per cent in 2017. More specifically, the group and sectoral trends in labour productivity growth during the periods of implementation of the BPoA and the IPoA have resulted in contrasting trends in the international productivity comparison between different LDC subgroups and ODCs.

The positive development of Asian LDC productivity outlined in the previous subsections have allowed them to just about keep pace with the growth of productivity in ODCs. Nevertheless, even the

Figure 2.6
Sectoral dispersion of labour productivity by contry groups, 2001–2017, selected years

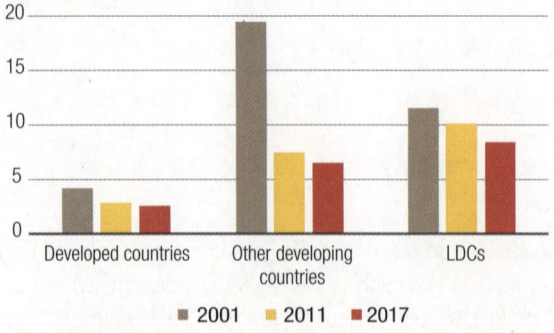

Source: UNCTAD secretariat calculations, based on data from UNCTAD, UNCTADStat database, and ILO, Key Indicators of the Labour Market database [both accessed May 2020].
Note: Ratio of maximum level of labour productivity among four sectors (agriculture, manufacturing, other industry, services) to minimum level.

best-performing LDC subgroup has not been able to narrow the gap with ODCs. The ratio of labour productivity of Asian LDCs to ODCs has oscillated around 20 per cent since the beginning of the century. African LDCs and Haiti, by contrast, have diverged from the ODC labour productivity level, even during the period of higher growth underpinned by high commodity prices of the 2000s. In 2001, the corresponding ratio was 22 per cent and higher than that of Asian LDCs. By 2017, the ratio for African LDCs and Haiti had declined to 17 per cent of that of ODCs and to a lower level than that of Asian LDCs (Figure 2.7).

The relative labour productivity in Island LDCs was as erratic as their absolute levels. While at the beginning of the new Millennium their labour productivity corresponded to two thirds of the level of ODCs, by 2017 it had declined sharply to 44 per cent, for the cyclical reasons mentioned above.

Labour productivity in LDCs has grown at a stronger pace than in developed countries since 2000. However, this was not sufficient to significantly close the enormous gap between the country groups. In 2017 the LDC labour productivity corresponded to just a minor fraction of the level of developed countries: 2.5 per cent (as compared to 1.7 per cent in 2001). While some convergence took place, it was marginal.

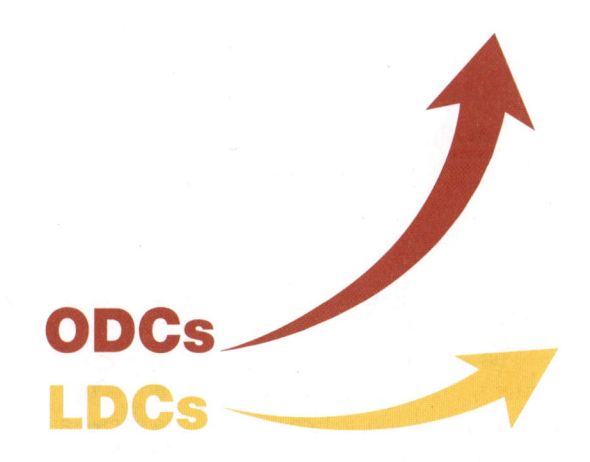

LDCs' progress on structural transformation and labour productivity has diverged from ODCs

3. Implications

The preceding analysis indicates that LDCs as a group have been diverging over the long term from ODCs, both in terms of the strength and direction of their structural transformation, as well as their overall labour productivity growth. The process was somewhat halted in the 2000s, thanks largely to the long commodities cycle but continued once

Figure 2.7
LDCs / ODCs labour productivity ratio by country groups, 2000–2017

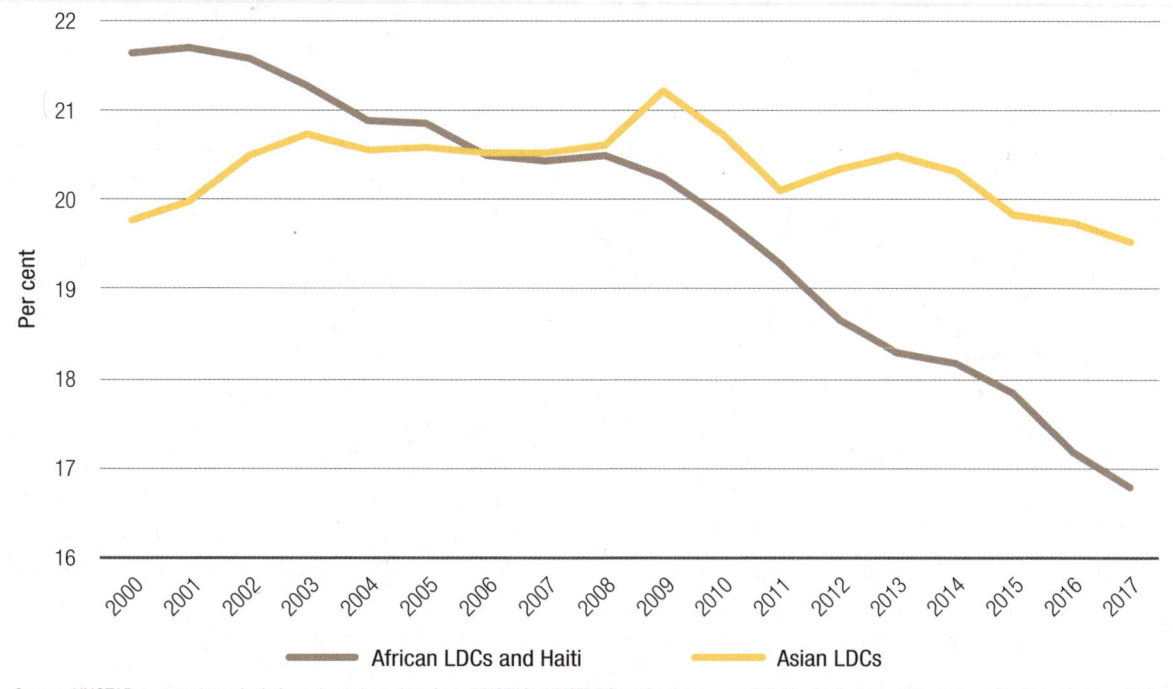

Source: UNCTAD secretariat calculations, based on data from UNCTAD, UNCTADStat database, and ILO, Key Indicators of the Labour Market database [both accessed May 2020].

Asian LDCs are undergoing a classical but shallow form of industrialization

again since the outbreak of the global financial crisis of 2008–2009. If this divergent trend is not reversed, LDCs as a group will not be able to overturn their long-term marginalization in the world economy. Reversing this trend, in turn, requires the acceleration of the building of productive capacities.

There is, however, a strong contrast between the three groups of LDCs in their structural transformation. Asian LDCs as a group are the ones undergoing what most resembles a classical process of industrialization, driven by Bangladesh, Cambodia, Myanmar, Lao People's Democratic Republic and Nepal. They have rising share of manufacturing in output and employment, specialization in manufacturing exports, the strongest performance in terms of labour productivity growth, shrinking of poverty and stronger progress in social outcomes. Still, there are some caveats to this apparent success story.

First, the importance of manufacturing in Asian LDCs remains lesser than in ODCs in terms of both employment and output (Table 2.3). Second, their industrial performance still trails well behind that of ODCs. The average of Asian LDCs UNIDO's Competitive Industrial Performance Index (0.0130) corresponds to one fourth of the average Index for ODCs (0.0508).[15]

Third, the industrialization these countries experienced corresponds to a "shallow" form of industrialization, typical of integration of low-income countries into GVCs. It means the establishment of some manufacturing activity, but with limited development of endogenous technological capabilities (Baldwin, 2016; UNCTAD, 2018a). The manufacturing of Asian LDCs is concentrated in a few industrial segments (especially garments and, to a lesser extent, textiles), which makes them highly vulnerable to developments in this industry. This was shown once again during the COVID-19 lockdown and the disruption of many global value chains (GVCs), which led to a sharp contraction of Asian LDC exports.

Fourth, countries such as Bangladesh, Myanmar, Lao People's Democratic Republic and Nepal, have to some extent built their manufacturing industry to serve foreign markets, while taking advantage of preferential market access conditions, especially the preferential treatment given to LDCs in major importing markets (particularly developed countries) (WTO, 2019). It is uncertain how this manufacturing sector will fare once these countries graduate form the LDC category, and eventually lose LDC preferential treatment. All these countries have entered the process of graduation from LDC status, or likely to do so in the near future. For their industrialization process to be sustainable, they need to broaden their industrial development and deepen their entrepreneurial and technological capabilities, so as to achieve what the *The Least Developed Countries Report 2016* characterized as "graduation with momentum" (UNCTAD, 2016a).

The process of structural transformation in African LDCs has been slower and the transfer of productive resources of higher-productivity sectors has been sluggish. The long commodity cycle of 2003–2011 has led to some degree of re-primarization of the commodity-dependent Africa LDCs. After the cycle finished, these countries found it difficult to establish new drivers of growth and diversification. The majority of the labour force remain concentrated in agriculture, where productivity has been growing but at a low pace. Most of the rural-urban migration has been absorbed in less knowledge-intensive service sectors, rather than in manufacturing or knowledge-intensive services, both of which tend to have higher labour productivity than less knowledge-intensive services. Thus, the challenge of diversifying their economy and developing high-productivity economic activities remains. Given the still very high share of employment in agriculture, these countries continue to have a very high potential for further structural transformation (McMillan et al., 2017). This supposes the following double contemporaneous challenge: (i) strongly accelerating the rhythm of agricultural labour productivity growth; (ii) generating employment in other sectors for their rapidly growing population (chapter 1). Moreover, these new jobs need to be of a considerably higher productivity level than that of agriculture.

Island LDCs have a differentiated profile. Most have the evolved towards an economic structure typical of SIDS. These countries diversified their economies towards services and focused strongly on tourism, which is a less knowledge-intensive and lower-productivity service sector. This generates vulnerability to developments in the global tourism economy, as once again sharply seen during the COVID-19 lockdown, which brought world tourism to virtual standstill. Timor-Leste, by contrast, is a typical oil-dependent country and the developments

---

[15] Unweighted average of the figure for 2017. UNCTAD secretariat calculation based on data from UNIDO (2019a).

in diversification and productivity are very strongly influenced by the international oil cycle.

These patterns of structural transformation highlight the vulnerability of LDCs to shocks in international markets and the need for the development of domestic markets, both in terms of supply-side (production) and demand-side (e.g. by developing consumer "taste" for domestic products). Even the virtuous processes of transformation and diversification have come to a halt because of the COVID-19 recession or, in some cases, gone into reverse. The recovery from the recession will need to be directed towards the objectives of virtuous structural transformation and towards building more resilient economies.

E. LDCs' productive capacities in the new decade

LDCs will need to analyze and take into account the developments raised in the preceding section as they prepare for the coming years, which will witness a coincidence of processes. The new decade starts with all countries struggling to cope with the consequences of the COVID-19 crisis, and recover from the deep recession it has caused. The international community is scheduled to adopt a new plan of action for the LDCs, and enters the final decade of the 2030 Agenda for Sustainable Development. LDCs will need to evolve productive capacities in such a way to ensure that it leads to the structural transformation of their respective economies and societies. This only will allow them to reach their development goals, including those contained in the 2030 Agenda for Sustainable Development and those to be adopted during UNLDC-V.

For all the discourse about "build back better" after COVID-19, it has to be adjusted to the conditions prevailing in LDCs. First, in most cases, the priority of these countries is not so much to build back as to develop new and superior productive capacities. This means either upgrading technologically the existing firms and farms or establishing new economic activities and sectors which did not exist previously. Second, the global COVID-19 crisis has not so much changed global realities as highlighted, sharpened or accelerated pre-existing trends, for example the acceleration of technological change, growing domestic and international inequalities, challenges to multilateralism, changing direction of globalization, and the effects of climate change, etc.

All of these pre-existing (and possibly accelerating) trends need to be taken into account by policymakers in LDCs and their development partners when

> **LDCs' priority is to develop new and superior productive capacities**

devising and implementing economic and social strategies and policies for the new period. Hereafter this section mentions some of the trends that will influence the development of productive capacities in LDCs during the 2020s. It then concentrates on one of them, namely the on-going technological revolution brough by frontier-technologies, and particularly digital technologies.

1. Trends affecting the future development of productive capacities

In the 2020s the development of productive capacities will be strongly influenced by developments in the global environment (as these are typically small open economies), and by the policies adopted by both LDCs and their development partners. Overall, this global environment will be strongly characterized by the lingering effects of the COVID-19 health and economic crises, and how international economic and political relations will evolve thereafter. Some broad trends will exert a particularly strong influence on the productive capacities of LDCs and their broader development prospects. These include the reorientation of international economic and political relations in the post-COVID-19 context, the future of globalization, GVCs, regional integration (UNCTAD, 2020a), progress in climate change and policies to tackle it, and the unfolding technological revolution (Fagerberg and Verspagen, 2020). Moreover, one specific feature of the LDCs is their very high rate of demographic growth, which entails the need to generate a growing number of jobs for annual arrival of new entrants in the labour market (chapter 1), let alone the growing demands for social services, the provision of which needs to be financed.

This report acknowledges the influence of these broad trends on future development of productive capacities in the new decade, but it does not try to speculate on future development on most of them. However, it does concentrate on the effects of the ongoing technological revolution brought about by frontier technologies. They have a direct impact on productive capacities worldwide and pose a major technological and economic challenge to LDCs. These challenges stem from the lingering low level of technological capabilities of most LDC (UNCTAD, 2007), and also from the fact that frontier technologies are created by technological developed countries to respond to the needs and challenges of their own countries. This means that these new technologies correspond to the economic (e.g. factor endowments) and social conditions of countries at the technological frontier. These conditions differ markedly from those of LDCs, which poses the question of the appropriateness of these new technologies to the conditions of LDCs.

The analysis of these issues is hereafter undertaken in three steps. First, the remainder of this chapter discusses the overall features of frontier technologies. Second, chapter 3 analyzes the state of development of productive capacities in LDCs. Third, chapter 4 asks how these new technologies are being taken up in LDCs, and how they can harness new technologies to strengthen their technological capabilities in a way that is appropriate to their natural, economic, social and demographic conditions.

2. The technological revolution

The world economy and society is being overtaken by a new technological revolution. It consists of the clustering of innovations in several key types of frontier technology, the most important of which are indicated in Table 2.5.

While still incipient, this technological revolution has some concrete features and visible outcomes, especially in technologically advanced countries.

Table 2.5
Frontier technologies

Field / Type	Main technologies
Digital technologies	Internet of Things (IoT)
	5G mobile broadband
	3D printing (additive manufacturing)
	Big data / Data analytics
	Blockchain
	Cloud computing
	Automation and robotics
	Quantum computing
	Artificial intelligence (AI)
Biotech	Genomics, bio-catalysis, agriculture
Nano-tech	Organic and inorganic nanomaterials
Green technnologies	Renewable energy, water management

Source: Adapted from UNCTAD (2018).

These technologies have the following characteristics (UNCTAD, 2018g):

- Different technologies build on each other;
- Technologies are converging through increasing use of digital platforms to produce new combinatory technologies (e.g. precision farming);
- Declining costs, especially in the case ICTs and photovoltaic panels;
- Growth and ubiquity of platforms of platforms, such as the Internet and global positioning systems (GPS);
- Digitalization; and
- Connectivity.

Some of these technologies are general purpose technologies (Bresnahan, 2010), and play a central role in growth as they are:

- Widely used and provide inputs to a large number of sectors;
- Capable of ongoing technical improvement, leading to cost reductions and quality improvements;
- Enable innovation in application sectors as they lead to increasing return to innovation through their interaction with these application sectors; and
- Affect all sectors of the economy eventually.

These technologies have a very strong potential impact on the development of productive capacities in LDCs in the new decade. However, this raises issues related to their diffusion and appropriateness. The dissemination of these technologies in LDCs and the potential that they have for boosting the development of productive capacities is analyzed in subsequent parts of this report. Given their increasing ubiquity, it is important for LDC policymakers to position themselves vis-à-vis these new technologies and, possibly, harness them to the extent that they contribute to reaching LDC development goals. Crucially, policymakers in LDCs and among their development partners need to realize the complementarity between the different elements of productive capacities in leading to structural transformation. This includes elements, such as the infrastructure analyzed above, the technological capabilities examined in chapter 4, and the other components of productive capacities and mutual linkages and trade-offs or synergies (analyzed in chapter 3).

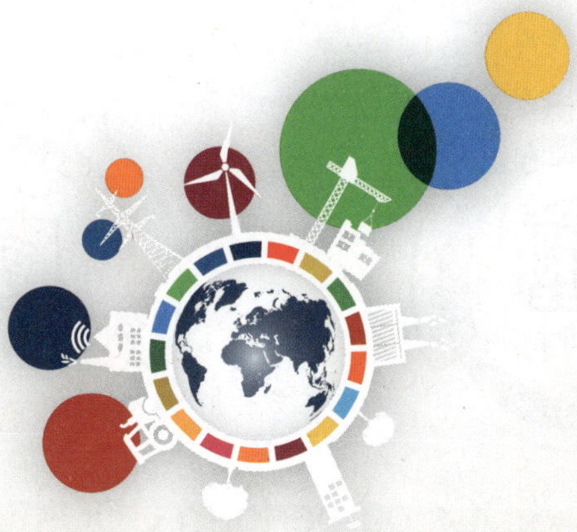

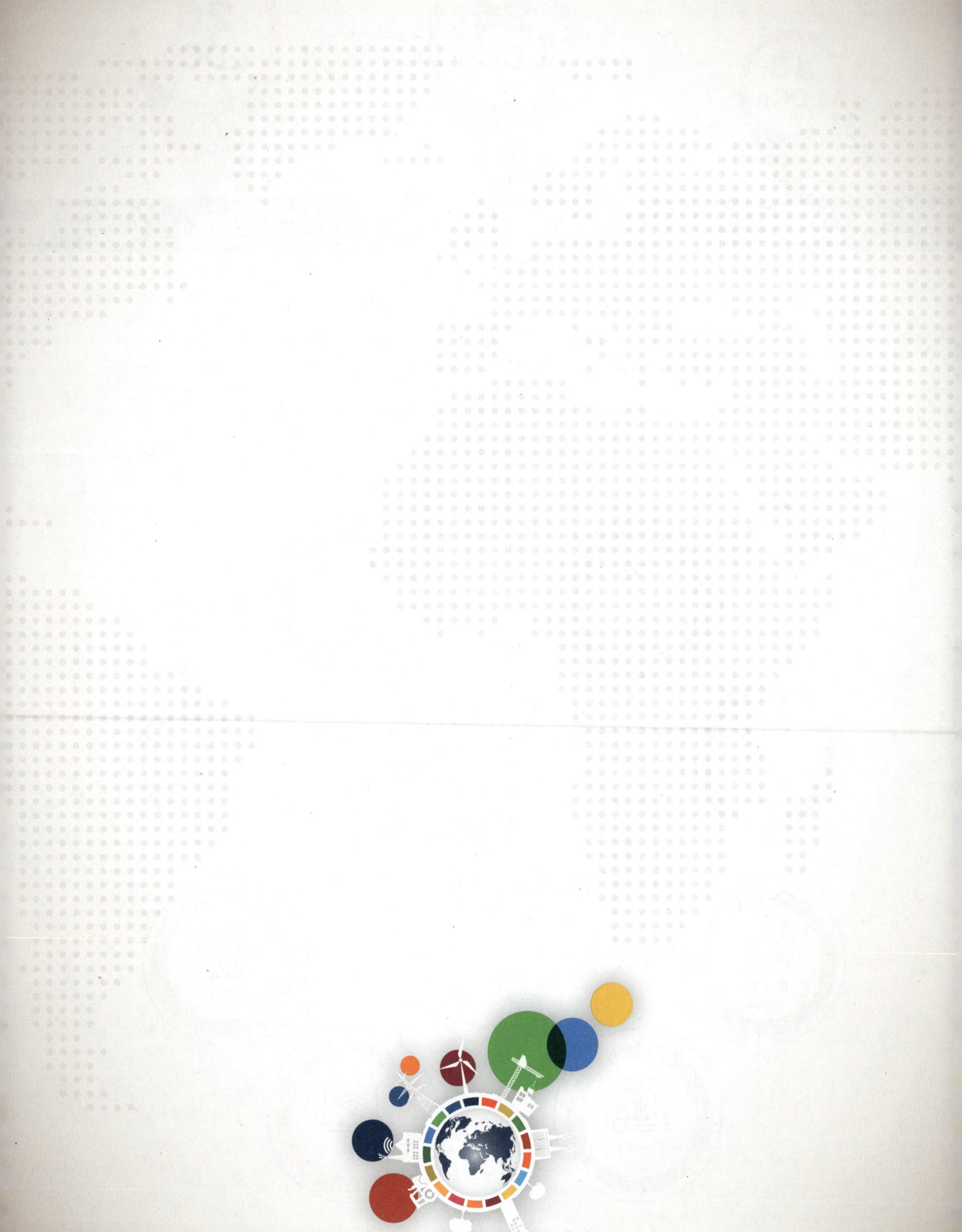

11 LDCs — 2001
18 LDCs — 2001
25 LDCs — 2011
6 LDCs — 2011
26 LDCs — 2018
6 LDCs — 2018

🔴 The number of LDCs with low productive capacities has increased over time

🟡 The number of LDCs with high productive capacities has decreased over time

- Human capital
- Natural resources
- Structural change
- Energy
- Private sector
- Transport
- Institutions
- ICT

PCI

LDCs outperform ODCs in the natural resources component

CHAPTER 3

Measuring productive capacities: LDCs' progress towards sustainable development

CHAPTER 3

Measuring productive capacities: LDCs' progress towards sustainable development

A. Introduction	**53**
B. The UNCTAD productive capacities index	**54**
1. Overview	54
2. Measuring progress and benchmarking with PCI	55
C. Assessing the progress of LDCs towards IPoA goals	**61**
1. GDP growth target and productive capacities	61
a. Productive capacity utilization and efficiency	62
b. Marginal impacts of the individual productive capacities, as per IPoA	65
2. Agriculture, food security and rural development	66
3. Trade and commodities	69
4. Human and social development	74
a. Education and training	74
b. Population and primary health	77
5. Multiple crises and other emerging challenges	80
6. Mobilizing financial resources for development and capacity-building	83
7. Good governance at all levels	85
D. Conclusion	**86**
ANNEX: A technical introduction to the UNCTAD Productive Capacities Index	**89**
a. Imputation of missing data	89
b. Forecasting	89
c. Multivariate analysis	89
d. Computing the PCI	90

A. Introduction

The structural economic problems of least developed countries (LDCs) have received considerable attention in the development discourse. Over the past 15 years or so, UNCTAD has consistently highlighted the need to develop the productive capacities of LDCs and support these countries with concrete measures to reduce their vulnerabilities. Among the measures it has proposed are diversifying and building the resilience of LDC economies, as well as increasing social development returns and boosting the poverty elasticity of growth. The productive capacities needed to transform LDC economies are broadly described in Chapter 1 and referenced throughout the report. This chapter demonstrates that efforts to monitor the progress made by LDCs in attaining internationally agreed objectives, notably the Istanbul Programme of Action for the Least Developed Countries (IPoA) and the Sustainable Development Goals, could be enhanced by measuring the productive capacities of the countries across all possible dimensions.

With less than a decade left to implement the 2030 Agenda for Sustainable Development, building the productive capacities of the LDCs could help the countries to ramp up progress on several Sustainable Development Goals. A steady rise in productive capacities is necessary to boost economic development impacts, including reducing extreme poverty (Sustainable Development Goal 1). The comparative advantages of LDCs in natural resources and abundant labour have not been efficiently exploited to enhance productive activities that could help these countries achieve higher levels of economic development. With the labour force in LDCs increasing by 2.7 per cent per annum in 2011–2019, these countries have a unique opportunity to bolster agricultural productivity (Sustainable Development Goal 2) and industrial growth (Sustainable Development Goal 8), particularly if improvements to labour productivity are contemporaneously implemented with surges in other productive capacities, such as energy (Sustainable Development Goal 7), structural change, information technology, infrastructure, transport linkages and private sector (Sustainable Development Goals 8 and 9).

This chapter builds on the concept of productive capacities outlined in chapter 2 and will demonstrate its policy relevance. An overview the UNCTAD productive capacities index (PCI) is presented and applied to assess the progress that LDCs have achieved over time. Since graduation from the LDC status is a fundamental goal of all international support measures (ISMs) specific to LDCs, the analysis appraises the performance of individual countries as they progress towards graduation, and the overall objective of the IPoA to enable half of the LDCs to meet the graduation criteria by 2020.

> **A steady rise in the productive capacities of the LDCs is necessary to achieve the SDGs**

The chapter further highlights areas in which LDCs have made notable progress and where they could have done better. The multidimensionality of the productive capacity categories implies that improvements, or lack of traction, in some productive capacity categories may affect progress in other categories. The analysis advances the view that building productive capacities is a viable framework for operationalizing development policy; however, to be effective the different capacities in the economy must complement one another as a system; linkages among countries also play a critical role for diversification and building export capacities.

The literature on measuring productive capacities proposes a large choice of indices; however, most of them measure productivity at the sectoral or aggregate economic level and are used to explain dynamic effects of growth on the structure of economies over time (Kalirajan and Salim, 1997; Nordhaus, 2002; Gagnon, 2007). In this approach, growth performance is explained by decomposing the marginal contributions of various inputs, particularly of labour (Scarpetta et al., 2000). The UNCTAD PCI is an aggregate measure which incorporates not just the endowments of a country but also how it transforms its resources and benefits from interlinkages with other countries. Although the methodology and indicators for measuring productive capacities may improve in the future, the UNCTAD PCI is the most extensive in scope, content and technical effort.

The rest of the chapter is organized as follows. A brief description of the methodology for constructing the UNCTAD PCI is provided in section B, which includes an illustration of how the PCI is used to benchmark the progress made by LDCs in relation to other country groups. Section C provides an assessment of the progress achieved by individual LDCs towards the IPoA targets. The assessment is based on targets explicitly identified in the IPoA and includes a dimension of how productive capacities boost or impede the chances of countries achieving the targets. Section D concludes the chapter with some policy recommendations.

B. The UNCTAD productive capacities index

1. Overview

The UNCTAD PCI is the first comprehensive attempt to measure productive capacities in all economies. The index is multidimensional, country-specific and allows for a comparison of progress made over periods and across countries or regions (UNCTAD, forthcoming). It builds on a conceptual framework discussed in Chapter 2 that posits productive capacities on three pillars, namely productive resources, entrepreneurial capabilities and production linkages; together, these productive capacities determine the capacity of a country to produce goods and services and enable it to grow and develop (UNCTAD, 2006).

Guided by these imperatives, the UNCTAD PCI incorporates eight categories (subindices) containing indicators addressing various aspects of productive capacity. The subindices represent the main channels through which the productive capacities of a country develop (Figure 3.1), and include an active accumulation of factors of production, which form dynamic processes through which factor accumulation occurs, as well as the exogenous effects of the immersion of the LDCs into the global economy (UNCTAD, 2006). The technical details on how the PCI and its subindices are constructed, as well as the indicators that were used are described in the Annex to this chapter. It is important to note that the definitions of the subindices are quite broad, and their aggregation procedure is quite rigorous. The two aspects that must be borne in mind are that: (i) for the panel data, the indicators used to construct the index are treated as random variables; and (ii) the correlation structure between the domain for each subindex are maintained, hence the final index consistently represents all domains.

Unleashing the power of productive capacities for structural transformation and economic development can be achieved through better utilization of existing capacities and building new ones, as well as an active reassessment of capacity gaps. Adopting a productive capacities methodology allows LDCs to reframe the development discourse to better balance social and industrial priorities (UNCTAD, 2020d). When countries are compared through the lens of the UNCTAD PCI, the link between social development and other development priorities (e.g. infrastructure, private sector and trade) become apparent. This distinction and the synergies in the index's productive capacities categories are critical to the economic development process and to the policies supporting it.

As a data intensive composite measure, one of the unavoidable steps in the construction of the PCI is the data imputation of missing values. As explained in the Annex, there are several options for imputing missing values, including by using neighbouring countries as proxies. The process is not without controversy as it assumes that observations in one country are correlated with those of its neighbours, and that the measurement scale of the imputed variables is adjustable to an arbitrary choice of weights. In severe cases, imputed data can introduce bias and uncertainty about the true statistical properties of variables, resulting in misleading predictions and inferences (John et al., 2019). For the PCI, data imputation is unavoidable because of the number of indicators and countries involved. Also, the optional step of forecasting new values and the principal components analysis deals with any data entropy issues that arise due to induced imputation or other measurement errors. It has been shown that the method behind the PCI is robust, with the only limitation being the need to re-estimate the entire dataset when one or more data points change.

Figure 3.1
The PCI thematic structure

PCI
- Natural capital — Natural capital indicators
- Human capital — Human capital indicators
- Energy — Energy indicators
- Transport — Transport indicators
- Institutions — Institutions indicators
- ICT — ICT indicators
- Private sector — Private sector indicators
- Structural Change — Structural change indicators

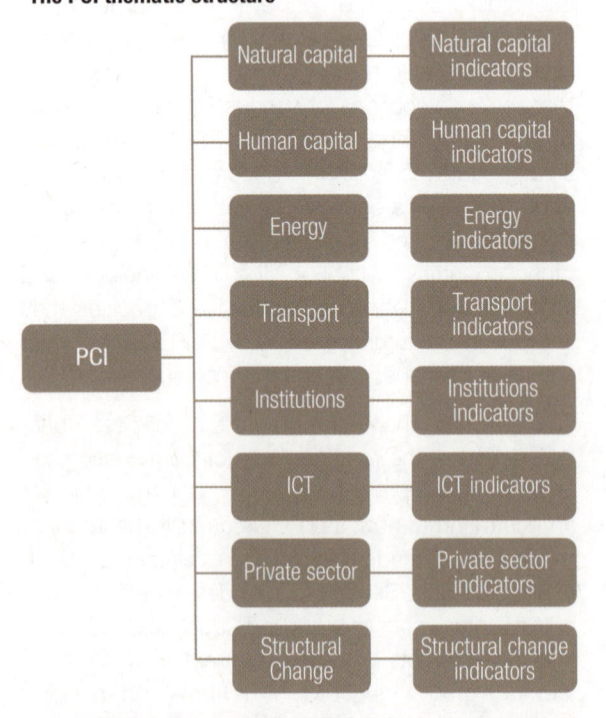

Source: UNCTAD, forthcoming. The UNCTAD Productive Capacities Index: The Methodological Approach and Results.

Re-estimation of the data points ensures consistency and a high correlation of alternative forecasts within entropy limits. However, the computation complexity and costs of iterations are not negligible in large datasets (Kim et al., 2019).

The other steps, also explained in the Annex, involve forecasting new observations and constructing the index using principal component analysis to reduce the dimensions represented by the original indicators. The principal component analysis explores the correlation structure and the variance of the observed data through a few linear combinations of the original data. The resulting linear combination is a latent factor that captures the information common to individual indicators in the cluster of variables forming a subindex. The final step applies the geometric mean to the subindices representing each category to reduce the level of substitutability between dimensions and control outliers and skewness in the distributions of the data. The resulting data contains a panel of 193 countries which make up the PCI and its components for the years 2000–2018.

2. Measuring progress and benchmarking with PCI

The PCI scale, both for the aggregate index and its subindices, ranges from 0 to 100, with 100 being the best score. PCI scores for LDCs varied from 9 (Niger and Chad) to 36 (Tuvalu), and the simple average for the group was 17 in 2011–2018 (Table 3.1). The scores for the seven Island LDCs are equal to or higher than the average for the LDCs and should be treated as a special case.[1] This is because the deflators used in the underlying variables include per capita and other measurement scales that tend to overcompensate for smaller countries. With this qualification, the PCI scores for a few non-island LDCs, including Bhutan, Bangladesh, Cambodia, Lesotho and Djibouti, are just slightly above the 75th percentile (19); Bangladesh and Cambodia, however, eclipse the group when small states are excluded. For the group, the median productive capacity score climbed from 14.9 to 17.2 in 2011–2018, and rose from 27.3 to 28 for other developing countries (ODCs).

A close examination of the subindices reveals significant disparities among countries. As a group, LDCs showed considerable depth in private sector capacity, with a median score of 65.2 and a maximum

The rate of change in productive capacities is very slow

of 85.1 (out of a possible 100). These scores represent, among others, liquidity of domestic credit markets to private sector (as a per cent of GDP), the cost of exporting/importing a container and lead times to export/import goods. The countries with the relatively higher scores in the energy productive capacity category are Bhutan, Nepal, Lao People's Democratic Republic, Guinea-Bissau and Myanmar, while the lowest ranked are Mali, Kiribati, Haiti, Benin and Togo. Oil and mineral resources exporters feature prominently in the natural resource category; however, the inclusion of land and forest area and flow measures of extraction and material intensity imply that the subindex does not distinguish between agrarian and industrial economies relying on extractives. As a result, Lesotho, Guinea, Liberia, Guinea-Bissau and Zambia top the group with scores ranging from 57 to 60, followed by predominantly agrarian countries (Malawi, Rwanda, Uganda, South Sudan and Burkina Faso), scoring slightly above the LDC average range of 47 to 49.

To illustrate the use of PCI in benchmarking the progress of LDCs, three clusters of least, average and high productive capacity LDCs were iteratively created for the years 2001, 2011 and 2018, respectively.[2] Countries were assigned to groups with the closest median PCI. The resulting distribution shows that productive capacities have slightly improved in the least productive cluster over the years, with the subgroup median PCI score rising from 18 to 22 in 2000–2018. However, in all clusters, the rate of change in productive capacities is too slow, and individual country performances have been lacklustre. Of note is the shrinking of the high-productive group from 11 countries in 2001 to only six in 2018 (Figure 3.2). It is important to note that the median PCI among the high-productive group rose from 23 to 29. Meanwhile, the low productive group expanded from 18 countries to 25 over the same period, while the number of countries in the average group ranged between 16 and 18 in 2001–2018. In addition, the composition of countries in the two

---

[1] The seven Island LDCs are Comoros, Kiribati, Sao Tome and Principe, Solomon Islands, Timor-Leste, Tuvalu and Vanuatu.

[2] The number of clusters was chosen arbitrarily, based on observed trends in trade, GDP and other characters which often result in natural clustering according to export specializations. For the interested reader, STATA and other statistical packages can automatically determine the optimal number of clusters (Makles, 2012).

Table 3.1
Productive capacities index scores of individual least developed countries and other country groups, average, 2011–2018

Country/Region	PCI total	Energy	Human capital	ICT	Institutions	Natural resources	Private sector	Structural change	Transport
Tuvalu	36	33	31	33	57	42	85	35	12.35
Bhutan	27	49	38	10	61	42	70	34	2.13
Vanuatu	26	29	31	8	57	34	77	36	5.26
Timor-Leste	23	32	29	7	53	37	67	31	3.11
Solomon Islands	22	34	30	5	46	49	77	27	2.42
Kiribati	21	25	39	7	56	16	76	16	6.44
Lesotho	21	33	31	8	50	60	67	42	0.63
Bangladesh	20	37	35	6	34	41	65	34	1.00
Cambodia	20	35	35	9	36	42	74	29	0.88
Djibouti	20	27	34	5	35	39	72	42	1.70
Sao Tome and Principe	20	28	34	9	47	39	69	32	0.87
Lao People's Democratic Republic	19	41	30	9	35	50	70	38	0.40
Nepal	19	41	38	7	36	36	64	34	0.49
Haiti	18	24	32	4	27	39	67	26	2.02
Yemen	18	29	28	7	16	35	69	33	1.25
Comoros	17	35	31	4	35	44	72	19	0.76
Ethiopia	17	34	27	3	32	43	62	25	1.60
Rwanda	17	31	33	5	51	48	67	28	0.30
Senegal	17	36	27	8	50	45	73	38	0.12
South Sudan	17	35	26	5	37	47	66	29	0.52
Uganda	17	34	27	5	39	48	65	36	0.31
United Republic of Tanzania	17	33	32	5	39	46	63	26	0.50
Zambia	17	36	27	6	47	57	50	30	0.27
LDCs average	**17**	**32**	**28**	**6**	**36**	**46**	**65**	**28**	**1.12**
The Gambia	16	29	25	8	37	49	76	30	0.18
Benin	15	24	26	6	47	41	71	31	0.17
Guinea	15	30	23	4	30	60	72	30	0.26
Liberia	15	28	30	4	36	59	68	25	0.19
Mozambique	15	33	23	4	39	53	70	31	0.29
Sudan	15	35	29	7	15	35	60	21	0.45
Togo	15	20	28	4	35	53	75	32	0.30
Angola	14	34	22	4	29	52	55	22	0.23
Malawi	14	30	33	3	44	49	65	25	0.23
Mauritania	14	27	25	6	34	50	70	31	0.09
Myanmar	14	38	32	5	28	40	69	28	0.14
Sierra Leone	14	27	30	5	38	57	72	14	0.16
Burkina Faso	13	27	21	5	44	47	62	19	0.18
Eritrea	13	38	20	1	17	54	58	36	1.33
Madagascar	13	31	25	2	36	50	71	32	0.12
Afghanistan	12	33	27	4	17	37	32	34	0.20
Burundi	12	31	26	2	25	52	59	19	0.27
Democratic Republic of the Congo	12	32	19	2	27	56	55	29	0.13
Mali	12	27	20	6	36	40	65	14	0.10
Guinea-Bissau	11	39	24	5	31	59	51	3	0.20
Somalia	11	34	19	2	3	55	69	21	0.88
Central African Republic	10	30	16	2	19	42	47	23	0.25
Chad	9	29	16	2	23	41	30	5	0.34
Niger	9	28	14	2	39	44	53	21	0.03
Other developing countries	**28**	**40**	**41**	**19**	**50**	**40**	**75**	**41**	**4.36**
Developed countries	**40**	**47**	**62**	**37**	**80**	**37**	**83**	**54**	**6.18**

Source: UNCTAD secretariat calculations, based on data from UNCTAD, UNCTADStat database [accessed May, 2020].

lower productive clusters changed significantly over the years. Bangladesh, Comoros, Djibouti, Gambia and Solomon Islands slid from the high productive capacity cluster into the average capacity

CHAPTER 3: Measuring productive capacities: LDCs' progress towards sustainable development

Figure 3.2
Clustering of LDC productive capacities, ranked by cluster-medians, 2001, 2011, 2018

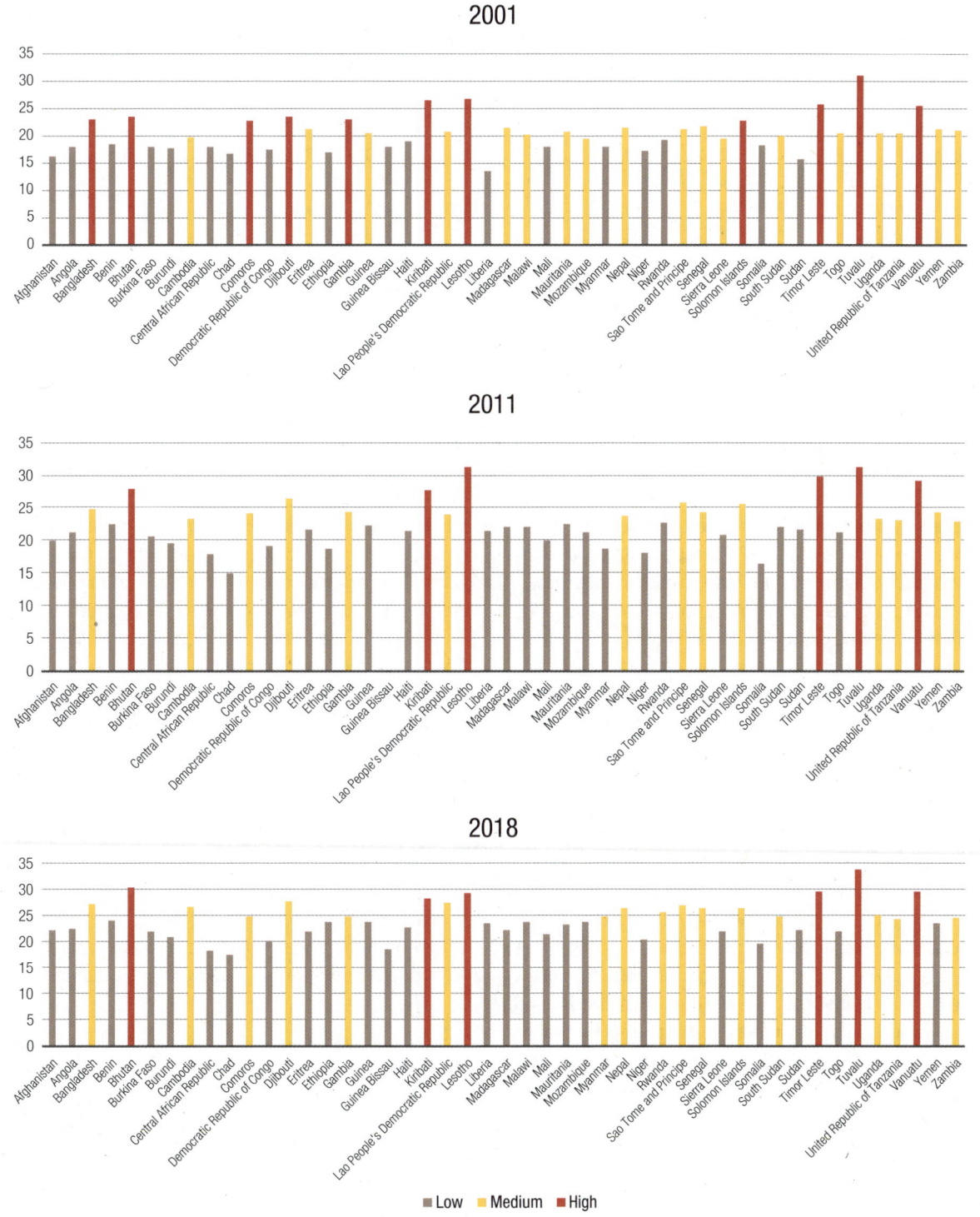

■ Low   ■ Medium   ■ High

Source: UNCTAD secretariat calculations based on data from UNCTAD, UNCTADStat database [accessed May, 2020].

group, while Eritrea, Guinea, Madagascar, Malawi, Mauritania, Mozambique, Sierra Leone, Togo and Yemen fell from the average capacity group into the least ranked cluster of productive capacities. Only two countries, Rwanda and Myanmar, climbed up the clusters in 2001–2018, moving from the least productive capacity group into the average group.

The disparities in economic development among LDCs and between LDCs and other country

Table 3.2
Productive capacities by country group, medians 2011 and 2018

	PCI total	Human capital	Energy	ICT	Institutions	Natural capital	Private sector	Structural change	Transport infrastructure
2011									
Developed countries	42.1	64.1	42.4	37	80.8	38.5	82.7	55.7	4.9
Least developed countries	14.9	27.8	30.1	3.7	36.9	44.5	66	28.4	0.3
Other developing countries	27.3	41.1	36.6	16.2	50.8	39.9	74.9	42.3	1.9
World	**26.2**	**40.5**	**36.1**	**15.8**	**50**	**40.3**	**74.1**	**40.5**	**1.6**
2018									
Developed countries	39.8	61.3	46.3	38.7	80.3	39.4	83.8	52.5	3.1
Least developed countries	17.2	28.7	31	6.8	36.9	46	69.3	30.9	0.4
Other developing countries	28	41.5	39.3	21.3	50.1	40.3	77.2	42	1.4
World	**27**	**40**	**38.7**	**20.4**	**49.9**	**40.9**	**76.5**	**40.7**	**1.3**
Percentage change (2011–2018)									
Developed countries	-5.4	-4.3	9.4	4.7	-0.6	2.2	1.4	-5.6	-36.3
Least developed countries	15.5	3.3	3	85.7	0	3.4	4.9	9	60.3
Other developing countries	2.5	0.9	7.6	31.3	-1.5	0.9	3.2	-0.7	-29.1
World	**2.9**	**-1.1**	**7.3**	**29.4**	**-0.2**	**1.5**	**3.2**	**0.6**	**-18.4**

Source: UNCTAD secretariat calculations, based on UNCTADStat database [accessed May, 2020].

groups can be explained by their PCI scores. When unbundled, some of the PCI components have been used extensively in the literature to explain differences in economic development among countries. For example, some studies consider the differences in factor productivity, especially of labour, and the accumulation of capital as the main reasons for the divergence (Hulten and Isaksson, 2007). However, total factor productivity only partially explains the underlying causes of the differences among heterogeneous groups of countries. Moreover, as shown in the schematic representation of the PCI, total factor productivity only accounts for the top two or three PCI subcomponents that are traditionally viewed as factors of production. Although the factor productivity decomposition approach explains most of the differences among high growth countries, there are limitations when these methods are applied to LDCs. For instance, the finding by Hulten and Isaksson (2007) that capital deepening was responsible for more than half of the growth rate of labour productivity in many countries may not generally apply to LDCs. As a summary measure, the PCI comprehensively incorporates the contributions of productive factors (e.g. labour, capital, technology and institutions), and other factors expanding the productivity of a country. The PCI analysis therefore provides better policy inferences relevant to the LDCs than the factor decomposition based on selected factors.

Benchmarking using PCI and other dimensions can help explain the differences among LDCs and between LDCs and other country groups. The PCI values do not reveal anything about past policies or systematic sources of vulnerability of the LDCs, but do show the extent to which countries have developed compared to others. The bottom 50 per cent of the LDCs added to their productive capacities faster than the lower half of the other country groups over the same period (Table 3.2). The LDCs posted major improvements in productive capacities related to ICT, transport infrastructure and structural change categories although, in absolute terms, their values in 2011 and 2018 on the bounded PCI scale (0.100) are too low compared to the scores of other country groups. Except for natural resources, LDCs lag behind ODCs in all PCI categories, and even more so in ICT, human capital and institutions. There are also significant differences among countries with respect to energy, private sector and structural change.

Other methods exist for estimating the efficiency of productive capacity utilization; these seek to extend the standard methods that end with the appraisal of resource endowments, policy and institutional differences, and the innate and structural characteristics that set countries apart.[3] The stochastic frontier discussed in section C estimates the efficiency of capacity utilization; however, it is sufficient to note that for benchmarking purposes countries with low productive capacities – mainly LDCs – are at the bottom of the economic

---
[3] The approach being described here belongs to a class of data-oriented method of estimating the relative efficiency of entities or decision-making units. The technical term for the assessment is data envelopment analysis, and it includes both non-parametric and parametric methods.

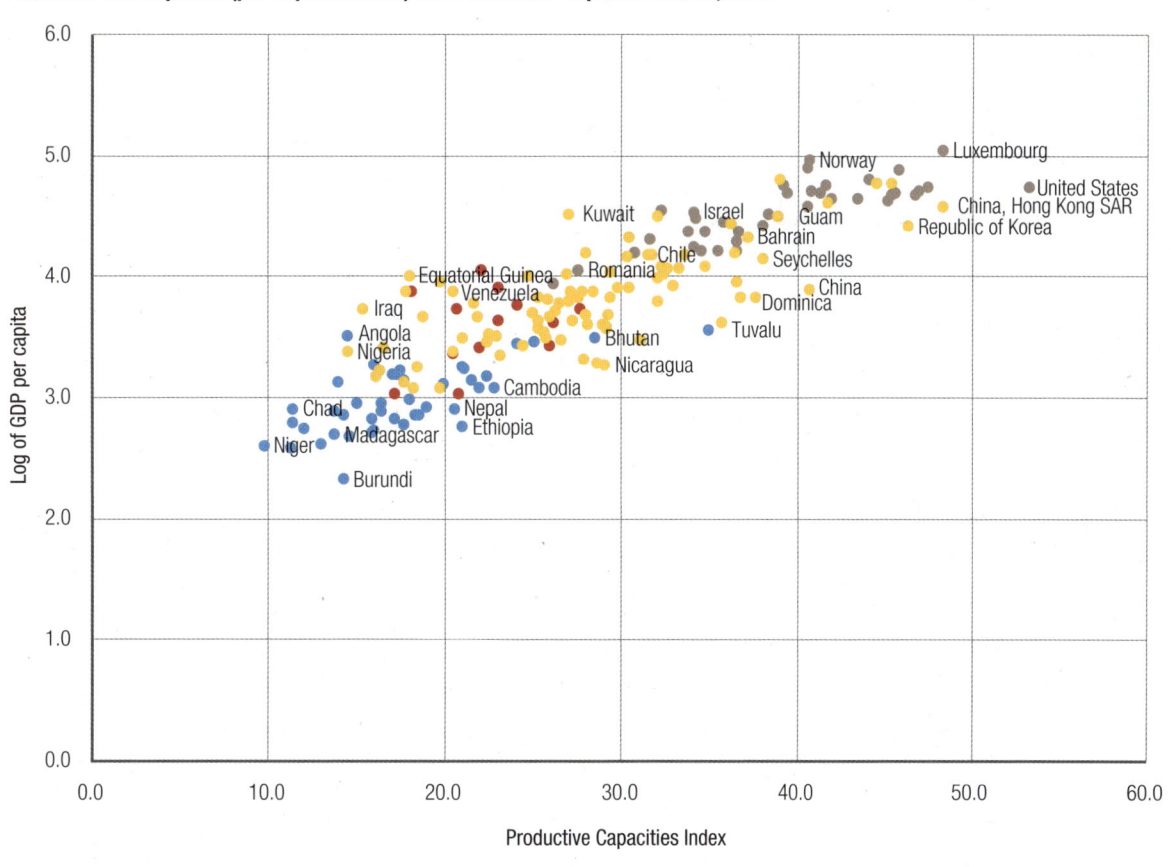

Figure 3.3
Economic development (per capita income) and Productive Capacities Index, 2018

Source: UNCTAD secretariat calculations, based on data from UNCTAD, UNCTADStat database [accessed May 2020].

development frontier, while ODCs are in the middle or catching up to the level of the developed economies (Figure 3.3).

The static picture shows how some LDCs (Angola, Bangladesh, Bhutan, Cambodia, Kiribati, Lao People's Democratic Republic, Lesotho, Solomon Islands, Timor-Leste and Tuvalu) are at the same level of development as ODCs. However, most LDCs are trapped in the low productive capacities cluster and appear to have no path out of this category. In 2018, the PCI of the top two developed countries ranged from 48 (LUX) to 53 (USA), except that LUX had a higher per capita income than the USA (Figure 3.4). The top LDCs scored between 28 and 35 on the PCI scale, and as a group, its exports remain highly concentrated, with the concentration index averaging between 0.43 and 0.45 in 2000–2018, while developed countries and ODCs averaged between 0.17 and 0.35, respectively.

Although the rankings by PCI scores show significant challenges among LDCs, the PCI scores of several LDCs (e.g. Bhutan, Myanmar, Rwanda and Tuvalu) show that with consistency, LDCs can breach the productive capacity of other country groups. A combination of other factors, including population size, geographical location and strategic linkages, play a favourable role for some economies. For example, Bhutan has very small population, comparable to that of Luxembourg, while China, Hong Kong Special Administrative Region and the Republic of Korea are quite populous. The strategic location of China, Hong Kong Special Administrative Region by the South China sea gives it a geographical advantage over the landlocked Asian LDCs, e.g. Bhutan and Nepal. In gravity theoretic terms[4], the pull factors of good regional neighbours in trade plays against most LDCs; for the Asian LDCs their proximity to more advanced economies have helped them, despite having lower factor endowments. The complementary trade structures of the subregion provide incentives for inter-industry trade to flourish among close neighbours. Kabir and Salim (2010) also found a negative elasticity of

---
[4] The traditional gravity theory of trade suggests that trade between countries is driven by geographic distance between them, relative economic sizes, similarities in consumer preferences, and cultural or historical linkages.

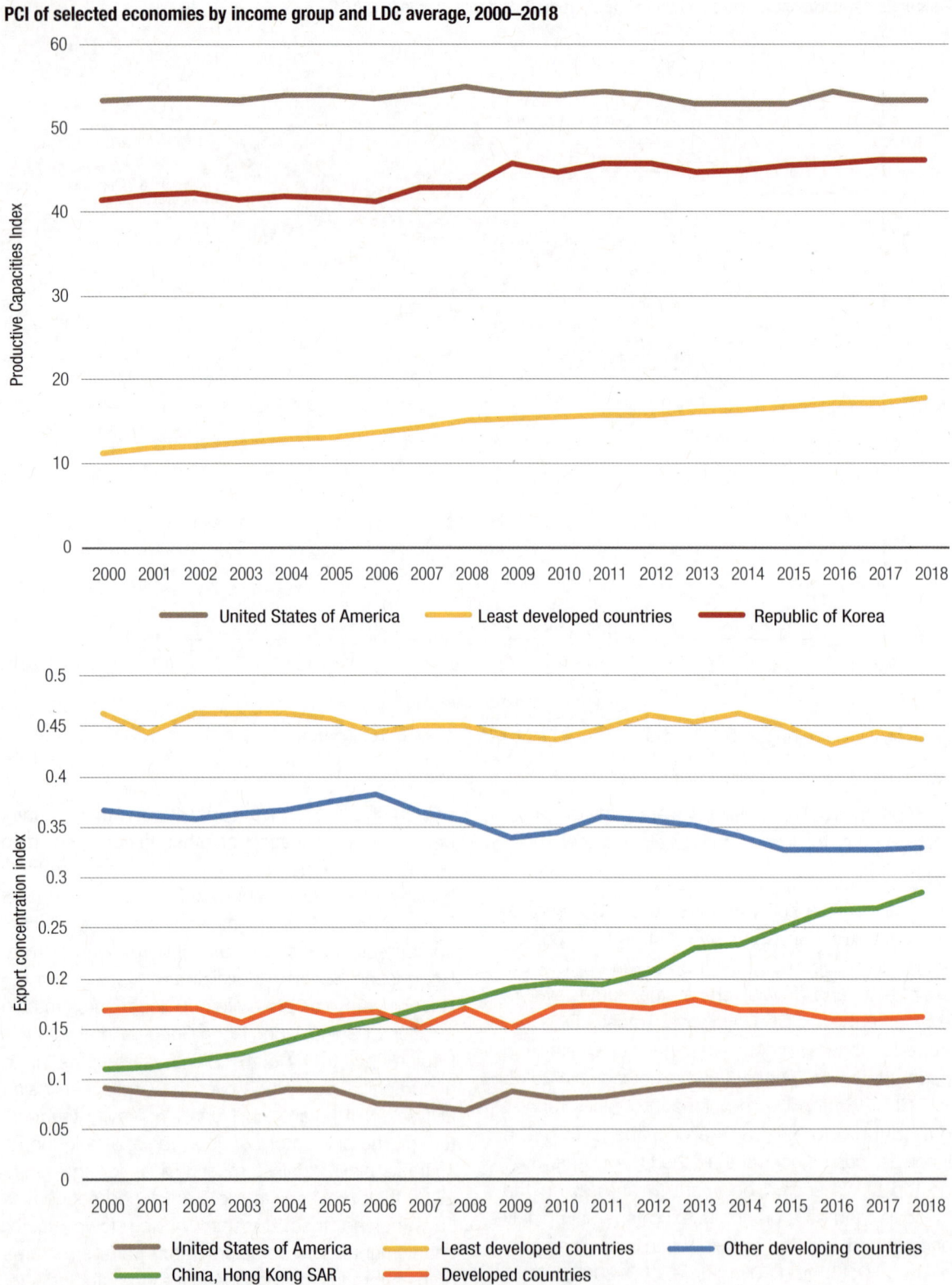

Figure 3.4
PCI of selected economies by income group and LDC average, 2000–2018

Source: UNCTAD secretariat calculations, based on data from UNCTAD, UNCTADStat database [accessed May 2020].

distance in the gravity analysis of the trading pattern of the Bay of Bengal Initiative for Multi-Sectoral Technical and Economic Cooperation, which may prove the value of having a good neighbour among Asian LDCs. This further highlights the importance of developing a diversified regional economy, with strong regional value chains among the contiguous countries, including among neighbouring LDCs. The discussion on what LDCs need to do to catch up with other developing countries is presented in sections C and D.

C. Assessing the progress of LDCs towards IPoA goals

UNCTAD has provided an assessment on the progress made by LDCs in meeting the IPoA objectives over several years (UNCTAD, 2017b and 2019c). This chapter presents the first occasion to extensively assess productive capacities, including their impacts on progress in other thematic IPoA priorities. The argument is that productive capacities are critical building blocks for the structural transformation, value addition and socioeconomic development of these countries. Moreover, since graduation from the LDC category is a key goal of all ISMs specific to LDCs, this section draws on insights on how other countries are performing and how well they are moving towards the overall goal of graduation. It also examines whether LDCs scheduled to graduate have accumulated enough basis to sustain the necessary momentum to nurture and generate lasting structural transformation.

1. GDP growth target and productive capacities

Robust GDP growth was considered critical to achieving the overarching goal of the IPoA. However, the target of at least 7 per cent GDP growth per annum has been elusive. Only 13 LDCs have ever attained the 7 per cent growth target during 2015–2018, and a smaller number still have managed to maintain the pace in successive years. Since 2011, GDP growth among developing countries slowed, and overall, the LDC growth trend was negative (Figure 3.5). The extent of the fallout from the recent COVID-19 pandemic is uncertain as the situation is still evolving. However, what emerged as a public health crisis has exposed the weak structures of LDC economies, their vulnerability to economic shocks, as well as their inability to mobilize productive capacities to adapt to changing market conditions.

Although LDCs made substantial progress in narrowing the GDP growth performance gap to ODCs, the LDCs as a group need to accelerate their growth to close the income gap with ODCs. In GDP growth terms, the

Figure 3.5
GDP growth rates for developing economies

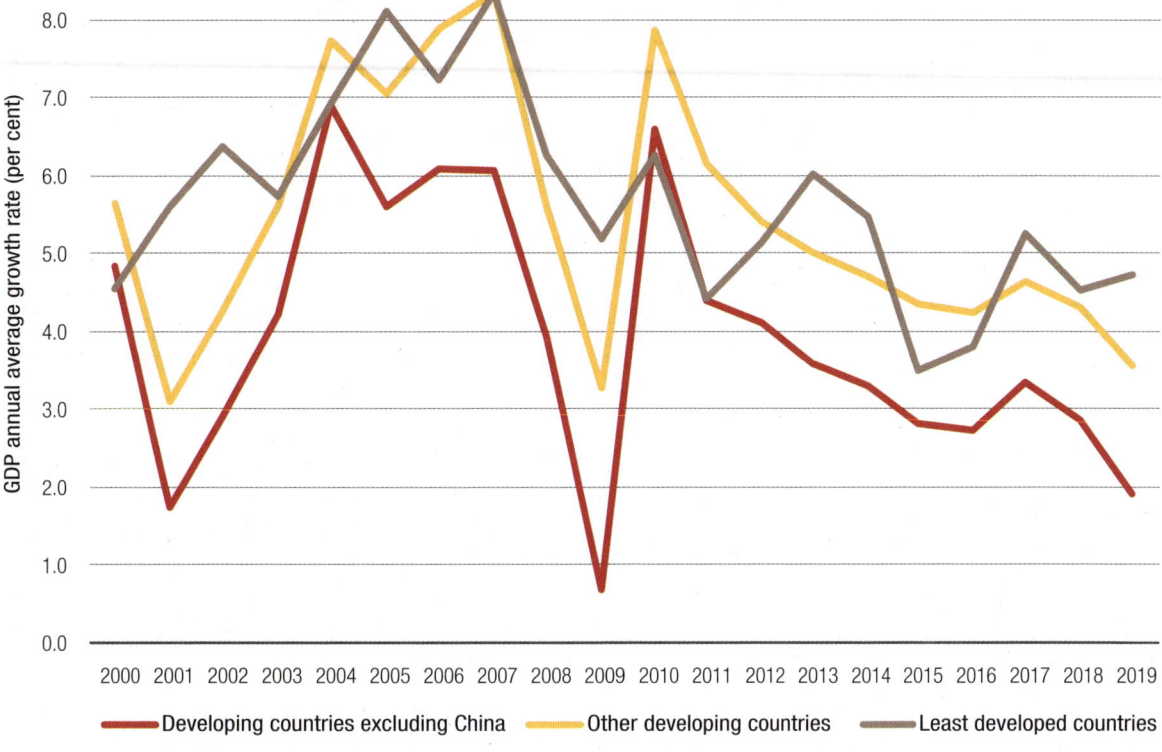

Source: UNCTAD secretariat calculations based on data from UNCTAD, UNCTADStat [accessed April 2020].

Figure 3.6
GNI per capita gap of least developed countries in comparison to other developing countries, average in current US dollars

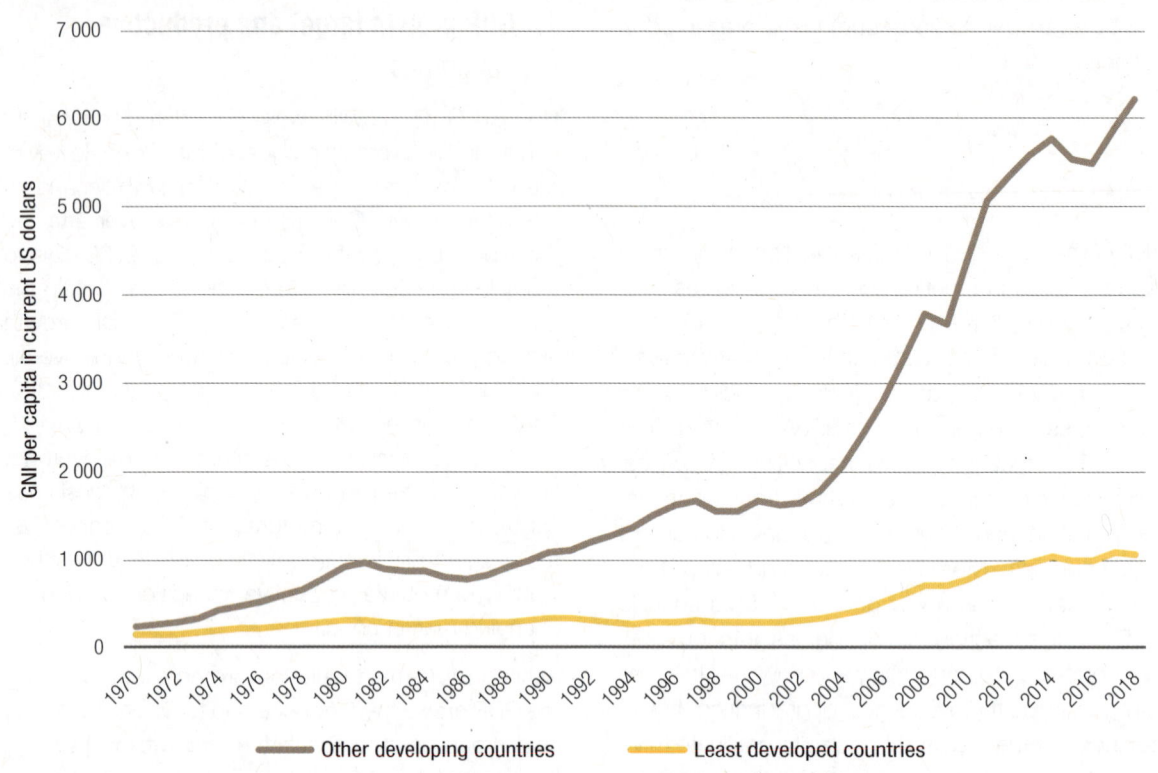

Source: UNCTAD secretariat calculations, based on data from UNCTAD, UNCTADStat database [accessed April 2020].

LDCs have narrowed the gap to within 1–2 percentage points, but in absolute terms the income gap measured in GNI per capita has widened (Figure 3.6). Actual growth rates tend to exaggerate the cyclical positions of countries (Scarpetta et al., 2000), and for small economies, market idiosyncrasies affecting cyclical and trend growth may cause policy paralysis. The GDP growth rate trend for LDCs is similar to that of ODCs (Figure 3.7); however, differences in relative economic sizes show that LDCs have been drifting further from ODCs and clearly highlight the need to track trend growth disparities and the policy variables that can shift it. It was evident at the beginning of the 1970s that LDCs were lagging ODCs, but the speed with which the gap grew in 2000–2018 is unprecedented. Both sets of countries almost quadrupled their average GNI per capita incomes, with LDCs edging slightly over $1000, while ODCs exceeded $6000 (Figure 3.6). If LDCs are to catch up to ODCs, they will have to keep "running while others walk" (Mkandawire, 2011).

a. Productive capacity utilization and efficiency

Cyclical noise aside, structural factors, including demographic changes, labour productivity differences and the state of technology, all play a critical role in explaining the growth potential of countries (Scarpetta et al., 2000). Per capita income is a suitable proxy for economic development as it takes demographics factors and an economy's size into account (Kopf, 2018). As explained in section B, the rising disparities in per capita GDP growth among the LDCs on the one hand, and between LDCs and other country groups on the other, is partly due to efficiency differences in the utilization of productive capacities.

The weight of, and changes to, the mix of productive resources, entrepreneurial capabilities and production linkages collectively determine the efficiency of a country to produce goods and services and enable it to make progress. The productive capacities, whether aggregated or clustered in their eight categories, imply an unobservable maximum level of output, $f(PCI) = Y(potential\ GDP,\ total\ or\ per\ capita)$, that a country can produce. The observed output may be sub-optimal if it is less than the potential output, or just right if the country efficiently utilizes its capacity, $y \leq Y = f(PCI)$.

A level of productive capacity may be associated with numerous output levels as countries differ in their utilization of productive capacities. A stochastic

CHAPTER 3: Measuring productive capacities: LDCs' progress towards sustainable development

Figure 3.7
Hodrick-Prescott filter trend growth rates of GDP per capita and real GDP[5]

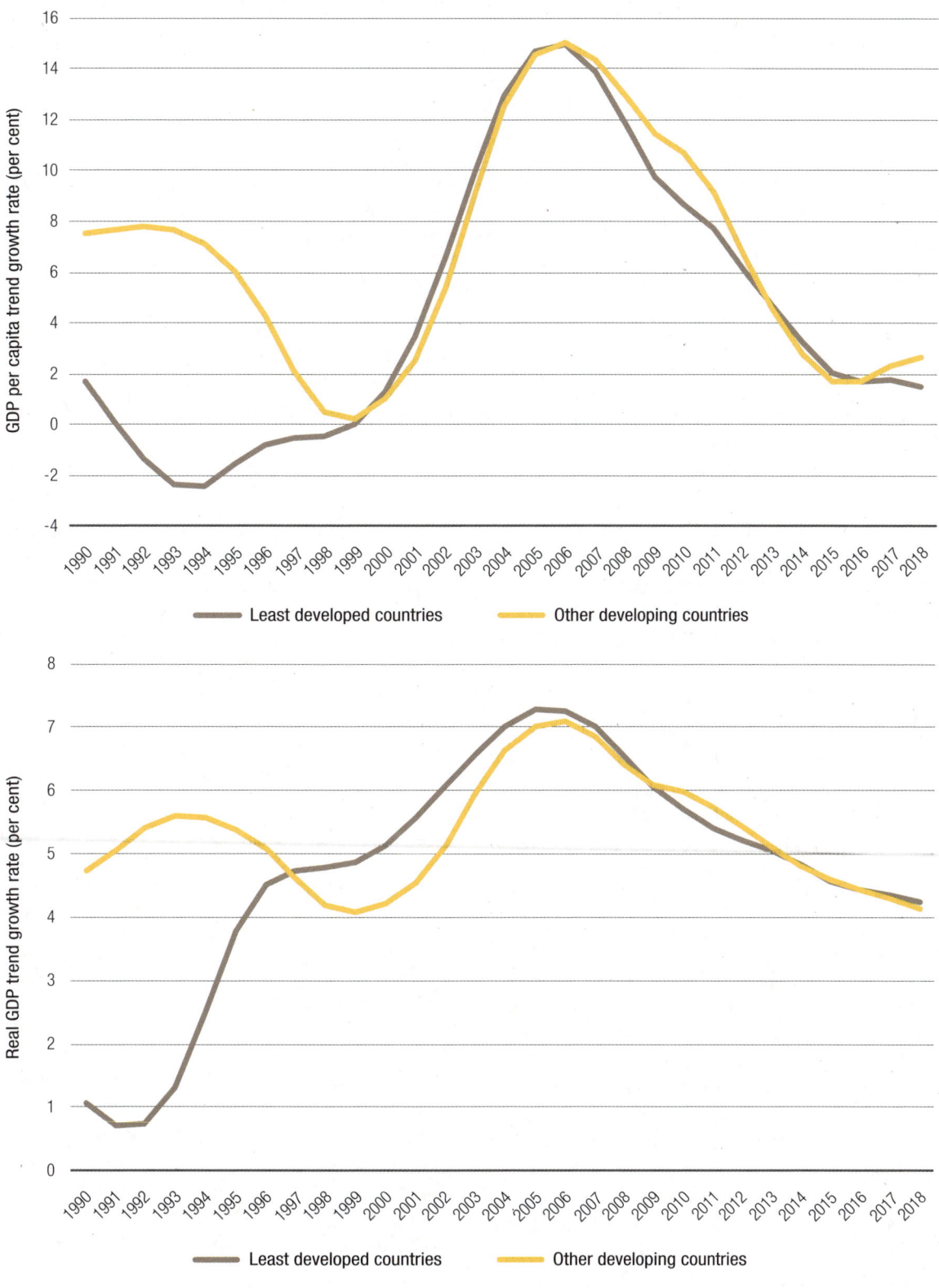

Source: UNCTAD secretariat calculation, based on data from UNCTAD, UNCTADStat database [accessed April 2020].

---

[5] The Hodrick-Prescott (HP) filter is a data smoothing technique used to decompose a time series into trend and cyclical components. In macroeconomics, the technique is used to isolate the impact of short-term fluctuations associated with a business cycle (de Jong and Sakarya, 2015).

Box 3.1 Stochastic frontier analysis at a glance

Stochastic frontier analysis is an extension of production analysis. It has its foundations in the analysis of production, cost and profit functions at firm level or the sector (Kumbhakar and Lovell, 2000; Kumbhakar et al., 2015). Given its microeconomic functions, the production frontier at the macroeconomic level represents the maximum output that can be produced from various input combinations (Kumbhakar et al., 2015).

$$y_{it} = f(X_{it}, \beta)e^{\varepsilon_{it}} \leq Y_{it}$$

Where y_{it} is the actual output of country i at time t as above, X_{it} is a vector of the eight categories of productive capacities, Y_i is the potential output, representing the maximum possible output that can be produced given the productive capacities level, and the error term $e^{\varepsilon_{it}} \equiv v_{it} + u_{it}$. It is assumed that the first part of the error term, v_{it} are symmetric identically independently distributed, representing a random distribution of output with zero mean and variance, σ_x whereas the second part, u_{it} have a truncated normal distribution. The stochastic frontier can accommodate both technical and time-varying technical inefficiencies, under various assumptions about the technical inefficiency relationship with the explanatory variables (Battese and Coelli, 1995).

The efficiency measure is given by the ratio of actual output to the potential output:

$$\frac{\text{Actual output}}{\text{Potential output}} = \frac{y_{it}}{Y_{it}} = \frac{f(X_{it},\beta)e^{\varepsilon_{it}}}{Y_{it}}$$

It follows that the efficiency values ranges from 0 to 1, with 1 being the most efficient. For recent discussions on the method, see Kumbhakar and Tsionas (2011).

---

frontier model accounts for these differences by imposing the same production technology (functional form) across all countries and decomposes the deviations from the frontier into inefficiency and noise components (see Box 3.1) (Wijeweera et al., 2010; Kumbhakar and Lovell, 2000; Kumbhakar et al., 2015).

A drawback to comparing LDCs with other country groups using data envelopment approaches is the fact that efficiencies are calibrated against the best performer included in the sample, and could be influenced by external factors which are not in the model (Erkoc, 2012). As a solution, the stochastic frontier model from which the results of the analysis in this chapter draws includes a specific dummy for LDCs. Moreover, since the objective of the analysis is to inform development policy of LDCs and comparing the progress of LDCs with other country groups, it would be uninstructive to estimate the productive frontier of only the LDCs. It is also possible to make two adjustments to the pooled panel data stochastic frontier. As previously proposed, adding a dummy for LDCs takes into account heterogeneity among countries, assuming that inefficiency is time-variant and that it persists at country level. Alternatively, two separate frontier models, one for LDCs alone and the other including ODCs can be estimated and checked for consistency against the pooled sample. For examples of these methods, see Guo et al. (2018) and Kumbhakar and Tsionas (2011).

As expected, the edge of the production frontier is filled by developed countries and other developing countries, with LDCs falling within the frontier (Figure 3.8). Angola, Tuvalu, Vanuatu and Sudan stand out as the most efficient in utilizing their productive capacities, but it must be noted that this relates to output measured by per capita income (Figure 3.9).[6] Although there is a positive relationship between productive capacities and per capita income, the marginal gain in per capita income from a unit increase in efficiency of utilization of productive capacity diminishes rapidly for LDCs compared to other country groups. This is because the sources of per capita income growth among LDCs are associated with an inconsistent performance in certain productive capacity categories; for example, they are stronger in the natural resources productive capacity category, but the utilization of that capacity is either weak or beset with vulnerabilities. The negative partial elasticity of natural resources on per capita income implies that an accumulation of natural resources wealth adds to GDP per capita at a decreasing rate (Table 3.3). The same is true for human capital and structural change, both of which return negative coefficients in the pooled estimation sample. LDCs have struggled to develop their human capital, leading to a weak performance on the variables in the human capital subindex, including years of schooling and health-adjusted life expectancy (HALE). On structural change, the elements in the subindex includes industrial ratio, which in some countries has been pushed up by an increasing

---

[6] Island LDCs appear as outliers in most of the results due to the usual measurement scale problem. Their small population sizes imply that they score better than other LDCs in productive capacity categories for which per capita variables are used. They also perform better in institutions and human capital, hence any comparison to other country groups should take these qualifications into consideration.

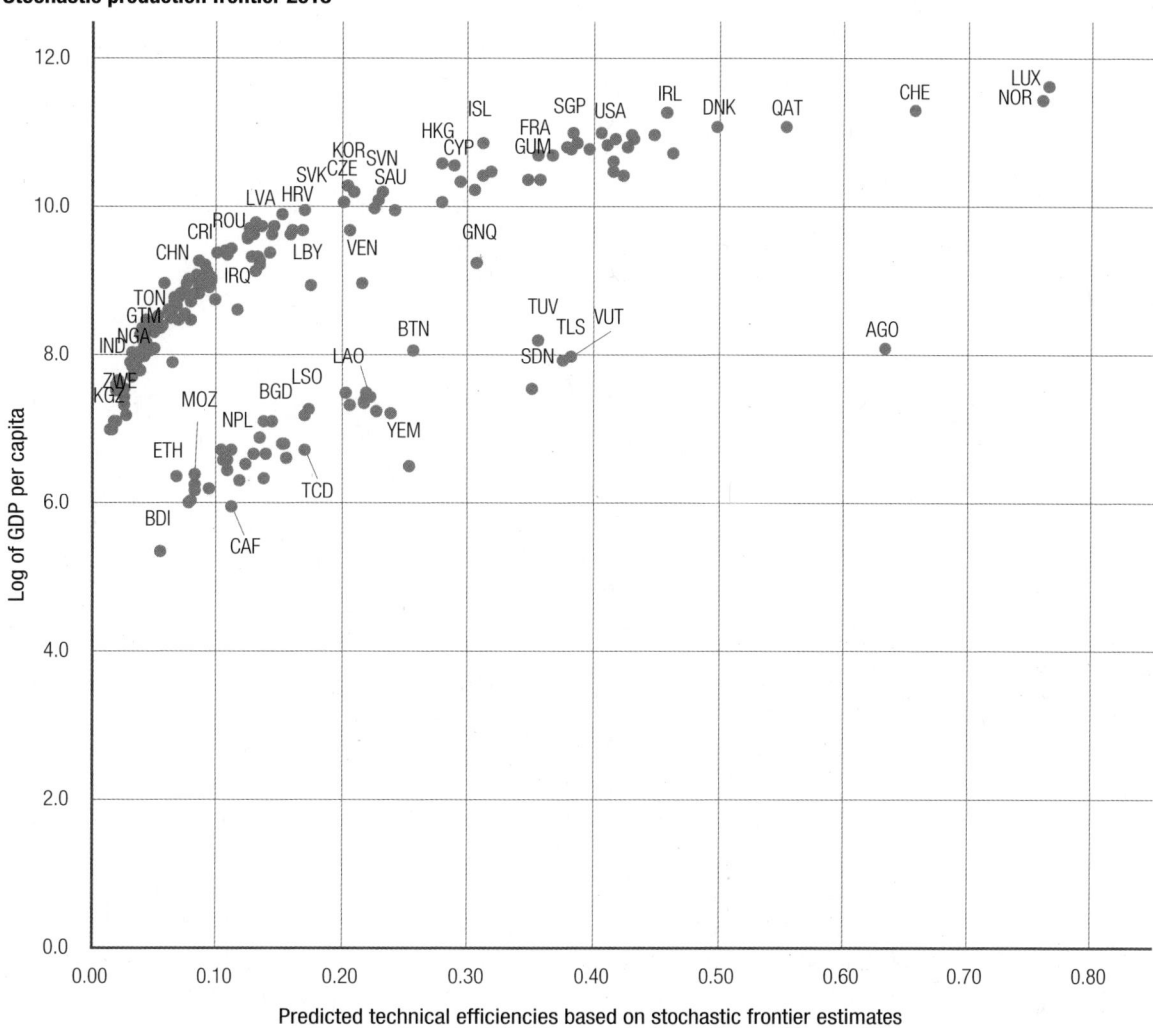

Figure 3.8
Stochastic production frontier 2018

Source: UNCTAD secretariat calculations, based on data from UNCTAD, UNCTADStat database [accessed May, 2020].

share of services rather than industrial growth.[7] Other elements, e.g. gross fixed capital formation and export concentration, have registered positive advances for the LDCs but not as significantly compared to other country groups included in the pooled sample. Of note also is the high negative impact of LDC dummy that confirms the divergence of income per capita between LDCs and other country groups.

The low efficiency in productive capacities utilization cannot be generalized across all LDCs. Per capita incomes grew significantly in several countries (e.g. Bhutan, Sudan and Tuvalu) between 2011–2018. However, other countries (e.g. Angola, Timor-Leste and Yemen) suffered setbacks in per capital incomes, despite making small gains in capacity utilization (Figure 3.9). The security situation in Yemen makes it a special case but the low per capita income reflects the impact of the conflict on the economy and people. For Angola, Bhutan, Sudan, Timor-Leste, Tuvalu and Vanuatu, the return on productive capacity utilization depends on natural resources that are extremely vulnerable to global economic shocks, natural disasters and environmental shocks.

b. Marginal impacts of the individual productive capacities, as per IPoA

The IPoA identifies infrastructure, energy, science, technology and innovation (STI) and private sector development as the critical productive capacities. The stochastic frontier estimates are consistent with previous UNCTAD findings that show that economic development is positively affected by infrastructure development, and that the level of industrial energy use is associated with a country's income level and stages

---

[7] The industrial ratio is calculated as the ratio of industry and services value added over total GDP, See the Annex for more details.

The Least Developed Countries Report 2020

Figure 3.9
Marginal change in per capita income, per unit of productive capacity utilization

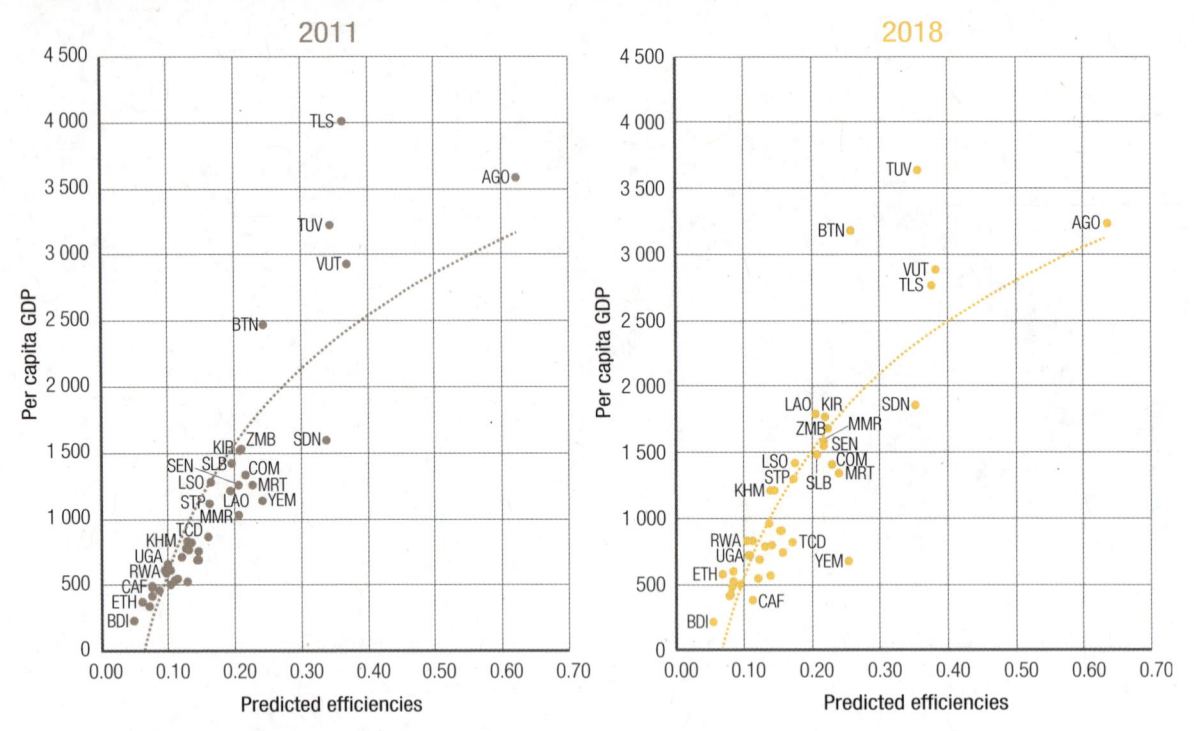

Source: UNCTAD secretariat calculations based on UNCTAD, UNCTADStat database [accessed May, 2020].

of development of a country. The stochastic frontier results suggest that a 1 per cent increase in energy infrastructure leads to only a 0.12 per cent increase in per capita income (Table 3.3). It will take a substantial boost in energy infrastructure to raise per capita GDP in LDCs: "the minimum level of electricity generation needed for productive use would mean an increase by a factor of between 3.4 and 6.8" (UNCTAD, 2017a).

Table 3.3
Partial elasticities of GDP per capita to productive capacity components based on the stochastic frontier estimates

Factor/productive capacity category	Elasticity of GDP per capita to factor change
Energy	0.120*
Human capital	-0.016
ICT	0.013*
Institutions	0.139*
Natural resources	-0.004
Private sector	0.030**
Structural change	-0.037*
Transport infrastructure	0.001*
LDC dummy	-0.051*

Source: UNCTAD secretariat calculations, based on data from UNCTAD, UNCTADStat database [accessed May, 2020].
Note: * significant at 5 per cent; ** significant at 10 per cent.

The confirmed positive roles of institutions, the private sector, ICT and transport infrastructure are also familiar; the negative impact of structural change may, however, not be so obvious. Structural change is a lengthy process and occurs at a pace determined by factors such as: (i) the growth dynamics in the economy; (ii) discoveries of new technology or natural resources; (iii) innovation and learning; and (iv) market forces (Islam and Iversen, 2018). As explained in Chapter 1, the sectors that have benefited the most from the structural shift in production in LDCs are not the sort of economic activities that would leverage growth. These activities include service sectors characterized by low wages, self-employment rather than job creation, high informality and income volatility (Bah, 2011). The blending of unproductive agricultural sector offering large numbers of employment opportunities, and an uncompetitive services sector with low productivity, high levels of informality and weak integration into global value chains, all contribute to reducing the impact of structural change on real GDP per capita (UNCTAD, 2018a).

2. Agriculture, food security and rural development

Agriculture plays a vital role in developing countries and provides one of the main opportunities for gainful employment and is one of the key sectors supplying essential food and raw materials to domestic and international markets. As a traditional sector, agriculture offers a livelihood to millions of people who would otherwise be unemployed. A rise in agricultural production shields people from hunger and poverty but during 2000–2019 low productivity and investment and other structural challenges have reduced the sector's contribution to economic growth. The role of agriculture in promoting structural change and productive capacities of LDCs are discussed in chapter 4. This section reviews the progress of LDCs on specific agriculture targets in the IPoA, namely progress towards eradicating hunger by 2020 and other indicators of structural change in the agricultural sector.

Agriculture is a priority because of the concentration of populations in rural areas, and the centrality of agriculture as a dominant employment sector in many LDCs (UNCTAD, 2015a). In 2011, the majority of the LDC labour force were employed in agriculture (58.8 per cent), and the situation has remained virtually unchanged with 56.1 per cent of the labour force still active in the same sector. A sharp divergence between the share of employment and value-added by agriculture flags rising inequality and poverty. For example, Liberia and Burundi have seen a sharp decline in the agriculture value-added share in GDP but without a corresponding fall in employment (Figure 3.10). A few countries, such as Sierra Leone and Chad, increased value-added from agriculture as employment shares receded. For example, Chad's

Figure 3.10

Change in employment and agriculture value added, per cent: 2000–2008

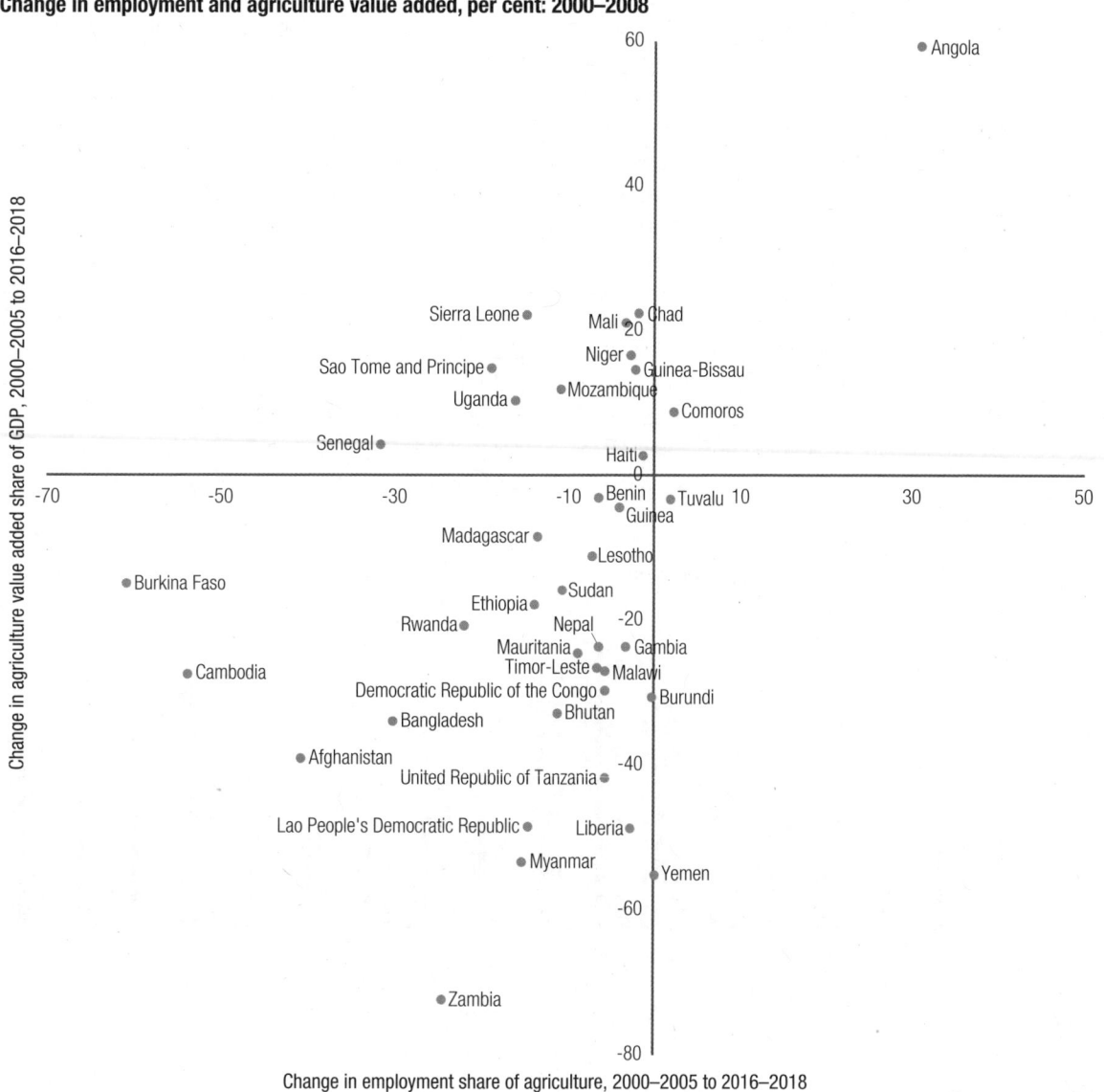

Change in employment share of agriculture, 2000–2005 to 2016–2018

Source: UNCTAD secretariat calculations, based on data from World Bank, World Development Indicators database [accessed April, 2020].

agriculture value-added rose from 38 per cent in 2000–2005 to 47 per cent in 2016–2018 but employment only dropped marginally from 83 to 82 per cent of the total.

There has also been a growing disconnect between agriculture and food security, with some of the countries employing the largest proportion of the labour force in agriculture also appearing among the food insecure. FAO estimates that the global number of those that are food insecure is 2 billion. In LDCs, the number of chronically hungry people rose from 194.7 million to 225 million in 2014–2018 (FAO et al., 2019). UNCTAD estimates show that there has been a spike in chronically hungry people in Bangladesh, Malawi, Mozambique, Niger and the United Republic of Tanzania. The situation is extremely critical in countries where the number of severely food insecure is above two-fifths of the population, for example, Guinea, Lao People's Democratic Republic, Lesotho, Liberia, Malawi, Mozambique and Sierra Leone (Figure 3.11).

The centrality of agriculture in LDCs suggests that agricultural transformation may be the quickest path to poverty eradication and inclusive development. However, if the sector is to effectively reduce poverty, labour productivity in agriculture has to be raised considerably, as well as to a level which can generate an income above the poverty line, taking into consideration the high concentration of subsistence livelihoods in the sector (UNCTAD, 2015a). LDCs should not simply aim for food sufficiency and increase the production of agricultural commodities but should instead aim to achieve surpluses from which to earn re-investible returns. Burkina Faso and Bangladesh were able to change the structure of employment from one predominantly based on agriculture in 2000 to a more diversified labour force in 2019, without a net loss in the contribution of agriculture to GDP. Generally, an increase in labour productivity would lead to a change in the structure of labour employment over time, as labour shifts from more productive sectors to others. The concern with the instability of agricultural incomes through trade would become a secondary issue to building export capacity through productive labour and competitive agriculture. Only Liberia, Nepal and Lao People's Democratic Republic have substantially increased their value-added per worker during 2011–2017 compared to the previous decade, while the positions of Comoros and Kiribati are subject to the previously stated qualification about Island LDCs (Figure 3.12).

The widening agricultural productivity gap between LDCs and ODCs is consistent with the slow growth of investment in the agriculture sector, as well as a gradual shift in economic structure to high-value manufacturing and services sectors, which are typically labour saving in character. Investment in agriculture remained unchanged in many LDCs in 2001–2016. In Comoros, the relative share of investment in agriculture doubled with no visible gains in value-added, while investment dropped drastically in several other countries, as in the case of Ethiopia, Myanmar, Sudan and Niger (Figure 3.13). Several factors are responsible for this, including: (i) long-standing government neglect of the sector;

Figure 3.11

Prevalence of moderate or severe food insecurity in the adult population, 2015–2018

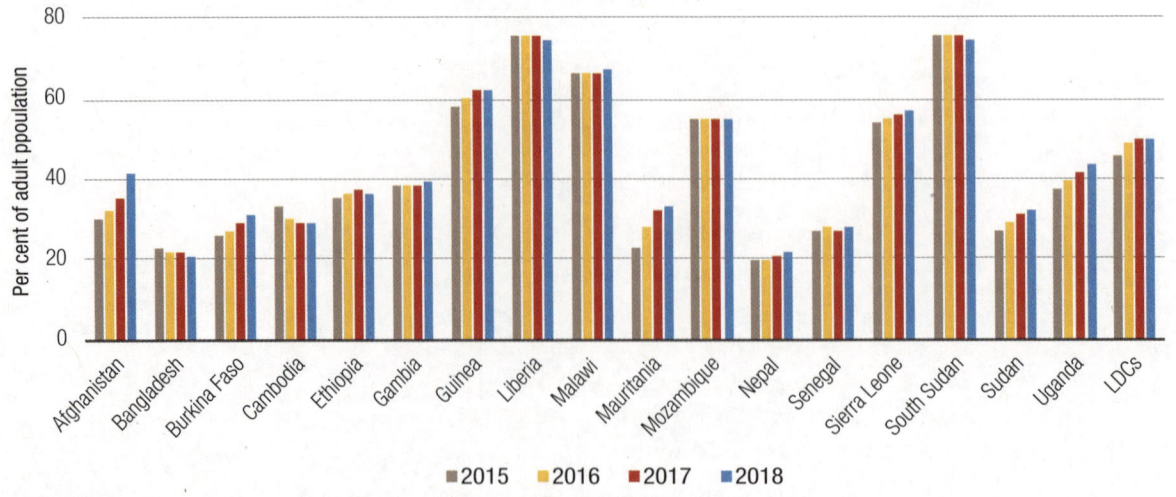

Source: UNCTAD secretariat calculations based on data from United Nations, Global SDG Indicators Database.
Note: Data missing for countries not included in the chart. LDC average is as provided by source.

Figure 3.12
Agriculture value added per worker in dollars, at 2010 prices

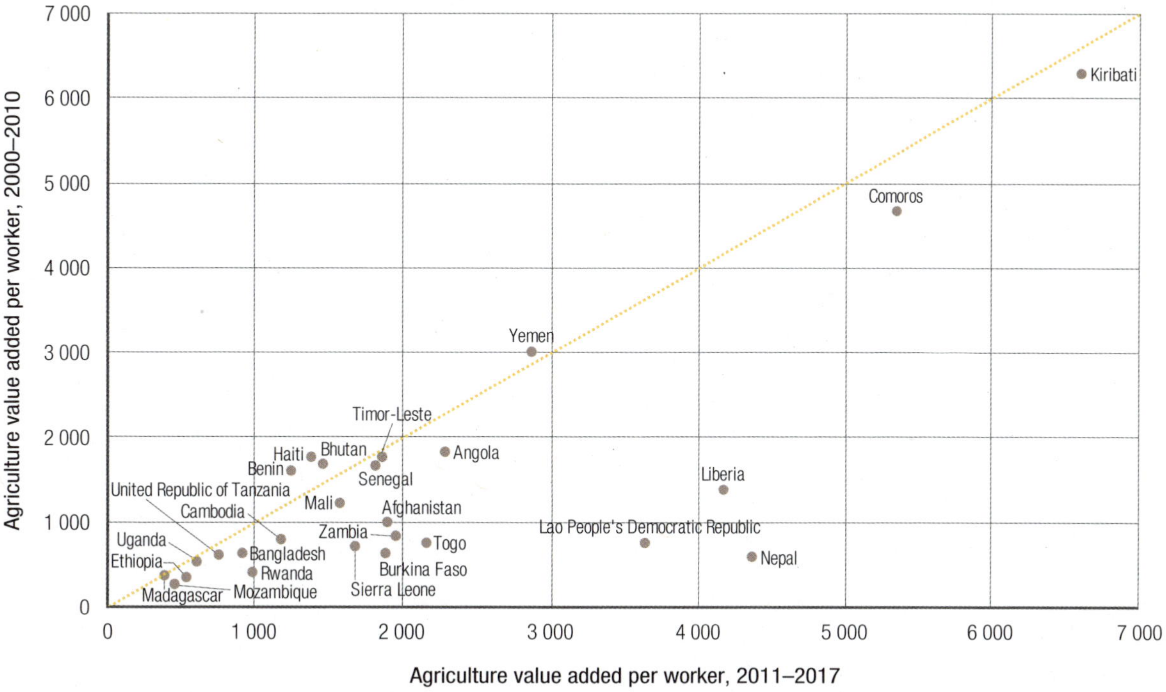

Source: UNCTAD secretariat calculations, based on data from World Bank, World Development Indicators database [accessed April 2020].

(ii) low investment by both the public and the private sectors; and (iii) low growth of land productivity (yields) and failure by the LDCs to improve labour productivity to the level comparable to ODCs. Global food supply chains have also become more capital intensive and concentrated, which contributes to inequality in food supply systems. As discussed in chapter 4, agricultural production boomed owing to green revolution technologies but a significant portion of the growth is due to extensification, i.e. the use of more natural resources (water, land), rather than intensification (Nkamleu, 2011; FAO, 2017).

The rise in food imports also implies a crucial role of income in the development of agriculture in the LDCs. The low productivity of agriculture in LDCs, as well as the changing pattern of food consumption expose the countries to large food import bills. According to UNCTADStat, in 2018 total LDC imports stood at $270 billion, $47 billion (17 per cent) of which was for food. However, the bigger LDCs, such as Bangladesh (15 per cent), Democratic Republic of the Congo and Ethiopia (9 per cent, respectively), also spend quite a lot on food imports. These are lost opportunities for LDCs that could benefit from close cooperation in trade, including agricultural commodities. Urbanization and income effects on food consumption patterns may also play a role in changing the structure of food production and trade among LDCs, as it is projected that by 2030 about 60 per cent of the population in developed countries will be based in urban areas (Cohen, 2006).

3. Trade and commodities

Trade and commodities are separate thematic priorities under the IPoA. However, due to their interrelatedness, the two are jointly discussed in this section. Despite duty-free quota-free market access for products originating in LDCs, their participation in world trade has not improved during the IPoA. The long-standing marginalization of LDCs in international trade has persisted as the commodities trade faltered under unfavourable commodity market conditions (UNCTAD, 2018b). Overall, the target of doubling the share of global exports from LDCs has failed to materialize. Instead, the LDC share in world merchandise exports deteriorated in five consecutive years to as low as 0.89 per cent in 2015 before recovering slightly to 0.98 per cent in 2018 (Figure 3.14).

World merchandise exports increased from $18 trillion in 2011 to $19 trillion in 2019, while those of LDCs also increased from $189 billion in 2011 to $192 billion in 2018 but faltered to $181 billion in 2019. There were notable declines in merchandise exports in 2015–2016, reflecting weak global demand, low

Figure 3.13
Gross fixed capital investment and value added in agriculture

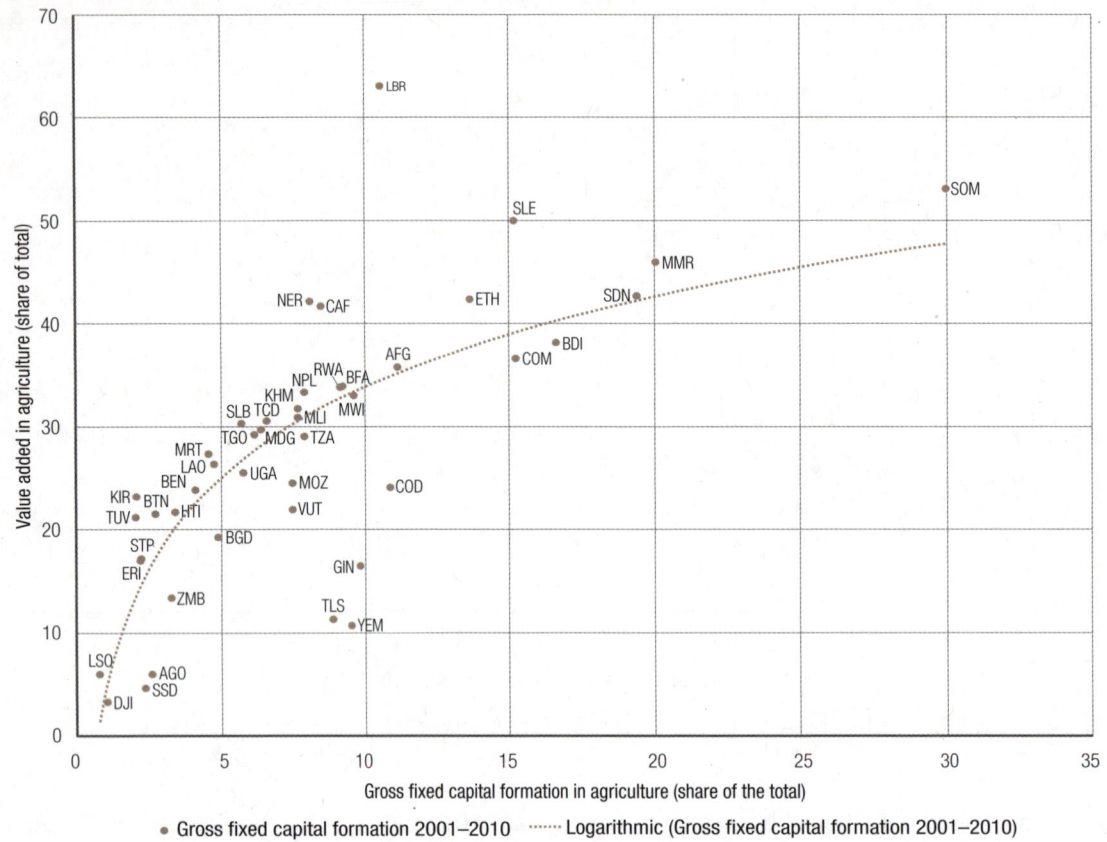

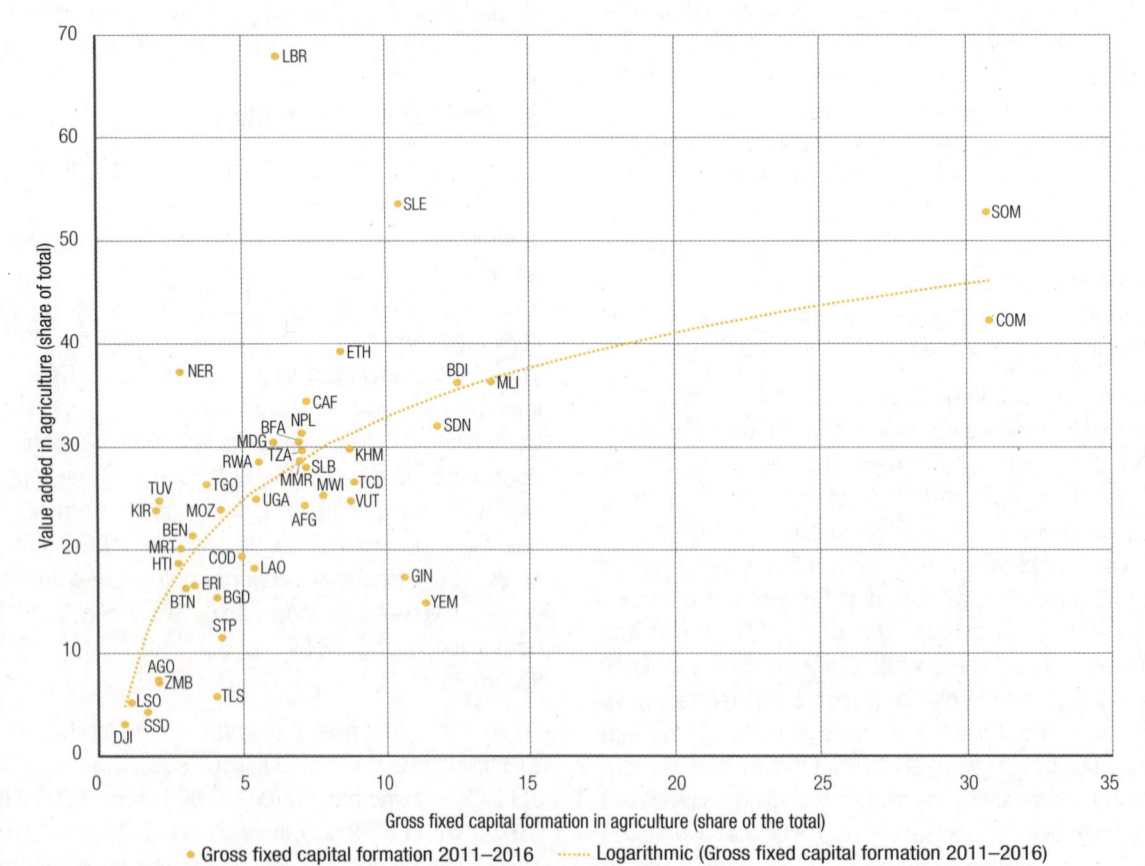

Source: UNCTAD secretariat calculations based on FAOSTAT [accessed April, 2020].

CHAPTER 3: Measuring productive capacities: LDCs' progress towards sustainable development

Figure 3.14
LDC exports as a share of world exports
(Per cent)

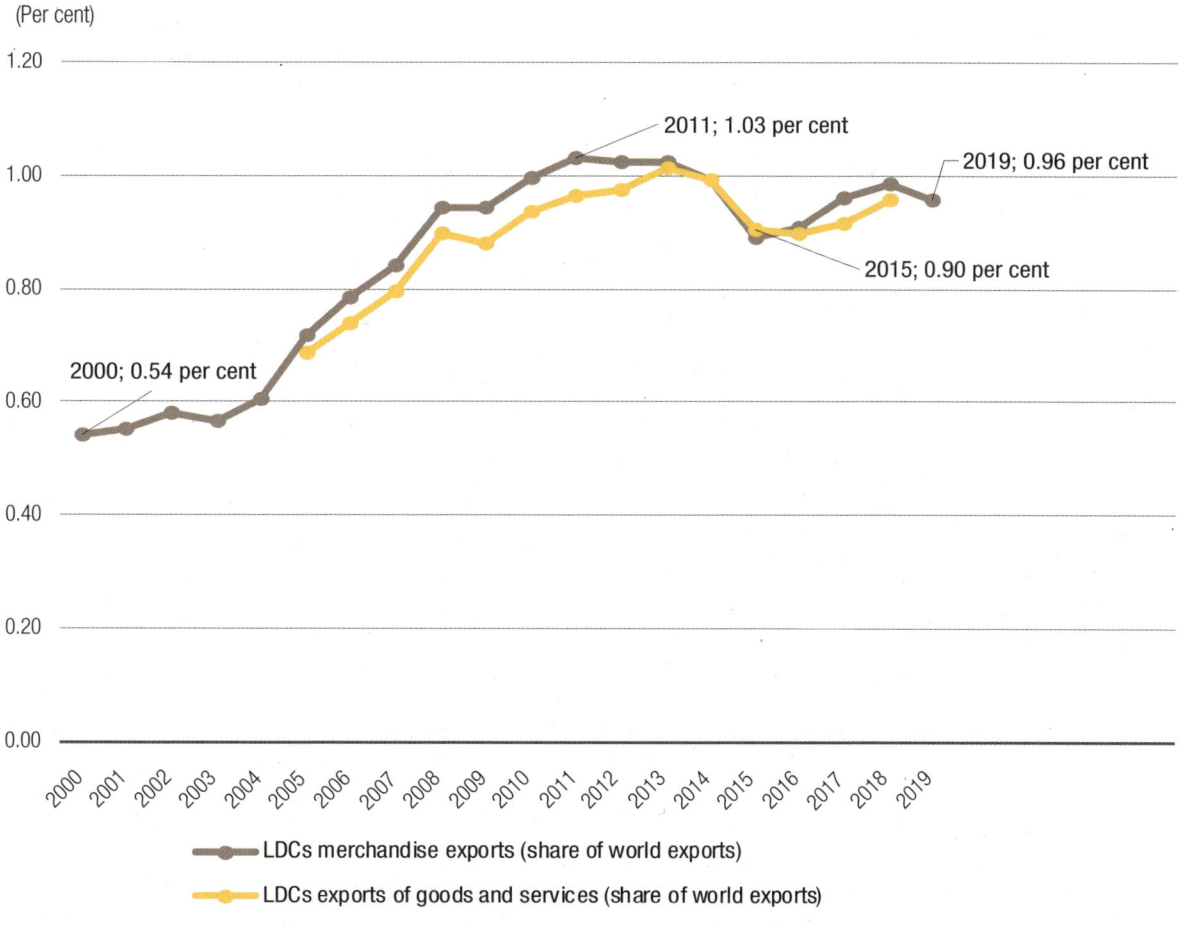

Key data points:
- 2000; 0.54 per cent
- 2011; 1.03 per cent
- 2015; 0.90 per cent
- 2019; 0.96 per cent

— LDCs merchandise exports (share of world exports)
— LDCs exports of goods and services (share of world exports)

Source: UNCTAD secretariat calculations based on UNCTAD, UNCTADStat database [accessed April, 2020].

commodity prices, dollar appreciation and production constraints (UNCTAD, 2016a). LDC exports continued to be dominated by a few countries, with the top 5 exporters (Angola, Bangladesh, Myanmar, Cambodia and Zambia) accounting for 62 per cent of all merchandise exports from LDCs in 2019.

Relative cost advantages and geographical advantages offering better linkages to global value chains have continued to play a critical role in boosting exports, particularly among Asian LDCs; African LDCs have for their part relied more heavily on their abundant natural resources. Structuralists, particularly those that view the market as the only determinant of trade, will point to the value differences in total factor productivity and other efficiency measures that affect the relative production costs. These Ricardian comparative advantages typically do not favour LDCs, except for labour-intensive sectors (agriculture and other non-extractive natural resources). Product varieties and dynamic export growth may foster an economy's capacity to trade and, if accompanied by buoyant growth, an economy may experience trade-led structural change over time (Gagnon, 2007).

What constitutes a structural change in the context of trade capacities is not a trivial matter, considering that not all commodities (sectors) are tradeable, and that sectoral composition based on GDP leaves out information about capacity utilization and productivity at the lowest level of aggregation. For example, it may not be immediately clear that higher productive capacities are associated with a lower product concentration of exports, except that most countries with PCIs between 15 and 30 have an export concentration of less than 0.5 (Figure 3.15). The product concentration index shows the extent to which the exports and imports of individual economies, or groups of economies, are dominated by a few products rather than being distributed among several products. The few LDCs with higher product concentrations in the 15–30 range of productive capacities are commodity-dependent

The Least Developed Countries Report 2020

Figure 3.15
LDC export concentration and Productive Capacities Index, 2000 and 2018

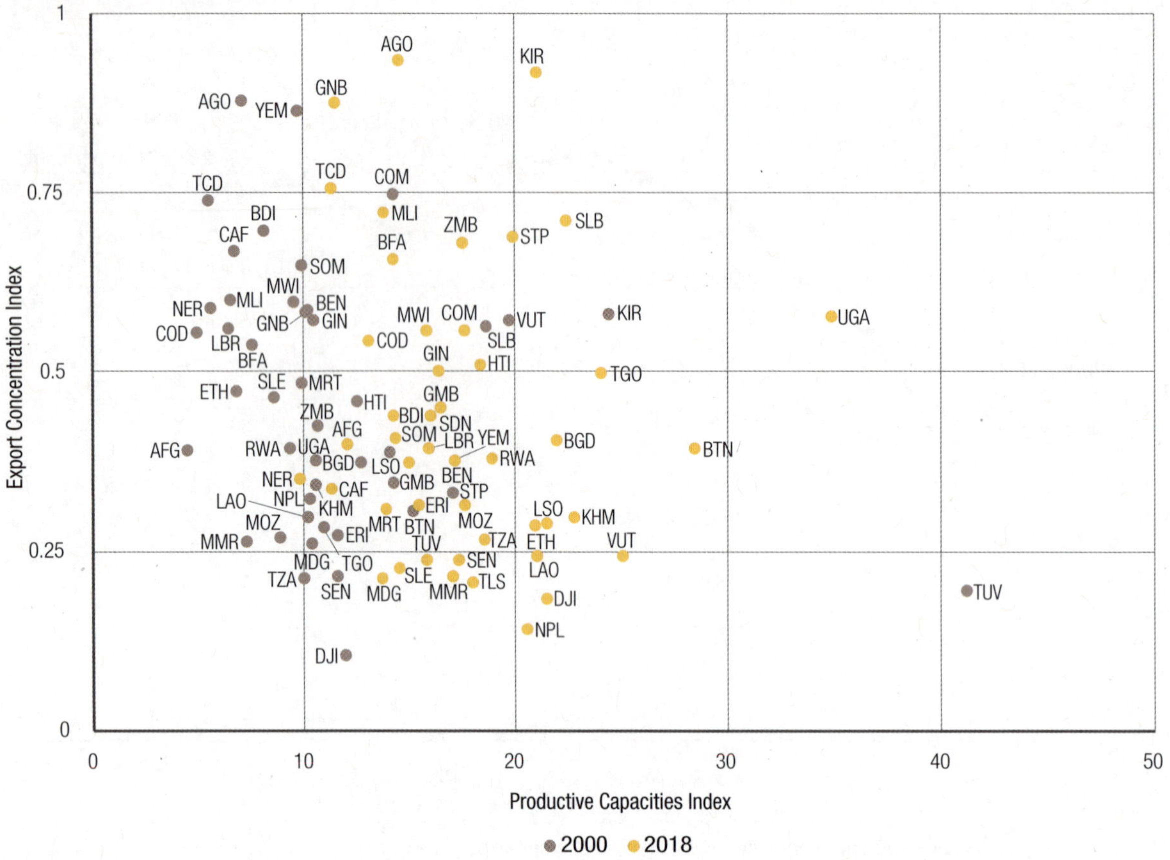

[Scatter plot with Export Concentration Index (y-axis, 0 to 1) versus Productive Capacities Index (x-axis, 0 to 50), showing data points for LDCs in 2000 (grey) and 2018 (yellow). Notable points include AGO, KIR, GNB, YEM near the top; UGA and TUV at higher Productive Capacities Index values.]

● 2000   ● 2018

Source: UNCTAD secretariat calculations, based on data from UNCTAD, UNCTADStat database [accessed May 2020].

exporters, including Angola (fuels), Zambia (metals), Malawi (tobacco), Kiribati (fisheries), and Sao Tome and Principe (cocoa). However, Bhutan, Cambodia, Nepal and Sierra Leone, all diversified their exports as their productive capacities increased.

The trade performance of individual LDCs has been variable but manufactured goods exports grew faster than other commodity types (Figure 3.16). An exception to this are Island LDCs that have seen ores and metals exports growing astronomically in 2011–2018, replacing fuels that were their main drivers during 2000–2010. However, the weight of their exports is too low compared to the other LDCs. Fuels have been on a downward spiral since the financial crisis of 2009, and sporadic spikes in fuel prices since then were insufficient to boost exports during 2011–2018. Fuel prices remained weak in 2019 and slipped further in the first quarter of 2020 as the effect of the COVID-19 pandemic on economic activities began to bite.

The concentration of primary commodities and fuels in exports have always been a source of concern for LDCs. With fuel and other commodities facing secular stagnation, the trade balance of LDCs with other country groups has deteriorated, further aggravating the marginalization in international trade that globalization was supposed to cure. Imports of goods and services rose sharply, jumping from $211 billion in 2010 to $338 billion in 2018, and imports accelerated by about $44 billion in 2015–2018 alone.

According to the IPoA, diversification of exports would mitigate the impact of external trade shocks due to the volatility of commodity prices. Specific productive capacities, e.g. better energy and transport infrastructure services, are positively associated with export diversification and overall trade performance. Generally, an increase in the share of manufacturing value-added is directly linked to export diversification, whereas natural resource endowments have the opposite effect through their tendency to trap countries into commodity specialization (Giri et al., 2019). Weaknesses in trade performance are linked to lack of industrial capacity and in some cases, the size of the economy (population) may also positively influence the diversification of exports (Osakwe and Kilolo, 2018). Improving human capital accumulation, institutions, reducing trade barriers and developing better industrial policies could also support export diversification. Giri et al. (2019) identified factors that predispose countries towards lower levels of export diversification but found that the relative influence of the size of an economy is less intensive than an abundance of natural resources.

The clustering of LDCs around various subcomponents of the UNCTAD PCI confirms the existence of specialization enclaves based on productive capacities which determine the level of export diversification and sophistication. Clustering around productive capacities is not a new phenomenon: it is a well-known concept in industrial economics as a process through which sectoral concentration of firms transform entire economies into national, regional or even global players in their value chains (Nadvi and Schmitz, 1994). The process of clustering around productive capacity subcomponents impacts the production and trade structures of countries. For instance, among agricultural commodity exporters, an expansion of transport infrastructure, private sector capacities, institutions, ICT and structural change, could trigger diversification and value addition, as these productive capacities are negatively correlated with agricultural raw material exports (Table 3.4). In itself, the productive capacity potential of natural resources is a deterrent to structural change, while the accumulation of quality labour plays a role in value-added exports growth because human capital is negatively correlated with primary exports (agricultural raw material exports, ores/metals and fuels), but positively correlated with manufactures, high technology and services exports.

Manufacturing and agriculture in LDCs may be negatively affected by industrial policy and infrastructure quality. Efforts to diversify LDC exports should focus on reducing trade costs, which account for a large share of transaction costs. Poor infrastructure prevents LDCs from fully utilizing their productive capacities, and an improvement in the transport sector alone could significantly alter trade specializations. The LDCs exporting manufactures are generally countries that have transformed their export structures over time (UNCTAD, 2015c), with transport connectivity and structural change at the centre of that transformation. In contrast, countries with static trade structures have not developed much capacity in infrastructure and scored poorly in structural change and other productive capacity subcomponents.

Figure 3.16
Commodity export growth rates for LDCs: 2000–2018

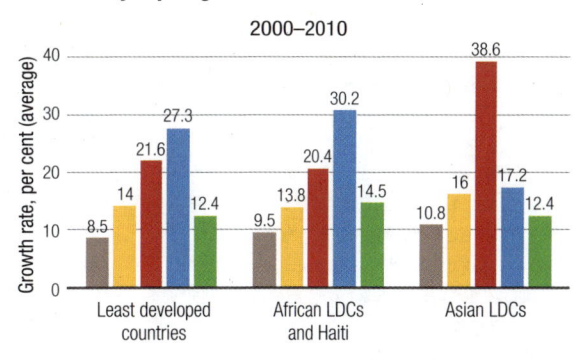

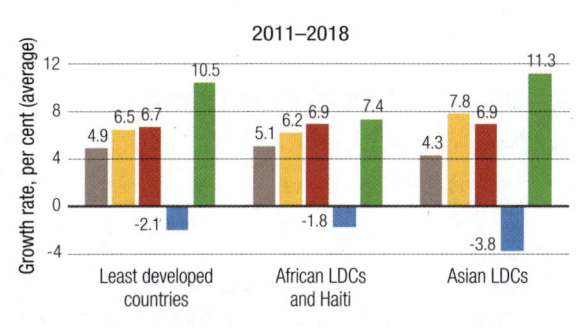

- Agricultural raw materials
- Primary commodities, precious stones and non-monetary gold, excluding fuels
- Ores, metals, precious stones and non-monetary gold
- Fuels
- Manufactured goods

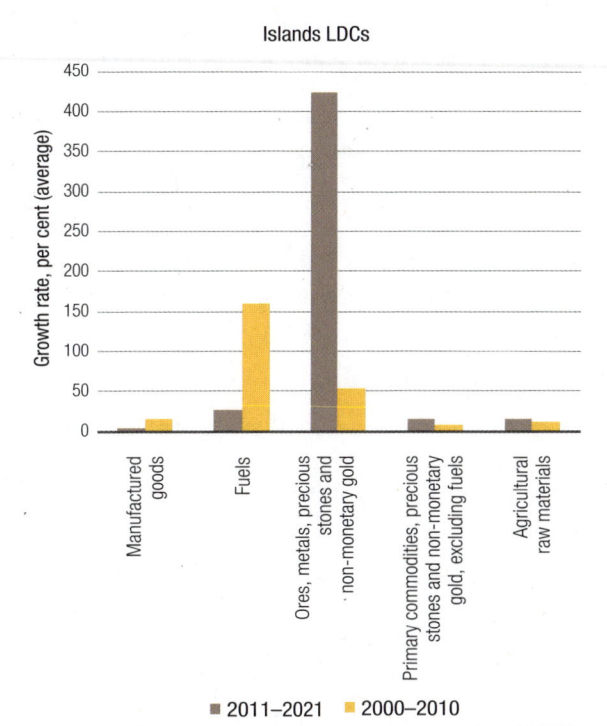

■ 2011–2021   ■ 2000–2010

Source: UNCTAD secretariat calculations, based on data from UNCTAD, UNCTADStat database [accessed April 2020].

Table 3.4
Pairwise correlations between components of the productive capacities index and major export commodities

Export type	Natural resources	Energy	Transport	Human capital	Institutions	Private sector	Structural change	ICT
Agricultural raw materials (SITC2 less 22, 27 and 28)	-0.0669**	0.014	-0.1616*	0.0098	-0.1495*	-0.0236	-0.0881*	-0.0817*
All food items (SITC 0+1+22+4)	0.0093	0.1877*	-0.1689*	0.1396*	-0.0721**	0.0654**	0.0525	0.0032
Ores and metals (SITC 27+28+68)	0.3053*	0.0991*	-0.1091*	-0.0584	0.0984*	-0.1293*	0.023	0.0271
Fuels (SITC 3)	0.1623*	0.0395	-0.0745**	-0.1422*	-0.1129*	-0.1572*	-0.1250*	-0.0129
Manufactured goods (SITC 5 to 8 less 667 and 68)	-0.0679**	0.1459*	-0.0196	0.2383*	-0.0257	0.0666**	0.1050*	0.0444
High-skill and technology-intensive manufactures	0.0316	0.1296*	-0.1682*	0.1019*	0.1060*	0.0308	0.1208*	0.0524
Low-skill and technology-intensive manufactures	0.0691**	0.2807*	-0.1145*	0.3405*	0.1369*	0.1193*	0.1299*	0.1296*
Labour-intensive and resource-intensive manufactures	-0.0739**	0.1384*	-0.0103	0.2320*	-0.0339	0.0643**	0.0993*	0.0397
Service exports	-0.134*	0.359*	0.139*	0.263*	-0.107	0.012	0.161*	0.183*
Commercial services exports	-0.121	0.348*	0.108	0.229*	-0.108	0.019	0.140**	0.175*

Source: UNCTAD secretariat calculations, based on data from UNCTAD, UNCTADStat database [accessed May 2020].
Note: * significant at 5 per cent; ** significant at 10 per cent.

4. Human and social development

The IPoA lists the human and social development priorities as education and training; population and primary health; youth development; shelter; water and sanitation; gender equality and empowerment of women; and social protection. LDCs have made mixed progress on these priorities, with a few positives in some areas but have generally disappointing when considered as a whole. LDCs have a youthful population, which account for close to 60 per cent of the total population. The youth population will increase by 62 per cent over the next three decades, surging from 207 million in 2019 to 336 million in 2050 (UN DESA, 2019). Among the goals of the IPoA is to build on the educational and skills capacity of youth and ensure their full and effective participation in society. Several countries have tailored their social policies to include specific interventions to enable them to reap dividends from their youthful population. However, LDCs faced several challenges in human and social development. For instance, while working-age cohorts are on the rise, not enough jobs are being created to accommodate them and reduce the burden of dependency (Ashford, 2007).

a. Education and training

Progress on education and training was measured through primary school enrolment and completion rates. While primary school enrolment rates are above 90 per cent in some LDCs, many others still have low enrolment rates. The goal of universal primary education with increased quality in outcomes will not be achieved in 2020 and may become harder to attain in the next decade. Of grave concern are countries that have seen an increase in the proportion of dropouts among school-age children, including in Eritrea, Sao Tome and Principe, South Sudan and Sudan (Figure 3.17). In Burkina Faso, Central African Republic, the Democratic Republic of the Congo, Djibouti, Eritrea, the Gambia, Guinea, Mali, Mozambique, Niger, Senegal, South Sudan and Sudan, more than 20 per cent of school-aged children have dropped out of school – setting the dropout threshold at 5 per cent of school-aged children would almost double the number of countries affected by this phenomenon.

Apart from challenges carried forward from the era of the Millennium Development Goals, with its focus on basic education at the expense of the transition from primary to secondary education, it is well established that the quality of education facilities, curriculum and other supporting environments for learners contribute to increasing enrolment and retention; however, the best measure of progress are retention and success rates at higher levels of education. The cost of fees has fallen but the cost of other household expenditures on education, e.g. learning materials, have risen. These costs may be too high for the poor, for example, in some urban locations of the United Republic of Tanzania, where monthly household expenditures on education per child were higher than the average monthly household expenditure reported in World Bank's Living Standards Measurement Study (Dennis and Stahley, 2012).

Gross secondary school enrolment rates reflect the struggles that countries are facing in retaining children in school. Of the countries with data, Bangladesh, Bhutan, Nepal, Tuvalu, Timor-Leste and Sao Tome and Principe have made significant strides in increasing gross secondary enrolments to well above 60 per cent. However, several other countries, e.g. Niger, Central African Republic and the United Republic of Tanzania, have stagnated at less than 30 per cent. As expected, gross enrolment

CHAPTER 3: Measuring productive capacities: LDCs' progress towards sustainable development

Figure 3.17
Children out of school
(Per cent of primary school age)

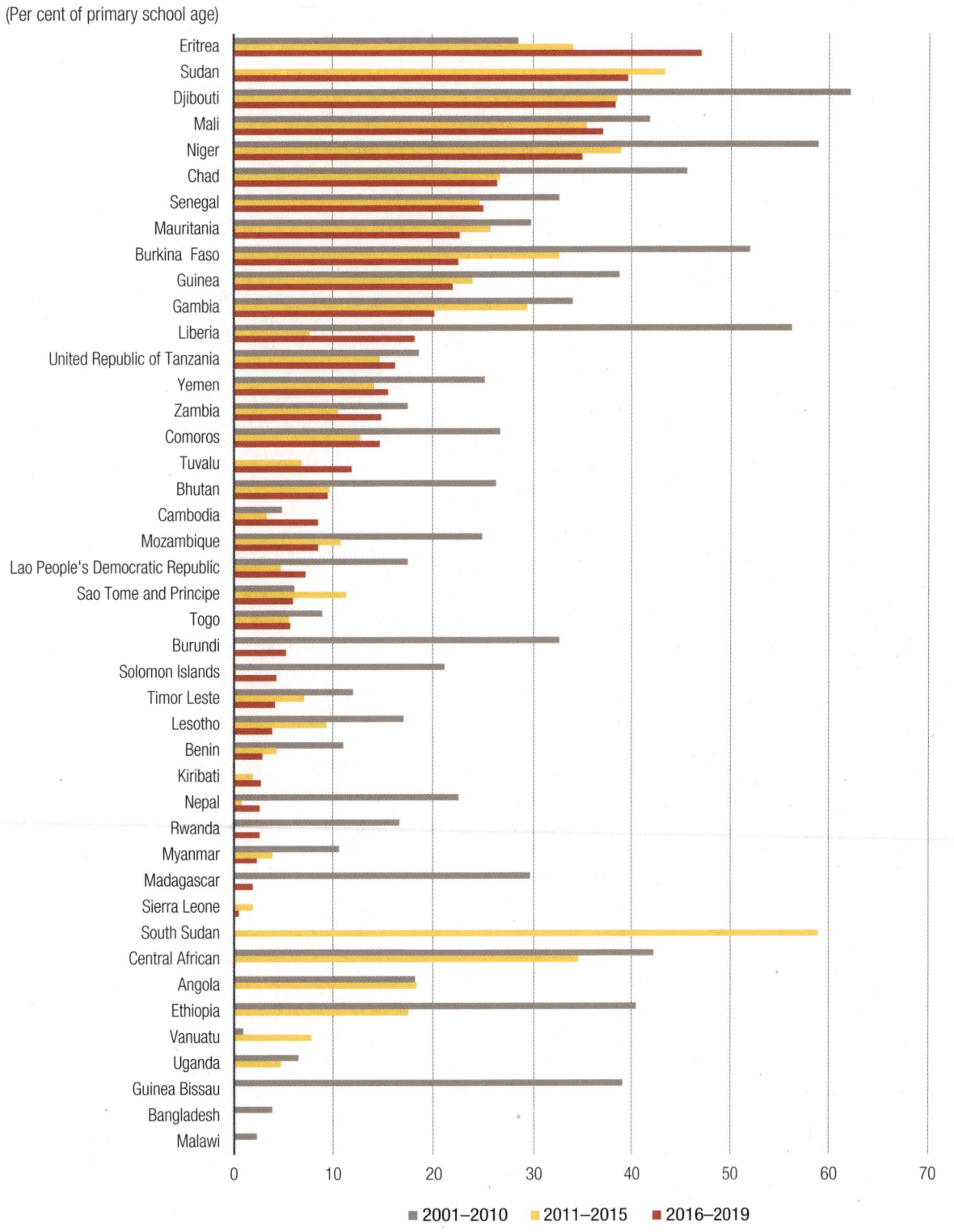

■ 2001–2010   ■ 2011–2015   ■ 2016–2019

Source: UNCTAD secretariat calculations, based on data from World Bank, World Development Indicators database [accessed April 2020].

is positively associated with both total PCI and the human capacity subcomponent (Figure 3.18). Secondary enrolment rates have improved for some countries but the bottom three countries have remained unchanged during 2000–2018, with Bhutan replacing Kiribati at the top of the list. Notable improvements were also recorded in secondary enrolment in Bangladesh, Djibouti, Nepal, Sao Tome

75

The Least Developed Countries Report **2020**

Figure 3.18
Gross secondary enrollment and productive capacities

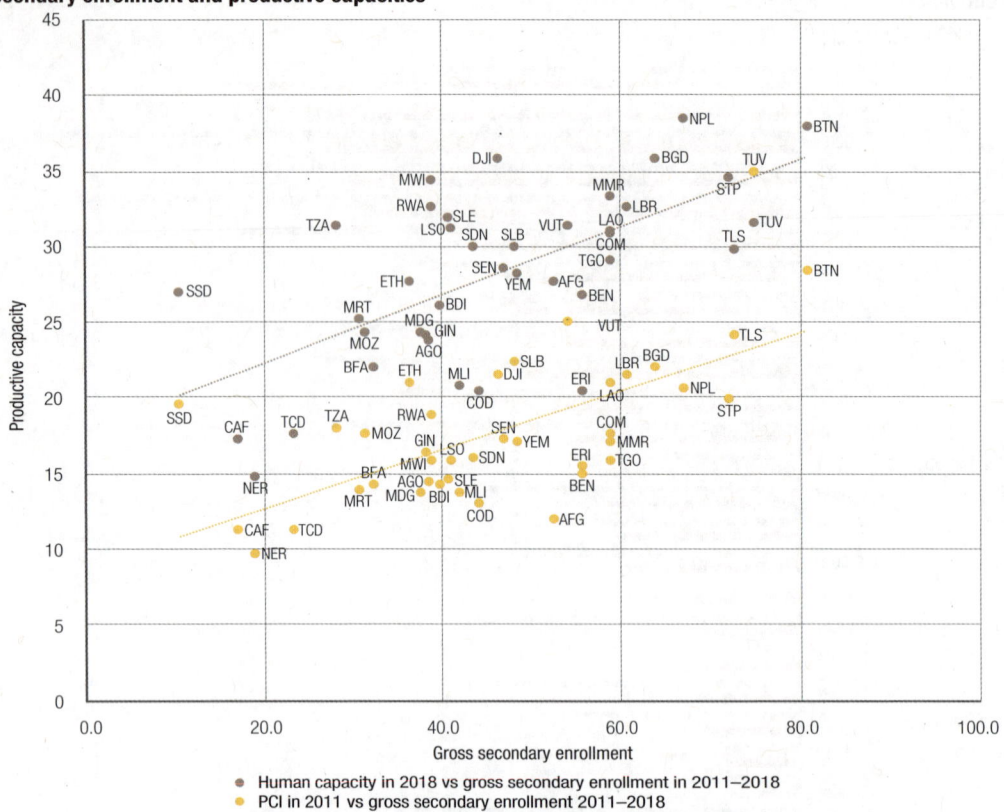

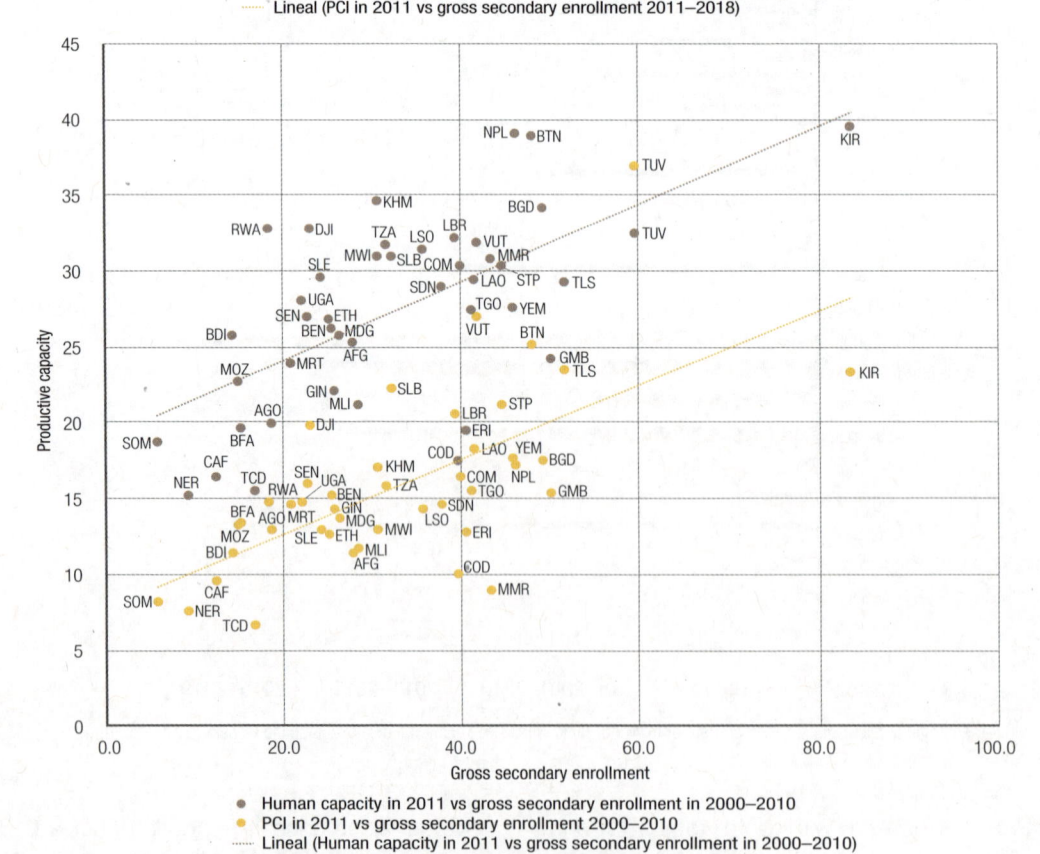

Source: UNCTAD secretariat calculations, based on data from UNCTAD, UNCTADStat database and data from World Bank, World Development Indicators database [accessed April 2020].

and Principe and Timor-Leste, which are reflected in the sizeable productive capacities gains achieved by these countries over this period.

b. Population and primary health

Concerned with high child and maternal mortality rates, the prevalence of communicable diseases including, among others, HIV/AIDS, malaria, tuberculosis, and other major diseases, the IPoA set population and primary health targets to reduce their burden on LDCs. It also encouraged countries to provide universal access to reproductive health by 2015 and promote access to medicines and invited international partners to assist in this regard. The COVID-19 pandemic has exposed the interlinkages among public health, the environment, and the economy, and need for better healthcare services across countries, including the access to medical supplies at critical moments.

Global efforts to reduce under-five mortality have yielded positive results in many countries, with the average under-five mortality rate dropping from 93 deaths per 1000 live births in 1990 to 39 in 2018 (Children: reducing mortality, 2019). However, for LDCs, Goal 3.2 of the Sustainable Development Bank of reducing under-five mortality to – at most – 25 per 1000 live births in every country by 2030 is unlikely to be met, judging from the progress made since 2011. Only the Solomon Islands and Tuvalu have already met the target, while 38 of the 47 LDCs have under-five mortality rates hovering above the world average of 39 in 2018. The only positive development is that every country has recorded some progress but that the number of preventable deaths from diseases or treatable remains too high. In light of the COVID-19 pandemic, strengthening health systems in the most vulnerable countries remains necessary but future efforts should focus on better targeting and upscaling of interventions, particularly in rural areas, as well as supporting the development and transfer of technology to produce affordable, safe, effective and good quality medicines in the developing countries.

The technology gap in developing countries with respect to the manufacture of influenza vaccines has been highlighted by Friede et al. (2011). The concentration of production capacity in a few countries in Europe and North America is a global public health risk that can be reduced by scaling up the WHO initiative on technology transfer and non-exclusive licences on specific vaccines and other types of medicines. Ideally, patents and R&D are best left to market forces but public funding is needed in the case of R&D. Moreover, capacity development and technology transfer to developing countries

Strengthening health systems and technology transfer in pharmaceuticals are priorities for the LDCs

are a global public good. Technology transfer is ineffective in the absence of intra-industry productivity spillovers, support for R&D, and the capacity to absorb and utilize the technology (UNCTAD, 2014). Although technology transfer is heavily constrained in sectors with high value intellectual property (e.g. pharmaceuticals), innovative policies could diminish the distortion caused by patent misuse and practices that impede trade (UNCTAD, 2018c). The pooling of resources and specialized skills through special mechanisms, including those under the auspices of WHO and WTO, could help to delink R&D costs in new medicines for diseases affecting populations in LDCs (Røttingen and Chamas, 2012).

Apart from the health challenges facing children and expectant mothers, shelter, water and sanitation are the other priorities of the IPoA. They are also covered in Goal 11 of the Sustainable Development Goals on sustainable cities and communities, and Goal 6 of the Sustainable Development Goals on clean water and sanitation. The number of people currently living in inadequate housing in the LDCs is quite high, and the problem of inadequate shelter is not limited to urban dwellers. However, based on available data, the proportion of the urban population living in slums ranged from 95 per cent in the Central African Republic to 21 per cent in Lao People's Democratic Republic (Figure 3.19). The problem of slums may signal a dichotomy between unproductive rural economies and growing urban economies which is better at attracting excess rural labour as the socioeconomic opportunities are more interesting. However, the continuing existence of slums reflects: (i) a lack of public and private capacity to mobilize adequate housing investments and infrastructure services for urban populations; (ii) a policy failure to attract investments in rural and urban economies; and (iii) a general weakness in social development policies (Marx et al., 2013).

Between 2000–2010 LDCs have made gains on the UNCTAD productive capacity subindex on human capital but progress since 2011 has been lacklustre. Some countries have continued to grow their human capital, although at a marginal page and others have lost momentum. This is due to stalling progress on years of schooling as dropouts piled up, while other

Figure 3.19
Proportion of the urban population living in slums
(Per cent)

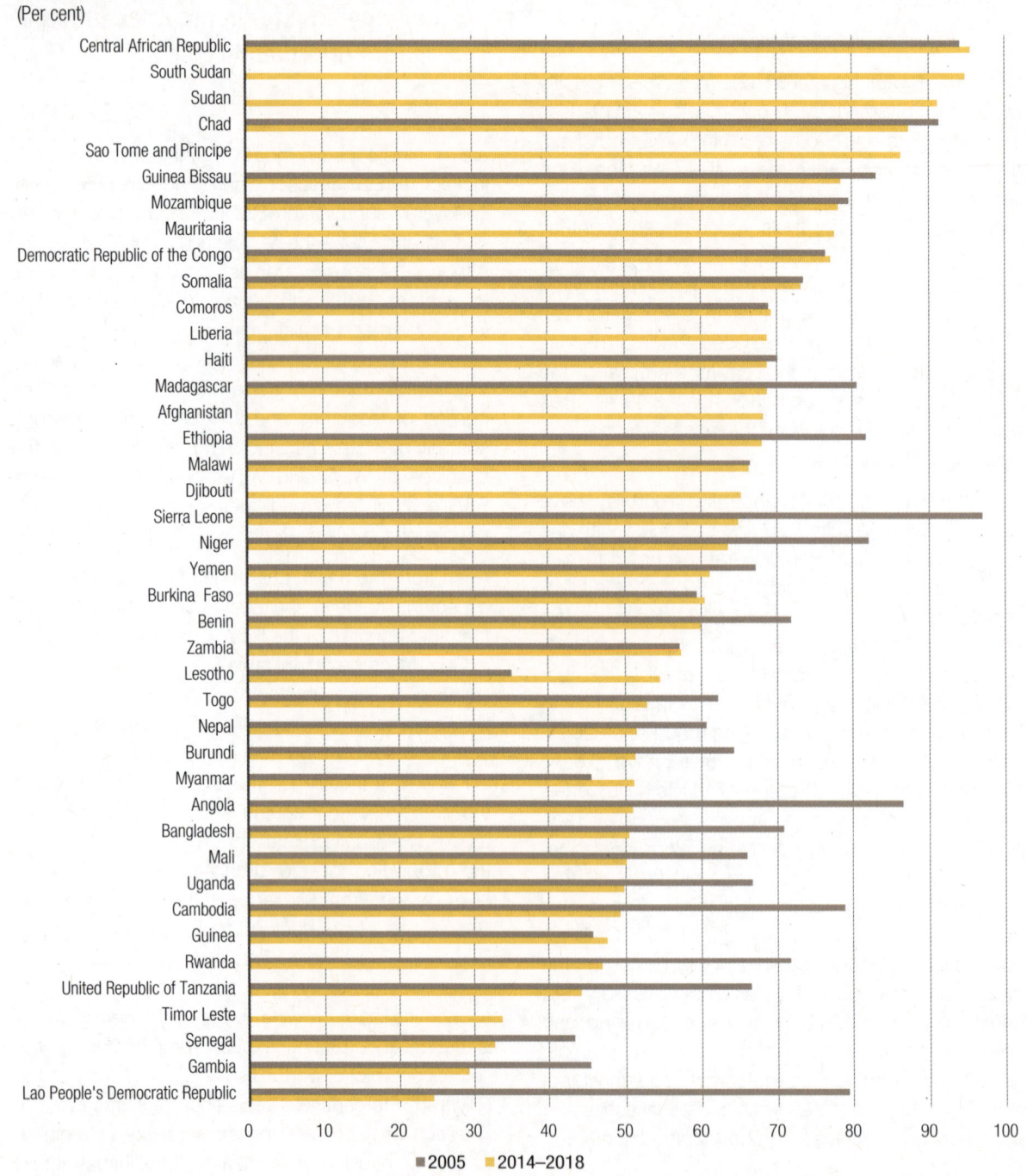

Source: UNCTAD calculations based on data from the UN Habitat, Urban Indicators Database.

components (e.g. life expectancy) have not improved by much. The upper limit of the human capacity index achieved hovered around 38–39 among the best LDC performers, with the low performers scoring less than 20 (Figure 3.20). In contrast, among ODCs, the worst performer in terms of human capital development (at 23) was close to the LDC median (26) in 2018, while the best performer in LDCs in 2018 (at 39), which was three points below the median human capacity index (at 42) for ODCs.

Human capital development is the main driver for productive capacity development. Ultimately, human beings determine investments in technology and knowledge, including in how existing production systems are utilized and the structural changes necessary to improve production systems.

CHAPTER 3: Measuring productive capacities: LDCs' progress towards sustainable development

Castellacci (2011) explains the widening gulf in economic development between country groups in terms of the technology gap (or distance to the frontier). The two dimensions of the technology gap, namely: (i) adaptive capacity, i.e. the ability to mimic advanced technologies; and (ii) absorptive capacity, i.e. the extent to which countries produce new advanced knowledge, are both heavily dependent on human capital and the stock of machines. There is, therefore, a need for LDCs to embrace a knowledge-based, productive capacities-centred view of development, with emphasis on developing the absorption, adaptation and organizational dimensions that drive technological change.

Skills acquired through education and work determine the utilization of all other productive capacities including hard and soft assets (e.g. infrastructure, institutions and policies). In general, if LDCs are to catch up to the level of ODCs, they should at least attain the same level of human capacity development, which can be best done through tangible investments in education and training, and targeting the right demographic

Youth population in the LDCs

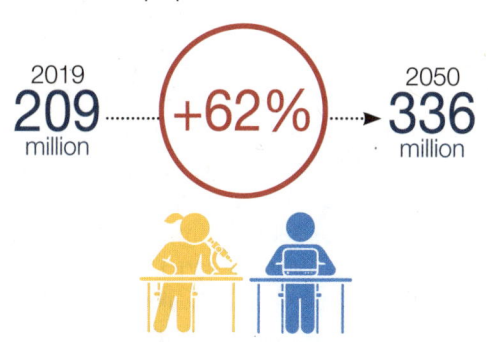

2019: 209 million · · · +62% · · · ▶ 2050: 336 million

Quality education and training for the youth will be key in reducing the technology gap between LDCs and other developing countries

group. With low education and health outcomes in LDCs, there is every likelihood that LDCs may be in the second and third industrial revolution phases of development, with oil and other primary commodities

Figure 3.20

Human capital component of the Productive Capacities Index, LDCs and ODCs

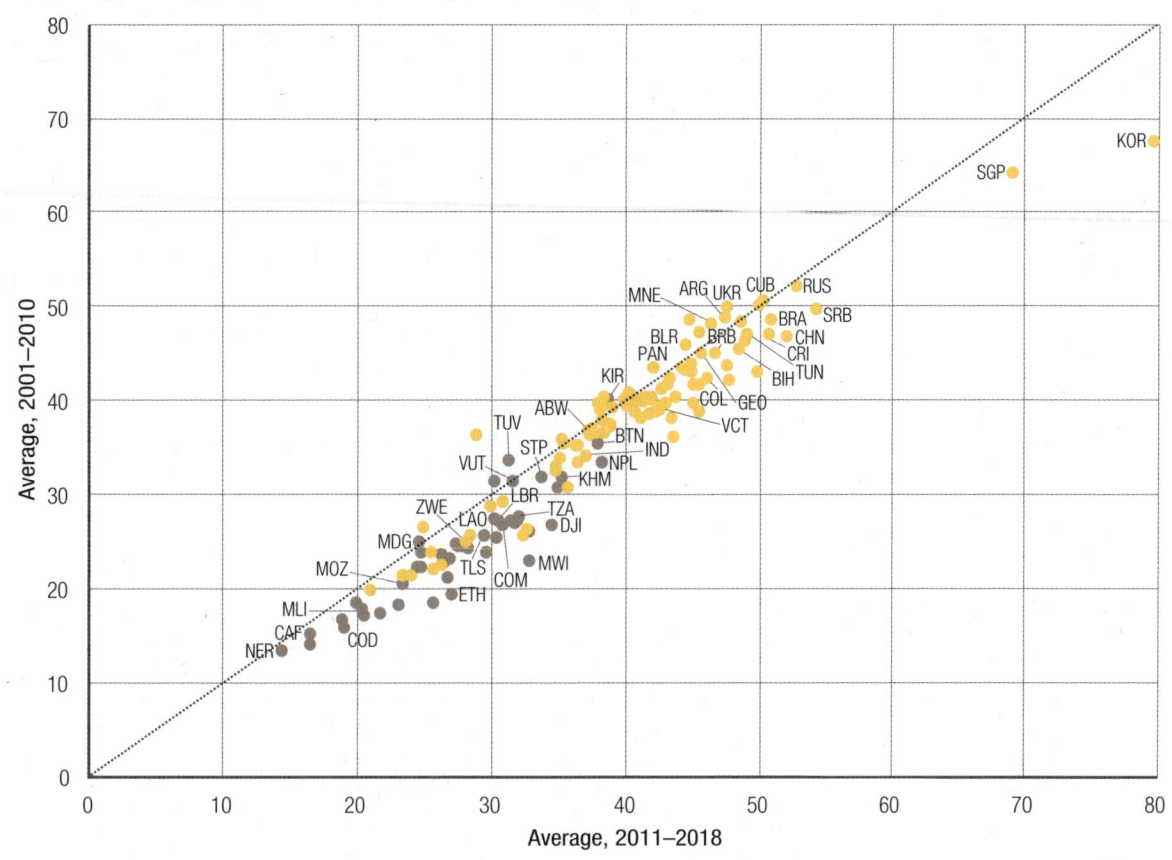

● Least developed countries   ● Other developing countries

Source: UNCTAD secretariat calculations, based on data from UNCTAD, UNCTADStat database [accessed May, 2020].

remaining as the mainstay of their economies. LDCs have low technology development and investment in learning compared to ODCs, or the frontier countries already tearing into the mesosphere of the Fourth Industrial Revolution (4IR), as well as perfecting its use of big data, the internet of things, artificial intelligence, nanoscience and nanotechnologies (Gauri, 2019). If artificial intelligence is the stratosphere of 4IR and the heartbeat of the digital economy, LDCs should not underrate the value of innovation, knowledge and the linkages created through innovation. As highlighted earlier, the difference between countries on the edge of the stochastic production frontier and those falling within (Figure 3.8) is due to variations in innovation and knowledge. Similarly, the difference between the best performers and the ODCs, particularly Singapore, and the Republic of Korea, is down to disparities in educational attainment and overall human assets.

5. Multiple crises and other emerging challenges

The vulnerability of LDCs to various shocks, including commodity price vagaries, financial and economic downturns, climate change and natural disasters, remain a concern. Several factors, such as conflict and weak institutional and governance systems, heighten the risk exposure to specific shocks. The IPoA sought to contribute to building the resilience of LDCs to withstand multiple emerging crises as they seek to attain sustainable development. Graduation from the LDC category is a fundamental goal of the IPoA, as well as other ISMs focusing on LDCs, but progress towards this goal has been disappointing.

A comparison of graduated countries and countries scheduled to graduate reveals some fundamental issues concerning the economic vulnerability of LDCs. Specifically, the performance of the countries during the IPoA implementation period shows that, with respect to economic vulnerabilities, there are important similarities and differences among graduated countries and those scheduled to graduate, or among those that have met one or more graduating criteria (Table 3.5).

The graduation threshold for the economic vulnerability index (EVI) is a score below 32. Some LDCs were able to lower their EVI scores in 2011–2020, but the vulnerability scores of 24 LDCs have worsened, and include countries such as Angola, Benin, Comoros, Guinea, Mali, Sao Tome and Principe, Sierra Leone and Timor-Leste (Figure 3.21). Fewer countries (21 in all) are below the 45-degree line in the figure, which indicates a higher economic vulnerability score in 2020 compared to 2011. However, a handful of countries met the criterion in both 2011 and 2020, and include Bangladesh, Central African Republic, Guinea, Myanmar, Nepal, Sao Tome and Principe, Togo and Uganda. Based on the average change in EVI scores over the period, the median was 0.09 per cent (Afghanistan), but the best performer in reducing vulnerability over the period was Liberia (-3.3 per cent) and the lowest Angola (+1.6 per cent).

The LDC with the highest reduction in economic vulnerability is Liberia, a coastal country with relatively stable structural variables (Figure 3.22). For example, its population in low elevated coastal areas grew marginally from 10.8 per cent in 2011 to 11.7 per cent in 2020, while the share of agriculture, fisheries and forestry in GDP remained above 70 per cent. The lower score in economic vulnerability was driven mainly by a fall in agricultural instability and individual victims of natural disaster. There were also reductions in export concentration and export instability, which are linked to positive dynamics in the agriculture sector.

Except for the group of countries that meet two graduating criteria, the country groups in Table 3.5 have lower average EVI scores in 2020 compared to 2011. However, they all scored poorly since the graduation threshold for the EVI is below 32.

Table 3.5

Country groups by graduation status and criteria

Countries that graduated	Countries scheduled for graduation	Countries that met two criteria in 2018	Other LDCs with GNI> $2,460
Botswana (1994)	Vanuatu (2020)	Bangladesh	Angola
Cabo Verde (2007)	Angola (2021 – GNI only criteria)	Kiribati	Bhutan
Maldives (2011)	Bhutan (2023)	Lao People's Democratic Republic	Kiribati
Samoa (2014)	São Tomé and Príncipe (2024)	Myanmar	Timor-Leste
Equatorial Guinea (2017 – GNI only criteria)	Solomon Islands (2024)	Nepal	Tuvalu
		Timor-Leste	Vanuatu

Source: UNCTAD secretariat elaboration, based on information from the United Nations Committee for Development Policy website, URL: https://www.un.org/development/desa/dpad/our-work/committee-for-development-policy.html [accessed April 2020].

Figure 3.21
Economic and environmental vulnerability index, 2011 and 2019

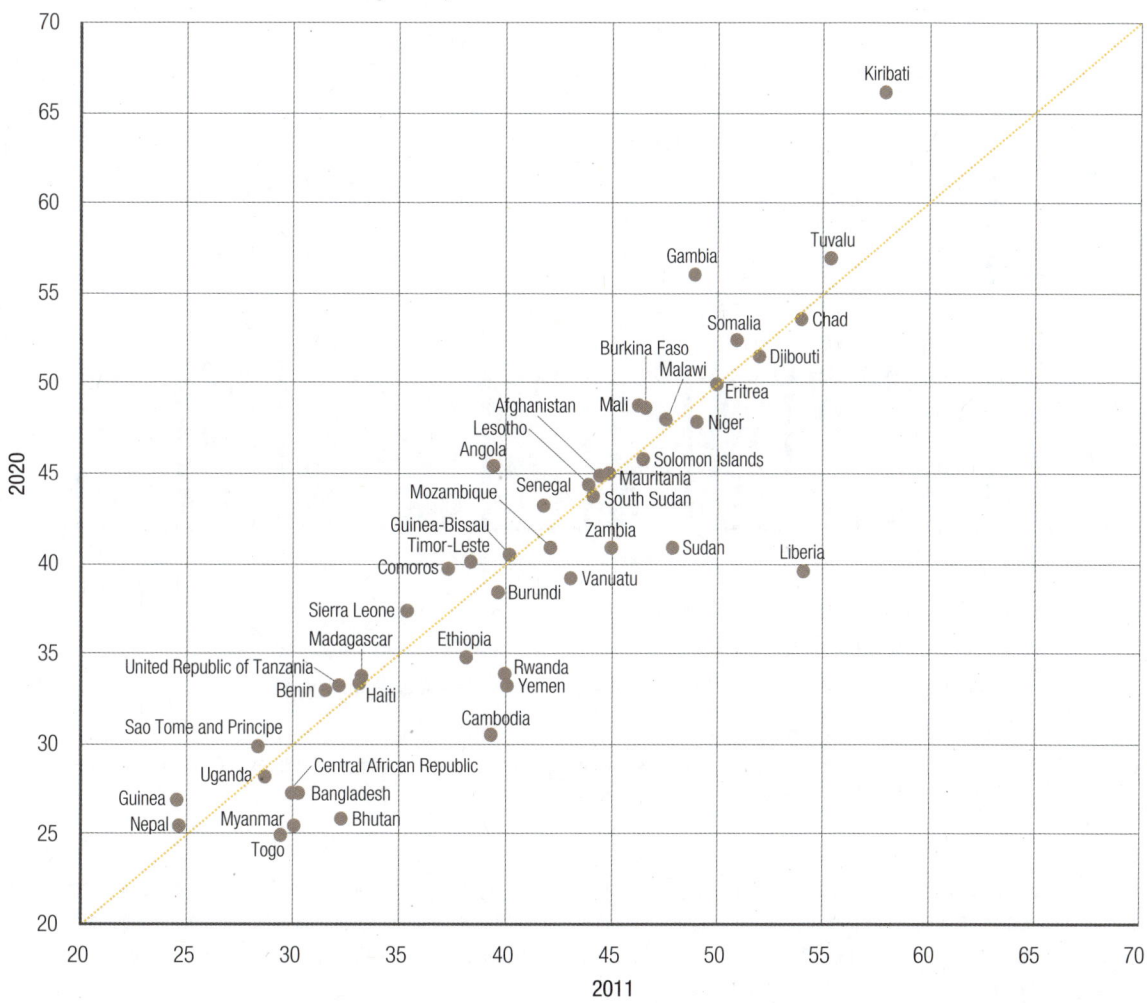

Source: UNCTAD secretariat calculations, based on data from United Nations Committee for Development Policy Secretariat. Time series estimates of the LDC criteria [April 2020].

As can be expected, countries with the lowest values happened to have graduated in both years.

Those LDCs that are scheduled to graduate have a higher than average EVI index and are far above the

Table 3.6
Correlation between economic vulnerability and productive capacities

	Country groups based on Table 3.5				Other country groups	
	Graduated	**Scheduled to graduate**	**Countries that met two criteria in 2018**	**Other LCDs with GNI greater than $2,460 (in 2018)**	**LDCs not in graduation frame**	**Other developing countries**
Energy	0.4748*	0.4041*	0.081	-0.5408*	0.0418	-0.1466*
Human capital	0.4240*	-0.3890*	-0.6985*	0.6186*	0.1026*	-0.1289*
ICT	0.0261	-0.9279*	-0.2813*	0.3446*	-0.0234	0.0176
Institutions	0.1889	-0.3757*	-0.2878*	0.5182*	-0.0787*	0.1109*
Natural resources	-0.2003	0.0361	0.4823*	-0.7855*	0.1177*	0.047
Private sector	0.2004	0.2669	-0.4468*	0.6007*	0.0326	-0.1790*
Structural change	-0.1215	-0.1367	0.3355*	-0.0333	-0.2798*	-0.3669*
Transport infrastructure	0.6829*	0.6268*	-0.2735*	0.6491*	0.0958*	0.3700*

Source: UNCTAD secretariat calculations, based on data from UNCTAD, UNCTADStat database and data from United Nations Committee for Development Policy Secretariat. Time series estimates of the LDC criteria [April 2020].

Note: * significant at 5 per cent.

Figure 3.22
Liberia: Economic vulnerability and subindices, 2011–2020

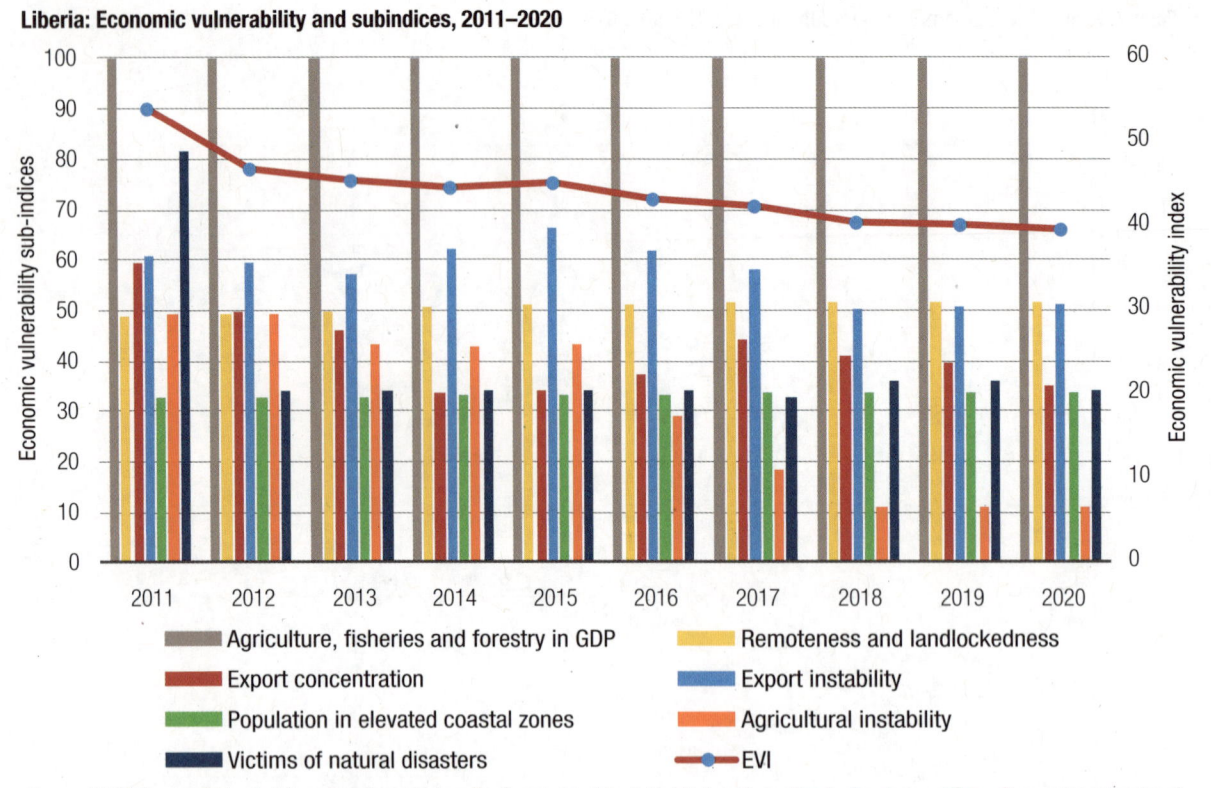

Source: UNCTAD secretariat calculations based on data from the Secretariat of the United Nations Committee for Development Policy. Time series estimates of the LDC criteria. [Latest available update, April 2020].

threshold. It follows that countries in this group will graduate based on the GNI per capita indicator and the human asset index, as graduation only requires two out of the three criteria to be fulfilled. The result highlights the need to address the sustainability of momentum after graduation, particularly as the risk of falling back into the LDC category increases for countries that graduated only on the basis of their GNI per capita income criterion. In such cases, it is critical to question whether graduated countries, regardless of the criteria that was used, should be granted a grace period in which they could lower their economic vulnerability before losing all their LDC-related support measures and exemptions.

A further examination of the relationship between economic vulnerability and the PCI shows that structural change is associated with lower economic vulnerabilities for all country groups in Table 3.5, except for LDCs that met two graduation criteria in 2018. Natural resources are also associated with a lower EVI for countries that graduated, as well as LDCs with a high GNI in 2018. By contrast, human capital, ICT and institutions are associated with lower economic vulnerability for countries scheduled to graduate. Beside the overlap in the graduation-framed subgroups, the countries that met the two criteria were more vulnerable in the natural resources dimension which they compensated with a higher GNI, a vibrant private sector or better transport infrastructure.

An important asymmetry is also observed between the countries that graduated from the LDC category and the entire set of ODCs. Components such as energy, human capacity, ICT, institutions, private sector and structural diversity, were all found to be associated with the lower economic vulnerability of ODCs, but natural resources and transport infrastructure had the opposite effect. For countries that graduated from the category, energy, institutions, transport infrastructure and human capital are associated with higher economic vulnerability, with only natural resources contributing significantly to lowering economic vulnerability. This confirms the observation that graduated LDCs, or those scheduled to graduate based on the income criterion, do so based on the wealth of their natural resources. The weaknesses exposed by their low score in other productive capacity components should be the focus of their policies if they aspire to reach the level of ODCs. This is clear from the productive capacity components associated with lower economic vulnerability scores among ODCs.

LDCs reduced their economic vulnerability by a 5 per cent mean reduction between 2011 to 2019 but countries that managed to lower their EVI scores either did so through improved trade or production indicators from outcomes of better productive capacities which, in turn, boosted economic performance and diversification. However, 12 out of 47 LDCs have become economically vulnerable since 2011. Graduated countries performed consistently better in 2011–2019 on both the total EVI index and its subcomponents, whereas countries scheduled to graduate met the criteria set in the human asset index and GNI per capita, giving a high group mean compared to the mean of all other LDCs. Some Island LDCs will struggle to lower their overall EVI score as they have small populations, a large proportion of people living in low coastal areas and their remoteness, which accounts for almost half of the total EVI index are structural and impossible to change with policy over the short term.

6. Mobilizing financial resources for development and capacity-building

A major feature of the development finance architecture promoted by the Addis Ababa Action Agenda is the promise for larger and more diversified development finance for developing countries. However, the growing gap between investment requirements and mobilized resources highlights the importance of bolstering tax capacities in developing countries to achieve Goal 17.1 of the Sustainable Development Goals. Domestic resource mobilization is constrained by their small economic bases, as well as their ability to implement broader and progressive taxation. It also corresponds to the capacity to close leakages through international cooperation on investment, taxation, combating illicit financial flows, and other avenues to leverage finance.

Among LDCs with recent data for 2011–2018, tax revenue to GDP averaged less than 20 per cent. Low savings are typical of small economies but a higher gross fixed capital formation of above 25 per cent of GDP shows that the investment climate in LDCs is still healthy. However, it is important to note that capital formation in LDCs is driven mainly by public spending on infrastructure and other durable assets. The external resource gap (i.e. the difference between the gross fixed capital formation rate and the gross domestic savings rate) of LDCs with data was 15.6 per cent of GDP in 2015–2018, up from 13.8 in 2011–2014 (Figure 3.23).

Typically, external resource gaps are wider in smaller economies that have very low savings. The

Figure 3.23
Savings, investment and external resource gaps

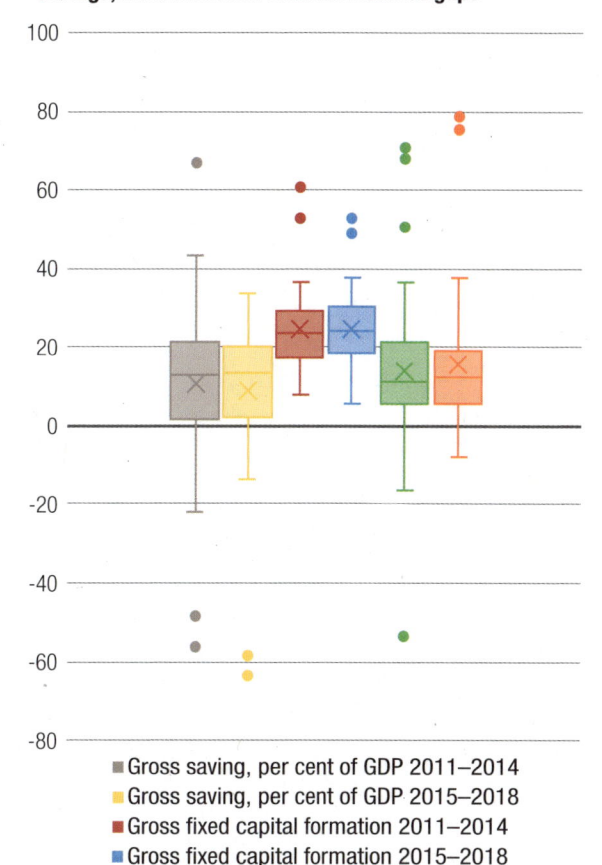

- Gross saving, per cent of GDP 2011–2014
- Gross saving, per cent of GDP 2015–2018
- Gross fixed capital formation 2011–2014
- Gross fixed capital formation 2015–2018
- External resource gap 2011–2014
- External resource gap 2015–2018

Source: UNCTAD secretariat calculations, based on data from World Bank, World Development Indicators database [accessed April 2020].

gap becomes a concern if the countries involved continue to record negative trade and balance of payments scores. As emphasized in this chapter, LDC trade deficits are worsening their long-standing marginalization in international trade. For most LDCs, the investment gap in 2015–2018 was narrower than in 2011–2014 as investment demand fell due to secular stagnation in commodity markets (Figure 3.24). In general, the LDCs should boost private sector investments to achieve structural transformation, which is the best route out of the primary commodity trap. Arguably, a higher allocation of credit to the private sector may indicate a healthy domestic financial environment that is supportive of productive investments, even though these claims may include credit to state-owned enterprises (Khaltarkhuu and Sun, 2014).

The relationship between productive capacities and domestic resource mobilization arises from utilization; in other words, a country with better

The Least Developed Countries Report **2020**

Figure 3.24
External resource gaps as a percentage of GDP, 2011–2014 and 2015–2018

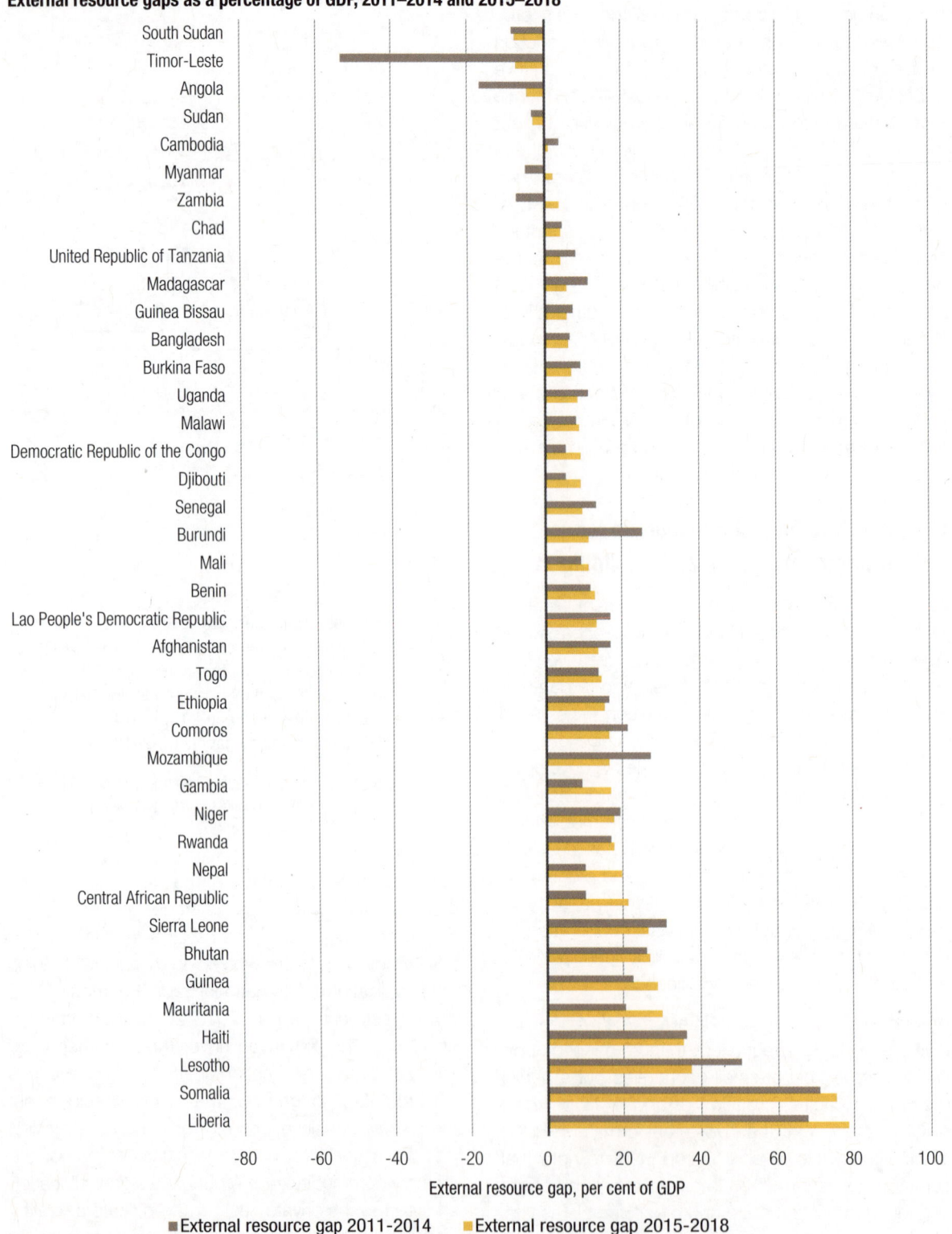

■ External resource gap 2011-2014   ■ External resource gap 2015-2018

Source: UNCTAD secretariat calculations, based on data from World Bank, World Development Indicators database [accessed April 2020].

utilized productive capacities has more means to generate a higher national income and therefore tax revenue. There is a two-way relationship between tax revenue and productive capacities, depending on the role of fiscal policy in stimulating growth and the real economy. The correlation between tax revenue and the various productive capacity components, except natural resources were significant and positive, suggesting that natural resource-rich countries have failed to broaden their tax bases to efficiently boost tax revenue. This result is consistent with the observation that resource-rich countries, e.g. Angola and Sudan, could improve the efficiency of their tax collection systems through a rationalization of their tax revenue components. Also, the level of revenue collection is still too low relative to their economy sizes (UNCTAD, 2019b).

A strategy for boosting economic growth and domestic resource mobilization is private sector-led development. Countries that need to transform their economies are also, by default, the same countries that have failed to attract competitive private investment, except for the countries with natural resources capacity. The complementarity between industrial policies and structural transformation policies derive from the common goal of cultivating positive feedbacks and interlinkages in the economy, even though the former may focus on a narrow set of industries. Policies to diversify the economy should, therefore, be consciously designed to stimulate private sector development, particularly in sectors shunned by market-seeking investors. It should, however, be noted that emerging activities will, by necessity, spring from existing capabilities including the labour, capital, technology, knowledge and skills developed over time (Brooks, 2007).

7. Good governance at all levels

Among the specific objectives of the IPoA was to enhance good governance at all levels by, among others, strengthening the capacity of governments to play an effective role in their economic and social development. LDCs made progress on some governance indicators in 2011–2018 but there are still several countries with on-going conflicts or recovering from past conflicts. Globally, the population of forcibly displaced people in 2018 was 70.8 million (UNHCR, 2019), 33 million of whom originated from LDCs (Figure 3.25). The situation of internally displaced people (IDPs) and refugees scattered in neighbouring or more distant countries challenges the perception of improved governance, particularly in countries with large populations of forcefully displaced people.

The acute rise in the number of displaced individuals from 16.8 million to 33 million in 2011–2018 is a growing problem in LDCs. Conflict-affected or post-conflict LDCs, e.g. Afghanistan, the Central African Republic, the Democratic Republic of Congo, Eritrea, Ethiopia, Myanmar, Somalia, South Sudan, Sudan and Yemen,

Figure 3.25
Population of displaced people in least developed countries, 2018

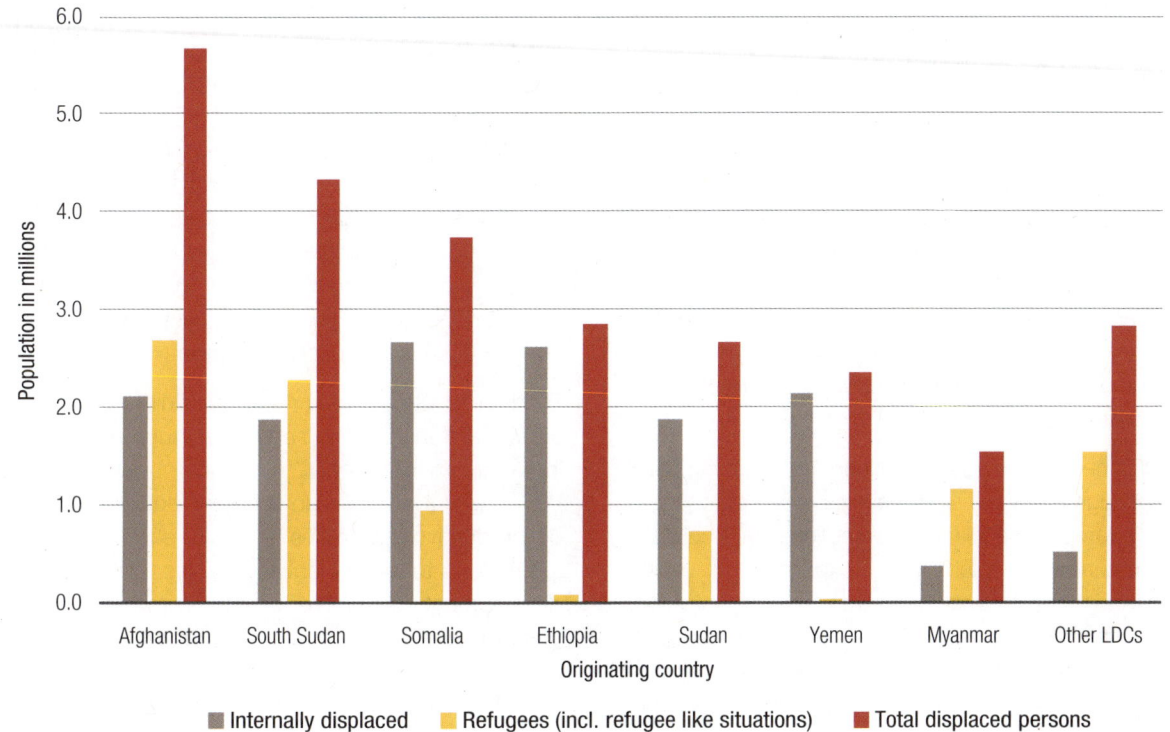

Source: UNCTAD secretariat calculations, based on data from UNHCR, Refugee Population Statistics Database [accessed April 2020].

> **Transformational policies can unleash the dynamic impacts of productive capacities on the economy**

have significant numbers of IDPs. Pockets of IDPs can also be found in Mali, Chad and Niger, as well as in other LDCs. These displaced populations, together with conflict-related deaths, exert a substantial drag on governance appraisals of LDCs.

The World Bank's Worldwide Governance Indicators (WGI) project has provided data on six broad dimensions of governance over the period 1996–2018, and covers indicators, such as voice and accountability, political stability and absence of violence, government effectiveness, regulatory quality, rule of law, and control of corruption (Worldwide Governance Indicators, 2020). An analysis of these indicators shows that several LDCs made progress in some areas but regressed in others. Based on this analysis, Rwanda scores relatively well on aggregate, while Somalia is the lowest ranked among African LDCs and Haiti. It should be noted that despite its overall ranking, a country may perform poorly or better in some governance dimensions; one example of this is the case of Rwanda which is ranked low on voice and accountability. Similarly, Bhutan and Tuvalu have a better overall governance scores among Asian LDCs and Island LDCs, respectively, while Yemen and Comoros were the lowest ranked in their respective subgroups.

The shared trait among the countries that were ranked highly on governance in the African and Asian LDC subgroups are their strong performances in government effectiveness and control of corruption. Island LDCs performed strongly on voice and accountability, as well as political stability and absence of violence. Asian LDCs also shared high rankings in political stability and absence of violence; but the best ranked African country was rated poorly on these components.

LDCs need to improve on all aspects of governance, as subgroup dimensions reveals areas of concern. For example, the Island LDCs have socially cohesive communities, which may explain their stable political systems and strong rankings on voice and accountability. However, their close communities may be contributing to lowering the quality of regulatory systems, fuelling corruption and reducing government effectiveness. In contrast, African countries have more fragmented societies, which may explain the lower ranking of political stability and absence of violence, as well as on voice and accountability. The role of social cohesion and social capital in economic development has been studied extensively by others (e.g. Woolcock et al., 2000). Corruption erodes trust in societies and breeds contempt for the government at all levels. Both the failure by the state to control corruption and the loss of trust in government by citizens can be detrimental to social inclusion and social cohesion (Sapsford et al., 2019).

Further analysis of the WGI and PCI reveal that better-governed countries generally have higher per capita GDPs, although not exclusively. A typical dilemma for resource-rich economies is their tendency to overly rely on the income weight when benchmarking their economic development against other countries. However, the insights provided by the PCI are revealing: well-governed countries tend to have better productive capacities, and the income distortion on economic ranking dissipates (Figure 3.26). This is clear in the case of Angola, Sudan and Zambia, and to some extent, Timor-Leste and Cambodia.

D. Conclusion

The chapter has analysed the progress that LDCs have made towards attaining the goals of the IPoA. This section further explores the implications of the lack of progress or improvements made on some dimensions of productive capacities, as well as the interactions among them. Overall, LDC progress towards achieving the targets of IPoA was unsatisfactory and lacked traction in many respects. Using UNCTAD's newly launched PCI revealed that an increasing number of LDCs are trapped in low productive capacities and find themselves in a specialization cul-de-sac. Specialization enclaves have always existed, driven by commodity dependence (African LDCs and Island LDCs), or market interlinkages (among Asian LDCs), but the persistence of crisis-linked setbacks affecting some LDCs are a new phenomenon.

Productive capacities are key building blocks for structural transformation and trade but their dynamic impacts on the economy will not come alive until they are activated by government policy. The state of productive capacities in LDC economies limit the extent to which public policies can influence development; for some of them, moreover, their geographical location and subregional dynamics have compounded the challenge. The analysis of the productive capacity categories suggests a trade-off among the building blocks, with most of the categories having complementarity impacts;

CHAPTER 3: Measuring productive capacities: LDCs' progress towards sustainable development

Figure 3.26
Worldwide governance index rankings and the UNCTAD PCI

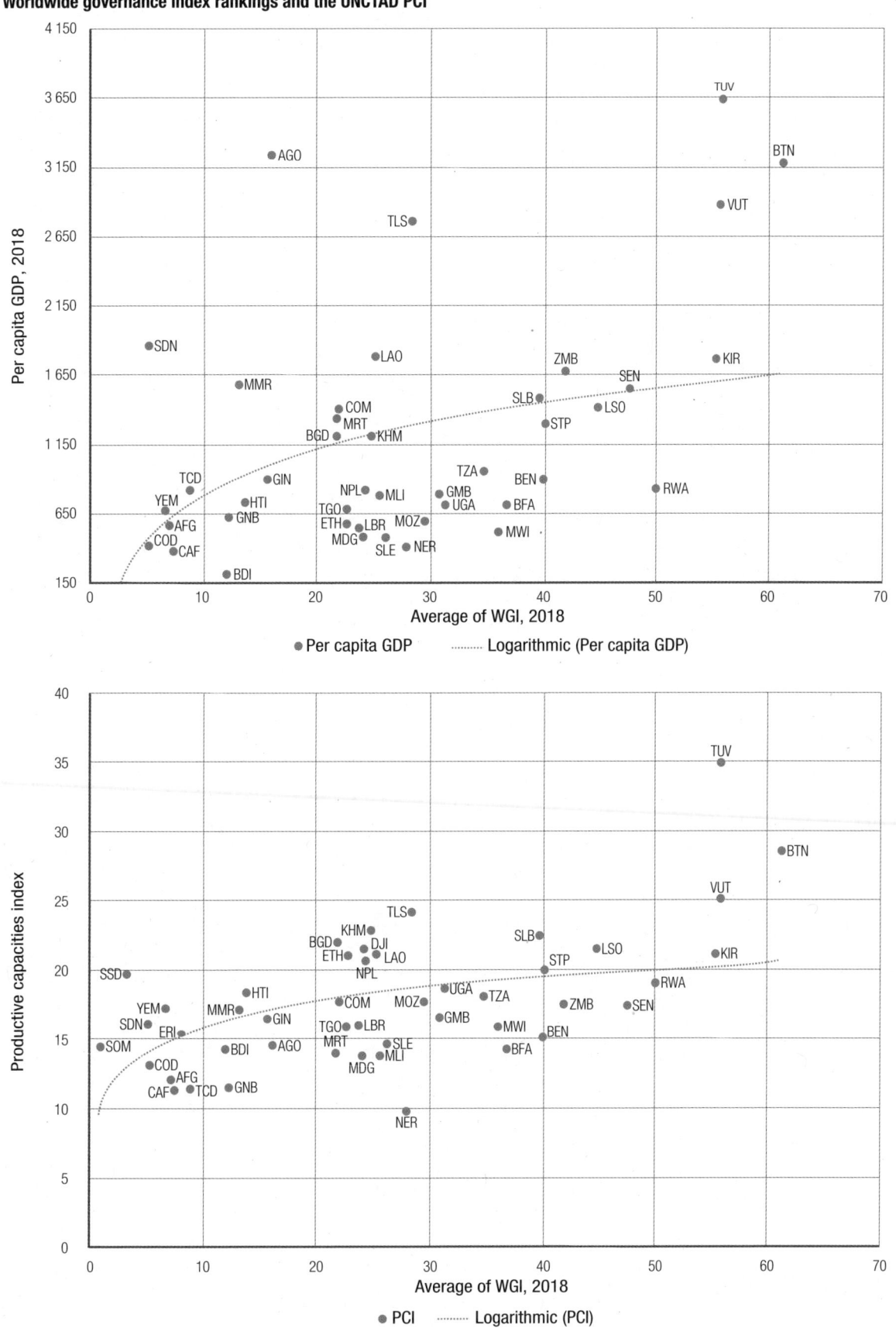

Source: UNCTAD secretariat calculations, based on data from UNCTAD, UNCTADStat database and data from World Bank, World Development Indicators database [accessed April 2020].

87

however, the existence of non-conventional negative correlations among the categories suggest low synergy. LDCs need to exploit complementary trade structures offered by their subregional markets. Asian LDCs could, for example, value their neighbours for providing the necessary inputs, including the technology they need, and as markets for the goods and services they export. African and Island LDCs also need to exploit their subregional markets but they will have to invest more in interlinkages, institutions and infrastructure.

Productive capacities subcomponents may impact economic sectors and individual LDCs differently. However, for primary sectors, such as agriculture and natural resources, a strong human capacity could be the trigger for structural reforms. Agriculture is a special sector for LDCs because of the critical roles it plays in employing most of the labour force and as a source of exports and supplier of raw materials. The dilemma for policymakers is to work out how to reduce dependence on unproductive labour that dampens the contribution of agriculture to poverty reduction, while at the same time as ensuring a sustainable livelihood for a growing population. Structural change capacities in LDCs also fail to elicit the same effect on growth as they do in ODCs because the burgeoning services sector is not driven by improvements in labour productivity but rather joblessness and widespread informality.

Building productive capacities is a slow process. Although productive capacities among LDCs have improved, three key trends have emerged, namely: (i) countries have progressively enhanced their capacities; (ii) countries have increased their capacities at a declining pace; and (iii) others have stagnated or regressed. As explained above, these have also meant specialization enclaves developing alongside stagnating productive capacities. Breaking these patterns of specialization would require altering not just the mixture of productive capacities but also the drivers of specialization. For example, energy capacity is positively related with both agriculture and manufacturing, but as noted earlier, the industrial-scale energy investment needed to spark value addition in agriculture and expansion of manufacturing capacity is in multiples of the current level (UNCTAD, 2017c). Moreover, policy-induced changes in economic orientation may reduce some of the inefficiencies observed. For example, export-promotion in narrowly defined sectors may be placing an undue burden on some economies, leading to some of the distortions related to economic structure. Some of the commodity-dependent economies are extremely vulnerable to the vagaries of global markets due to their inadvertent policy discrimination against other economic sectors (UNCTAD, 2015b).

LDCs have missed many opportunities to build human capital and promote human development more widely. While the available indicators do not comprehensively capture human and social development, they nevertheless highlight the need to reduce inequalities, build resilient communities and eliminate all forms of poverty. In line with what UNCTAD has been advocating over the years, LDCs should take advantage of their youthful population to close the widening gap between them and the ODCs. To do this, they need to ensure that youth are productive and not used a source of cheap labour in agriculture and other sectors. Uneducated and untrained labour remains an unproductive and underutilized resource, hence the key to reaping the demographic dividend and bridging the technology gap between LDCs and ODCs is to refocus public investments in education and training by bringing the skills development and knowledge at the centre of the efforts.

It is getting harder for LDCs to graduate from the category. The few countries that have graduated have done so based on their large natural resource capacity. However, natural resources also pose the a great source of instability to exports and may raise the vulnerability of the countries. The result is that economic vulnerability persists, even after countries have graduated from the LDC category. There may be a need for the international community to agree on specific support measures for those countries in the graduation frame, as well as to recently graduated countries to ensure a sustainable momentum. A differentiated support structure seems inevitable given the low graduation rates, and the slow progress towards graduation among the LDCs.

ANNEX: A technical introduction to the UNCTAD Productive Capacities Index

The following material draws from the methodological note about the UNCTAD PCI (UNCTAD, forthcoming).

The Productive Capacities Index (PCI) is a composite of an initial list of 46 indicators extracted from various sources (Appendix Table 3.1). It is calculated as a geometric average of eight domains or components, namely, natural capital, human capital, energy, transport, ICT, institutions, structural change and the private sector. The categories are selected based on their relevance to conceptual and analytical framework for building productive capacities. Mathematically, the PCI is defined as follows:

$$PCI = \sqrt[N]{\prod X_i^{PCA}} \qquad (1)$$

Where X_i^{PCA} is the weighted score extracted from the principal component analysis on the i-th category, for $i = 1,\ldots, N$ categories. The *PCI* values range from 0 and 100, with 100 being the best score.

The process of constructing the index consists of a sequence of data-intensive steps as follows. The steps were implemented in R-programming language, a free software widely used for data management and statistical analysis.

a. Imputation of missing data

Data for each country, calendar years and indicators are difficult to come by. Data imputation for missing values is therefore an unavoidable exercise when organizing data for a large set of countries. Two approaches were used: the first involved extending data for missing years, and it works only if there is an acceptable set of existing data points from which the missing data can be inferred by way of simple interpolation; the second case is more challenging, as the data for countries with missing observations are imputed from the closest neighbouring economies with identified observations. By design, per capita incomes are used as weights in calculating imputed values, but other suitable weights may also be used. This is operationalized through the following expression:

$$x_i^{NA} = \log(y_i) * \left(\frac{1}{5} \sum_{j=1}^{5} \frac{x_j}{\log(y_j)} \right) \qquad (2)$$

Where x_i^{NA} is the imputed value for country *i* from observations, x_j of the neighbouring countries, for $j = 1,\ldots,5$ while y_j is the *j - th* country's per capita income.

b. Forecasting

It may be desirable in some cases to obtain new observations for each indicator. New observations may be generated by using an Auto Regressive Moving Average where *AR(p)* and *MA(q)* are selected by Bayesian Information Criterion or by using local linear forecast using smoothing splines (Hyndman et al., 2005). Applied to the PCI, the two forecast methods yield highly correlated estimates with the correlation coefficient of the observations,

$$\rho(PCI_{splines}, PCI_{ARMA}) = 0.99 \qquad (3)$$

Similarly, the forecast error show high correlation with the real *PCI*, but *ARMA* achieves a slightly lower mean squared error than the local linear forecast based on smoothing splines,

$$\begin{cases} MSE(splines) = E[\Sigma(x_{i,splines} - \hat{x})^2] = 0.004 \\ MSE(ARMA) = E[\Sigma(x_{i,ARMA} - \hat{x})^2] = 0.002 \end{cases} \qquad (4)$$

c. Multivariate analysis

In this step, the Principal Component Analysis (PCA) is applied to reduce the dimensions of the data by extracting a group of factors that best represented the original data. The resulting factor weights are then used in the weighting of the individual indicators to construct the PCI components.

In this context, PCA is used to cluster individual indicators and capture the information common to individual indicators into a latent factor. In the PCI framework, weights are applied to the indicators to capture their common information. Moreover, such weights only measure the explanatory capability of each of the indicators in terms of the overall variance in the data, and therefore do not imply any form of ranking of their theoretical importance.

The first step in PCA is to check the correlation structure of the data, thus explaining the variance of the observed data through a few linear combinations of the original data. Correlated principal components indicate that they are measuring the same domain, while lack of correlation highlights divergence of latent structures of the variables. Then, a certain number of latent factors are identified to represent the data. In this context, each of the selected factors fulfil the following binding constraints:

- The factor's eigenvalue is greater than one; and
- The factor explains at least 10 per cent of total variance.

Finally, the PCI category scores are built on the F_i scores of the rotated factors, weighted by their respective share of total explained volatility. The scores are standardized as below.

$$X_i^{PCA} = \frac{F_{i,o} - F_{i,min}}{F_{i,max} - F_{i,min}} \quad (5)$$

d. Computing the PCI

The overall PCI scores are obtained by aggregating the individual scores for each of the eight categories. This is done by using the geometric mean, instead of the arithmetic mean because the geometric mean reduces the level of substitutability between dimensions and is less sensitive to outliers, thus reducing the effect of skewed PCI components. This choice is fully justified by the theoretical framework underlying the productive capacities, where a balanced mix of inputs is necessary to foster economic development.

$$PCI = \sqrt[N]{\prod_{i=1}^{N} X_i^{PCA}} \quad (6)$$

Where X_i^{PCA} are the scores of PCI categories extracted using principal component analysis.

The final step is to estimate the significance and internal consistency of each category. This is done using Cronbach's alpha, a widely used measure for assessing the reliability or internal consistency of a set of scale or test items. Generally, the higher the Cronbach's alpha, the more intercorrelated the indicators are among themselves. For this reason, Cronbach's alpha was applied to assess the level to which the set of indicators for each category adequately represent a single unidimensional latent construct, namely, the PCI categories, and how the categories correspond to the overall PCI. The Cronbach's alpha is defined as:

$$\alpha = \frac{M_i}{M_{i-1}} \left(1 - \frac{\sum_{j=1}^{M_i} \sigma_{I_j,i}}{\sigma_i}\right) \quad (7)$$

Where M_i is the total number of weighted indicators in the category i, $\sigma_{I_j,i}$ is the variance of the indicator j and σ_i is the total variance of the category i.

Interested readers will find a practical illustration of this step in the methodological note referred to above. The indicators and the data sources used in constructing the PCI and its subindices are outlined in the table below.

Annex Table 3.1

Indicators used in constructing the PCI and its subindices

Category	Indicator Name	Source
Energy	Share of people with access to electricity	World Bank, Sustainable Energy for All (SE4ALL)
	Transmission and distribution losses as share of primary supply	IEA Statistics © OECD/IEA
	Renewable energy consumption (share of total final energy consumption)	World Bank, Sustainable Energy for All (SE4ALL) database from the SE4ALL Global Tracking Framework led jointly by the World Bank, International Energy Agency, and the Energy Sector Management Assistance Program.
	GDP per kg of oil consumption	IEA Statistics © OECD/IEA 2014 (iea.org/stats/index.asp), subject to iea.org/t&c/termsandconditions
	Total primary energy supply per capita	IEA Statistics © OECD
	Total energy consumption per capita	IEA Statistics © OECD

Annex Table 3.1 (continued)

Category	Indicator Name	Source
Human capital	Expected years of schooling (years)	UN Development Program
	Research and development expenditure (share of GDP)	UNESCO Institute for Statistics
	Researchers in R&D per million people	UNESCO Institute for Statistics
	Health Adjusted Life expectancy (years)	IHME, http://ghdx.healthdata.org/gbd-2017
	Health expenditures (% GDP)	World Health Organization Global Health Expenditure database
	Fertility rate	United Nations Population Division. World Population Prospects: 2019 Revision. (2) Census reports and other statistical publications from national statistical offices, (3) Eurostat: Demographic Statistics, (4) United Nations Statistical Division. Population and Vital Statistics Report (various years), (5) U.S. Census Bureau: International Database, and (6) Secretariat of the Pacific Community: Statistics and Demography Programme.
Information & Communication Technologies	Fixed broadband subscriptions per 100 people	International Telecommunication Union (ITU)
	Number of mobile subscriptions per 100 people	International Telecommunication Union, World Telecommunication/ICT Development Report and database.
	Number of fixed lines per 100 people	International Telecommunication Union, World Telecommunication/ICT Development Report and database.
	Secure internet servers per million population	WDI (Infrastructure)
	Number of internet users (percent of population)	International Telecommunication Union, World Telecommunication/ICT Development Report and database.
Institutions	Control of corruption	World Governance Indicators
	Government effectiveness	World Governance Indicators
	Political Stability and Absence of Violence/Terrorism	World Governance Indicators
	Regulatory quality	World Governance Indicators
	Rule of law	World Governance Indicators
	Voice and accountability	World Governance Indicators
Natural capital	Agricultural land (share of land area)	Food and Agriculture Organization
	Forest area (share of land area)	Food and Agriculture Organization
	All extraction flows over GDP	http://www.materialflows.net/
	Material Intensity	Own computation on UN Stat National Accounts – Analysis of Main Aggregates (AMA) and materialflows.net. Material Intensity is the total extraction flows over industrial value added
	Total natural resources rent (share GDP)	Sustainable Development Goals
Private sector	Domestic credit to private sector (% of GDP)	International Monetary Fund, International Financial Statistics
	Cost to export a container	World Bank, Doing Business project
	Time to export (days)	World Bank, Doing Business project
	Cost to import a container	World Bank, Doing Business project
	Time to import (days)	World Bank, Doing Business project
	Enforcing contracts (time to enforce days)	WDI (Private Sector)
	Starting a business (time in days)	World Bank, Doing Business project
	Trademarks applications	WIPO
	Patent Applications	WIPO
Structural change	Export concentration index	UNCTADStat
	Economic complexity index (value)	Own Computation on trade data (UNCTAD)
	Gross fixed capital formation (% of GDP)	UN Stats, https://unstats.un.org/unsd/snaama/
	Industrial ratio	Own computation on UN Stat National Accounts – Analysis of Main Aggregates (AMA). Industrial ratio is Industry and Services over total GDP
Transport	Air transport registered carrier departures worldwide per 100 people	International Civil Aviation Organization
	Air transport freight (million ton-km)	International Civil Aviation Organization
	Air passenger per capita	Own computation
	Logarithm of km roads / 100 sq. km. land	International Road Federation, World Road Statistics
	Logarithm of total km rail lines per capita	Own computation on WDI Database Archives

Tacit knowledge is a critical component of technological capabilities

...but it is hard to share or teach

It resides in firms' employees

With limited industrialization, LDCs struggle to leverage the digital 4th industrial revolution

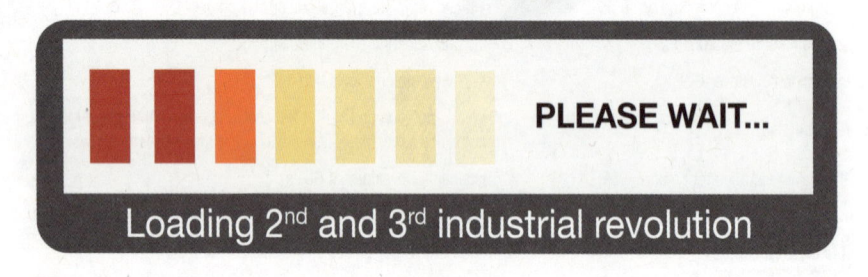

PLEASE WAIT...

Loading 2nd and 3rd industrial revolution

Technological capabilities acquisition by firms is not automatic

PROMOTE UPGRADING

INCENTIVES
- Scale in operations
- High value segments in supply chains
- Past accumulation of production capabilities and tacit knowledge

FOSTER INERTIA

DISINCENTIVES
- Low value segments in supply chain
- Lack of investment capital
- Need for specialized and matching human and capital assets
- Poor trade facilitation infrastructure

CHAPTER 4

Transition to the digital economy: technological capabilities as drivers of productivity

CHAPTER 4

Transition to the digital economy: technological capabilities as drivers of productivity

A. Introduction — 95
1. Legacy and digital technologies: interdependencies and critical links — 96
2. What makes digital firms different — 97
3. The role of technological capabilities in firms' digital transformation — 98
   - a. Defining technological capabilities — 98
4. The technological capabilities firms will need — 99
   - a. Business and managerial capabilities — 100
   - b. Data management capabilities — 100
   - c. Dynamic marketing capabilities — 100

B. Agriculture — 101
1. The innovation context — 101
   - a. The smallholder challenge — 101
   - b. The productivity challenge — 102
   - c. Public research and development — 104
   - d. Farm size — 104
   - e. Introduction to agriculture 4.0 technologies — 104
2. Agriculture case studies — 105
   - a. Case study 1: expanding access to mobile telecommunications to boost agricultural development in Myanmar — 105
   - b. Case study 2: LDC experience in the use of drones in agriculture — 107
   - c. Case Study 3: The emergence of agritech entrepreneurs in LDCs — 108

C. Manufacturing and services — 109
1. The innovation context — 109
2. Manufacturing and services case studies — 111
   - a. Case study 4: Ethiopia's footwear industry under threat from digital transformation — 112
   - b. Case study 5: Uganda's Kayoola Bus initiative — 114
   - c. Case study 6: Trade and logistics services — 115

D. Case study synthesis — 118

E. Conclusions — 119

A. Introduction

Technological capabilities are an indispensable component of the productive capacities needed by economies to climb up the economic development ladder. This chapter examines the technological capabilities that LDC firms need to engage with, in particular the digital technologies of the Fourth Industrial Revolution (4IR technologies), and the digital connectivity at the heart of these technologies. It also covers the role of public policies in helping firms to acquire the technological capabilities for their effective participation in the global digital economy.

The Sustainable Development Goals committed the international community to strive for universal and affordable access to the Internet in LDCs by 2020, as well as ensure gender parity in access to basic services, including technology, by 2030. This places the interdependence between the goals of closing the digital divide and fostering the technological capabilities for the Fourth Industrial Revolution (4IR) squarely on the international and national development agenda of LDCs.

Digital technologies underpin ever greater swathes of transactions and the digital economy is increasingly inseparable from the functioning of the economy as a whole (UNCTAD, 2019a). LDCs have enhanced their investments in core traditional and ICT infrastructure to strengthen the industrial base of their economies. Some have chosen areas where there may be quick wins to be realized from digitalization – e-commerce can be considered as low-hanging fruit for LDCs to benefit from digitalization (UNCTAD, 2019a). However, because e-commerce mainly covers the trade and market exchange aspects of the economy, it constitutes an inadequate basis to capture the policy implications of the diverse changes that a digital economy implies for productive activity and the behaviour of economic actors. Therefore, it is essential to address the broader attributes and aptitudes which firms must have to build and maintain their competitiveness in the digital economy. Technological capabilities are at the heart of these attributes and aptitudes and assume prerequisite status for building and maintaining long-term competitiveness.

It is critical that development policies take account of national and regional strategies which support and incentivize investment in the acquisition of tangible and intangible technological capabilities. Some estimates suggest that firms with traditional business models and technologies in LDCs may still have a shelf life of two to three decades (Akileswaran and Hutchinson, 2019) if they don't adopt new technologies; however, policymakers need to act sooner rather than later. This is evidenced by the already apparent trend of a widening digital divide between and within countries. UNCTAD research on the changing digital landscape since the great financial crisis of 2008–2009 reveals that, while the COVID-19 crisis has accelerated the uptake of digital solutions and gave a solid boost to the global transition to a digital economy, it has nonetheless also exposed the existing chasm between the connected and the unconnected (UNCTAD, 2020d), and facilitated the entrenchment of the market power of already dominant players, especially digital frontrunners, across various industries in global markets. The literature also highlights a widening performance divide between more and less productive firms that might be driven by digitalization (OECD, 2019).

Digital economy policy implications surpass promoting e-commerce

The findings of Rapid eTrade Readiness Assessments undertaken by UNCTAD in 24 LDCs show that in addition to deficiencies in infrastructure and related access problems, LDC firms face significant gaps in relevant skills and capabilities. The assessments also reveal that traditional programmes of support to small and medium-sized enterprises (SMEs), e.g. through loan programmes and trade shows, are unlikely to be effective in addressing these issues.

Compelling claims about the unprecedented opportunities digital technologies represent currently dominate the normative discourse on sustainable development. These claims possess intuitive appeal and are fuelling technological optimism[1] across a variety of economic and social sectors, and also extending into the sphere of development cooperation. The optimism hinges on two central predictions about the impact of 4IR in contexts of LDCs: (i) the predicted ability of these new technologies to induce the creation of new business models and value propositions that stimulate inclusive growth; and (ii) the potential of latecomer countries, such as LDCs, to leapfrog development. Through a review of the current state of knowledge on the process of technological capabilities acquisition and evolution, and selected case studies on 4IR technology adoption in LDCs, this chapter sets out to critically assess how these two predictions fare in reality, and

---

[1] https://www.weforum.org/agenda/2019/09/why-the-4ir-is-a-fast-track-to-african-prosperity/ accessed 4 June 2020.

the lessons that can be learnt. The chapter builds a picture of some of the technological capabilities needed by firms to adopt and effectively utilize these technologies by specifically focussing on capabilities of relevance to the agriculture, manufacturing and services sectors.

1. Legacy and digital technologies: interdependencies and critical links

The emergence of advanced and interdependent technologies underpinning the digital economy is a source of disruptive change to the functioning of the world economy and has impacted the landscape of international trade. LDCs are admittedly not at the epicentre of this evolution and remain far from the technological frontier but their economies are inextricably linked to these developments because globalization has cemented interdependencies between economies. The deployment of advanced technologies across the world will shape LDCs' prospects for structural transformation, be it directly through their own choice to develop productive capacities, or indirectly through the impact on them of the actions of their competitors and/or trade partners. In international markets driven by global value chains (GVCs), these trends are typically mediated by lead firms and influence the relative competitiveness of participating LDCs. In domestic markets, these trends have the potential to reconfigure the complex network of intra- and intersectoral linkages underpinning the creation of value and the appropriation and retention of value along supply chains.

Development trajectories are also path-dependant, and entailing successive industrial revolutions built on technology adoptions introduced in preceding revolutions. According to UNIDO, the majority of low- and middle-income countries, including LDCs, are clustered in the first and second industrial revolutions. Their economies are characterized by limited production bases and low technological adoption. Most LDCs struggle with the application of second and third industrial revolution technologies. These economies potentially face the most severe challenges in absorbing 4IR technologies (UNIDO, 2019a), and remain encumbered with the challenges of facilitating the emergence of inclusive digital economies and struggling to assure the preconditions for the application of second and third revolution technologies. They are consequently at risk of being excluded from the current industrial revolution and its potential benefits of wage or productivity growth (Van Reenen, 2019).

Figure 4.1

Production technologies: From the first industrial revolution to the fourth

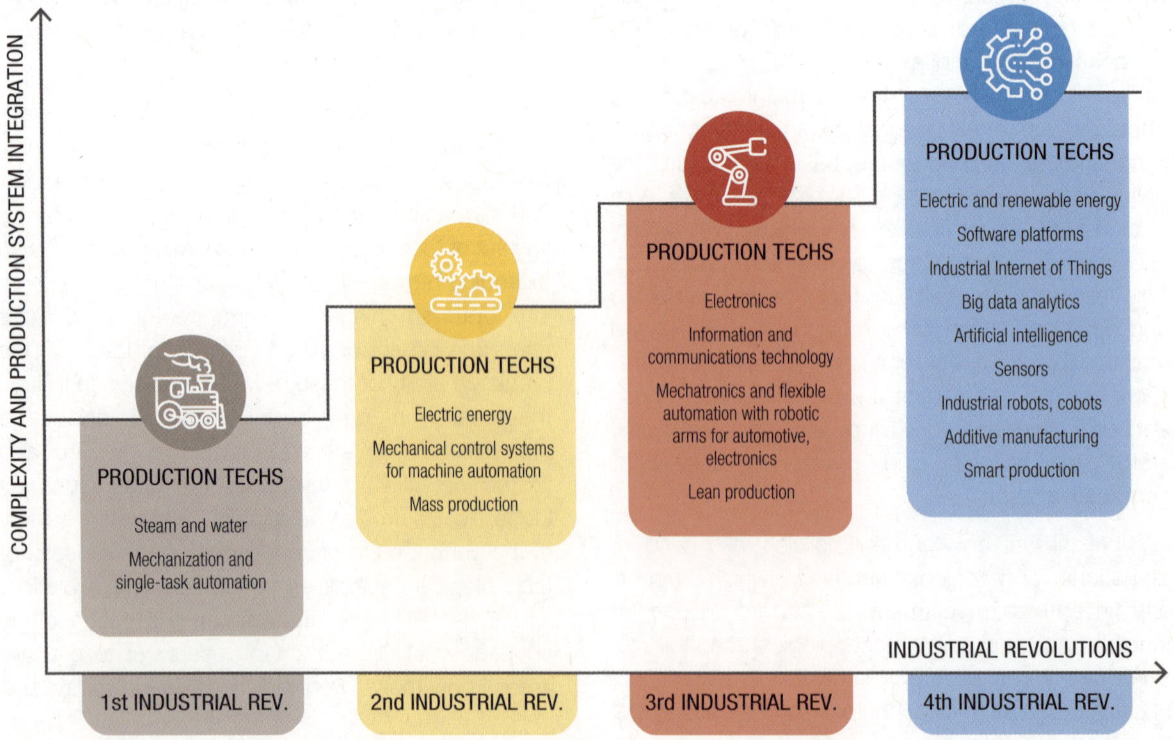

Source: Andreoni and Anzolin (2019); UNIDO (2019a).

There is also an interdependence between traditional and new technologies. Digital technologies offer opportunities for productivity improvements and leapfrogging; their economic and developmental impact is largely dependent on the broader status of technological upgrading and infrastructural provision in the economy. For example, many digital technologies rely on the adequate provision of hard and soft infrastructure to fully unleash their economic potential. Accordingly, access to the Internet represents a dimension of connectivity that is reliant on pre-existing technologies, such as electricity or transport infrastructure. In 2018 barely 52 per cent of the LDC population had access to electricity, imposing severe constraints on the scope for e-commerce growth. Likewise, and as underscored by various UNCTAD eTrade Readiness Assessments, inadequate regulatory frameworks and weak postal systems pose additional challenges. Moreover, leveraging 4IR technologies is often contingent on the availability of complementary end-use machinery, digital data and achieving sufficient scale to justify the fixed costs of physical and other related investments.

The advent of the digital economy has blurred the traditional distinction across economic sectors and enabled some services to assume features traditionally ascribed to manufacturing, for example enabling productivity spillovers and scale and network economies (UNCTAD, 2016; Rodrik, 2016; Nayyar et al., 2018; Hallward-Driemeier and Nayyar, 2017). Advanced digital technologies have facilitated and complemented a deepening specialization in, and expansion of, the range of tradeable services that fuels the so-called trade in tasks and the ascendance of the services sector as a source of value addition (Baldwin and Robert-Nicoud, 2014; Beverelli et al., 2017). In particular, the "servicification" of manufacturing has manifested in the increased reliance on services as inputs acquired, as activities undertaken within firms, and sold bundled with goods, or as stand-alone outputs. Manufacturing firms increasingly derive value-added from the inclusion of digital-intense services in their production processes, including through developing customer-centric business models in which value is co-created with consumers. They also progressively undertake wholesale, retail and transport services (Miroudot, 2017). A similar, albeit more incipient, process of servicification is occurring in agriculture with digital platforms (e.g. farming apps) with smart logistics and distribution services also beginning to drive productivity and diversification (Krishnan et al., 2020: 10). Patterns of structural change in LDCs (chapter 2) suggest that services segments offer limited scope for intersectoral productivity spillovers, being instead more readily associated with under-employment (UNCTAD, 2018). Such services segments fail to generate the productivity increases needed to stimulate sufficient demand for productive labour and trigger structural transformation. Against this backdrop, it is important to qualify the optimism that may be expressed for a shift to services as an alternative pathway to structural transformation for LDCs.

2. What makes digital firms different

The rapidly changing nature of technology creates difficulties in pinning down a definition of the digital economy (Barefoot et al., 2018). UNCTAD (UNCTAD, 2019a, 2017) adopts a broad approach that distinguishes between the core, narrow and broad scopes of the digital economy whereby the digital and information technology sectors are positioned at its core (Figure 4.2). The analysis in this chapter will address firm-level aspects of the digitalized economy encompassing precision agriculture, industry 4.0, and the algorithm-driven economy.

It is important to emphasize that access to information and communication technologies (ICTs) is an indispensable gateway to unlocking the promise of the digital economy. ICTs enable greater leverage of current systems and information; however, they complement rather than compete. Thus, firms that operate in an environment that is increasingly permeated with digital

Figure 4.2
A representation of the digital economy

- Broad scope: Digitalized economy
- Narrow scope: Digital economy
- Core: Digital (IT/ICT) sector

e-Business, e-Commerce, Industry 4.0, Precision agriculture, Algorithmic economy, Digital services, Platform economy, Sharing economy, Gig economy, Hardware manufacture, Software & IT consulting, Information services, Telecommunications

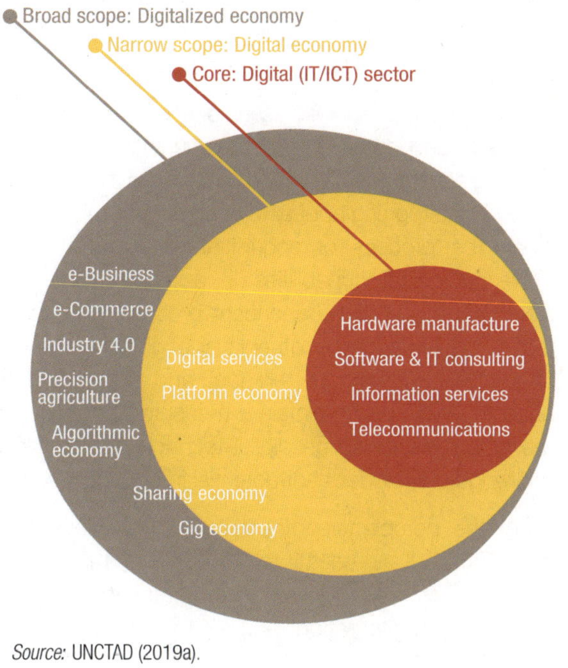

Source: UNCTAD (2019a).

Figure 4.3
The capabilities escalator

- Invention capabilities
- Technological adoption capabilities
- Production capabilities

LEVEL OF DEVELOPMENT

Source: Cirera and Maloney (2017).

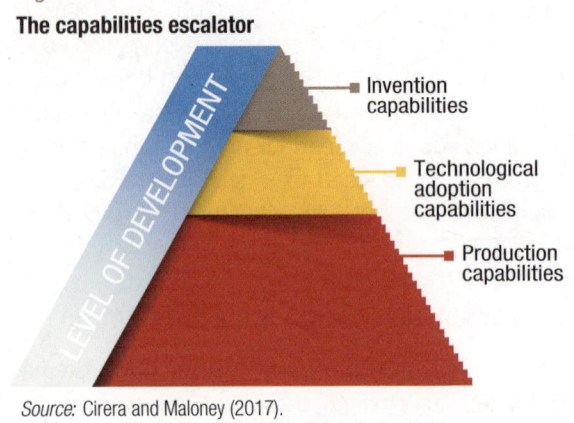

technology do not automatically transform into digital firms (OECD, 2019). This gives rise to the paradoxical co-existence of rapid technological change and slow productivity growth that has been documented in developed and developing countries (Johnson, 2019; OECD, 2019). Cirera and Maloney (2017) propose a capabilities escalator which depicts the sequential nature in the process of technological capabilities acquisition, and notes the truism that firms do not naturally move by themselves up the escalator, despite proven high returns. This assertion appears to be borne out by a global survey on digital business which found that the vast majority of businesses have yet to undergo successful digital transformation (Palmer et al., 2017, 2018).

Lall (1992) argues that, over the medium-to-long term, economic growth arises from the interplay of incentives and capabilities. Thus, capabilities define the best that can be achieved, while the incentives guide the use of the capabilities and stimulate their expansion, renewal, or disappearance.

This already signals that assertions on the potential for LDCs and other developing countries (ODCs) to leapfrog development ought to be qualified. Discourses around leapfrogging appear to be especially misplaced when the process of acquisition and deployment of technological capabilities is appreciated as an incremental and path-dependant process. The signs that ICTs have added another layer of global inequality offer clear evidence of this fact and underline the need to infuse and maintain a measure of nuance in the global discourse on digital technologies and the challenge of their dormant potential in LDC contexts.

From the perspective of enterprise behaviour and capabilities, it is useful to understand the digital transition of firms as an incremental process of digitization, digitalization, and digital transformation. Digitization addresses the core of the digital economy, whereby physical data is converted into digital data using ICTs. Digitalization is the use of digital technologies and digitized data to impact how work is done (*Bloomberg*, 2018). Digitalization necessarily depends on the availability of digitized data but does not inherently result in a fundamental change to existing production systems. ICTs help firms to deliver short-term improvements, or streamline and optimize existing processes, such as fulfilling procurement needs by undertaking purchases online.

According to Savić (2019), digital transformation assumes an umbrella role, encompassing digitization and digitalization as its constituting components. Dynamic and continuous changes in production systems can be expected to be at the centre of digital transformation and the lagged emergence of productivity impacts (OECD, 2019). Accrued advantages go beyond improving operational performance and reducing costs, although at different intensities across business lines and firms, the use, collection and analysis of data is increasingly an integral part of business models. Thus, digitally transformed firms are better understood as data-driven firms making strategic decisions based on data analytics and interpretation. This data-driven approach enables such firms to develop, identify and exploit new business models and revenue streams using ICTs and digital technologies.

Achieving digital transformation is the most challenging stage of the digital transition. It requires investments in long-term growth drivers for the vast majority of firms that are not born digital. It thus carries the greatest burden of the risk that typically characterizes investments (regardless of whether for short- or long-term gain) made by firms, particularly as complementary investments in skills, organizational changes, process innovation and new systems and business models, involve a high degree of trial and error and take time (OECD, 2019). Moreover, during this time of adjustment and experimentation, productivity growth may be low and can turn negative. A related concern is the limited number of firms in LDCs with surplus investment capital available for innovation (UNCTAD, 2018; UNIDO, 2019b), particularly entrepreneurial ecosystems in these countries are dominated by capital-scarce micro and small enterprises

3. The role of technological capabilities in firms' digital transformation

a. Defining technological capabilities

Technological capabilities are fundamental elements of productive capacities and are key to increased productivity, competitiveness and profitability for the firm. They play a central role in the integration and participation of firms and economies in industrial revolutions because they turn tangible, physical or intangible assets or resources (e.g. ICTs) into outputs of greater value. Cimoli et al. (2009) emphasize the linkages between micro-learning dynamics, economy-wide accumulation of technological capabilities and industrial development. Technological capabilities comprise that broad range of effort every enterprise undertakes to absorb and build upon knowledge utilized in production, as well as acquiring additional capabilities as an automatic result of that production process, i.e. learning by doing (Biggs et al., 1995; Cirera and Maloney, 2017; UNCTAD, 1999).

Economic literature recognizes the distinction between production capabilities that make use of existing technologies and organizational configurations to operate or maintain existing production systems and technological capabilities that enable firms to improve or develop new technologies and processes needed to realize a change in production systems (Bell and Pavitt, 1993; Cirera and Maloney, 2017; Lall, 1992; UNCTAD, 2020a). Like other technologies, 4IR technologies encompass elements of explicit[2] and tacit knowledge. The two types of knowledge are interdependent (Garcia, 2014) but the greater weight of tacit knowledge in the innovation process often underpins production systems change at the firm level. Tacit knowledge is present in individuals (employees) and firm processes, culture and values (Haldin-Herrgard, 2000). It is an invisible component of the innovation process[3] not easy to aggregate or disseminate and constitutes a source of sustainable competitive advantage (Thum-Thysen et al., 2017; UNCTAD, 1999; UNDP, 2017; Zhu, 2019). The increased reliance on intangibles is one characteristic of digitally transformed firms (OECD, 2018).

The investments of firms in technological capabilities are mediated by the entrepreneurial ecosystem, macroeconomic policy orientation and power dynamics within production chains. For example, an important aspect of firm operations in LDCs is that they have largely been driven by FDI-led integration into GVCs, and as part of national export strategies capitalizing on low cost and relatively low skill labour,

---

[2] Explicit knowledge is general, conventional and easy to express and thus possible to share, codify and convert as principles, formulae, data, processes and information.

[3] The development of technological capabilities is not the same as the ability to undertake leading edge innovation. However, innovative capabilities are an important element of technological capabilities (Biggs et al., 1995; Cirera and Maloney, 2017).

Supply chain governance influences investment in capabilities

as undertaking repetitive tasks requiring little in the way of technological capabilities. Such FDI seldom requires sophisticated technological capabilities; furthermore, productivity in labour-intensive services reliant on mainly low education labour cannot be readily increased through capital accumulation, innovation or economies of scale (Hallward-Driemeier and Nayyar, 2017), as the low education of employees becomes a significant barrier. Under these circumstances, the disincentives these factors can impose on investments in innovation by LDC firms cannot be overlooked.

The governance structure of supply chains has an important bearing on decisions on technological adoption and investments in technological capabilities. The benefits from technological investment are typically unevenly distributed between lead and follower partners within GVCs; elevated risks exist when players assuming the cost and risk of investment may not be the ones who can capture the resulting value. Similarly, firms at the same or proximate stage of the chain are rivals/potential rivals. These inherent conflicts of interest between GVC partners will be magnified rather than diminished by 4IR technologies, which have more complex skill requirements and other disincentives for technology transfer (Hallward-Driemeier and Nayyar, 2017; Manyika et al., 2013; UNCTAD, 2018, 2020b). For instance, Baker and Sovacool (2017) review the public policy support for increased solar and wind technology adoption in South Africa and provide evidence that tensions can arise between the commercial priorities of multinationals and the goals of local content regulations. The same case study also highlights the role of international standards in limiting the localization of renewable energy technology capabilities to the lowest skill segment of the industry. The literature highlights the role of investments in specialized assets, such as complementary technologies, distribution channels and logistics networks, in helping firms to bridge the disjuncture between value creation and value capture that typifies GVC regimes (Sako and Zylberberg, 2019).

4. The technological capabilities firms will need

The universe of technological capabilities that will be important for firms' transition to digital status

Technological capabilities are interdependent

is likely to be as vast as the number of processes, procedures, product lines, business models and strategies that firms might choose to pursue to set themselves apart from their competitors. Capabilities are likely to also vary by: sector; the segment of the production network that firms are active in; and the nature of the interactions they may have with other firms in the production network. They are likely to differ also by orientation, for example, whether a firm pursues an export orientation as its main strategy. They are equally likely to be influenced by internal factors that relate to lack of access to investment capital and low staff complements, particularly in respect of micro and small enterprises that make up the majority of firms in LDCs (UNCTAD, 2018). In LDCs, factors external to the firm can impose severe impediments. It suffices to provide examples of key technological capabilities found in the growing body of literature on the digital economy of broad application to the sectors discussed in this chapter. The interdependencies between the categories of capabilities presented makes it difficult to distinguish between them and they are presented here for illustrative purposes and to enable a discussion, rather than to suggest definitional boundaries.

a. Business and managerial capabilities

Among relevant technological capabilities highlighted in the literature are a variety of organizational and managerial skills that are commonly found across all firms and sectors, namely: goal-setting; problem-solving; decision-making; recruitment; continuous training and/or reskilling of talent; identification of business domains and activities that would most benefit the firm from rapid digitization; sourcing the right technologies and defining digitization targets and identification of best-fit suppliers; tracking and identification of competitors areas of competitive advantage, etc. Cirera and Maloney (2017) identify basic managerial skills as central to the introduction of new processes, technologies, and products, noting the severe scarcity of these capabilities in developing countries. They state that few firms can articulate long-run strategic or innovation project plans. Moreover, few have human resource strategies that could support the latter. They caution policymakers against equating innovation policy to frontier science and technology policy. There is a need for sustained policy interventions to help the learning or relearning process in firms' upgrading (Biggs et al., 1995; UNCTAD, 1999).

b. Data management capabilities

Data management capabilities across all stages of information processing from data capture and data management, data transformation to data delivery can be considered primary operational capabilities and supporting capabilities (Bärenfänger et al., 2015). They include capabilities on information processing, operational business intelligence, analytics and cognitive computing (Knabke and Olbrich, 2018; Mikalef et al., 2018; Pappas et al., 2018).

c. Dynamic marketing capabilities

Dynamic marketing capabilities guide innovation and aim to meet customer needs and include a variety of skills and are impacted by ownership characteristics, entrepreneurial orientation and industry partnerships (Xu et al., 2018). Dynamic marketing capabilities call for adaptability and engagement in vigilant market learning, that enhances deep market insights with an advance warning system to anticipate market changes and unmet needs; also needed is adaptive market experimentation to continuously learns from experiments and open marketing to forges relationships with strategic partners (Day, 2011; Diyamett and Mutambla, 2014; Jiang et al., 2019; Kamasak, 2017; Whitfield et al., 2020; Xu et al., 2018). Dynamic marketing capabilities include sensing capabilities that can anticipate trends; integrating capabilities associated with new operational routines; and learning capabilities needed to revamp and adapt in response to new knowledge (Surmeier, 2020). Dynamic marketing capabilities are key for high-velocity industries and sectors that operate in dynamic international markets, such as tourism. They are relevant to GVCs and rely extensively on combined knowledge derived from global and local contexts.

The remainder of this chapter discusses six case studies of digital technology deployment in the agriculture, manufacturing and services sectors in LDCs. The case studies highlight some of the constraints posed by the lack of technological capabilities and areas where policy support will be critical to unlocking the potential of the digital economy in LDCs.

B. Agriculture[4]

1. The innovation context

Global population trends demand additional efforts to keep food production at levels consistent with population growth and environmental imperatives (FAO, 2017, 2018a, 2009). The Green Revolution yielded a quantum leap in food surplus and led to each farmer feeding about 155 people. It is estimated that for the current revolution and projected population up to 2050, one farmer will need to feed more than 265 people (EY Global, 2017). Other related pressures include more diets of meat and dairy products, and increased global demand for food, land, energy, water and resources, such as phosphate for fertilizers. Agriculture also competes with urbanization if real estate development encroaches on farm land (Abu Hatab et al., 2019; FAO, 2018b, 2017; Streatfield and Karar, 2008).

Afghanistan, Angola, Burundi, Chad, the Democratic Republic of the Congo, Gambia, Malawi, Mali, Niger, Senegal, Somalia, the United Republic of Tanzania, Uganda and Zambia (FAO, 2017) are among the LDCs experiencing the most rapid rates of population growth. Asian and African LDCs are experiencing high rates of urbanization and remain reliant on food imports. Food-insecure countries are considered ill-positioned to guarantee adequate agricultural production to meet the global food challenge (FAO and Collette, 2011; Aminetzah et al., 2020; Schmidhuber and Meyer, 2014; UNCTAD, 2013). There is also increased interest by global business in agriculture as a growth sector, and the World Bank (2008) considers that growth in agriculture is three to four times more effective in reducing poverty than growth in other sectors.

a. The smallholder challenge

The United Nations General Assembly officially declared 2019–2028 the Decade of Family Farming. This makes this segment of farmers a key target of development cooperation efforts aimed at the modernization of agriculture in LDCs and complements the designation of 2020–2030 as the Decade of Action on the Sustainable Development Goals. Eighty percent of the farmland in sub-Saharan Africa and Asia is managed by smallholders; island LDCs and Haiti are likewise dominated by smallholders (Cayeux et al., 2017; UNCTAD, 2018).

The predominance of smallholders is a common feature across LDCs

The predominance of smallholders is a unifying profile across LDCs, as is their co-existence with usually larger commercial farmers and the predominantly rural nature of agriculture. This underpins differing abilities to use the same assets, including technology and resources in responding to market opportunities. This difference also applies within and across countries. The potential for differences between farms in scale, wealth and resources, including the influence of security of tenure status can be significant. In addition to limited technological capabilities and financial resources, heterogeneity in constraints, capabilities, resources, attitudes, priorities and cultural norms impact adoption decisions. Moreover, extension services in LDCs have been a prime target of downsizing in reforms under development cooperation programmes in the past (FAO, 2005). Smallholders[5] have an extensively documented history of low rates of technology adoption, including dis-adoption (Chandra and McNamara, 2018; Glover et al., 2019; Iiyama et al., 2018; Llewellyn and Brown, 2020; Moser and Barrett, 2003; Mukasa, 2018; Udry, 2010; Vercillo et al., 2020; Yigezu et al., 2018)

New technologies are often closely associated with the youth and strategies addressing youth employment. Such discourses often intersect

---

[4] Agriculture is broadly defined to include the cultivation of crops, rearing of animals, forestry and fisheries.

[5] The term "smallholder" does not have a widely accepted definition. This chapter adopts the FAO's definition (FAO, 2012a).

with the fate of smallholders through an implied "fix" that proposes to simultaneously address the productivity challenge in agriculture by substituting (older) subsistence farmers with dynamic young and tech-savvy entrepreneurs.

b. The productivity challenge

Making agriculture more efficient alongside other sectors of the economy is a key motivation for pursuing innovation in agriculture in line with the classical paradigm of structural transformation. Smallholders are widely recognized as being less productive and profitable, and are acutely vulnerable to climate change. Agricultural productivity measured as total factor productivity (TFP) (Figure 4.4), is lower and growing more slowly in LDCs than ODCs (chapter 2). It is the long-standing preoccupation in developing countries to raise the incomes of subsistence farmers and productivity of livelihoods. Eighty percent of production increases in developing countries are projected by the Food and Agriculture Organization of the United Nations (FAO) to come from increases in yields and cropping intensity (FAO, 2009).

Total Factor productivity (TFP) increases if total output grows faster than total inputs. Increasing agricultural TFP is important because it results in better jobs for agricultural workers who remain in the sector while fostering a more rapid transition of workers from agriculture to industry and services, where TFP growth is expected to be higher (UNCTAD, 2015; World Bank, 2011). The reliance on productivity reflects agriculture's dependence on inherently limited natural resources like land and water (Fuglie et al., 2020).

The TFP of Asian LDCs has steadily accelerated, albeit at a slower pace during the early years of the IPoA implementation and surpasses that of other LDCs. African LDCs and Haiti have experienced prolonged periods of stagnation in their TFP, which assumed a downward trend by the start of the implementation of the IPoA. The progress of TFP in island LDCs is volatile and in a general trend of decline; all of which points to LDCs embarking on the digital transformation of their agriculture sectors from different starting points.

In developing countries, women could increase yields on their farms by 20–30 per cent if they had the same access to productive resources as men (UNCTAD, 2015; FAO, 2011). Gender-sensitive deployment of digital technologies represents a double-dividend in terms of closing productivity gaps, while achieving enhanced gender equality (Box 4.1). Studies on land and agriculture in developing countries show that gender inequalities, compounded by an increased feminization of agriculture, affect rural and agricultural development. Increased feminization of agriculture has been linked to a variety of factors, including male rural out-migration, a growing number of women-headed

Figure 4.4
Agriculture Total Factor Productivity index
(2005=100)

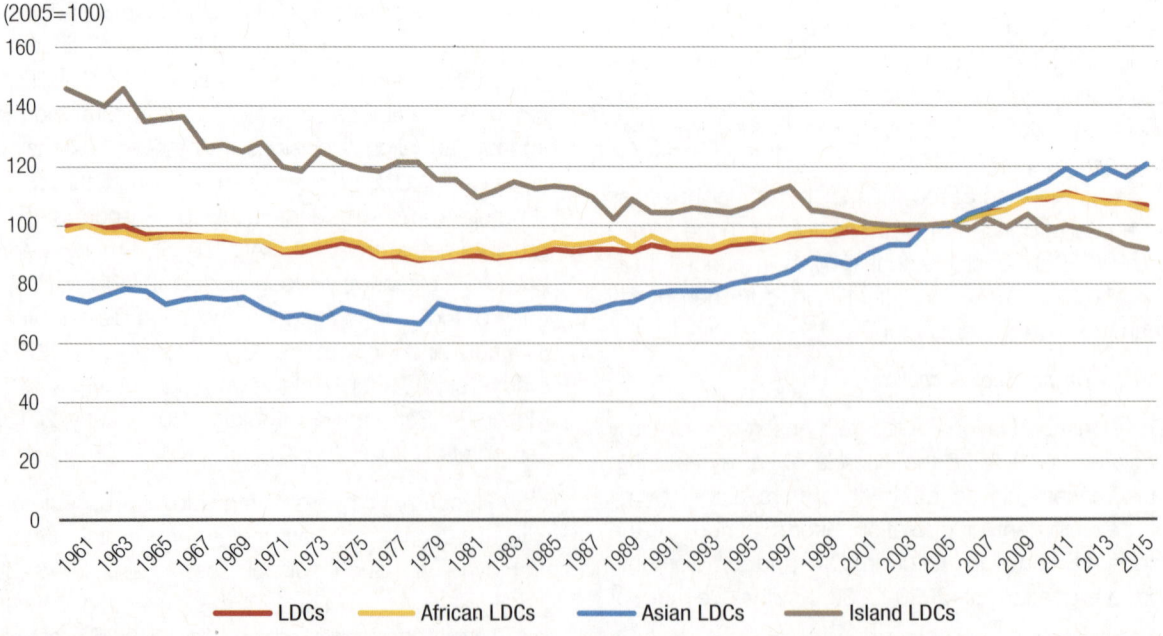

Source: UNCTAD secretariat calculations, based on data from United States Department of Agriculture, United States Department of Agriculture database [accessed April 2020].

Box 4.1 **Digital technologies and the gender gap in agricultural productivity**

The gender gap in agriculture productivity has been widely cited and studied in the literature. The difference in agricultural productivity between men and women has been quantified for five African LDCs (Ethiopia, Malawi, Rwanda, Uganda and United Republic of Tanzania) as ranging from 11 per cent in Ethiopia to 28 per cent in Malawi. Gender differentials in the access to machinery and technology explain 8–18 per cent of the gap, driven mainly by lower cash incomes and access to finance (UN WOMEN, 2019). Using national data from the Uganda National Panel Survey for 2009–10 and 2010–11, Ali et al. (2016) estimate a productivity gap of female farming of 20–30 per cent, mainly attributable to greater burdens of childcare. Gender differentials in access to inputs such as labour supply, land, pesticides and equipment, credit, information, skills, and extension services contribute to poorer productivity outcomes in agriculture for women (Huyer, 2016; Oseni et al., 2015; Obisesan, 2014).

Digital technologies cannot solve all constraints faced by women farmers, especially not those influenced by societal norms, their societal status and those specific to the acquisition of technological capabilities. However, they could potentially increase female agricultural productivity by improving operational performance and reducing costs through providing access to digital services (e.g. financial services), market information and enhancing their agricultural knowledge. Studies on gender equality in climate-smart agriculture confirm a positive impact of higher access to ICTs in increasing yields (Mittal, 2016; Huyer, 2016). Murray et al. (2016) argue that failing to incorporate gender equality into climate change adaptation will likely increase global gender inequalities overall. Global System for Mobile Communications (GSMA) estimates that closing the gender digital gap could deliver an additional $700 billion in GDP growth, primarily through benefits from providing necessary information and support in work and education (GSMA, 2020a).

Women are often predicted to benefit more from digital solutions then men, particularly in cultures where, due to social norms, they are more confined to their homes with much less access to farmers' associations and peer information and knowledge (CTA, 2019). Examples of specific initiatives targeting women farmers in LDCs and ODCs are scarce and the availability of gender disaggregated information on agricultural digital solutions is limited. However, with most agricultural digital solutions available through mobile phone applications and the most productivity enhancing solutions often requiring a smartphone (case study 3); before women can use a mobile or smartphone, they have to own one, be able to use it, know how to read, have internet access, and have the electricity to recharge it in the first place. Despite improvements in internet network coverage in most LDCs, barriers to mobile internet services for women persist. Excluding variance due to societal specificities, the literature cites women as disproportionately affected by barriers that limit mobile technology deployment for productive uses, such as low levels of literacy, low mobile ownership and urban-rural divides in access; factors often compounded by unaffordability of technology (mobile phones) and mobile data (case study 3), low digital skills, safety and security concerns. In some contexts, women may need to secure their families' consent to own a mobile phone and in poor families, the use of a single mobile phone may be shared by several family members.

Across developing countries, women generally have lower access to ICT infrastructure, which prevents them from benefitting equally from digitalization. Many digital solutions reach less women than men. Based on country case studies conducted by CTA only 17 and 10 per cent of the registered users of Digitalisation for Agriculture (D4Ag) solutions in Ethiopia and Senegal, respectively, were women. Despite improvements from a low of 27 per cent in 2017, only 54 per cent of women in low- and middle-income countries were connected in 2019. The gap is largest in South Asia, where females are 51 per cent less likely to use mobile internet, followed by Sub-Saharan Africa with 37 per cent (GSMA, 2020a). Large variation exists between rural and urban areas. For example, the gender gap in rural Uganda is four times higher than in urban areas, and in Senegal, women are 32 per cent less likely to use mobile Internet in rural areas, as opposed to only 11 per cent less likely in urban areas. Differentials also exist in the frequency of the use of mobile Internet and in the access to sophisticated services (GSMA, 2020a; Huyer, 2016).

Rwanda provides a stark reminder of why notions of access should be nuanced as, 4G LTE coverage reached 90 per cent of the population but Internet usage remains at 8 per cent (AfterAccess, 2018). Reasons for lagging uptake vary across countries, but the majority of women polled by an AfterAccess survey stated "no access device" (10 to 77 per cent of respondents) and "do not know what Internet is" (0 to 45 per cent), rather than "no mobile coverage" (0 to 4.2 per cent). The gender gap goes beyond telecommunications coverage and the development of digital agricultural applications. Moreover, many agricultural solutions using ICTs are under way in LDCs but their full potential for closing the gender gap is yet to be realized because digital businesses often view male farmers as the "lowest-hanging fruit" (CTA, 2019). A recent study in Malawi found no gender gap in learning but suggested a gendered-gap in the perception of transmitted information (BenYishay et al., 2020). Studies also emphasize that technology itself is not sufficient, "it needs to be understood in the context of local knowledge, culture, gender relations, capacities, and ecosystems" (Huyer, 2016: 122) underlining the need for nuanced responses to the gender problems in digitalisation. This will require, as a first step, enhancing the availability of gender disaggregated data and information on literacy, access and usage of digital agricultural solutions by farmers in order to deploy tailored support to enable greater possibilities to leverage digital technologies for agricultural development. In addition, technological empowerment requires to be backed by social empowerment (Singh et al., 2019).

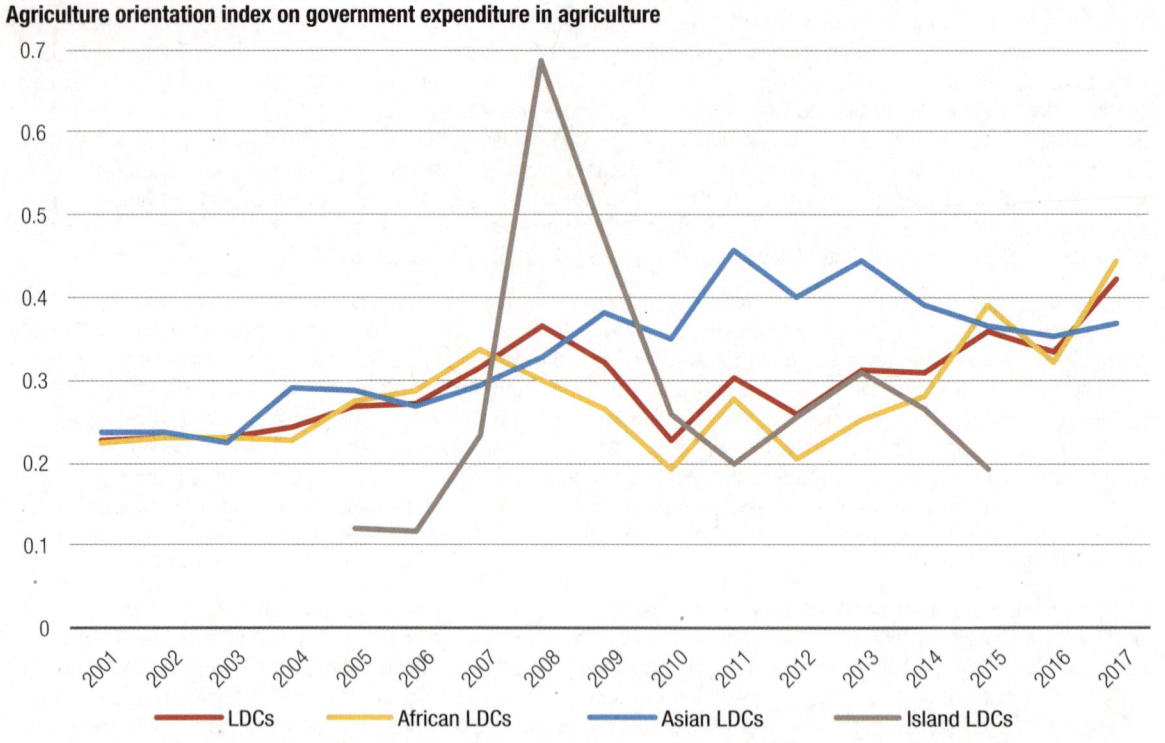

Figure 4.5
Agriculture orientation index on government expenditure in agriculture

Source: UNCTAD secretariat calculations, based on data from FAO, FAOstat database, URL: http://www.fao.org/faostat/en/#data/IG [accessed April 2020].

households, and the development labour-intensive cash crops (e.g. horticulture).[6]

c. Public research and development

Agriculture's dependence on inherently limited natural resources (land and water) makes it heavily dependent on productivity for growth, which in turn places a premium on agricultural research and development (R&D). The private sector typically under-invests in this area, especially for indigenous crops. In the presence of this market failure – climate change, which is a threat multiplier – public investment is assigned a specific indicator under Goal 2 (Indicator 2.a.1) and is monitored globally through the Agriculture Orientation Index. The Agriculture Orientation Index is defined as the ratio between the agriculture share of government expenditure and the agriculture value added as share of GDP.

Expenditure across all LDCs (Figure 4.5) shows vulnerability to shocks, with African LDCs and Haiti as a group showing the greatest improvement, albeit from a lower base than Asian LDCs, during the IPoA implementation. However, the index for all LDCs remains low and well below 1, which reflects the low agriculture orientation of public expenditures.

d. Farm size

Recent research suggests that there is no economically optimal agrarian structure, although some farm sizes may face productivity disadvantages depending on their country's level of economic development and circumstances (Fuglie et al., 2020). This means incentives rather than size are the main obstacles to adoption. Factors such as modern supply chains increasingly erode the productivity advantages of small farmers by creating economies of size. Size economies may also be significant in acquiring information and accessing services for farm, financial, risk, and marketing management.

e. Introduction to agriculture 4.0 technologies

Agriculture 4.0 (Figure 4.6) technologies comprise, among others, biologicals, digitalization and big data, imagery and sensors, and robotics and automation, and have myriad applicability and interconnectivity that impacts the entire agricultural value chain from input supply to the end customer. Agriculture 4.0 has an enhanced focus on farm management tools, the internet of things (IoT) and the use of big data to drive greater business efficiencies in the face of rising populations and climate change. IoT is deployed through agricultural machinery and

---
[6] See for example: Behrman et al., (2011); UN WOMEN (2019); Ali et al., (2016); Akter et al., (2017); Uzoamaka et al., (2019); Murray et al., (2016); Huyer, (2016); Oseni et al., (2015); Donald et al., (2020).

Figure 4.6
Agriculture 4.0 technology map

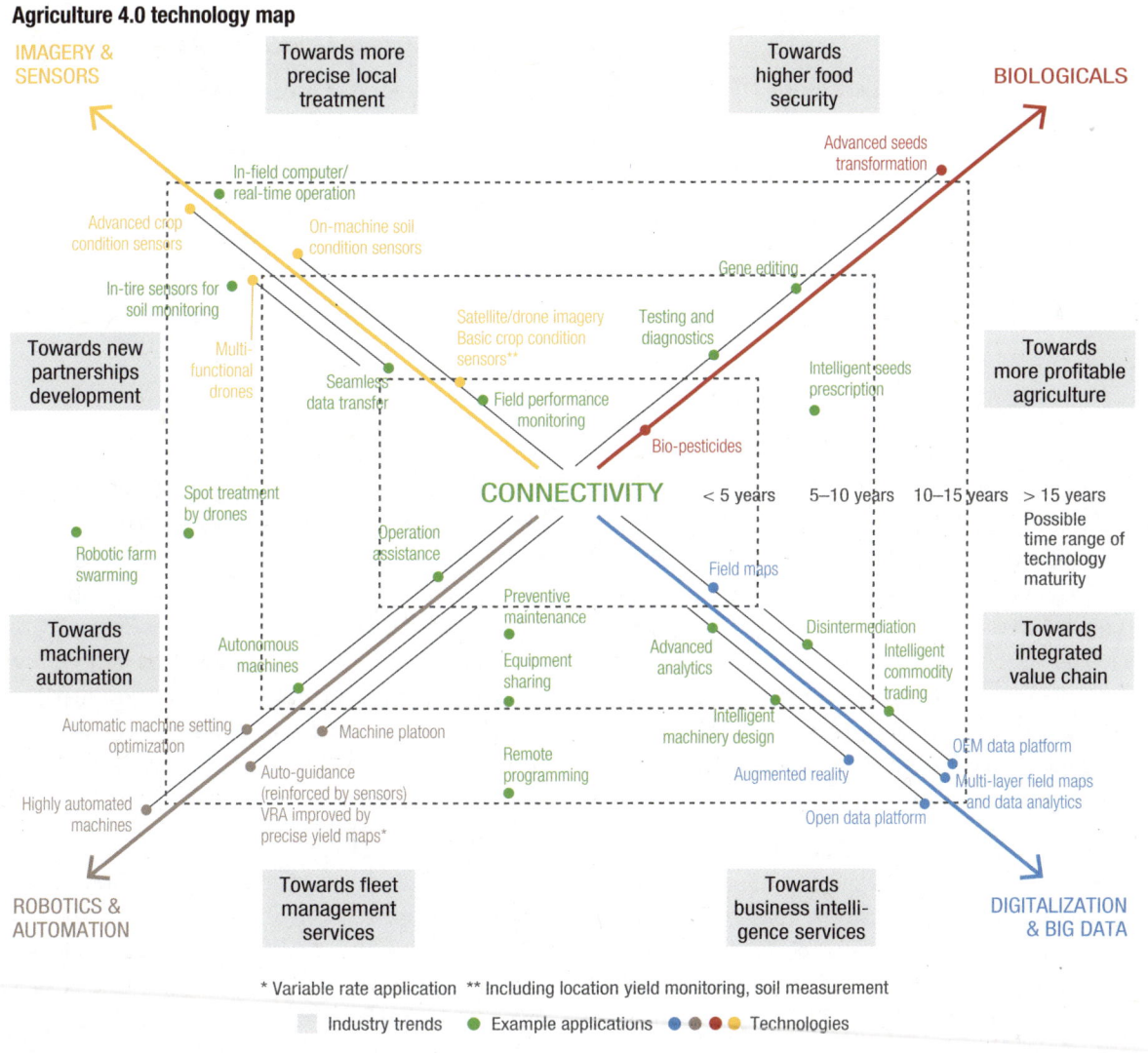

Source: Roland Berger (2019).

gadgets, such as drones that provide imagery of field conditions, connected tractors and robots, etc. (De Clercq et al., 2018; Agricultural Transformation Consultation Team, 2019; Talavera et al., 2017; National Research Council, 1997; Chandran, 2019; Tantalaki et al., 2019). They are frequently employed as part of precision agriculture[7] (Jones et al., 2017; Mulla and Khosla, 2015; Allen, 2019; European Commission, 2017; Klerkx et al., 2019; Saiz-Rubio and Rovira-Más, 2020; Tantalaki et al., 2019; Wolfert et al., 2017). However, challenges remain given the need for local adaptation (Tantalaki et al., 2019).

---

[7] Precision agriculture is also known as precision farming. This farm management approach uses ICTs and a wide array of items such as GPS guidance, control systems, sensors, robotics, drones, autonomous vehicles, variable rate technology, GPS-based soil sampling, automated hardware, telematics, and software (Roland Berger, 2019).

2. Agriculture case studies

The case studies address the two central predictions concerning the impact of digital technologies outlined. This section covers three case studies. The Myanmar case study helps us to assess how far the diffusion of core ICTs have induced a significant uptake of digital technologies by farmers. Two subsequent case studies focus on specific manifestations of digitalization through the rise of mobile app- and drones-based agritech services.

a. Case study 1: expanding access to mobile telecommunications to boost agricultural development in Myanmar

Myanmar has gone from minimal mobile connectivity to one of the world's fastest growing mobile market. The government's 2012–2015 Framework for Economic and Social Reform set a target of

The Least Developed Countries Report 2020

Figure 4.7
Digital agriculture use cases in Myanmar

Examples of digital tools	Digital procurement	E-Commerce	Smart farming	Information services	Weather and climate services	Digital Finance
Farmtrek	◆	◇	◇	◇	◇	◆
Golden Paddy	◆	◇	◆	◆	◆	◇
Greenway	◆	◆	◇	◆	◆	◇
Htwet Toe	◇	◇	◇	◆	◆	◆
Site Pyo	◇	◇	◇	◆	◆	◇
Tun Yat	◇	◇	◆	◇	◇	◇

Source: GSMA (2020b).

reaching 80 per cent mobile phone penetration by 2015, with a view to broadening access to rural areas, lowering transaction costs and to establish the foundations for eGovernment (Arnaudo, 2019).[8] By 2016, smartphone penetration reached 83 percent in urban areas and 75 percent in rural areas,[9] including 32 million farmers. However, Internet penetration stood at 41 per cent[10] in January 2020, notwithstanding a mobile broadband market driven by increasingly faster speeds as 4G and eventually 5G networks are rolled out (BuddeComm, 2020)

Agriculture is the logical focus of mobile value-added services for the private sector, including mobile telecommunications providers as the sector provides a livelihood to about 70 per cent of Myanmar's population, and dominated by small-scale farmers. Growth in the sector is vulnerable to climate change and extreme weather events. The ratio of extension staff to farm family is nearly 1 to 585, where an extension worker covers 5,081 acres of cropland. Productivity is low due to, among others, inadequate supply of public research and extension services; poor value chain facilities and services; low supply of certified and improved seeds; low input (fertilizer and chemicals) quality; and poor knowledge among farmers about proper fertilizer usage.[11] While the Government of Myanmar strongly encourages organic farming, farmers prefer chemical fertilizers for faster and higher yields.

From the perspective of consumer access to Internet services, the country is considered to have leapfrogged fixed access. Fixed broadband penetration lags due to a limited number of fixed lines and the dominance of the mobile platform. Unwillingness by operators to invest in fixed broadband infrastructure (BuddeComm, 2020) means that the basis for data analytics remains low, despite the apparent exponential uptake of mobile connections. In addition, demand for electricity outpaces supply. A disparity between smartphone and digital finance penetration is apparent (Roest and Konijnendijk, 2018).

Agritech solutions are at the forefront of Myanmar's emerging digital economy. Digital agriculture solutions are predominantly smartphone apps marketed directly to farmers. Most focus on the access to services, specifically advisory services, crop price data, and weather information – relatively low complexity solutions. One start-up enables users to hire agri-machinery, however, infrastructure remains a challenge. For example, (Figure 4.7) shows the use cases of the country's most established digital value-added services in agriculture.

In terms of gender, data show that women in Myanmar are 10 percentage points less likely than men to report mobile phone or internet usage (Htun and Bock, 2017; World Bank, 2020).

Anecdotal evidence suggests farmers limit mobile phone use to voice calls, Internet access to social networks and sending messages. Farmers also repurpose existing social media platforms to stay rather than gravitating to apps.[12]

---

[8] One of the least virtually accessible points on earth after North Korea, Timor-Leste and Eritrea (Arnaudo, 2019).

[9] https://www.statista.com/statistics/1063852/myanmar-smartphone-penetration-by-region/ accessed 6 July 2020. According to (GSMA, 2020b), mobile broadband connections reached 44 million or 75 per cent of total mobile connections in 2018.

[10] https://datareportal.com/reports/digital-2020-myanmar accessed 6 July 2020.

[11] Farmers often underapply or over apply fertilizers.

[12] Apart from the in-text references, this case study is also based on Arnaudo, (2019); Aye, (2018); BuddeComm, (2020); Devanesan, (2020); Htun and Bock, (2017); GSMA, (2020b); Roest and Konijnendijk, (2018); Sparling, (2018); USAID, (2015); World Bank, (2020).

Figure 4.8
Key M2M applications
(Percentage share in number of deployments)

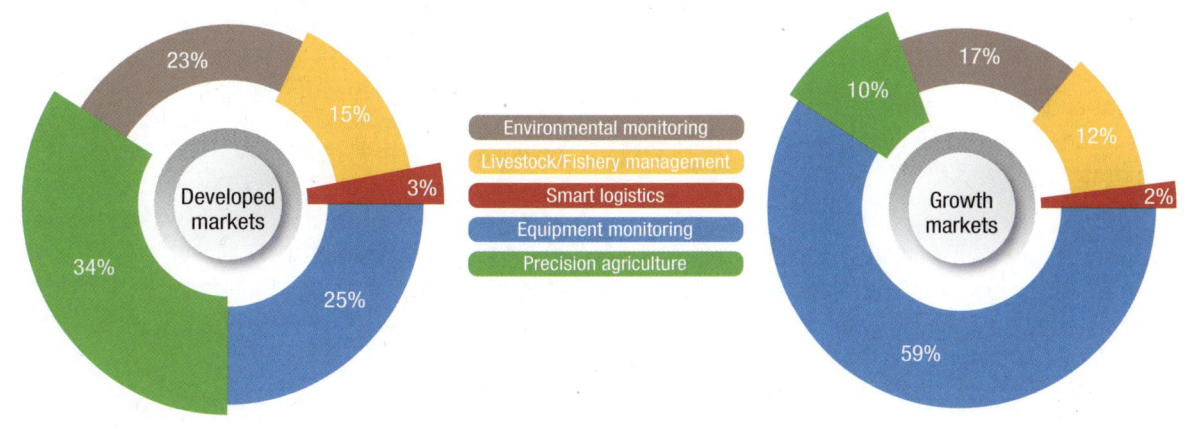

Developed markets: Environmental monitoring 23%, Livestock/Fishery management 15%, Smart logistics 3%, Equipment monitoring 25%, Precision agriculture 34%

Growth markets: Environmental monitoring 17%, Livestock/Fishery management 12%, Smart logistics 2%, Equipment monitoring 59%, Precision agriculture 10%

Source: PwC (2017).

b. Case study 2: LDC experience in the use of drones in agriculture

Agriculture is a leading sector for the application of unmanned aerial vehicles (UAVs) or drones. According to FAO (2018c), agri-business is the pre-eminent sector for the civilian use of drones, thanks to innovation in areas of miniaturization, batteries, imagery and remote communications. The literature on the use of UAVs to study crops in LDC smallholder systems is still limited (Chew et al., 2020), and mostly focused on the potential of the technology or donor project achievements. Concerns linger that the technology will remain out of reach for the majority of farmers for some time to come (Chandran, 2019; European Commission, 2018a). Compared to other precision agriculture digital technologies, drones are a more recent and less mature tool. Drone data is highly contextual; satellites orbiting much farther cannot compete (Yonah et al., 2018). Globally, motivations and use cases vary considerably.

In agriculture, drones are not a stand-alone technology. To create decision-level actionable agricultural intelligence, data from drones is most useful when complemented by data from other digital technology which draws on a variety of digitized location-specific agricultural information – making the total cost of technology (including maintenance) a critical factor in farmer adoption decisions and requiring public investments in digitized agricultural information (e.g. land and soil registries).

Among more advanced developing countries where an already existing stock of farm machinery and equipment is larger, machine to machine (M2M)[13] adoption is outpacing precision agriculture (Figure 4.8).

The technical base for fully locally operated drone systems may be sufficient in certain LDCs, for example Togo[14] has a drone factory and pilot school[15] and Malawi's University of Science and Technology is implementing drone training. However, there are still a limited number of local businesses active in drones services (Knoblauch et al., 2019).

To serve as an optimized decision tool, data from drones typically requires contributions and collaborations across several technical disciplines, including agronomists, farmers, GIS experts, surveyors, aviation experts, engineers (including software engineers) (FAO, 2018c). Specialists with digital capabilities are often required to design and interpret the predictive analytics and impact models used to generate actionable intelligence (de Jesus, 2019).

Lack of certainty that a farmer can effectively translate the information into actions that guarantee increased profitability, is a constant.[16] The substantial capital investment and technical expertise to be acquired and properly utilized makes drones acquisition difficult for many small- and medium-sized farms to justify

---

[13] Machine-to-machine communication, or M2M, is two machines "communicating," or exchanging data, without human interfacing or interaction. This includes serial connection or wireless communications in the industrial IoT.

[14] https://cio-mag.com/agriculture-de-precision-un-deploiement-de-drones-a-partir-du-togo-annonce/ accessed 13 July 2020.

[15] http://www.commodafrica.com/10-09-2019-le-togo-abritera-le-futur-centre-de-formation-des-pilotes-de-drones-agricoles-dafrique-de accessed 10 July 2020.

[16] http://m.theindependentbd.com/printversion/details/160688 accessed 10 July 2020.

M-agriculture dominates digital agriculture solutions in LDCs

the cost and less likely to benefit from economies of scale, even in developed country contexts (European Commission, 2018a).

Inadequate infrastructure (Internet connections for real-time output and data platforms facilitating integrated software analytics), lack of regulatory capacity, lagging standards development worldwide remain major bottlenecks in LDCs. Drone regulation, albeit inadequate, exists in Bangladesh, Benin, Burkina Faso, Lao People's Democratic Republic, Madagascar, Malawi, Niger, Rwanda, Senegal, United Republic of Tanzania, Vanuatu and Zambia. Minor references are included in aviation regulations in Chad, Mali, Mauritania, Togo and Uganda. Currently, the literature points to the need for a balance between public safety and reliable commerce with underlying trade-offs between over-regulation and promoting private enterprise.

Identified challenges linked to the application of agricultural drones in LDC-specific contexts include:

- inadequate access to electricity (for charging batteries) and spare parts;
- producing maps, 3D models, and other useful data outputs requires considerable computing power; lack of specialized software and adequate computing power, or Internet and mobile data allowing rapid connectivity to access cloud-computing services hinders timely production of actionable insights;
- presenting actionable insights in a way that can be easily understood by farmers;
- intense intercropping or high diversity of crop types often limit drone capabilities; monoculture systems are easier to assess;
- sustainable in-country operations and maintenance require local capacity building and partnerships with local universities and schools of technology;
- the possession of additional knowledge and analytics tools will not bring benefits on its own because local context and local idiosyncrasies count; drone deployment is "localized-knowledge-intensive", requiring local technological capabilities.[17]

c. Case Study 3: The emergence of agritech entrepreneurs in LDCs

GSMA (2016) states that mobiles offer a unique opportunity for agricultural value-added services (Agritech or Agri VAS). The market potential has been described as nearly limitless (Manhas, 2019). According to GMSA, the largest potential LDC markets for Agri VAS in 2020 are Ethiopia, Bangladesh, United Republic of Tanzania and Angola.[18] Global investments were estimated at nearly €2 billion in 2017 (Tsan et al., 2019). Investment in Africa-based start-ups remains small representing only 3–6 per cent of all tech start-up investment in 2018 (Tsan et al., 2019).

M-agriculture refers to agricultural services, technology dissemination and communication using mobile devices, such as mobile phones, laptops and other wireless enabled devices. The complexity of M-agriculture varies from low to high. Examples of low, medium and high complexity can be found in LDCs. However, there are indications in sub-Saharan Africa that entrepreneurs, users and governments' readiness for sophisticated solutions cannot match the scale of global innovation, which indicates a lack of managerial and business capabilities. Moreover, there are currently relatively limited M-agriculture employment linkages, although agri-finance is a potentially valuable area for start-ups (Chandran, 2019; GSMA, 2016; Tsan et al., 2019). However, it requires a unique set of capabilities that ICT/tech-oriented entrepreneurs usually lack (GSMA, 2020), and a lack of resources to recruit and retain talent. Unlike tech start-ups, mobile operators can scale up but they are not proficient in agriculture extension and advisory services. Partnership models underpinned by dynamic marketing capabilities between mobile operators, public agriculture organizations and institutions are emerging as a standard. The general and specific barriers linked to business models (Table 4.1) require technological capabilities to overcome. Common features and issues include:

- Digital agriculture solutions across LDCs come mainly in the form of apps (mAgriculture) that are marketed directly to farmers.
- The predominant Agri Vas use case are advisory services and information services.
- Agritech struggles to bring projects to scale, has low numbers of repeat users and most business models remaining unproven; highly

---

[17] Apart from the in-text references, this case study is also based on Chandran, (2019); Chew et al., (2020); de Jesus, (2019); European Commission, (2018a); FAO, (2018c); Knoblauch et al., (2019); PwC, (2017); Yonah et al., (2018).

[18] Modelled potential based on the size of the rural and agricultural population and the largest growth of agricultural workers with a mobile phone between 2014 and 2020.

Table 4.1
Business model features and barriers

Business model	Key feature	Specific barriers	General barriers
Direct revenue – B2C	Smallholder farmers pay a fee to use the service	Poor rural smallholder farmers have low disposable income and, consequently, very low ability and willingness to pay	Poor network coverage in rural areas where most smallholder farmers live
		High in marketing cost to drive initial uptake and maintenance costs to sustain user interest	Cost of ownership of mobile devices is still prohibitive for many poor rural farms
		Commoditisation of information as farmers discovered cheaper information sources	High cost of acquiring and maintaining content, particularly in markets with underdeveloped agriculture ecosystems
		Strong tendency of farmers to share information amongst themselves, creating many indirect users	
Direct revenue – B2B	Agribusiness pay for farmers to access the service	Limited scope for scale in market having weak agriculture ecosystems	Forging agreements with critical partners, such as content providers
		Some mobile operators may have limited skills and experience in managing enterprise relationships	
		Market decentralisation if agribusiness develop inhouse systems in attempt to reach farmers directly	Language and literacy barriers, especially in multilingual countries
Direct revenue – hybrid	Agri VAS generates revenue from both smallholder farmers and enterprise customers	Creating value for both sets of customers may prove expensive, especially content development and delivery	Growing involvement of women in farming activities and overall gender gap in rural areas
Indirect benefits	Mobile operator provides support for the service on expectation of increased subscriber uptake, average revenue per user appreciation from network usage and customer loyalty	Difficulty in quantifying indirect benefits to the mobile operator could negate the business case for continued support	Technology barriers, especially among older farmers and women in rural areas, leading to high education costs
Subsidized model	Donors/NGOs fund the service, mainly for developmental purposes or private companies fund the service as part of corporate social responsibility effort	Continued support depends on the primary objectives of the main donor	Forming strategic partnerships between mobile operators and third-party Agri VAS providers to ensure sufficient value creation for both parties
		A change in the main donor's funding strategy could lead to a scaling back of operations or complete closure	

Source: GSMA (2016).

active sub-Saharan users are estimated to range 15–30 per cent.

- The high cost of mobile data services is a significant barrier to wider usage in LDCs (Figure 4.9).
- Farmers are reluctant to adopt apps for a variety of reasons, e.g. preferadvice from peers or consider variation in crop yields subject to numerous unknowns too costly to concurrently control.
- Agri Vas may appeal more to farmers of high-value horticulture.
- Agritech is heavily dependent on donor funding and has difficulty securing additional private investment funding, especially in Africa; investment in complementary infrastructure (such as farmer registries, digital agronomy data, soil mapping, pest and disease surveillance, and weather data infrastructure etc.) is lacking.
- Uptake by women farmers is low in Africa and addressing equity issues is beyond the technological capabilities of ICT/tech-based entrepreneurs.[19]

C. Manufacturing and services

1. The innovation context

Globally the largest traded sector, manufacturing is valued for its labour absorption, higher paying jobs generating capacities and has the highest job multiplier effect on other sectors of the economy. It is also often a driver of innovation. Economic theory emphasizes the main role a robust manufacturing sector plays in sustaining long-term economic growth. Manufacturing is central to achieving Sustainable

---
[19] Apart from the in-text references, this case study is also based on Chandran, (2019); Baranuick, (2018); Bloomberg.com, (2020); Grow Asia, (2019); GSMA, (2020b, 2016); ITU, (2020); Manhas, (2019); Merriott, (2016); Thu, (2020); CTA, (2019b).

The Least Developed Countries Report 2020

Figure 4.9
Mobile-data-and-voice basket in PPP$, 2019

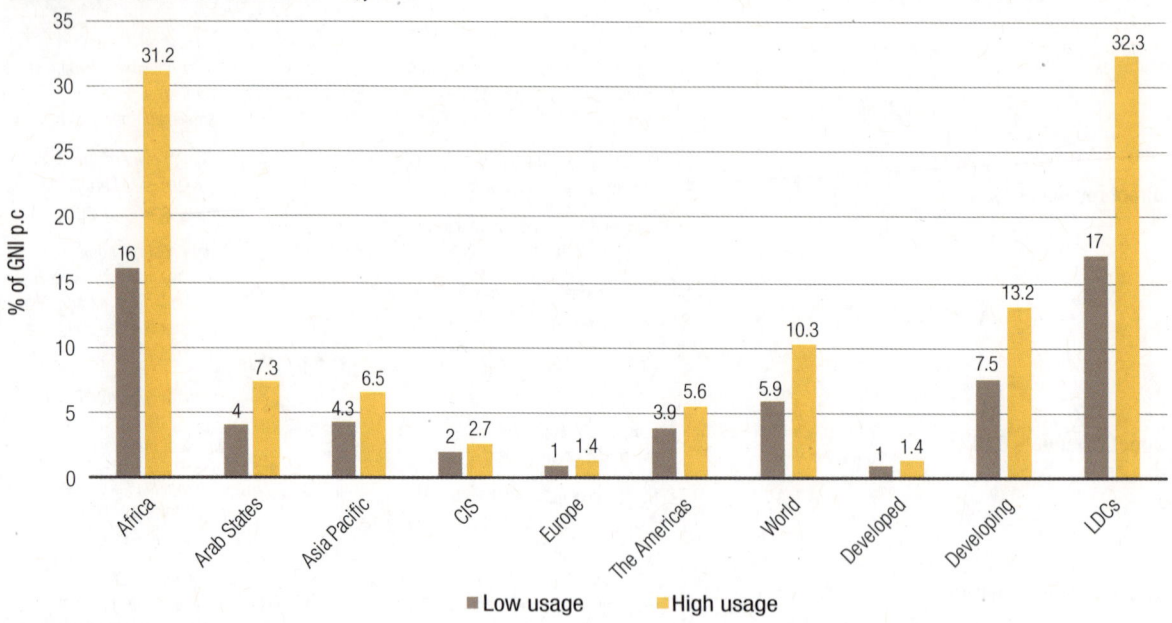

Region	Low usage	High usage
Africa	16	31.2
Arab States	4	7.3
Asia Pacific	4.3	6.5
CIS	2	2.7
Europe	1	1.4
The Americas	3.9	5.6
World	5.9	10.3
Developed	1	1.4
Developing	7.5	13.2
LDCs	17	32.3

(% of GNI p.c)

Source: ITU (2020).

Development Goal 9. Target 9.2 of the same Goal aims to "significantly increase" the level of industrialization in developing countries. The ambition of LDCs is to double their share of manufacturing in GDP.

The slow appearance of high-value manufacturing sectors and concerns around premature de-industrialisation in many developing countries, lends urgency to an accelerated reset of LDC manufacturing sectors to foster competitiveness and sustainable development. Manufacturing is key to the achievement of Goal 9 and is traditionally regarded as a critical sector to foster structural transformation.

As documented in chapters 2 and 3, most LDCs have been unable to sustain long periods of industrialization, and achieve a modest integration in global markets; had they done so, they would have registered a slow expansion into higher productivity activities characterized by a re-allocation of labour largely flowing from higher to lower productivity sectors and insignificant technological spillovers across sectors. Manufacturing value added (MVA) is low, and in some cases diverging from other country groupings (UNCTAD, 2019). LDCs experienced a period of deindustrialization in the 1990s when MVA per capita decreased at an annual rate of 2.7 percent. Despite MVA per capita growth of 4.1 percent per year from 2000 to 2016, difficulties in expanding manufacturing sectors has meant that the capacity of LDCs has continued to lag other regions (UNIDO, 2019b). Burundi, Chad and Malawi industrial sectors are falling farther behind on progress towards reaching Target 9.2 (doubling the share of MVA and manufacturing employment as a percentage of total employment) (UNIDO, 2018; UNCTAD, 2020b, 2020a). On current trajectories, LDCs are unlikely to achieve these targets by 2030.

LDCs have predominantly looked to foreign direct investment (FDI) and trade strategies to industrialize and access technology, not least because of the limited size of their domestic markets and low purchasing power of their consumers. This process has been reinforced by the emergence of global value chains, and as industrial processes increasingly embrace modern information technology, traditional manufacturing and production methods are experiencing digital transformation. Digital technologies are driven by a convergence of advancements in sensors, advanced materials and robotics with digital platforms, artificial intelligence and big data analytics. 4IR technologies enable mass customization and hyper-personalization of consumption through additive manufacturing (3D-printing), production-as-a-service through digitization, and new business models (e.g. the shared and on-demand economies). Fifth-generation wireless technology (5G) is expected to revolutionize digital manufacturing as it promises ultra-fast bandwidth speeds and massive connectivity to support a wider range of devices and services and process innovations. According to a survey on business preparedness for a connected era, overall, IoT is expected to have the most profound impact

Figure 4.10
Industry 4.0 technologies by most profound impact

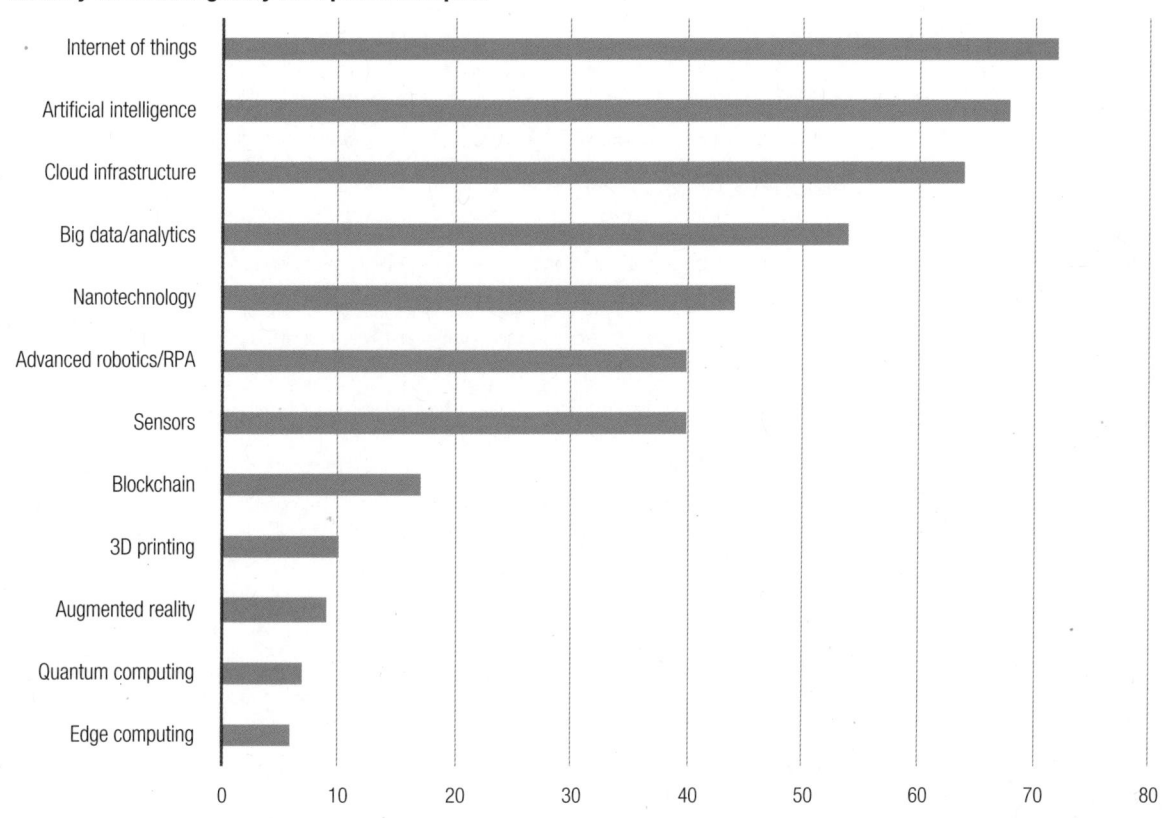

Technology	Value
Internet of things	~72
Artificial intelligence	~68
Cloud infrastructure	~64
Big data/analytics	~54
Nanotechnology	~44
Advanced robotics/RPA	~40
Sensors	~40
Blockchain	~17
3D printing	~10
Augmented reality	~9
Quantum computing	~7
Edge computing	~6

Source: Deloitte (2020); N=2,029.

(Figure 4.10) (Deloitte, 2020).[20] Currently, the three most significant challenges in applying industrial IoT technologies are the lack of interoperability standards, data ownership and security concerns, and under-qualified operators (Deloitte, 2017a).

Table 4.2 summarizes some of the most important pervasive and secondary technologies, including ICT, sensors, advanced materials and robotics in manufacturing. When integrated into future products and networks, these could collectively facilitate fundamental shifts in how products are designed, made, offered and ultimately used by consumers.

Additive manufacturing presents an interesting case because experimentation in LDCs is already taking place (Box 4.2), particularly in 3D printing. However, generally, 3D printing is still underdeveloped at the global level. It currently does not scale well; even as the range of printable materials is expanding. The Atlantic Council cautions that foresights that suggest monumental change is imminent are one of the fallacies surrounding 3D printing (Gadzala, 2018).

Enabling national economies and industries to take advantage of advanced manufacturing technologies like 3D printing will depend on support from governments and businesses alike to build 3D printing ecosystems by putting key elements of policies, research, education and commercialization together.

2. Manufacturing and services case studies

This section discusses three case studies. The first explores the prospects for Ethiopia's footwear industry in the light of the diffusion of 4IR technologies in the global industry. The second describes Uganda's efforts to use industrial policy to foster domestic solar vehicle manufacturing industry, thereby using renewable energy, an example of frontier technologies. The Uganda case study provides a relevant illustration of how LDCs can use an available window of opportunity to leverage industrial policy to expand their production bases using second and third industrial revolution technologies and business models. The third case study on trade and logistics provides insight on the potential of advances in supply-chain technologies for the manufacturing industry, and how this dovetails with measures to enhance trade facilitation, generally, in LDCs.

---

[20] For more detailed explanations on each of these technologies see (Ezrachi and Stucke, 2016; UNCTAD, 2017, 2019a; UNIDO, 2019a).

Table 4.2
Pervasive technologies and likely future impacts

Pervasive technology	Likely future impacts
ICT	Modelling and simulation integrated into all design processes, together with virtual reality tools allows complex products and processes to be assessed and optimised with analysis of new data streams.
Sensors	Integration of sensors into networks of technology will revolutionise manufacturing. Newly available data streams will: support new services; enable self-checking inventories and products; self-diagnosis of faults before failure; and reduce energy usage.
Advanced and functional materials	New materials will incorporate: reactive nanoparticles; lightweight composites; self-healing materials; carbon nanotubes; and biomaterials and 'intelligent' materials providing user feedback.
Biotechnology	Greater use of biology by industry; new disease treatment strategies; bedside manufacturing of personalised drugs; customised organ fabrication; engineered leather and meat; sustainable production of fuel and chemicals.
Sustainable/green technologies	Reduction of resources used in production; clean energy technologies; improved environmental performance of products; minimized use of hazardous substances.
Secondary technology	
Big data and knowledge-based automation	Enhance on-going automation of tasks; increased volume and detail of information captured; better understanding of customer preferences and possibilities of customised responses.
Internet of things	Business optimization; resource management; energy minimization; remote healthcare; autonomous products with embedded sensors.
Advanced and autonomous robotics	Obsolescence of routine operations in: healthcare and surgery; food preparation and cleaning; autonomous and near-autonomous vehicles; enhanced development of computer vision, sensors and remote-control algorithms; smart 3D measurement and vision to track human gestures.
Additive manufacturing (3D printing)	Essential 'tool' for waste reduction; reduction in weight; reduced inventories; flexibility in manufacturing location; product personalization; and consumer self-manufacture.
Cloud computing	Computerized manufacturing execution systems (MES) in real-time for enhanced productivity; supply chain and customer relationship management, resource and material planning.
Mobile internet	Ubiquitous smartphones for general purpose supply chain, assets, maintenance and production management; directed advertising; remote and personalised healthcare. Linking of battery technology, low energy displays, user interfaces; nano-miniaturization.

Source: UNCTAD compiled from Gadzala (2018); Deloitte (2017); Foresight (2013).

a. Case study 4: Ethiopia's footwear industry under threat from digital transformation

Ethiopia has implemented tax incentives for investment in high priority sectors, including leather and leather goods. Currently, the main investors in Ethiopia's footwear production are Chinese manufacturers. Of the 24 million pairs of shoes produced annually, only 15 percent are exported to international markets. Over 90 per cent of the exports are generated by FDI-originated plants. The bulk of production is destined for higher profitability domestic and regional markets.

Frey and Osborne (2013) estimate that up to 85 per cent of Ethiopian manufacturing may be under threat from automation, and that Ethiopia faced the inflection point between 2038 and 2042 (Banga and te Velde, 2018). The foundational requirements for advanced manufacturing, e.g. low tele- and internet-density, low broadband, etc. are not readily or currently available in Ethiopia. Low teledensity, coupled with low Internet and broadband penetration, with 4G only available in the capital, mean the foundational requirements for advanced manufacturing are absent. Ethiopia currently has the infrastructure potential to use only basic to intermediate cloud computing applications (e.g. email, web browsing and video conferencing) (Banga and te Velde, 2018). Ethiopia's industry is further challenged by unreliable electricity supply,[21] logistical bottlenecks and contraband. Investments in 5G will enable local manufacturers to run precision, high-output, and mostly automated operations but the government has yet to develop the necessary regulations; in addition, the oversupply of 4G mobile Internet, which consumers cannot afford, has left carriers on the continent worried about returns on investment.

---

[21] https://agoa.info/news/article/15316-ethiopian-footwear-on-the-rise-includes-data.html accessed 14 June 2020.

Box 4.2 3D Printing and manufacturing in LDCs

Some LDCs are developing nascent capacity in this technology: in Togo, an inventor realized the first 3D printer created entirely from recycled electronic waste to print small objects like medical prostheses;[22] in Malawi, an entrepreneur printed plastic face masks during the COVID-19 pandemic; in Uganda, Comprehensive Rehabilitation Services Hospital partners and Canadian organizations created prosthetic limbs more efficiently; and lastly Ethiopia launched its SolveIT![23] competition to create 3D printers in 2017.

Adoption of 3D printing technology is also occurring in developing countries neighbouring African LDCs. Algeria and Nigeria acquired skills training programmes in advanced manufacturing technologies and supported innovative local entrepreneurship. The tech garage in Lagos birthed Elephab, a technological start-up initiative to locally prototype and 3D print replacement parts for various industries[24, 25]. Morocco hosts the global centre of expertise for 3D printing for the Thales Group, it has also inaugurated the Industrial Competence Centre to develop and print intricate metal parts for the aerospace sector.[26] Similarly, a public-private partnership (PPP) between Aeroswift and the Council for Scientific and Industrial Research (CSIR) in South Africa is building the world's most extensive and fastest additive manufacturing system to 3D print titanium aircraft parts from powder.[27] South Africa currently hosts 49 businesses to provide 3D printing services, including in jewellery, tooling, and prototyping consulting and design services and supply of 3D printers.[28]

The take-up of 3D printing in South-East Asian LDCs (Myanmar, Lao Democratic People's Republic, Cambodia) is thought to be low at 1-2 per cent, and far overtaken by their developing country neighbours. Their proximity to more advanced developing countries and the role of South-South cooperation could be a critical advantage for some LDCs. Neighbours in South East Asia – Singapore, Thailand and Malaysia – are lead adopters of 3D printing, accounting for about 80 percent of the market by value. Others in the region are focused on developing related infrastructure and skills.

Sources: Gadzala (2018); AMFG (2019).

The footwear industry faces global headwinds from 3D printing, which currently accounts for 10 percent of global production but is expected to become the largest 3D printed consumer product segment, with a projected growth of $6.3 billion overall revenue opportunity over ten years (Sher, 2019). Several footwear industry leaders now use 3D printing to produce insoles for sandals, moulds and prototyping. Final parts already represent 34 per cent of all revenues associated with 3D-printed footwear parts. Much of the footwear industry's prototyping and mould-making services are currently undertaken in Asia.

While 3D printers still generally do a poor job of handling soft, flexible materials, the threat from 3D is not trivial considering that American sportswear brand Nike has re-shored manufacturing from China, Indonesia and Viet Nam to the United States. Germany's sportswear brand Adidas has followed suit. Both brands can access computerized knitting, robotic cutting and additive manufacturing in their home countries using automated computerized processes maintained by highly skilled workers maintained by highly skilled workers (EIU and UNDP, 2018). Should more lead firms accelerate their automation agenda, exporters such as Ethiopia would see their low-wage production undercut by European low-wage robot production (EIU and UNDP, 2018).

Assuming the 3D soft materials challenge will eventually be overcome, this may offer only temporary respite to Ethiopian and other LDC producers, e.g. Cambodia (Gadzala, 2018). In addition, for African LDCs, the future success of continental initiatives such as the African Continental Free Trade Area, (AfCFTA), Boosting Intra-African Trade and the Single African Air Transport Market. A significant regional market for Ethiopia's low-wage footwear products will be contingent on the impact of regional competition, other African countries have begun footwear production and the global industry might continue to relocate production to countries that proactively invest in capabilities to adopt and apply 4IR technologies.

---

[22] https://globalvoices.org/2013/12/18/made-in-togo-a-3d-printer-made-from-recycled-e-waste/.
[23] http://addisstandard.com/news-local-3d-printer-solveit-2019-top-prize-winner/.
[24] http://www.3ders.org/articles/20161123-ge-opens-lagos-garage-new-home-for-nigerian-3d-printing-innovation.html.
[25] https://www.3ders.org/articles/20171004-nigerian-startup-elephab-aims-to-increase-local-manufacturing-with-3d-printing.html.
[26] http://www.mcinet.gov.ma/en/content/thales-launches-global-centre-expertise-morocco-specializing-metal-additive-manufacturing.
[27] https://3dprint.com/166672/south-africa-aeroswift-project/.
[28] http://www.rapdasa.org/members/ accessed 19 July 2020.

Prepare and incentivize industry for digital transformation

A 2014 survey of 79 firms in the fashion industry (51 per cent of whom were leather and leather goods manufacturers) found that only 25 per cent possessed ISO certification, and the level of adoption of hard[29] and soft[30] process and product technologies was limited (Mekasha, 2015). Many local factories did not have a systematic approach to managing the production process and developing human capacity to ensure that machinery performs efficiently and effectively. Although some local tanneries and footwear factories in Addis Ababa have similar or identical equipment to those used in Italy, Turkey and India, deficiencies in process management, information handling, work task and workplace design and motivation has meant quality is an issue for many factories. Interactions with buyers, suppliers and other producers play a bigger role as channels through which Ethiopian firms acquire knowledge (Gebreeyesus and Mohnen, 2011), with inter-firm interactions locally still weak, despite the government's policy goal of promoting clusters.

The Ethiopian footwear industry faces near-term decisions to make on how it should prepare and incentivize its industries for digital transformation. Active engagement will require work to build robust technological capabilities. Ethiopia's education policy already focuses on digital literacy. However, while its ICT-focus supports students to be effective users of technology more needs to be done to transition students from being technology consumers to being creators. This requires the development of knowledge, skills and understandings of the underlying concepts of information systems, data and computer science that underpins the digital economy. In 2018 the University of Addis Ababa launched courses and workshops on data science and machine learning in 2018 but the focus is not on manufacturing. The prospects of Chinese investors accelerating digital transformation in the industry are uncertain. For example, while 72 per cent surveyed in China have adopted industrial IoT applications, only 46 per cent had clear-cut industrial IoT strategies and plans (Deloitte, 2017). Given the significant weight of FDI, Ethiopia could also consider reforming its investment regime to favour tax incentives for manufacturers to introduce apprenticeships and on-the-job training, including in more advanced production locations.[31] The country could also benefit from modernizing its industrial policy and developing job-creating service sectors linked to servicification (Akileswaran and Hutchinson, 2019).[32]

b. Case study 5: Uganda's Kayoola Bus initiative

Uganda's capital city is the backbone of the economy, generating over 60 per cent of its GDP. Most people in the capital, Kampala, commute by foot or low capacity transportation modes, including private vehicles. The estimated resident population is 1.5 million, with a daytime population of over 4.5 million people, leading to extreme traffic jams, massive losses in productivity and air pollution. In the past decade, at 162(μg/m3) pollution is up to six times higher than World Health Organization Air Quality Guidelines (25 μg/m3).[33] The Uganda National Environment Management Authority (NEMA), estimates that about 140,000 litres of fuel is burnt daily by idling cars, which is equivalent to almost US$134 000 worth in fuel consumption.[34]

In response, the government put in place strategies to ramp up domestic research and development established the Ministry of Science, Technology and Innovation in 2016, and tasked it with creating an enabling policy environment for STI and national development. It enacted the National Science, Technology and Innovation Policy (2009), the National Development Plan II and Vision 2040. Uganda's 2016/2017 Budget committed 30 billion Uganda Shillings (about $9 million) to support innovations and technology research. An additional $4 million was allocated to finance talented youth in the ICT sector. The government has initiated other measures to fund and support innovation and collaborative research and development, especially with the private sector. It has also leveraged the Kyoto Protocol's Clean Development Mechanism (CDM) to launch the Kiira Electric Vehicle Project.

The project evolved from staff and students' extracurricular activities at the Makerere University

---

[29] Hard technologies are those relating to facilities, equipment, robotics and computer aided manufacturing.
[30] Soft technologies are those related to management and information system such as total quality management (TQM), just in time (JIT), enterprise resource planning (ERP).
[31] For example, Switzerland has concluded agreements with 13 countries outside of the EU to help develop job and language skills [https://www.swissinfo.ch/eng/apprenticeship-agreements/29274220, accessed July 2020].
[32] Apart from the in-text references, this case study is also based on (Gadzala, 2018; Akileswaran and Hutchinson, 2019; Banga and te Velde, 2018; Deloitte, 2017; Frey and Osborne, 2013; Gebreeyesus and Mohnen, 2011; SmarTech, 2019; Mekasha, 2015; EIU and UNDP, 2018).
[33] Exposure to contaminated air may narrow or block blood vessels. It could lead to a heart attack, chest pain, stroke, or other respiratory diseases such as asthma, chronic bronchitis, lung cancer, and pneumonia.
[34] https://www.kcca.go.ug/news/316/#.XuT8Si17HOR.

College of Engineering, Design, Art and Technology (CEDAT). It grew into a national programme championing value addition in the domestic automotive industry. Kiira Motors is fully owned by the government and is funded through the Presidential Initiative on Science and Technology.[35] The project has designed and manufactured a prototype 35-seater electric bus, which relies on two lithium-ion batteries and 2-speed pneumatic shift transmission.[36] Power is supplemented by solar panels on the roof to increase the bus's range of distance up to 80 kilometres without refueling. The Kayoola solar bus prototype cost $140,000 to produce but is projected to cost $45,000 once mass production is under way.

Kiira Motors Corporation (KMC) partnered with CHTC Motors of China to acquire technological capabilities. The partnership agreement explicitly includes requirements for technology transfer, capacity development for Ugandan engineers and practical training on bus manufacturing with a view to establishing a modernized local industry; under the agreement, CHTC is also required to supply parts that are not readily available in Uganda. These collaborative efforts are expected to foster broader development of high-tech firms, and other spin-off industries in the economy.

The floor of the bus is made of bamboo, the interior is mainly plastics and aluminium with a steel superstructure and body panels; mostly sourced locally and providing opportunities for supply chain localization. KMC is developing a comprehensive local content policy to support local participation in the automotive industry. Just over 100 local firms have been identified as potential component suppliers through the Uganda Manufacturers Association (UMA). Truck and bus manufacturing lines and a regional facility for contract assembly planned to be developed along. Strategies targeting the youth are also in place. It is envisaged that locally manufactured components and items could include automotive batteries, paints, brakes, various metal components, seats, plastic mouldings for the interior panels and fibreglass rooftops, although until local capabilities have been sufficiently developed, all components are expected to be imported.[37]

Forward-looking public policy has catalytic impact

It has yet to be established if the initiative has any potential or whether it can achieve scale and profitability. However, the case highlights the potential of strategic forward-looking public policy to have catalytic impact, and illustrates how systems thinking and collaborative public investments can lower risk and facilitate systemic diffusion of technological capabilities. It also establishes that innovation is present in LDC contexts and the benefits that can still be reaped by LDCs at each stage of the technology escalator.

c. Case study 6: Trade and logistics services

Effective supply chain management is a critical element in the manufacturing industry and has increasingly been elevated as an independent function. It ensures that raw materials arrive at production sites on time and that finished products are efficiently delivered to markets and consumers. Industry 4.0 induces firms and industries to rethink the design of their supply chains. Firms nowadays increasingly need to take account of trends, such as growth in trade with rural areas, pressures to reduce carbon emissions, consumer preferences for online purchases and availability of digitally skilled labour that add to the challenges that logistics face. A significant proportion of supply functions involve services activities in trade and logistics. Digital technologies can be a source of innovation in all these sectors by contributing to increased efficiency and competitiveness of supply and trade processes. Like manufacturing production processes, supply-chain management applies digital innovations (e.g. IoT, advanced robotics, analytics, and big data) to jump-start performance and customer satisfaction. According to McKinsey & Company (Bradley et al., 2020; Bughin et al., 2017; Gezgin et al., 2017), the implications for revenues, profits, and opportunities from the deployment of digital technologies in supply chain management are potentially dramatic for firms. Business and trade models driven by e-commerce also have the potential to reduce transaction costs, enhance remote goods and services delivery, and contribute to market integration. According to ITC,[38] emerging success

---

[35] The initiative works through various bodies including the Uganda Industrial Research Institute (UIRI), the Uganda National Council of Science and Technology (UNCST), Makerere University Institute of Science and Technology/Food Science, and the various research stations across the country. http://www.statehouse.go.ug/presidential-initiatives/science-and-technology

[36] Kayoola Solar bus: http://kiiramotors.com/edvehicles/kayoola-solar-bus/.

[37] https://www.256businessnews.com/kiira-motors-identifies-a-century-for-local-content-in-automotive-value-chain/

[38] ITC (2018). What sells in e-commerce: New evidence from Asian LDCs. International Trade Center. Geneva. Online at https://www.intracen.org/publication/What-sells-in-e-commerce/.

> **Advanced technologies have the potential to boost trade facilitation**

stories in cross-border e-commerce by LDCs, including Bangladesh, Cambodia, Lao People's Democratic Republic, Myanmar and Nepal, engaging in merchandise transactions in agricultural products, food and beverages, textiles and crafts on Alibaba's B2B platform. B2C trade dominates e-commerce in other LDCs, such as Rwanda, where it is mainly dedicated to the airline, hospitality, health, banking, food delivery and courier services sectors. Similarly, in Uganda, customer-facing mobile app-enabled platforms connect customers to service providers (such as motorbike taxis) and boost the sales of many small Ugandan traders.[39]

The potential application of digital technologies to trade facilitation ranges from establishing paperless trading to enhancing the efficiency of transportation infrastructure and transportation flows, including postal services in the case of e-commerce.[40] For example, the COVID-19 pandemic has increased business to consumer (B2C) and business to business (B2B) e-commerce – it is expected that this trend will endure. At the firm level, business and trade models driven by e-commerce have the potential of reducing transaction costs, enhancing remote goods and services delivery, and contributing to market integration. The global value of e-commerce sales (B2B and B2C) reached nearly $26 trillion in 2018, accounting for 30 percent of world GDP; an annual increase of 8 per cent (UNCTAD, 2020c). The bulk of these dividends were, however, realized in developed and ODCs, not LDCs. Of economies that benefitted the least, LDCs accounted for 90 per cent.[41]

Enhancements to optimize supply chain management increasingly explain the widening disparity in profits and degrees of operational excellence in the global corporate-performance race. Digital supply chain require in-firm technological capabilities, and also at the level of the environment in which industries operate. For business, paperless trade provides a unique opportunity to reduce trade costs by streamlining information flow, and simplifying the exchange of required documents or contractual arrangements for cross-border trade in goods and services, thereby curbing cumbersome regulatory procedures. In LDCs, the private sector often battles physical infrastructure bottlenecks and lengthy custom procedures. For example, digital trade facilitation measures are estimated to reduce trade costs for businesses by up to 40 per cent in LDCs in Asia and the Pacific (Duval et al., 2018) The trade and logistic transparency and performance of LDCs will increasingly be contingent on if digitalization is effectively mainstreamed in trade facilitation reforms with the aim of enabling the efficiency of logistics systems, especially in LDCs that are, or seek to position themselves, as transit hubs.

Advanced technologies, including drones, mobile applications and blockchain have the potential to boost cross-border trade facilitation and supply chain management.[42] For example, drones have been used for underwater inspection and port infrastructure maintenance, inspecting bridges and tunnels, and monitoring traffic. Blockchain has the potential to revolutionize the tracing of goods, their content and original source unlocking dividends in terms of customs clearance and settlement, cross-border cooperation, tax compliance and a variety of payment transactions (UNECE, 2020).

Raising the efficiency of logistics and distribution channels at the level of the economy, a key factor for economic competitiveness and integration into global and regional value chains, is critical for landlocked and coastal LDCs and is a vital complement to the internal efforts undertaken by firms to enhance their individual performance.

The digitalization of border procedures has yielded tangible outcomes across LDCs. In Senegal, automated and digitalized custom clearances, the implementation of the e-trade data platform and paperless administration system for cargo-preclearance have all contributed to significant reductions in time and costs. Registration time for custom declaration decreased from 2 days to 15 minutes, customs pre-clearance process dropped from 2 days to 7 hours, and clearance for exports and imports decreased from 14 days and

---

[39] UNCTAD (2020. Ugandan e-commerce platforms power recovery from COVID-19 crisis. Online at https://unctad.org/en/pages/newsdetails.aspx?OriginalVersionID=2442.

[40] WEF (2017). Supply Chain and Transport Briefing. Geneva. World Economic Forum.

[41] The Index is calculated as the equally weighted average of four indicators: account ownership at a financial institution or with a mobile-money-service provider (% of population above 15); Individuals using the Internet (% of population); Postal Reliability Index; and, Secure Internet servers (per 1 million people).

[42] International Finance (2019). Technology uptake drives African logistics innovation. Logistics Magazine, September-October issue. Online at https://internationalfinance.com/technology-uptake-drives-african-logistics-innovation/.

CHAPTER 4: Transition to the digital economy: technological capabilities as drivers of productivity

Figure 4.11
Regional trade facilitation scores by dimension

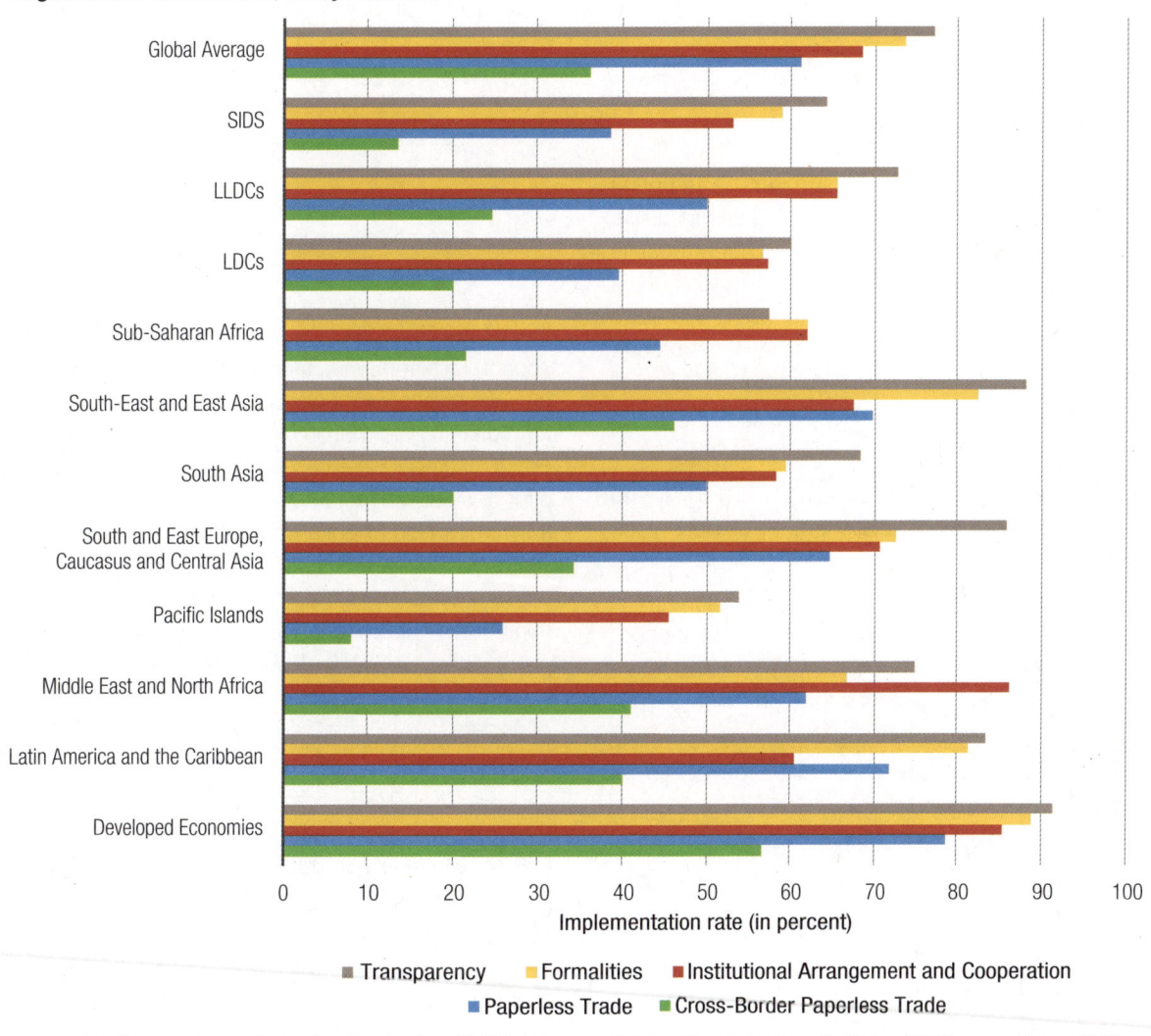

Implementation rate (in percent)

Categories (top to bottom): Global Average, SIDS, LLDCs, LDCs, Sub-Saharan Africa, South-East and East Asia, South Asia, South and East Europe, Caucasus and Central Asia, Pacific Islands, Middle East and North Africa, Latin America and the Caribbean, Developed Economies.

Legend: Transparency ■ Formalities ■ Institutional Arrangement and Cooperation ■ Paperless Trade ■ Cross-Border Paperless Trade

Source: UNCTAD secretariat compilation, based on data from UN Global Survey on Digital and Sustainable Trade Facilitation, 2019 [accessed August 2020].

18 days to 1 day, respectively; time for removal of goods from ports decreased three to two days (UN-OHRLLS, 2017). In Eastern African Community (EAC) member countries, the implementation of electronic cargo tracking systems contributes to reduced transit time, enhanced cargo safety, and helps traders and customers to better predict the arrival of shipments, while at the same time as boosting revenue collection for customs and other trade-related authorities (Kilonzi and Kanai, 2020)). Nevertheless, the UN Global Survey on Digital and Sustainable Trade Facilitation 2019,[43] shows that LDCs lag global implementation of enhanced trade facilitation measures. LDCs implemented 20.16 per cent and 39.64 per cent of cross-border paperless trade[44] and paperless trade,[45] respectively, of measures foreseen by the WTO Trade Facilitation Agreement that came into force in 2017, compared to respective global averages of 36.15 and 62.76 per cent (Figure 4.11).

---

[43] The UN Global Survey on Digital and Sustainable Trade Facilitation, Online at untfsurvey.org, 2019.

[44] *Cross-border paperless* trade measures in the UN Survey accounts for laws and regulations for electronic transactions, paperless collection of payment from a documentary letter of credit, electronic exchange of SPS Certificate, recognized certification authority, electronic exchange of Customs declaration.

[45] *Paperless trade* measures account for automated customs systems, electronic application for custom refunds, e-payment of customs duties and fees, electronic application and issuance of preferential certificate of origin, electronic submissions of air cargo manifests, internet connection available to customs and other trade control agencies, electronic single windows systems, electronic submission of customs declarations, electronic application of import and export permit.

> **Deep understanding of digital technologies is needed for policy decisions**

With such notable successes, it might be tempting to assume that digitization is advancing well in LDCs. However, digitalizing trade facilitation is not without its challenges for them. Policymakers will need to have a thorough understanding of digital technologies to make the right investment decisions in infrastructure, technologies and appropriate regulatory frameworks/ capacity, and identify and develop talent to avoid stranded assets (both human and physical).

An UNCTAD assessment (UNCTAD, 2019b) found that the key underlying challenges in LDCs include aspects linked to the lack of technological capabilities and barriers to their acquisition, including:

- Limited awareness by policymakers, businesses and consumers of the relevance of e-commerce to their business transactions.
- Low access to and limited experience of online payments, contributing to the prominence of cash-based transactions.
- Weak institutional, legal and regulatory environments, including for consumer protection.
- Lack of digital business development skilling, especially for MSMEs.
- Pervasive barriers for women and the youth.

Supply-chain transformations at the firm and industry level encompass technology and operations, and call for appropriate and targeted investments underpinned by market intelligence and experience. Strengths in organizational culture and strategic long-term visions (intangible technological capabilities) underpin firm potential in the global corporate-performance race, as do the magnitude and the scope of digital investments, including in developing supporting talent and capabilities to build and reinforce operational agility along multiple dimensions. LDC firms are acutely disadvantaged in all respects. Moreover, with the function often located in multinational lead firms' headquarters, already severe challenges to technological capabilities transfer are further constrained in LDC firms located far from the centre of power of international production networks.

As the characteristic convergence of digital technologies in 4IR deepens and accelerates intersectoral linkages and interdependence, policymakers in LDCs will need to adopt integrated cross-cutting and coherent policy approaches to strengthen and grow the industrial bases of their respective economies.

D. Case study synthesis

Much of the literature on digital technologies in developing countries and LDCs is focused on highlighting the potential benefits and uses of these technologies. All the case studies highlight the signs of the digital economy, such as the process of e-government, roll out of e-agriculture, universal/inclusive access to the Internet and mobile phones do not signify that economic actors will automatically mobilize available technologies for productive purposes. Policy strategies for digital transformation exclusively embedded within or substituted for by ICT strategies do not necessarily offer a window into the process of transition for firms from digitization to digital transformation. They may risk missing the mark. For instance, it could be argued that the returns to the diffusion of broadband in Myanmar might have been more far-reaching if the strategy were driven by a sufficiently balanced approach to consumption and productive sector-facing considerations. Nevertheless, while highlighting the dangers of narrow technology-centric approaches and consideration of firm-level dynamics, the case study confirms that government policies and frameworks can be powerful driving forces behind digitalization. Indeed, high-level political commitment to maximizing economy-wide benefits of ICTs is not always lacking in LDCs.

While instances of farmer acquisition of frontier technologies beyond AgriVas services are hard to find, the case studies show that farmers often lack the resources to move to a higher level in exploiting the technology. Many farmers and agritech entrepreneurs do not, as yet, have the skills, access to energy or affordable broadband to take advantage of digital technologies. Moreover, Agri VAS services (Myanmar, drones and agritech case studies) confirm that in LDC contexts, conditions for profitable agritech entrepreneurship and technological capabilities development are difficult. These are limited by factors that are internal and external to entrepreneurs. Lastly, the studies highlight signs that the balance of power in agriculture supply chains and value chains can be a significant impediment to the profitability of smallholders in LDC contexts.

Agritech entrepreneurs lack the critical range of digital technological capabilities to design and effectively deliver agritech business models that deliver profitability through scale, which requires both an increasing number of farmer adopting their apps and a critical mass of repeat users. LDC agritech entrepreneurs will need to build multidisciplinary teams and find innovative business models to develop increasingly complex products. The agriculture case studies underline requirements for increased partnerships and collaboration at meso and micro level, including across multiple disciplines by, among others, breaking down silos across technical disciplines, as this is a prerequisite for appropriate and viable digital solutions. Pools of digitally skilled talent and business advisory experts and advice on better business models is needed. The current overwhelming presence of donor, private sector and NGO project-type initiatives in agritech might make it difficult to identify and address skills and capabilities gaps in a systematic and targeted way, and potentially complicates coordination and the learning of lessons (UNCTAD, 2019c).

In all of the case studies, it is clear that adequate infrastructure and related services development will be key to driving structural transformation in LDCs. The case study on services and trade facilitation shows that improvements in the enabling environment and investments by firms are interdependent. LDCs with lower transport and communication costs can stimulate and enhance returns to technological capabilities investments made by firms. Leveraging joint investments could offer advantages in this respect. For African LDCs, the advent of the AfCFTA, might offer some impetus to counter technological inertia in forms, and generate opportunities for the uptake of digital technologies, digital transformation, new business models and attract investors.

The case study on Ethiopia's footwear industry provides valuable insights on how gains from traditional industrial and export orientation policies that have served LDCs well in the past are being rendered obsolete by the digital economy. Firms in these countries will increasingly be challenged by these trends. However, the Uganda case study also shows that strategic vision and deployment of traditional industrial policies and systems thinking remains relevant in some industries; it also confirms how such policies could have a catalytic impact by lowering firms' risks through socializing the costs of technological capabilities development. In such cases, the policy initiatives facilitate the movement up the technology escalator and systematizes the impact of technological advancement at meso levels.

E. Conclusions

Innovation is occurring in different LDCs but these initiatives are currently hamstrung by a lack of technological capabilities. Still, the possibility that

> **The discourse on leapfrogging understates the challenge faced by LDCs**

digital technologies uptake in some industries or sectors (e.g. retail services) might be easier, cannot be discounted. Notable example of successful cases of digital technology deployments provide encouragement but place in sharp relief key structural challenges in LDCs; they also confirm that the discourse on leapfrogging understates the magnitude of the effort in capital and human resources investments individual firms in LDCs need to make to leverage advanced technologies. Furthermore, it conceals the magnified threat of expanding new and further entrenching existing gender inequalities. More nuanced assessments are needed, especially in view of the lagged stages of technological capabilities acquisition and the complexity of 4IR technologies packaged in suites of converged technologies.

LDCs have three concurrent opportunities to pursue. The first lies in the need to continue to consolidate on gains already achieved in raising productivity and fostering structural transformation. As illustrated by the Uganda case study, this can be achieved by strategic use of industrial policies. Studies suggest that some LDCs have the necessary breathing space for traditional business models to succeed. The second opportunity lies in the use of digital technologies, especially ICTs, to accelerate and strengthen the latter process of consolidation – e-commerce being an obvious example. The third opportunity is to actively pursue the digital transformation of firms in the economy as this process is path-dependent and takes time. The size of investments and the breadth of the public policy reconfigurations needed to support digital transformation are likely to be substantial, and in a climate of habitually constrained LDC budgets, strategic choices with a focus on long-term gains will be crucial.

Digitalization implies investments in institutional and regulatory capacity in LDCs. A successful reset of LDC sectors and economies is contingent on bolstering institutional capacity to incentivize innovation. Policy design is likely to require deep insights and understanding on digital technologies and their application across different sectors. Goals on fostering inclusivity and consumer preferences will require policy responses on technological capabilities development that are calibrated to address socio-economic, geographic, infrastructure provision and technological development at the ecosystem and firm level. The role of public extension service provision in technology adoption by rural producers is another case in point. Maintaining policy coherence will be important.

For example, appropriately calibrated education, tax, and tariff incentives are implicated in fostering firm and industry level dynamic technological capabilities investment. Maximizing the return on investments in infrastructure will require LDC governments to pay closer attention to the impact of market concentration on the affordability of access to critical ICTs services, as digitalization can raise barriers to entry in digital markets and give rise to security and privacy concerns. While consensus has not been reached on the appropriate policy responses, a sentiment that is is gaining traction is that enforcement might need to be bolder, quicker and context-specific (European Commission, 2018b; Gökce Dessemond, 2019; OECD, 2018; Sodano and Verneau, 2014; UNCTAD, 2019d).

Another area that could benefit from greater policy coherence is engagement to reap the youth dividend. Currently, development discourses tend to readily associate youth and technology, and many projects currently target youth specifically in, for instance, agritech. This could inadvertently lead to overlooking the important role of on-the-job experience in fostering tacit capabilities acquisition and raising the quality of entrepreneurship across all sectors, if it lends to a disproportionate emphasis on self-entrepreneurship as an entry point for youth in LDCs (UNCTAD, 2018). The case studies also highlight the need for LDC policymakers not to overlook the manufacturing sector as an attractive area for engagement with the youth on technology adoption.

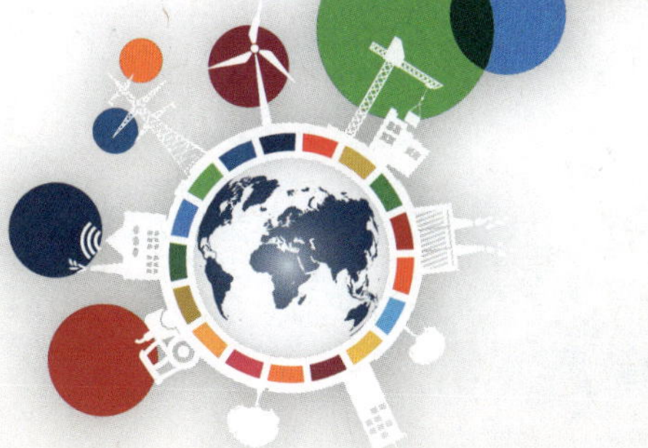

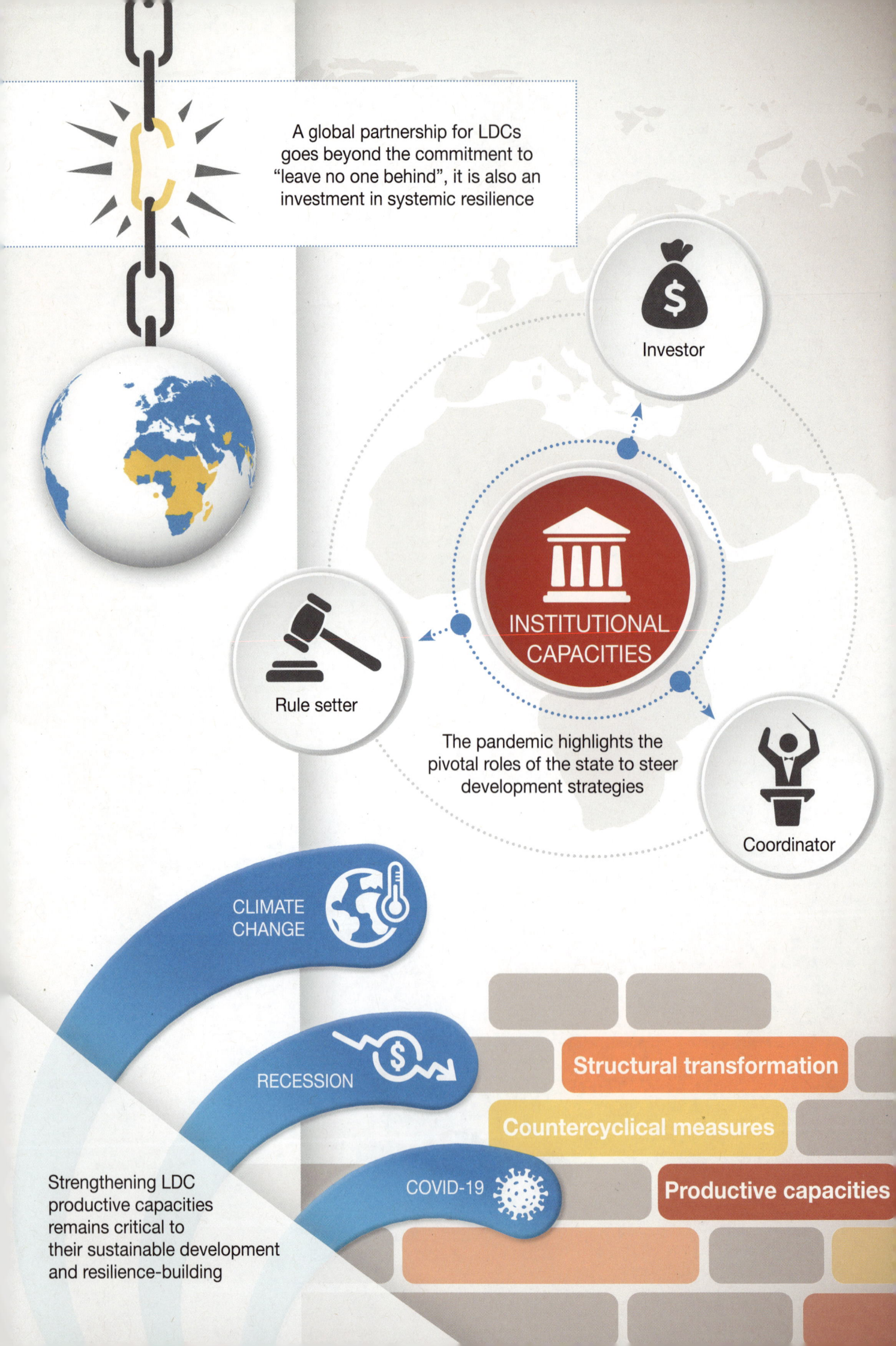

A global partnership for LDCs goes beyond the commitment to "leave no one behind", it is also an investment in systemic resilience

INSTITUTIONAL CAPACITIES

- Investor
- Rule setter
- Coordinator

The pandemic highlights the pivotal roles of the state to steer development strategies

- CLIMATE CHANGE
- RECESSION
- COVID-19

- Structural transformation
- Countercyclical measures
- Productive capacities

Strengthening LDC productive capacities remains critical to their sustainable development and resilience-building

CHAPTER
5

Policies to develop productive capacities in the new decade

CHAPTER 5

Policies to develop productive capacities in the new decade

A. Introduction	**125**
B. Putting productive capacities at the core	**126**
1. Macroeconomic and financial policies	127
a. Countercyclical policies	*127*
b. The role of the state	*130*
c. Financial policies	*131*
2. Sectoral and industrial policies	131
a. Employability and labour market policies	*132*
b. Policies for science, technology and innovation	*132*
c. Rural development policies	*134*
d. Industrial policies	*134*
e. Trade policy	*136*
f. Policy priorities for the development of productive capacities of LDC sub-groups	*138*
C. What can the international community do?	**138**
1. LDC stakes in systemic issues	138
a. Strengthening multilateralism	*139*
b. Sustainable development finance	*140*
c. Debt issues	*141*
d. Climate finance	*142*
e. Illicit financial flows	*142*
2. Stronger international support measures for LDCs	143
a. Trade ISMs	*143*
b. Technology ISMs	*144*
c. Reinforcing the effectiveness of ISMs	*145*

A. Introduction

The emergence of advanced technologies and the rising importance of related services are radically transforming the prospects for trade and industrialization in developed and developing countries alike. Meanwhile, the fallout from the COVID-19 pandemic increasingly appears set to have long-lasting effects on the global economy and erode many of the achievements made towards meeting the Sustainable Development Goals. While least developed countries (LDCs) are not at the epicentre of either of these two trends, the impact of the pandemic is exerting wide-ranging impacts on their sustainable development prospects and will continue to do so for the foreseeable future. Against this backdrop, this chapter outlines key policy options to foster the development and full utilization of the productive capacities of LDCs. In addition, with an eye on the preparations for the Fifth United Nations Conference on the Least Developed Countries (UNLDC-V), this chapter charts critical elements for the international community as it considers how best to support LDCs in the new decade.

The structure of the present chapter is (loosely) based on that of the Istanbul Programme of Action (IPoA) and distinguishes actions undertaken by LDCs and by development partners. The chapter is structured into two main sections. Section B presents policy options for policymakers in LDCs to consider as they seek to put the development of productive capacities at the core of their development strategies. Section C is instead mainly directed to the international community, and outlines concrete proposals to enhance the effectiveness of international support measures (ISMs) in favour of LDCs. While this subdivision was adopted for conceptual clarity, it is worth highlighting that these two levels of analysis and policy action are complementary.

As shown in earlier chapters, the development of LDC productive capacities is largely – but not exclusively – an endogenous process: the pattern of LDC integration in the global economy inevitably exerts a far-reaching influence on their needs, policy space, available means, as well as the viability of given policy measures. Therefore, while LDCs have the primary responsibility for their own development, the international community has an important role to play in supporting their quest for sustainable development.

These considerations are all the more relevant in the context of the unprecedented shock that humanity has experienced in 2020. This new decade simultaneously marks the remaining horizon of Agenda 2030 for Sustainable Development and the implementation of

> **Persistent divergence between LDCs and other countries undermines sustainable development for all**

the next programme of action for LDCs, to be adopted during UNLDC-V. While there will inevitably be an understandable temptation to prioritize domestic concerns in the policy discourse, it is fundamental that the international agenda adequately reflects the interests and needs of LDCs, particularly as the IPoA is likely to remain largely unfinished business by 2021. Currently accounting for 14 per cent of the world population, the 47 LDCs are home to more than 50 per cent of the people living with less than $1.90 per day at a global level. Representing the main locus of extreme poverty worldwide, they remain, now more than ever, "the battleground on which the 2030 Agenda for Sustainable Development will be won or lost" (UNCTAD, 2015a: 14).

Yet, the call for an authentic global partnership in support of LDCs goes well beyond the moral commitment to "leave no one behind"; in an increasingly interconnected world, it also reflects long-term considerations related to global public goods, potential spillovers across nations and ultimately to the world's systemic resilience. The rapid cascading effect of a health shock (COVID-19) on a wide swathe of dimensions ranging from the socioeconomic sphere to the environmental one, has underscored critical elements of systemic interdependence that can no longer be overlooked (OECD, 2020b; Ungar, 2018). This has placed renewed emphasis on inclusivity/universality, the fundamental role of international cooperation, and adds a new strategic dimension to the call for ensuring that LDCs do not fall behind. Low socioeconomic development is typically regarded as an influential driver of instability, conflict and migration, particularly when coupled with increasing pressure on natural resources, the intensifying adverse impacts of climate change and limited institutional capabilities (Hendrix and Salehyan, 2012; Mach et al., 2019; United Nations, 2019; Katie Peters et al., 2020). In this respect, the persistent divergence between LDCs and other countries might adversely affect political economy dynamics, and ultimately undermine sustainable development in neighbouring countries and beyond.

With over a billion people, a very young population structure, considerable natural resources but also entrenched vulnerabilities, LDCs inevitably represent

---

International support for structural transformation in LDCs is an investment in systemic resilience

---

"frontier economies", in which the recent wave of technological innovations could either unleash opportunities for inclusive growth – with positive repercussions on economic partners – or further entrench and widen existing divides, with all the attendant risks. Which of these two scenarios turns out to be closer to reality will largely depend on the achievement of a virtuous circle of structural transformation. In this perspective, revamping international support for productive capacity development and structural transformation in LDCs should be conceived as an investment in systemic resilience, and as part and parcel of a process of "building back better", as originally defined in the United Nations Sendai Framework for Disaster Risk Reduction 2015–2030 (United Nations, 2015b).

B. Putting productive capacities at the core

A growing consensus is emerging on the central role that productive capacities development plays in setting in motion the long-term process of structural transformation, which forms one of the pillars on which sustainable development rests (UNCTAD, 2006, 2014, 2018c, 2019b). As clarified in chapter 2, productive capacity development operates both within firms/sector, through capital deepening and productivity gains, and across sectors, as the acquisition of productive capabilities paves the way for the emergence of new products and higher value-added activities. This process hinges on a mutually reinforcing dynamic relationship between the supply and demand-side of the economy, whereby the expansion of aggregate demand creates the scope for intersectoral linkages, factor reallocation and pecuniary externalities that sustains the financial viability of investments. Productive capacity development fosters structural transformation and economic diversification, and has a knock-on effect on employment opportunities, inclusive growth and potentially also on resource-efficiency and environmental sustainability (UNCTAD, 2012).

Chapters 2 and 3 highlighted how efforts to develop productive capacities have been critical to the trajectory of a handful of best-performing LDCs;

they also drew attention to the fact that the general performance of most LDCs was rather lackluster, and fell short of the objectives enshrined in the IPoA. In this context, UNCTAD's Productive Capacity Index (PCI) provides a means to assess the performance of LDCs, benchmark progress made, and identify critical areas for improvement. A number of LDCs, including many of those in the process of graduation, have steadily increased their capacities, as measured by the sustained improvement in their PCI. However, a large group of them progressed at a markedly slowing pace, while many others stagnated or even fell behind. Additional analysis of the subcomponents of the PCI sheds more light on the effectiveness with which LDCs have translated productive capacity gains into higher per capita income. The analysis demonstrates that, on average, LDCs operate at less than 60 per cent of the maximum possible efficiency to raise their per capita incomes, with in particular elements related to natural resources, human capital and structural change being either underutilized or ineffectively combined with other facets of productive capacities. Beyond pointing to considerable margins for improvements, these findings highlight the intrinsic complementarity of the various productive capacity components, and show how the PCI can be unpacked, in a sort of country-level diagnostic, to identify the most binding constraints to inclusive growth.

More generally, the findings of this report underscore the risk of a widening gap between LDCs and other countries (whether developing or developed), as well as persistent vulnerabilities among even the best performing LDCs, which are currently close to the graduation milestone. Against this background, the centrality of productive capacity development remains of paramount importance in building the resilience of LDCs and, as such, forms the core of strategies geared towards "graduation with momentum" (UNCTAD, 2016a). While this key message is not entirely new, it remains as topical as ever, not only because the 2030 Agenda for Sustainable Development calls transformative change, but also because its main tenets have been further vindicated by the COVID-19 crisis. Indeed, the transmission of the shock, as well as the sharp asymmetries in the capacity of different countries to respond to it, once again expose the vulnerabilities stemming from weak productive capacity development. Equally, in the wake of the COVID-19 crisis potential tensions have emerged between the (over)emphasis on efficiency and specialization as opposed to redundancy, local embeddedness and connectivity (OECD, 2020b; Ungar, 2018).

As the fallout from the pandemic threatens to roll back the clock on several areas of progress achieved by many LDCs in recent years, only a sustained recovery rooted in the structural transformation of LDC economies can avert the dangers of a decade of anemic growth. Accordingly, productive capacity development needs to be integrated into COVID-19-related responses. This does not involve neglecting the containment of the health emergency, nor its immediate socioeconomic costs but rather implies addressing these critical needs in a sustainable way, by addressing their root causes and building long-term resilience. For instance, fostering greater inclusivity is not only a social goal in itself; if articulated strategically, related measures can also represent a way to break poverty traps which constrain LDC domestic markets and foster a denser network of supply-demand linkages. This adds further emphasis to the importance of integrating short-term policy responses with longer-term support to a broad-based recovery, underpinned by the creation of sufficient levels of productive employment.

The objective of setting in motion the process of structural transformation through the development and full utilization of LDC productive capacities will require tailored policies at all levels. For the sake of clarity, the sections below make a distinction between macroeconomic and financial policies (affecting broad macroeconomic aggregates) from meso/sectoral-level ones. Notwithstanding this conceptual distinction, what matters in practice is their interplay and the underlying incentive structure they shape. Hence, the importance of policy coherence and coordination across different ministries and stakeholders cannot be overemphasized.

1. Macroeconomic and financial policies

Integrating a developmental approach into macroeconomic policies requires moving beyond a narrow focus on preserving stability, and acknowledging that the expansion and full utilization of productive capacities is itself a crucial policy objective, which cannot automatically be achieved through a laissez-faire approach. In the context of technological gaps in LDCs, the process of capital accumulation and technological upgrading plays a key role in this respect, not only through demand multipliers but also by supporting the emergence of new activities, goods and sectors. The key policy priority for LDCs is thus to preserve stable macroeconomic fundamentals, while concurrently pursuing a concerted investment push to redress or close long-standing infrastructural and technological gaps. Achieving this calls for an expansionary fiscal

> Only a recovery rooted in the structural transformation of LDC economies can avert a decade of anemic growth

policy, buttressed by an accommodating monetary policy that maintains inflation in check but also keeps interest rates reasonably low, as well as, where possible, an exchange rate policy designed to facilitate the process and ease pressure on the balance of payment (UNCTAD, 2018c).

Until recently, many LDCs have displayed some signs of progress in relation to the above macroeconomic objectives, as they maintained fairly sound fundamentals and significantly boosted investment ratios. This process, however, had come at the cost of widening current account deficit and soaring indebtedness, with only modest benefits in terms of structural transformation (UNCTAD, 2019b). The current conjuncture, marked by the COVID-19 pandemic, has put an abrupt end to this situation, and even threatens to reverse some of the modest gains recorded so far. In so doing, the downturn is once again underscoring the structural constraints to LDCs macroeconomic policy options, ultimately stemming from the weak development of productive capacities and the associated dependence on external finance.

a. Countercyclical policies

More so than in 2009, at the beginning of 2020 the fiscal space of LDCs was already seriously constrained by their limited economic size, lukewarm dynamism, widespread informality, coupled with persistent pitfalls in tax structure and revenue administration systems and limited progress at an international level in tackling illicit financial flows (UNCTAD, 2019b, 2020g; UNECA, 2019). These factors, coupled with LDC limited ability to borrow domestically, have restricted the scope for counter-cyclical fiscal policy at a time of unprecedented need; likewise, LDC monetary and exchange rate policies were inevitably constrained by structural current account deficits, heightened dependence on sensitive imports, and a worsening debt sustainability outlook (UNCTAD, 2019b). On the one hand, sluggish improvements in the financial development and the shallowness of domestic bond markets (absent in many LDCs) have crippled the effectiveness of monetary policy; on the other, the scope for using exchange rate devaluation to sustain aggregate demand is undermined by both the reduction in global demand and a corresponding rise in the costs of critical imports and debt services,

Without international assistance LDCs cannot finance adequate policy responses to the COVID-19 crisis

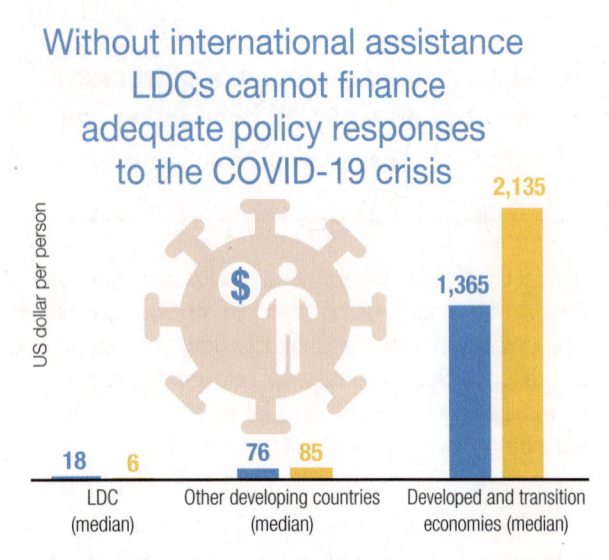

US dollar per person

	Additional spending or foregone revenues	Liquidity support
LDC (median)	18	6
Other developing countries (median)	76	85
Developed and transition economies (median)	1,365	2,135

with the ongoing fall in foreign direct investment (FDI) and remittances adding to the shortage of foreign exchange (chapter 1).

While the exceptional severity of the COVID-19 crisis called for bold countercyclical policies, along the lines of the "whatever it takes" motto, most LDCs have been unable to afford the sizeable policy packages adopted elsewhere, notably in developed countries (Figure 5.1).[1] Regardless whether one considers fiscal support measures, such as additional spending and forgone revenue, or liquidity support measures (e.g. contingent liabilities, equity injections, loans, asset purchase, or debt assumptions), the imbalance in the magnitude of policy responses across different groups of countries stands out clearly, when seen relative to each country's GDP (Panel A), and more so still when expressed in per capita dollar terms (Panel B). This calls for greater solidarity, as stronger international support will be indispensable to avoid catastrophic outcomes. At this stage, averting a deeper and more prolonged downturn appears to be the top priority to minimize long-term scars to the productive sectors, which could pose even more serious challenges to the attainment of the Sustainable Development Goals. The International Labour Organization (ILO) has warned that working-hours losses in the first half of 2020 could be equivalent to over 400 million full-time jobs worldwide, and that 1.6 billion workers in the informal economy are at an immediate risk of seeing their livelihoods reduced (ILO, 2020b). Other research work has raised profound concerns about the challenges faced by enterprises and small businesses (UNECA, 2020; Le Nestour and Moscoviz, 2020; *Reuters*, 2020b; Bosio et al., 2020). Similarly, numerous studies have highlighted the harsh impact the downturn could have on global poverty and food insecurity, potentially giving rise to path-dependency turning transient forms of poverty into chronic ones (Gerszon Mahler et al., 2020; Sumner, Hoy, et al. 2020; Valensisi, 2020; UN, 2020; Laborde et al., 2020).

Overall, these analyses point to the risk that a protracted recession could cause permanent job destruction, threaten enterprise survival – with related losses in terms of tacit knowledge and productive capabilities – and possibly have a long-term effect on potential output. Avoiding this dramatic outcome will be crucial to LDCs, as a prolonged crisis would further deteriorate an already weak entrepreneurial landscape characterized by a plethora of mainly informal survivalist businesses, a structure of firms largely skewed towards small enterprises, and limited access to credit for the private sector (UNCTAD, 2018a). According to early surveys, African firms during lockdown were operating at 43 per cent of their capacities, with labour-intensive sectors, e.g. manufacturing, transport, trade and tourism services, being the hardest hit (UNECA, 2020). Similar difficulties were reported in relation to the Asian garment industry, with supply chain disruptions compounded by a deep recession in key export markets (*Reuters*, 2020b). In this context, the deeper or longer the crisis the higher the risk of exacerbating the "missing middle" in LDCs, as the downturn threatens hard-gained entrepreneurial capabilities and ultimately jeopardizes a broad-based recovery.[2]

While the situation is still unfolding and it is too early to have a full picture, the emerging evidence points to the following priority areas for countercyclical policies:

1. *Protect employment and minimize income losses for own-account and informal workers*, who constitute the bulk of the labour force of LDCs;
2. *Preserve the viability of enterprises*, including micro, small and medium-sized enterprises (MSMEs) which have limited resources to weather the crisis and typically have reduced access to credit; and

---

[1] Data from ESCAP repository of policy responses to COVID-19 in Asia and the Pacific confirms this reading of the evidence, with Asian and Pacific LDCs typically unable to earmark to policy support packages more than 2–5 percentage points of GDP, unlike their richer neighbours.

[2] The expression "missing middle" refers to the relative lack of mid-sized enterprises in LDCs, whose entrepreneurial scene is dominated by a plethora of micro or small firms, and, at the other end of the spectrum, a few large enterprises with a disproportionately large footprint in terms of output, employment and exports (UNCTAD, 2018a).

CHAPTER 5: Policies to develop productive capacities in the new decade

Figure 5.1
Summary of fiscal measures in response to COVID-19 (selected countries)[3]

Panel A: Percentage of GDP

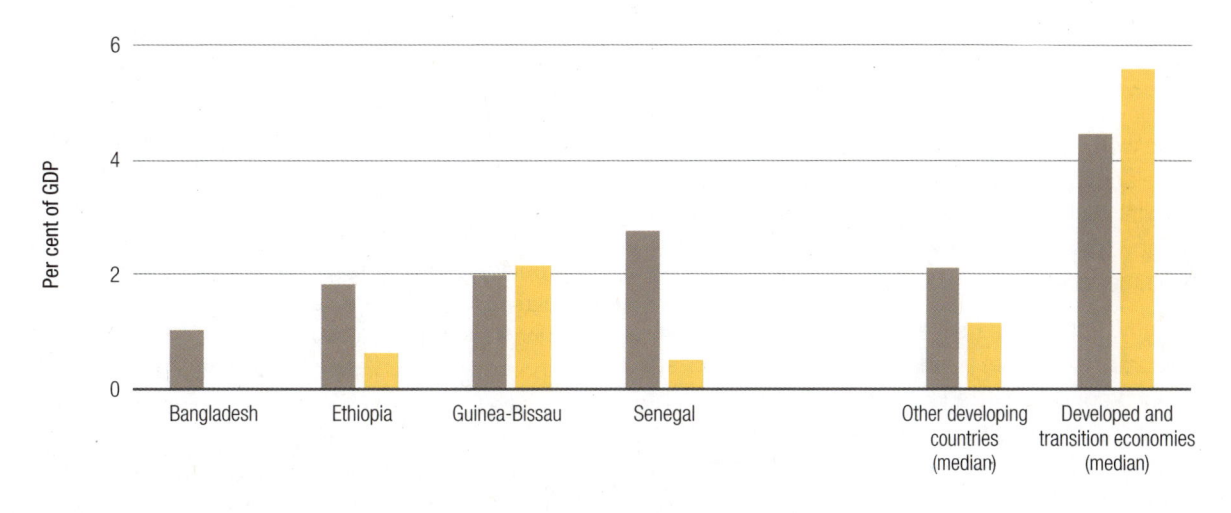

Panel B: Dollar per person

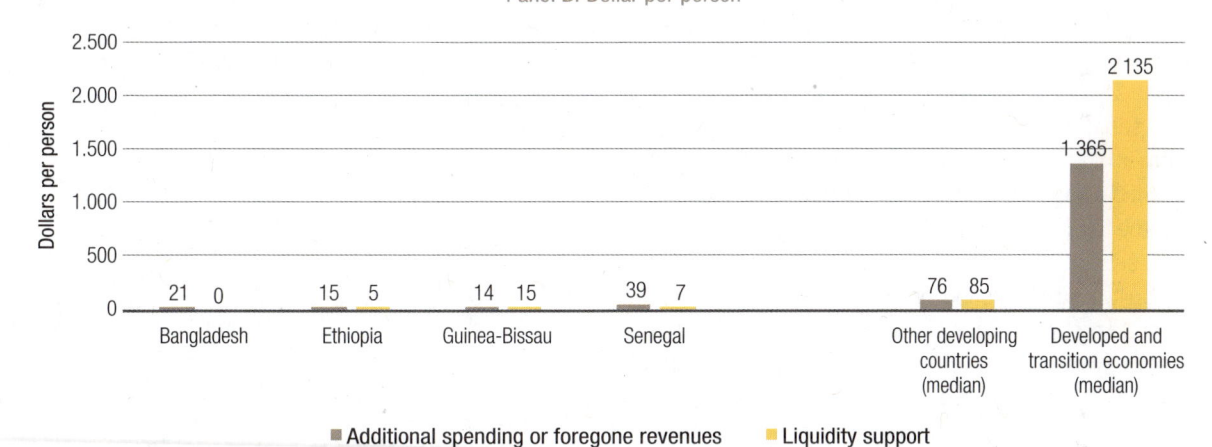

■ Additional spending or foregone revenues   ■ Liquidity support

Source: UNCTAD secretariat calculations, based on data from IMF (2020a) and UNCTAD, UNCTADStat database [accessed June 2020].

3. Provide support to poor households *and vulnerable categories*, notably women who tend to be over-represented in many of the sectors that have been the most heavily hit by the downturn.

Distinct countries have implemented these priorities differently, reflecting their specific contexts and institutional capacities, but the wealth of experiences across these countries provides useful lessons. In the wake of the pandemic, a large number of countries (including many LDCs) have extended social protection programmes or developed *ad-hoc* solutions to cushion the impact of the crisis on vulnerable groups. Concrete examples include: (i) public procurement or conditional cash transfers to support local production in Bangladesh and Ethiopia; (ii) tax exemptions/deferrals to support households and firms coping with liquidity constraints in Angola, Bhutan, Burkina Faso and Zambia;[4] (iii) enhancing infrastructural provision through

---

[3] Instead of aggregating across countries of diverse economic and population size, Figure 5.1 reports the median value (i.e. the value separating the higher half from the lower half of a distribution) for each country group, apart from LDCs which depicted individually. Other developing countries include: Argentina, Brazil, Chile, China, Colombia, Egypt, Ghana, Honduras, India, Indonesia, Kenya, Mauritius, Mexico, Nigeria, Pakistan, Peru, Philippines, Saudi Arabia, Singapore, South Africa, Thailand, Tunisia, Turkey, United Arab Emirates and Viet Nam. Conversely, developed and transition economies encompass: Albania, Australia, Belgium, Bulgaria, Canada, Czech Republic, Denmark, Finland, France, Georgia, Germany, Italy, Japan, Kazakhstan, Korea (Republic of), New Zealand, Norway, Poland, Romania, Russia, Spain, Sweden, Switzerland, The Netherlands, United Kingdom and the United States.

[4] The examples cited in this paragraph are drawn from the IMF repository of policy responses to COVID-19 and are only intended to provide concrete examples, and not the exhaustive list of policies taken by LDCs.

> The COVID-19 crisis has highlighted the pivotal role of the state as rule setter, coordinator and investor

public work schemes in, among others, Guinea, Sierra Leone and Uganda; and (iv) facilitating the emergence of digital businesses, as in the case of Senegal where the government fast-tracked the implementation of e-commerce policies.[5]

In many LDCs these schemes reflected timely but temporary initiatives and/or were characterized by incomplete coverage. Fiscal constraints and institutional challenges, notably the lack of systematic data on informal workers and people living in informal settlements, has rendered these vulnerable categories harder to reach with targeted extensions of existing social programmes. The lack of universality, however, implies weaker countercyclical effects and higher social costs. Moreover, the *ad-hoc* nature of such schemes makes them less suitable to respond to other longer-term shocks where risk pooling might be critical, as is the case for climate change and extreme weather events. A progressive move towards universal social protection schemes can nonetheless be built upon existing initiatives and judiciously paced to respond to mounting socioeconomic needs without creating excessive fiscal imbalances. This process could also pave the way for discussions on creating more sustainable financing options and on channeling funds to programmes linking short-term relief with measures conducive to the longer-term development of productive capacities. Conditional cash transfers linked to training and upskilling programmes, or public work schemes to improve the provision of infrastructure in slums and rural areas, are but two examples of these potential linkages (UNCTAD, 2013a).

b. The role of the state

Interestingly, the COVID-19 crisis has brought to the fore a renewed debate on the pivotal role of the state as a "rule setter", but also as a "coordinator" and an "investor", as well as related emphasis on institutional capacities to steer development strategies and design policy measures to respond to exogenous shocks. The role of public investment remains particularly critical for LDCs, both in the short term – to contain job losses and support unskilled workers – and also over the long term – for redressing supply-side bottlenecks (UNCTAD, 2017a, 2018d, 2019b). In this respect, pervasive market failures, ranging from sunk costs and scale economies to complementarities and the public goods nature of the underlying infrastructure, suggest that governments have a fundamental role to play in crowding-in private investments. Rural areas, in particular, have suffered massively from under-investment in basic infrastructures (e.g. irrigation, transport/storage facilities, electrification); these gaps weigh down the potential supply response on the parts of LDC farmers, further limiting the scope for viable rural non-farming activities (UNCTAD 2015a, 2018a). Equally, the poor quality of infrastructural provision in many LDC cities and peri-urban areas compromises the competitiveness of manufacturing and services firms, forcing them to incur disproportionate costs for electricity or connectivity, thus dampening the prospects for both traditional and digital businesses. In this context, public investment will continue to play a crucial role in the shift towards greener and climate-resilient infrastructures, supporting a more sustainable recovery.

Even in sectors where innovations, such as mobile telephony or decentralized electricity generation, have tempered some of the traditional market failures associated with infrastructure and paved the way for a greater involvement of private actors, the role of the state should evolve, but cannot retrench. History shows that not all areas of this "social overhead capital"[6] lend themselves equally well to the involvement of the private sector, hence public investment remains crucial to avoid the under-provision of specific infrastructural services, as well as to strike an appropriate balance between financial viability and affordability. Moreover, technological transitions occur over lengthy periods of time, especially infrastructure development, and entails the coexistence of different technology vintages (Grubler, 2012; UNCTAD, 2017a). Hence, the role of the state remains critical in ensuring that systemic considerations, including competition issues and the interrelatedness/inter-operability of different technologies are duly accounted for, and that the overall investment push is closely integrated with the country's development strategies, including in relation to the interface between infrastructural development and productive sector dynamics. Moreover, the development of traditional or digital infrastructure

---

[5] https://unctad.org/en/pages/newsdetails.aspx?OriginalVersionID=2342.

[6] The concept of "social overhead capital" is used to identify the source of certain basic services required in the production of virtually all commodities. In its most narrow sense, the term refers to transportation, communication, and power facilities.

sectors should be seen not just as a response to existing and latent demand but rather through strategic lenses as: (i) forming part and parcel of the process of structural transformation; (ii) contributing to value addition by offering possibilities of technological development and skills accumulation; and (iii) a potential source of spillovers to other sectors.

c. Financial policies

The emphasis on investment goes hand in hand with domestic resource mobilization and effective financial intermediation, as it combines adequate incentives for broadening access to financial services guided by sound regulations and supervision (UNCTAD, 2018c, 2016c). Given the shallowness of the financial sector in most LDCs, the main long-term priorities in this respect are: (i) the development of viable secondary markets for government securities and long-term financial instruments denominated in local currency; (ii) the strengthening of the banking sector to cater for the diversified needs of private enterprises and consumers; and (iii) the consolidation of national and regional development banks. The progress made thus far under the IPoA has, in most cases, been lackluster and marked by sluggish improvements, and a persistently large share of unbanked firms and individuals, notably among women and MSMEs (UNCTAD, 2018a, 2018c). Moreover, the portfolio of available financial instruments is limited and does not always meet the requirements of all segments of potential customers; unlike large firms or high turnover businesses, the distinct needs of other private actors, in particular SMEs and agricultural producers, remain inadequately catered for. Improving this situation requires creating an effective and reliable institutional framework, capable of mobilizing domestic savings and intermediating them, while also upgrading prevailing technologies and business practices.

The COVID-19 pandemic has exacerbated liquidity constraints and has presented a major stress-test for an underdeveloped financial sector that has long struggled to ensure that credit reaches those most in need. In the wake of the pandemic, many LDCs swiftly adopted measures to alleviate constraints linked with their tight finances, cutting rediscount rates, adopting credit support schemes (for instance through loan guarantees), lowering reserve requirements, as occurred among others in Angola, Bangladesh, Cambodia and the Democratic Republic of the Congo. In responding to the crisis, several LDCs also moved to integrate the use of digital technologies in social welfare programmes through digital cash transfers, or by supporting the extension of digital payment and financial services, as in the case of Mozambique, Togo and Uganda. These encouraging initiatives provide a wealth of experiences from which to draw important lessons for the future; however, more needs to be done to strengthen financial intermediation, particularly if the sector is to pave the way for structural transformation and productive capacity development.

2. Sectoral and industrial policies

Beyond the pure macroeconomic realm, the COVID-19 pandemic has underscored the fundamental importance of so-called meso-level policies, which decision-makers use to steer the development of specific economic activities according to the national development strategy. These encompass policies applied horizontally (i.e. across all sectors), as well as vertical policies concerning only selective sectors or activities. Though straightforward in conceptual terms, this distinction is somewhat blurred in practice, as policy implementation is contingent on the prevailing characteristics of the sectoral composition of output and entrepreneurial landscape; hence, these policies are often lumped together under the rubric of "industrial policies".

Calls to rethink industrial policies have received a fair amount of attention in recent years (Crespi et al., 2014; OECD, 2016; UNCTAD, 2018g, 2016b, 2014), but it was their swift deployment – even by countries supposedly preaching a more laissez-faire approach – that has decisively brought them back to the fore of the political debate in the wake of the COVID-19 pandemic. A detailed, comprehensive discussion on meso-level policies for productive capacity development in the context

Strategies for productive capacity development need to speak to the political economy of each country

Digitalization and 4IR call for prioritizing access to technologies

of African and LDCs can be found elsewhere (UNCTAD, 2018c, 2020d). What this section does, instead, is to highlight those critical policy elements that have acquired renewed relevance and/or are set to play a fundamental role during the next programme of action for LDCs.

The importance of meso-level policies cannot be fully grasped without considering the fundamental role of employment creation and labour reallocation in the process of structural transformation, and the concomitant effects this may have on aggregate productivity growth and poverty reduction (chapter 2). With the labour supply in LDCs expected to increase by an average 13.2 million workers per year over the next decade, sustainable development will inevitably hinge on the capacity of LDC economies to generate sufficient opportunities for productive employment outside the agricultural sector, and thus ultimately affect both the direction and pace of their structural transformation process. Addressing the employment challenge calls for a multipronged approach which simultaneously supports labour demand in higher-productivity labour-intensive sectors and enhances the employability of youth entering the labour market. Macro-policies focused on investment should intrinsically support employment creation. Besides, a growing number of LDCs have embarked in reforms to improve their respective business environment and trade facilitation frameworks in order to lower administrative costs for potential entrepreneurs, including self-employed and own-account workers who constitute the backbone of the labour force of LDCs (chapter 4 and UNCTAD, 2018a). Such measures have the merit of cutting red tape, lowering barriers to entry, promoting greater competition and facilitating self-employment; nevertheless, the extent to which business environment reforms contribute to productive capacity development ultimately depends on the prevailing type of entrepreneurship they foster. Lacking broader shifts towards higher-productivity sectors, these measures alone are unlikely to change the patterns of entrepreneurship characterizing many LDCs, dominated by survivalist forms of entrepreneurship (UNCTAD, 2018a). Targeted forms of support to labour-intensive but relatively high-productivity sectors covering, among others, rural non-farming activities, light manufacturing, installation/maintenance of mechanical equipment, business services and ICTs, stand a better chance of combining employment creation with productivity-enhancing structural change.

a. Employability and labour market policies

Beyond improving the entrepreneurship framework, rapid job creation will inevitably require enhancing the employability of youth entering the labour market. Investments in education and upskilling are thus of paramount importance, particularly as shortages of skilled labour are often cited among the main obstacles faced by firms operating in the LDCs. This is set to become an even more binding constraint with the emergence of advanced technologies. Action in this respect could involve improving the quality of secondary education and bolstering technical and vocational training programmes as these could make an important contribution to enhancing human capital in LDCs. Given the increasing degree of specialization and complexity of new technologies, however, decisive action is also required to boost tertiary education, particularly in relation to science, technology, engineering, and mathematics (STEM) disciplines. Strengthening consultations with the private sector and business associations could lead to a better alignment of curricula with market needs; enhancing international university collaboration (especially at the regional and South-South levels) could also be particularly important. Beyond formal education, the potential contribution of apprenticeships, on-the-job training, adult education and retraining should also be explored, especially in view of the potential inputs employers could provide to the upskilling process (UNCTAD, 2020d).

b. Policies for science, technology and innovation

The second horizontal issue of crucial relevance for the future prospects of LDCs is technological upgrading. The surge of digitalization and the Fourth Industrial Revolution (4IR) have brought renewed emphasis on access to technologies as key drivers of development prospects. However, while advanced technologies create additional opportunities for employment and productivity growth, serious concerns have been voiced about the extreme divides in their creation and diffusion, as well as the potential of some digital technologies to give rise to excessive market power and rent-seeking behaviour (chapter 4 and UNCTAD, 2018d, 2019d; UNIDO, 2019a). The fact that the ten technologically frontrunner economies account for 90 per cent of the patents and 70 per cent of exports of advanced digital production technologies, speaks volumes to the risk of widening technological divides (UNIDO, 2019a).

The pivotal role of technologies for sustainable development is all the more critical to the post-COVID-19 scenario, as the fallout from the pandemic is likely to accelerate some facets of the ongoing process of industrial digitalization and servicification. Value chains are set to undergo far-reaching reconfigurations to: (i) reduce excessive dependence on key suppliers; (ii) encourage reshoring and regional embeddedness, and (iii) boost overall resilience (Baldwin and Evenett, 2020). While these trends are unlikely to reverse globalization, they have nonetheless critical implications for the industrialization prospects of developing countries, as some authors had warned before the outbreak of the COVID-19 crisis (Rodrik, 2018; Baldwin and Evenett, 2020). Most importantly, the advent of advanced technologies may reshape comparative advantages, thereby potentially weakening the importance of low-labour costs for investors' locational choices.

For LDCs, all of this implies that the long-standing challenges in upgrading their technological base and setting in motion meaningful technology transfer will likely become even more daunting in the future, for at least three reasons. First, their positioning in the global division of labour could be further marginalized, should their distance from the technological frontier grow wider and the digital divide persist. Emerging evidence points to serious risks in this respect, as LDCs are overwhelmingly "laggards" in relation to advanced digital production technologies applied to manufacturing, with only four countries classified as "latecomers" (Ethiopia, Malawi, Uganda and Zambia), and one country (Bangladesh) designated as a "follower" (UNIDO, 2019a).[7] Equally worrying, no LDC appears to be meaningfully engaged in the production and trade of advanced digital technologies, being at most importers of such technologies (chapter 4). Such a lopsided pattern of engagement as "users" vs "producers" of advanced technologies points to deep-seated challenges not just in terms of adoption, but more so in domesticating frontier technologies, adapting their design to the reality and comparative advantages of LDCs, and engaging in the manufacturing stages of these technologies. This is reminiscent of the trajectory followed with mobile

---

[7] UNIDO's approach defines as "frontrunner" as the leading 10 economies engaged in patenting advanced digital production technologies; the categories of "followers" and "latecomers" are defined in terms of decreasing engagement in patenting advanced technologies or trading related goods, with "laggards" displaying very little or no engagement. The dimensions considered to obtain this classification include the average values of patent, export and import activity.

No LDC appears to be meaningfully engaged in the production and trade of advanced digital technologies

telephony: its rapid penetration in LDCs provided some developmental benefits and enabled some instances of leapfrogging but the full developmental benefits of these technologies in terms of manufacturing and structural transformation have remained elusive (Juma, 2015, 2017).

Second, in a context of weak global demand and increasing drive for resource efficiency, the failure of LDCs to break their dependence on primary commodities and spur industrialization will continue to be their Achille's heel. This is especially the case if the establishment of forward linkages in commodity sectors remains elusive and if commodity-related goods continue to be exported in forms that embody limited domestic value addition (UNCTAD, 2019g). Current production activities inevitably constitute the main source of potential learning and innovation opportunities for a firm, and hence have a crucial bearing on the accumulation of productive capabilities and tacit knowledge. Accordingly, history shows that developing a certain basis of industrial capabilities is critical for the adoption and domestication of advanced technologies; it also presents advantages when reaping the benefits of learning-by-doing to climb the technological ladder. Yet, since the beginning of the decade more than half of the LDCs have witnessed premature de-industrialization, reflecting a decline in the relative weight of their respective manufacturing sectors in total value added. Moreover, engagement in advanced digital technologies and research and development (R&D) activities is largely concentrated not only in terms of countries, but also within larger firms, due to the pervasiveness of economies of scale and scope (UNCTAD, 2018d; UNIDO, 2019a). Therefore, without dismissing the "advantages of backwardness" à la Gerschenkron, the lopsided nature of the LDC entrepreneurial landscape – dominated as it is by MSMEs with little capital and technology/knowledge-intensive activities – represents an additional challenge.

Third, advanced technologies will no doubt have to play a critical role in LDC mitigation and adaptation efforts, LDCs being particularly exposed to climate change and extreme weather events (UNCTAD, 2010, 2016a, 2017a). Commodity sectors, in particular,

> **Policies to promote technological upgrading and innovation ecosystems are pivotal**

are extremely susceptible to climate change, as it is expected to reduce yields for major crops and more broadly to affect millions of people relying on natural resources for their livelihoods (Zhao et al., 2017; Ray et al., 2019; UNCTAD, 2019h). Equally, it will also impinge on the fundamentals of hard commodity markets, especially (but by no mean exclusively) fuels (UNCTAD, 2019h). Much-needed policies to reduce greenhouse gas emissions in line with the Paris Agreement will inevitably depress fossil fuel demand and increase the risk of "stranded assets" – a possibility that should be carefully accounted for in the development strategies of resource-rich LDCs.[8]

Policies to promote technological upgrading and enhance science, technology and innovation (STI) ecosystems are set to become even more pivotal in the future. Maintaining and, wherever possible, increasing investment in basic research and related facilities/institutions is an inescapable priority, not only nationally but also at the regional and subregional level. Similar investments should be accompanied by ambitious measures to boost human capital accumulation, particularly by boosting competencies in STEM disciplines. Besides, governments should strengthen the incentives for bolstering technology absorptive capacity, while actively promoting experimentation. In this respect, more can be done to catalyze collaboration and knowledge-sharing between private actors, research institutions and public bodies, and encouraging more rapid technology experimentation and domestication. Ongoing responses to the COVID-19 pandemic provide some success stories, one example being the rapid development of testing kits in Bangladesh, Senegal and Uganda (Mahmud, 2020; UNECA, 2020). A more proactive approach on the part of public institutions and regulatory bodies could help in supporting technological upgrading by private actors, for instance by raising awareness on the available policy space (notably in relation to the LDC flexibilities under the Agreement on Trade-Related Aspects of Intellectual Property Rights – TRIPS), or by having patent offices or other public authorities periodically disseminate lists of expired patents to interested parties and business associations.[9] Enhanced South-South cooperation could also play a conducive role in strengthening national and regional capacities for technological upgrading in countries of the Global South.

c. Rural development policies

Going beyond horizontal issues, a focus on agriculture and rural development remains a critical priority for inclusive and sustainable growth in the LDCs, particularly as the agricultural sector still employs the bulk of the labour force, a large percentage of whom are women, and plays a pivotal role in terms of poverty reduction and ensuring food security (chapter 2). The growing pressure on natural resources coupled with the looming threat of climate change leave little alternative to tackling the sector's chronic productivity gaps, and to gradually shift away from the reliance on exports of cash crops, often in the context of buyer-driven value chains. If harnessed judiciously, rapid urbanization can provide a powerful demand multiplier to sustain investment in agriculture and strengthen intersectoral linkages, thus establishing a virtuous circle between domestic demand and supply (chapter 4). This calls for broadening access to the inputs needed by the distinct agro-ecological and farm systems, stepping up measures to tackle scale issues in input supply, and exploring the scope for diversification into higher value-added products (UNCTAD, 2015a). It also implies strengthening R&D and extension services to promote the use of appropriate and climate-resilient seed varieties (including by nurturing and adding value to traditional knowledge), as well as supporting the pursuit of market differentiation, certification schemes and enhanced value addition through agro-processing.

d. Industrial policies

If agriculture cannot be disregarded, in most cases it is the emergence of viable manufacturing hubs which remain the fundamental engine for growth, structural transformation and sustainable development in LDCs. This prominence was retained in the context of the Sustainable Development Goals which, in Goal 9, explicitly refers to "sustainable industrialization". This consideration, which is the traditional premise of industrial policies, ultimately stems from the

---

[8] "Stranded assets" refer to assets that, prior to the end of their economic life (as assumed at the investment decision point), are no longer able to earn an economic return. In the context of climate change, this typically refers to fossil fuel resources, exploration/production/processing facilities and other infrastructure which may need to be mothballed to limit global warming to well below 2°C.

[9] Under Article 66.1, LDCs are not required to apply the provisions of the TRIPS Agreement (other than Articles 3, 4 and 5) until 1 July 2021.

conclusion that the manufacturing sector can provide a greater scope for increasing returns, learning by doing and technological spillovers than other sectors. The advent of digitalization, servicification and 4IR may warrant some rethinking of the above premise, as some features traditionally ascribed to manufacturing, e.g. spillovers, scale economies and innovation, are increasingly shared by services sector firms (UNCTAD, 2016b; Rodrik, 2016; Nayyar et al., 2018; Hallward-Driemeier and Nayyar, 2017). This, however, does not completely overturn the argument in favour of developing a sound industrial basis, at least not for countries such as LDCs as their structural characteristics – notably low levels of industrialization and human capital – remain far from those of knowledge-based economies (UNCTAD, 2016b; Rodrik, 2016; UNIDO, 2019a; UNCTAD, 2020d). Moreover, the importance of a manufacturing base was once again highlighted in the context of the reaction to the spread of the pandemic (chapter 1).

One of the key lessons of the COVID-19 fallout is that resilience requires adaptability and, to borrow from the terminology of Hausmann and Chauvin (2015), a capacity to adapt "moving to the adjacent possible", which are both contingent on the pre-existing capabilities.[10] Being able to rapidly adjust from the production of textiles to that of personal protective equipment (PPE) (Venter, 2020; Moyo and Lozansky, 2020), or from alcoholic beverages to disinfectant (Munnik and Chen, 2020), requires firms with productive capabilities and that are able to identify potential opportunities and work out what adjustments they need to make to competitively respond to market changes. Equally, the opportunity to engage in the adaptation and production of advanced technologies largely depends on the presence of a certain manufacturing basis and the acquisition of complementary skills (UNCTAD, 2020d; UNIDO, 2019a). The latent spillovers in this discovery process imply that investment in different and complementary types of productive capabilities should be actively encouraged by LDCs as a fundamental step in establishing and advancing their industrial competitiveness (Hausmann and Rodrik, 2003). Servicification, digitalization, along with the growing importance of distribution and logistics, have blurred the distinction between the manufacturing and

---

[10] In this context, the idea of "moving to the adjacent possible" refers to the incremental process of economic diversification, through step-by-step "jumps" from the existing products to nearby possibilities, characterized by broadly similar requirements in terms of underlying knowledge and productive capabilities, but higher levels of sophistication.

Developmental opportunities in high-productivity services are contingent on a vibrant industrial basis

services sectors, and underscored the emergence of services segments that may offer large scope for spillovers. Yet, these services subsectors are typically underdeveloped in LDCs, and unlikely to provide opportunities for both productivity growth and job creation for unskilled labour (Nayyar et al., 2018). Many of the developmental opportunities in high-productivity services are ultimately contingent on a vibrant industrial basis, as a key source of demand in the case of business services, logistics and distribution, or through synergies and complementarities with the design and production of the goods embodying knowledge-intensive services (e.g. the installation and maintenance of machinery and mechanical equipment).

From a policymaking perspective, rather than framing the discussion as a dichotomy between manufacturing-led versus services-or an agricultural-led model, the advent of new technologies puts a premium on the systemic coherence of the policy framework. This entails designing policies that strategically target synergies and complementarities across sectors, with a view to gradually enhance an economy's sophistication. It also involves awareness of the political economy dimensions underlying technological change and its potential distributional effects. The accelerating penetration of new technologies makes skills acquisition and technological upgrading ever more relevant, since the capabilities to adapt and undertake incremental innovation can play a key role in "directing" technical change towards more appropriate, inclusive and socially desirable outcomes. A notable example of this is decentralized renewable-based electricity generation, which has the potential to foster rural electrification and reduce rural-urban inequalities; however, if left to unfettered markets, its rollout it could fall short of what is required for structural transformation (UNCTAD, 2017a).

Lacking a viable industrial basis, current trends suggest that LDCs will struggle to move beyond the role of late followers in the use of advanced technologies, i.e. they are likely to remain importers and consumers, rather than producers and innovators. This situation calls for a bold and proactive industrial policy framework, which favours pragmatic

Coherence between trade policy and agricultural/industrial objectives is a priority

experimentation and coordination by all relevant stakeholders to address market failures and nudges firms to gradually sharpen their competitiveness edge, as well as support linkages development and the process of self-discovery inherent to the climbing up the sophistication ladder (UNCTAD, 2020d, 2018b; Hausmann and Rodrik, 2003; Chang and Andreoni, 2020). Simultaneously, policymakers should be wary of potential rent-seeking – hence careful to build-in sunset clauses and closely monitoring the outcomes of the support/protective element provided – but also creative in defending and make full use of available policy space.

The global on-going response to the COVID-19 pandemic has provided numerous concrete examples of industrial policy options, thanks to an unprecedented level of mobilization, albeit under faltering multilateral leadership. These responses range from the strategic use of public procurement to advanced market commitments (which lower risks and entice investment in R&D), and from swift legal action to ensure that intellectual property rights (IPR) flexibilities are actionable to proactive efforts aimed at facilitating coordination among all relevant stakeholders. More broadly, a large number of developing countries have recently deployed other policy tools, including local content requirements as targeted Special Economic Zones (SEZs) (Oqubay and Lin, 2020; UNCTAD and FAO, 2017; UNCTAD, 2020a). The success record of these industrial policy measures remains somewhat mixed: upgrading opportunities and spillovers to the rest of the economy have not always materialized or been commensurate to the related costs. Nonetheless, when part of a holistic policy framework and designed in a balanced pragmatic manner, industrial policies have been instrumental to industrial upgrading (UNCTAD, 2020d).

e. Trade policy

Beyond the domestic border, another key policy priority for LDCs is to enhance the strategic coherence and articulation of trade policies and align them with sectoral agricultural/industrial policy objectives. Harnessing international trade strategically to achieve diversification is part and parcel of that systemic policy coherence that was referred to above. Regional integration, in particular, can provide a powerful engine to attain larger economies of scale, harness trade complementarities and gradually enhance an economy's competitiveness and sophistication. It can also prove instrumental in attracting FDI and enhancing the scope and developmental effectiveness of integrating regional and global value chains. The experience of many LDCs, particularly in Africa, suggests that trade liberalization has at times been rolled out in a rather haphazard way, with tariff structures that are not necessarily conducive to the establishment of a national/regional industrial basis, or with measures sequenced in ways that ultimately hinder national competitiveness (UNECA, 2015; UNCTAD, 2019c, 2009). This reasoning applies not only to tariff liberalization, but also to non-tariff measures (NTMs). The supply disruptions caused by the COVID-19 pandemic are a stark reminder of the magnitude of the costs and frictions related to transport and trade facilitation issues, as well as to other NTMs. This serves as strong reminder of the need to implement the African Continental Free Trade Area. Similarly, broad regional integration schemes, e.g. the Association of Southeast Asian Nations (ASEAN) or the South Asian Free Trade Area (SAFTA), could be instrumental to the recovery of Asian LDCs, and could prove particularly valuable for countries graduating from the LDC category in the future (UNCTAD, 2016a).

International trade, with its inherent focus on country-specific endowments, geography and specialization pattern, provides an excellent example that there is no "one size fits all" approach, just as there is no single pattern of structural transformation. The mainstream prescription of pursuing export-led growth risks falling victim to a fallacy of composition, especially in the current depressed context: not all countries can simultaneously export their way out of the recession. Moreover, even when accounting for their small share of the global market, it remains clear that unless LDCs can attain a gradual diversification of their exports, they will at least partly compete with one another in markets related to a narrow range of products. Hence, to be successful, strategies geared towards productive capacity development should address the context-specific realities of each individual country, whether in relation to their international trade or their own "internal integration", which is often overlooked in the development discourse but remains crucial notably for relatively large LDCs.[11]

---

[11] According to Wade, "(a)n economy with high internal integration, has a well-filled input output matrix – a dense set of links between sectors (…) and a structure of demand such that a high proportion of domestic production is sold to domestic wage earners" (Wade, 2004: xlviii).

CHAPTER 5: Policies to develop productive capacities in the new decade

Box 5.1   **Using the PCI to identify common challenges in productive capacity development**

This box illustrates how the PCI can be used to identify common challenges in LDC productive capacity development in a "theory-blind" manner. To do so, a K-means clustering analysis has been performed along the eight underlying dimensions of the PCI, using values for the year 2018. This analysis identifies a partition of the n observations into k clusters in which each observation belongs to the cluster with the nearest mean (cluster centroid). The exercise was repeated for a number of clusters ranging from two to ten, and then the preferred number of clusters was selected based on the Calinski-Harabasz pseudo-F statistics (which describes the ratio of between-cluster variance to within cluster variance).

The resulting centroids are reported in Box Table 5.1. Besides, since it would be impossible to graphically represent all the eight dimensions of the PCI, to provide a visualization of the clusters the latter are aggregated into three components – namely infrastructural, structural change and institutional (as illustrated in the table) – using the geometric mean, thus mimicking the aggregation procedure adopted in the construction of the PCI itself. Further, the clusters are graphically represented in Box Figure 5.1, which drops the structural change dimension along which the variability is anyway extremely limited across LDCs.

Box Table 5.1

Mean values of Productive Capacity Index dimensions, within-cluster

	Infrastructural component			Structural change component			Institutional component	
	Energy	ICT	Transport	Human capital	Structural change	Natural capital	Private sector	Institutions
Blue cluster	19	5	13	34	12	59	61	22
Red cluster	17	6	12	38	14	62	72	40
Green cluster	23	8	17	42	16	48	79	51

Source: UNCTAD secretariat calculations, based on data from UNCTAD (forthcoming).

Box Figure 5.1

Visualization of LDC clustering according to PCI dimensions, 2018

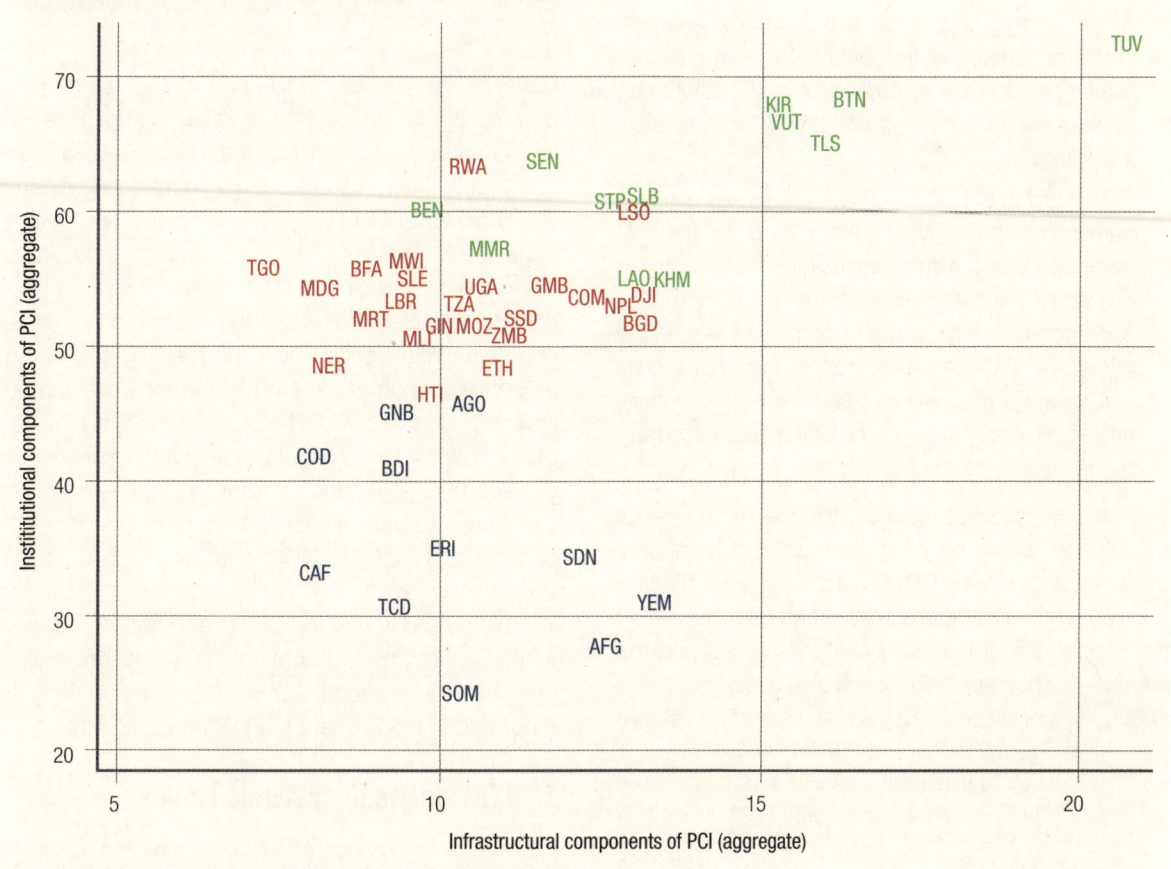

Source: UNCTAD secretariat calculations, based on data from UNCTAD (forthcoming).

> **LDCs need a more conducive international environment and support to develop their productive capacities**

f. Policy priorities for the development of productive capacities of LDC sub-groups

The importance of country-specific factors has been highlighted repeatedly in this report, and the need for them to inform strategies for the development of LDC productive capacities. From a broader policy perspective, though, it is instructive to go beyond the heterogeneity of the LDCs and identify broad commonalities across them, which point to specific sets of policy priorities. As shown in Box 5.1, a way to do so is through clustering the eight dimensions of UNCTAD's PCI to detect similar challenges in productive capacity development. Interestingly, this exercise reveals three broad typologies of LDCs:

1. A group of mainly conflict and post-conflict countries, characterized by low average levels of productive capacities across all dimensions, but whose most binding constraints appear to stem from the institutional dimension (blue cluster);

2. A second group with similarly low average performance along five of the PCI dimensions, but far better track record in terms of institutional, private sector and human capital components (red cluster);

3. A third group of LDCs with typically higher average human capital, private sector and institutional component and with a significantly lower footprint on natural capital (green cluster). This latter group, encompassing eight of the 11 countries meeting the criteria for LDC graduation in 2018, is composed by LDCs with a relatively diversified export structure, and smaller countries with far better average quality of the infrastructural provision.[12]

The above exercise points to the fundamental importance of accounting for political economy dynamics and related institutional challenges in shaping the viability of LDC development strategies, as well as the importance of human capital investment and the pattern of export specialization. It also underscores the peculiarities of island LDCs, whose level of productive capacity development might be relatively encouraging by LDC standards, but whose economic vulnerability remains extremely high. More broadly, the evidence presented here reinforces the relevance of "graduation with momentum", which views graduation not so much as an end in itself, but rather as a milestone in the long-term process of structural transformation, whereby developing productive capacities is key to building resilience in turbulent times (UNCTAD, 2016a).

C. What can the international community do?

Considering that structural transformation is largely an endogenous process occurring within a given economy, the preeminence of domestic policymaking for productive capacity development is rather straightforward. This is also consistent with the positions stated in the IPoA, and later reaffirmed in the Addis Ababa Action Agenda, that LDCs "have the ownership of and primary responsibility for their own development" (United Nations, 2011: 10). Nonetheless, in an increasingly interdependent world, the unfavourable terms of LDCs' integration into the global economy inevitably shape their development needs, policy space, available means of financing, and more broadly the overall viability of given policy measures.

Renewed assistance on the part of the international community is needed at a challenging time for multilateralism; support is needed to create a more conducive international environment and sustain the aspirations of LDCs to develop their productive capacities. Indeed, this recognition constitutes the raison d'être of the LDC category itself, whose continued relevance was demonstrated in earlier chapters. This position is reinforced by the recent recommendation of the Committee for Development Policy that the UNLDC-V Conference adopt the theme "Expanding productive capacity for sustainable development" as the organizing framework for the new programme of action for LDCs for the decade 2021–2030 (CDP and UN DESA, 2020). With this in mind, this section discusses how the international community can strengthen its support to LDCs, first by highlighting the significant stakes they have in systemic issues, then by moving to recommendations related to LDC-specific ISMs.

1. LDC stakes in systemic issues

The structural nature of LDC vulnerabilities implies that they are at the forefront of the looming crises confronting the multilateral system and its capacity

---

[12] The three LDCs meeting the criteria for LDC graduation in 2018, but not included in the second cluster are: Angola, as an oil exporter representing a case of graduation based on income-only criterion, and Bangladesh and Nepal, both narrowly belonging to the middle cluster, but located at the fringes of the upper cluster.

to adequately provide global public goods, redress entrenched inequalities, and support sustainable development and resilience building. This is immediately evident in relation to the containment of COVID-19, but the same point also applies to securing adequate access to sustainable development finance, preserving financial stability and addressing the impact of climate change and biodiversity losses. Given their heightened exposure to shocks (chapter 1), LDCs cannot but be among the most fervent supporters of a revamped and more effective multilateral system, capable of addressing today's global challenges and creating a more conducive international environment. While their marginal economic weight mirrors their limited say on systemic issues, the stakes for LDCs in the related debates could not be higher. Hence, they would definitely stand to gain from a greater voice and representation in global fora. Symmetrically, disregarding their legitimate interests may come at a cost not only to the LDCs themselves but also to other countries as a result of potential spillovers related to global health, financial stability, environmental considerations but also, more positively, to pecuniary externalities within the global economy.[13]

a. Strengthening multilateralism

Even prior to the COVID-19 pandemic, the Inter-Agency Task Force on Financing for Development warned that "international economic and financial systems are not only failing to deliver on the SDGs, but ... there has been substantial backsliding in key action areas" (United Nations, 2020a: xvii). The COVID-19 crisis and ensuing global recession have deteriorated the outlook further, exposing weak policy coordination and absent global leadership. The risk that the COVID-19 pandemic could be used to justify a retreat from multilateral cooperation and lukewarm efforts towards achieving the Sustainable Development Goals and the Paris Agreement, should be met with a resounding call for renewed and strengthened multilateralism, capable of furthering systemic resilience. This entails revamping support to vulnerable countries, as well as addressing long-standing flaws in the prevailing multilateral trade and financial architecture (UNCTAD, 2020h, 2017e, 2019b).

In the trading sphere, especially in the early phase of the crisis, unilateral trade-restrictive measures, such as border closures, export and travel bans or aggressive public procurement practices, created shockwaves in markets of sensitive products (e.g. medical equipment and food), leaving import-dependent countries such as LDCs vulnerable to price hikes and supply disruptions (Baldwin and Evenett, 2020; UNCTAD et al., 2020). These perverse dynamics have partly eased with time, as countries reverse export bans and resort to regional procurement schemes, similar to the one adopted by the Africa Centres for Disease Control and Prevention (CDC), and a range of international cooperation initiatives emerging in multiple directions, North-South, South-South and even South-North (UNCTAD et al., 2020; UNCTAD, 2020i; AUC, 2020; Izmestiev and Klingebiel, 2020). Nonetheless, realizing a free, fair, non-discriminatory, transparent, predictable and stable trade and investment environment and keeping markets open remains vital to ensure availability of essential goods and promote a strong economic recovery (UNCTAD et al., 2020).

An LDC post-COVID recovery requires the reform of the international financial architecture and a Marshall Plan

In the financial sphere, the COVID-19 crisis has vindicated some of the arguments made in *The Least Developed Countries Report 2019*, and recalls the dynamics of balance-of-payment-constrained growth models (Thirlwall, 1979; Bacha, 1990; UNCTAD, 2019a). The multifaceted shock prompted by the COVID-19 pandemic triggered declines in public revenues and a largely exogenous deterioration of the balance of payments, through falling commodity prices and collapsing global demand, FDI and remittance flows (chapter 1 and UNCTAD, 2020h, 2020a; Baldwin and Weder di Mauro, 2020a, 2020b). In turn, the resulting exchange rate dynamics increased the cost of sensitive imports (food, fuels and medical equipment), while typically also worsening their debt sustainability outlook (UNCTAD, 2020j). The COVID-19 pandemic also further exacerbated LDC structural weaknesses, and led to widening of

---

[13] The fact that sustained growth in emerging markets pulled the global recovery in the aftermath of the 2008–2009 financial and economic crises provides a relevant example of these pecuniary externalities.

LDCs' foreign reserves drained by COVID-19 outbreak

"twin deficits" of government budget and current account, which have heavily constrained the scope for proactive policy responses by these countries.

Stronger international cooperation is sorely needed to reform the prevailing international financial architecture that has shown itself incapable of ensuring adequate access to international liquidity and long-term development finance to LDCs – all of which has undermined sustainable development and resilience building. While LDCs might have some room to enhance domestic resource mobilization, improve cost-effectiveness of public spending and strengthen national competitiveness, this is patently insufficient in the current context (UNCTAD, 2019b). With daunting investment needs and heightened external resource dependence, they are essentially constrained by an international monetary system which imposes the burden of adjustment on debtors and deficit economies (UNCTAD, 2015d, 2019b). This situation contributes to global deflationary pressure and exacerbates global inequalities, as the world's most vulnerable countries have had to cope with an unparalleled economic shock with little means at their disposal. The asymmetric role of international reserve currencies for developed and developing countries is at least partly to blame for this outcome, which further aggravated LDCs' vulnerabilities. Not only reserves hoarding (as a form of self-insurance) may entail sizeable opportunity costs for cash-strapped economies but exchange rate dynamics tend to ultimately undermine their usefulness precisely in times of crisis. While the foreign reserves of LDCs have historically been limited and have for the past four or five years been on a downward trend, they have dwindled rapidly in the early phase of the COVID-19 outbreak, which also occurred in other developing countries (UNCTAD, 2020c; IMF, 2020b). Shortages of hard currencies were worsened by the amplifying and mutually reinforcing interactions between financial markets and currency fluctuations, with LDCs losing much-needed foreign exchange because of "flight to safety" dynamics, leading to what has been dubbed "original sin redux" (Hofmann et al., 2020).[14] This exerted additional pressure on foreign exchange, reducing LDC resilience to the crisis, as hard currencies constitute a lifeline to pay for supplies of sensitive imports. International financial institutions and regional development banks have reacted to this situation by mobilizing and/or redirecting significant additional resources (Djankov and Kiechel, 2020; AfDB, 2020). However, lacking the political will for a stronger concerted action, including fresh capital injections, their action has fallen far short of the $2.5 trillion package for developing countries that UNCTAD and the IMF have called for (UNCTAD, 2020c; *Reuters*, 2020a; Djankov and Kiechel, 2020).

Against this background, the cry for stronger multilateralism and more effective international cooperation could not resound more clearly. A sustainable recovery in LDCs inevitably warrants stronger mechanisms for the provision of international liquidity. This should include a fresh injection of Special Drawing Rights (the IMF's unit of account), under a more progressive allocation mechanism that could at least partly rebalance LDC marginal weight in IMF's quota system (UNCTAD, 2020c; Truman, 2020). While a multilateral initiative is increasingly necessary, the current conjuncture also calls for strengthening regional and South-South mechanisms for financial cooperation. This might include the expansion of concessional and non-concessional resources provided by regional development banks, or as appropriate, a currency swap and repurchase arrangements. Looking ahead beyond the COVID-19 outbreak, mechanisms for rapidly disbursing international liquidity and contingent financing are likely to play an even more essential role in the future as part of enhanced emergency responses to climate change and disaster risks. In light of their disproportionate vulnerability to natural disasters, whose frequency and intensity is increasing year by year, the needs of LDCs should be given particular attention.

b. Sustainable development finance

The inadequacy of the current international financial architecture becomes perhaps even more apparent in relation to the issue of access to long-term sustainable development finance, especially considering the formidable scale of the investment needs of LDCs. In 2017 UNCTAD estimated, for instance, that the total investment needed to achieve basic universal energy access in LDCs by 2030 would be in the order of $12–40 billion per year, while increasing supplies to fulfil the needs of transformational access would raise these costs even further (UNCTAD, 2017a). Similarly, with only less than one third of the population of LDCs using the Internet and disproportionately high

---

[14] The "original sin" refers to the fact that most countries cannot borrow abroad in their own currency (Hausmann and Panizza, 2003).

costs for ICT services, the investment requirements to bridge the digital divide in LDCs are also daunting (UNCTAD, 2019e, 2019d). Moving from infrastructures to human capital, substantial financing gaps have long emerged in relation to the health and education sectors, whose chronic underfunding situation has become irrefutable in recent months. In a nutshell, there can be no doubt that prospects for spurring the development of LDC productive capacities and meeting the 2030 Agenda for Sustainable Development will require a concerted investment push of unprecedented magnitude. Failure to do so might deepen existing divides, entrench inequalities and gender disparities in access to education and new technologies, all of which will have long-term effects on the attainment of the Sustainable Development Goals.

The scant resources of LDCs and their dwindling fiscal space calls for a Marshall plan with significantly bolstered aid flows to avert the consequences of a prolonged downturn and pave the way for a sustained recovery (UNCTAD, 2020b). Notwithstanding periodically reaffirmed aid targets – whether in total or specific to LDCs (respectively 0.7 per cent and 0.15–0.20 per cent of donor countries' gross national income – GNI) – only a handful of Development Assistance Committee (DAC) donors have delivered on their promises (UNCTAD, 2019b). Preliminary data for 2019, for example, show that ODA provided by OECD-DAC members only reached 0.31 per cent of their GNI; meanwhile, net bilateral aid flows to the LDCs reached $33 billion, increasing by 2.6 per cent in real terms after a drop in 2018 (OECD, 2020a). It is already clear that the COVID-19 outbreak will put additional pressure on aid budgets; yet, the cost of policy packages adopted by donor countries in the wake of the pandemic dwarfs the cost of meeting long-standing aid commitments, as reaffirmed in target 17.2 of the Sustainable Development Goals. UNCTAD recently estimated that had DAC donors met the LDC-specific target for aid allocation, LDCs would have received an extra $32–58 billion per year (UNCTAD, 2019b). It is hard to overemphasize the difference such resources could make in supporting a broad-based recovery in the world's most vulnerable and aid-dependent countries. Equally, similar gaps speak volumes to the fact that decade-long debates on mutual accountability do not remain dead letter, as do the declarations to reduce global inequalities in the 2030 Agenda for Sustainable Development Goals.

Beyond the size, the very modalities of aid delivery to LDCs have become increasingly complex, evolving in ways that might pose additional challenges to recipient governments, notably in terms of ensuring

The scant resources and fiscal space of LDCs call for a Marshall plan with significantly bolstered aid flows

aid coordination, ownership of and alignment with their development strategies (UNCTAD, 2019b). Contrary to long-standing recommendations stipulating that ODA to LDCs should essentially take the form of grants, concessional loans have accounted for a rising share of resources, surpassing 25 per cent of total ODA.[15] In addition, project-type of interventions – which are poorly reflected (if at all) in the government budget process – have accounted for the lion's share of net ODA disbursement, contributing only weakly to the reinforcement of institutional capacities, including in the health and education sectors. Finally, increasing access to private sector instruments has only marginally been successful in mobilizing additional resources for LDCs (whose perceived risk-profitability profile remained unattractive); however, these instruments risk hollowing out the role of governments in assessing alignment and additionality, and also risk potentially watering down the whole aid effectiveness agenda, and ultimately blurring the lines between aid and other official flows. While these trends are consistent with what happened in other developing countries, the heightened aid dependency and institutional weaknesses of LDCs could mean that their adverse effects on capacity development might be more pervasive. In light of this evolution of the aid architecture, coupled with growing demands for redressing entrenched inequalities and spurring social change, a revamped aid effectiveness agenda 2.0 is increasingly warranted to rebalance the power relationships between donor and recipient countries, as well as enhance the coherence between the means and ends of international cooperation (UNCTAD, 2019b).

c. Debt issues

Another long-standing systemic issue of immediate relevance to LDCs pertains to debt sustainability and the related absence of an effective framework for debt workout. As highlighted repeatedly by UNCTAD,

---

[15] The OECD's Recommendation on Terms and Conditions of Aid stipulated that ODA to LDCs "should be essentially in the form of grants and, as a minimum, the average grant element of all commitments from a given donor should either be at least 86 per cent to each least developed country over a period of three years, or at least 90 per cent annually for the least developed countries as a group" (OECD, 1978: 8).

LDCs would benefit from a concerted investment push informed by common but differentiated responsibilities

recent years have witnessed an extraordinary buildup of developing countries debt stocks, and the COVID-19 shock could be the perfect storm to trigger a wave of debt crises (UNCTAD, 2016c, 2018e, 2019b, 2020j; Djankov and Panizza, 2020; Kose et al., 2020). The scale of the problem for LDCs is hard to overstate: according to the debt sustainability assessments by the IMF and the World Bank, as of September 2020 14 LDCs were deemed to be at high risk of external debt distress, with five more in debt distress.[16] While the G20 decision to adopt to a temporary debt service standstill on bilateral official loan repayments from the so-called "IDA countries" represents a step in the right direction, it remains insufficient along several dimensions. First, the exclusive focus on the poorest countries leaves out many low- and middle-income countries that already face severe economic strains. Second, private creditors participation is sought only on a voluntary basis, and yet they are an important constituency for some LDCs, as well as for middle-income countries, where they hold the majority of the sovereign debt. Third, while this solution is temporary and does not affects debt stocks, it is increasingly clear that several LDCs will require significant debt relief if they are to rebound from the COVID-19 shock without compromising much-needed social spending. More broadly, for LDCs and other developing countries alike, there is a pressing need to adopt a standard framework for debt workout, particularly as the costs for coordination and potential litigation have increased over time with the broadening of the range of creditors and the associated complexity (UNCTAD, 2019b). LDCs would equally benefit from greater international support and technical assistance in improving debt reporting and management practices, including in areas such as data reliability, transparency, monitoring of contingent liabilities and debt incurred by state-owned enterprises (SOEs) (UNCTAD, 2018e, 2019b).

d. Climate finance

While the ongoing recession is understandably the main focus of current policy discussions, in the longer term the impact of climate change might well dwarf the COVID-19 shock, casting the whole debate on access to development finance in a different light. LDCs are predicted to disproportionately shoulder the adverse effects of climate change and could push tens of millions into extreme poverty, thereby worsening existing inequalities and creating what some have called a "climate apartheid" (United Nations, 2019, 2020b), underpinning their vital need for an adequate provision of climate finance. In this respect, if the availability of climate finance has increased in recent years, the fact remains that it falls significantly short of the promise to mobilize $100 billion per year by 2020, as agreed at the 15th Conference of Parties in Copenhagen (UNCTAD, 2019b). According to OECD estimates, in 2017 – the latest year for which data are available – climate finance reached globally $72 billion, including bilateral and multilateral public finance (attributed to developed countries), officially-supported export credits and mobilized private finance (OECD, 2019b). Of this amount, public climate finance accounted for $54 billion in 2017, consistent with a projected level of $67 billion in 2020 – a projection which did not take into account the COVID-19 shock. Moreover, the thematic breakdown of these resources remains heavily skewed: 73 per cent of the resources were channeled towards mitigation purposes, a further 8 per cent to cross-cutting issues, and only 19 per cent to adaptation. While the share of adaptation in public climate finance in 2016–2017 was significantly higher for LDCs (45 per cent), this composition remains only partly aligned with their conditions, considering their relatively small carbon footprint and their dire need for climate-resilient infrastructure. It is thus clear that LDCs would benefit greatly from the adoption of a concerted investment push informed by the principle of common but differentiated responsibilities and respective capabilities, such as those envisaged in the global green new deal (United Nations, 2015a; UNCTAD, 2019j, 2019b).

e. Illicit financial flows

Beyond ODA and external assistance, genuine support to the resource mobilization efforts of LDCs could go a long way in recovering much-needed financial resources. This applies notably to ongoing efforts to curb illicit financial flows. In 2015 it was estimated

---

[16] Countries at high risk include: Afghanistan, Burundi, Central African Republic, Chad, Djibouti, Ethiopia, Gambia, Haiti, Kiribati, Lao P.D.R., Mauritania, Sierra Leone, Tuvalu and Zambia; conversely Mozambique, Sao Tomé and Principe, Somalia, South Sudan and Sudan were classified as in debt distress. Data on Angola are not available as the country is not covered by the Debt Sustainability Framework for Low-Income Countries. Concerning the methodology of the Debt Sustainability Framework for Low Income Countries refer to IMF (2017); updated country assessments are available online at: https://www.worldbank.org/en/programs/debt-toolkit/dsa.

that illicit financial flows averaged 5 per cent of the GDP of LDCs and 36 per cent of their tax revenue, with some countries registering much higher outflows (UNCTAD, 2019b). Trade mispricing, in particular, appears to be heavily concentrated in commodity sectors, depriving many LDCs of much-needed revenues and foreign exchange, with adverse effects on a wide range of developmental outcomes (UNCTAD, 2019b, 2016d, 2020g, 2020b). Similarly, LDCs appear to be particularly exposed to base erosion and profit shifting by multinational enterprises and the challenges related to the taxation of increasingly digitalized business models. Moving towards a fairer international taxation system and strengthening the support for capacity development for LDC regulatory and tax administration bodies is thus an international imperative. In addition, it is essential to enhance cross-border financial transparency, strengthen international tax cooperation, and provide adequate technical assistance and capacity development for LDC tax administration entities. LDCs may also benefit from even small steps towards unitary taxation of multinational enterprises (i.e. taxing a multinational enterprise and its subsidiaries as a single firm based on its worldwide operations), thus reducing the incentive for tax competition and the use of tax havens, along the lines proposed by the Independent Commission for the Reform of International Corporate Taxation (UNCTAD, 2020g). LDCs are particularly exposed (at least in relative terms) to illicit financial flows but have a limited stake in related international initiatives, which gives rise to questions on their legitimacy.

2. Stronger international support measures for LDCs

Existing international support measures (ISMs) in favour of LDCs encompass a range of actions, commitments and provisions across the fields of development finance, trade, technology and technical assistance. Thoroughly reviewing all of them and rigorously assessing their impact on LDC economic performance is admittedly beyond the scope of this report.[17] Nonetheless, it is fair to say that existing ISMs have only had – at best – modest concrete impacts, as evidenced by LDC limited progress against the IPoA targets. This, in turn, reflects a combination of weak design, declining effectiveness, insufficient funding, inadequate institutional settings, or limited awareness and low uptake on the part of LDC themselves (UNCTAD, 2016a).

---

[17] For a comprehensive discussion on the different ISMs and related impact, refer to UNCTAD (2016a) and CDP and UN DESA (2018).

Enhanced international cooperation to stem illicit financial flows could generate much-needed resources for LDC recovery

a. Trade ISMs

Beyond development finance issues, ISMs in the areas of trade and technology are the most relevant to the present discussion on productive capacities for the next decade. Despite some progress at the technical level, the various forms of trade-related support for LDCs have fallen short of what was needed to double LDC share of world exports by 2020, as envisaged in the IPoA (paragraph 65) and in target 17.11 of the Sustainable Development Goals. These challenges are best epitomized by the mixed record of the major trade-related ISM – duty-free quota-free market access – which is enshrined in several World Trade Organization (WTO) ministerial declarations, as well as in target 17.12 of the Sustainable Development Goals.

Notwithstanding the rising number of developed and developing countries granting unilateral non-reciprocal preferences to exports originating from LDCs, this has typically played a subdued role in the evolution of LDC market shares in preference-granting countries, with relative price effects and other structural factors being more important drivers of performance (WTO, 2019). Preferential schemes differ widely in terms of coverage, preference margins, rules of origin and availability of alternative preferential arrangements, but several common factors have dampened their effectiveness. First, preference erosion tends to reduce the commercial value of these schemes over time; besides, their unilateral nature implies some degree of uncertainty and unpredictability, especially at a time when the international trade scene has become increasingly volatile and restrictive measures are on the rise.[18] Second and more fundamentally, lacking a broader action to support productive capacity development, these schemes appear to

---

[18] Recent examples of suspension of unilateral trade preferences include:
- the February 2020 decision of the European Commission to withdraw part of the tariff preferences granted to Cambodia under the Everything But Arms trade scheme due to the "serious and systematic violations of the human rights principles" (European Commission, 2020); and
- the July 2018 decision by the US President to suspend the application of duty-free treatment for all AGOA-eligible apparel from Rwanda, following the latter's ban on second-hand clothes and imports of shoes (TRALAC, 2018; AGOA info, 2018).

International support measures for access to technology are grossly inadequate

have done little to support LDC export diversification. Even though preference margins tend to be more lucrative on manufacturing products, few LDCs have been able to reap these benefits at the extensive margin, making good use of preferential market access to support diversification. However, given the persistence of primary commodity dependence in most LDCs, the potential gains from preferential schemes have failed to materialize, as the bulk of their merchandise is traded at the most-favoured nation (MFN) duty-free rate (WTO, 2019). Third, stringent rules of origin have at times undermined the utilization of preferential schemes on the part of LDC exporters by raising their costs of compliance, especially in the context of weak productive fabric and institutional framework (UNCTAD, 2018f, 2019g). A set of multilateral guidelines for simpler and more transparent rules of origin applicable to preferential trading schemes for LDCs have been developed in the context of the WTO, helping to catalyze reforms in the area and bring more attention the issues of transparency and predictability.[19] Yet, greater scope exists to improve the utilization rates of preferential schemes, especially with respect to some of the more recent preferential arrangements, which are characterized by a high proportion of eligible imports entering LDCs at the MFN rate.

More generally, the trade performance of LDCs is constrained by NTMs, including a wide range of requirements from technical standards or sanitary and phytosanitary (SPS) measures to anti-dumping, and other administrative provisions. Developed countries, in particular, tend to apply relatively more NTMs (i.e. regulating a larger share of their imports and using more regulations on each item) than other developing countries or LDCs, while the latter regulate their exports twice as frequently as developing or developed countries (UNCTAD and World Bank, 2018). The presence of NTMs is particularly large in sectors of fundamental importance for LDCs, such as agro-food, textile and apparel, whose impact often exceeds that of tariffs.[20] LDCs and small producers are disproportionately hit by NTMs, as the costs of compliance depend on a range of factors, including technical know-how, production facilities, hard and soft infrastructural base (notably quality assurance and standard-setting bodies).

The same broad reasoning applies to trade in services in LDCs: while services exports have increased significantly over the past decade, they remain below one per cent of the world total and are increasingly concentrated in a handful of countries. Moreover, they are mainly accounted for by tourism, transport, and distribution services, while more knowledge and ICT-intensive types of services, whose dynamism is underpinned by digitalization and servicification, play a subdued role. Work on the so-called "LDC services waiver" – allowing WTO members to grant preferential treatment to services and service suppliers from LDC members – began in 2011 precisely with the objective of better integrating LDCs into international services trade. Yet, notwithstanding some progress, nearly ten years down the line it is clear that this measure alone is unlikely to radically change the picture, as services market access comprises a mix of liberalization (i.e. removing discrimination), capacity development and regulatory reforms.[21]

b. Technology ISMs

ISMs related to access to technology lend themselves to an equally sobering assessment, a finding that raises very serious concerns at a time when digitalization threatens to widen existing divides, and challenge traditional business models. LDCs do benefit from a number of related special and differential treatment (SDT) provisions, including a waiver of most obligations under the WTO TRIPS Agreement until 2021 (under Article 66.1), as well as an exemption from provisions of the TRIPS agreement related to pharmaceutical products until 2033 (under TRIPS Council decision nr IP/C/73, dated 6 November 2015). Besides, developed countries "shall provide incentives to enterprises and institutions (…) for the purpose of promoting and encouraging technology transfer" to LDCs, under article 66.2 of TRIPS. In practice, however, this provision has translated into very few meaningful success stories (UNCTAD, 2016a), few LDCs have been able to make significant progress in technological upgrading through the strategic use of SDT measures, Bangladesh being perhaps the

---

[19] Decisions on preferential rules of origin for LDCs have been adopted in the 2013 and 2015 WTO Ministerial Conferences (respectively in Bali and Nairobi).

[20] Incidentally, this sectoral pattern is likely to have an adverse impact on gender equality, as women tend to be over-represented in the agriculture and garment sectors.

[21] As of October 2019, 51 WTO members (accounting for 86 per cent of global trade) had notified preferences to the benefit of LDC services and services suppliers.

main exception in relation to the rapid growth of its pharmaceutical industry (Nazim Uddin Bhuiyan et al., 2019; Helal Uddin Ahmed, 2019). Besides, the use of these flexibilities is at times restricted by WTO-plus obligations included in bilateral trade and investment agreements (UNCTAD, 2007), as recently reflected by the litigation risks associated with policy responses to the COVID-19 outbreak (Bernasconi-Osterwalder et al., 2020).

Beyond SDT, a host of technical assistance initiatives have also been rolled out in relation to climate technology transfer, notably under the United Nations Framework Convention on Climate Change (UNFCCC) technology mechanism and the Poznan strategic programme on technology transfer. Similarly, the LDC Technology Bank, established in 2011 but only operational as of 2018, has begun carrying out Science, Technology and Innovation Reviews and Technology Needs Assessments and taken action to promote access to research and technical knowledge and strengthen national academies of science. Despite these laudable steps, it is hard to avoid the conclusion that, overall, these measures are too piecemeal and underfunded in relation to LDC technological gaps, rendering technological upgrading in LDCs largely elusive. Besides, the complexity and fragmentation of the underlying mechanisms are challenging to navigate for LDC policymakers, undermining the effectiveness of related support (Brianna Craft et al., 2017; UNCTAD, 2016a).

c. Reinforcing the effectiveness of ISMs

Overall, these few examples underscore five main conclusions. First, *ISMs that are inherently rooted in some form of trade liberalization are unlikely to succeed in redressing LDC marginalization in international trade, without a congruous simultaneous effort to boost their productive capacities and spur diversification*. If anything, this trend is likely to be further reinforced in the context of on-going servicification and digitalization, given the growing interdependence they underpin across firms and economic sectors, as well as the pivotal role of connectivity and related infrastructures. In this respect, the strengthening of the Aid for Trade initiative, as a critical form of support to productive sectors and trade-related infrastructure, stands out as a necessary condition for the effectiveness of other trade-related ISMs. Equally, a strengthening of trade-related technical assistance, notably through the Enhanced Integrated Framework (EIF), would also be important.

Second, *the concrete impact of most ISMs ultimately hinges on the quality of LDC institutions*. This is particularly critical in addressing some of the hurdles

Stronger and more innovative ISMs are needed to prevent a further widening of technological divides

related to NTMs, digital trade and trade in services, where issues of transparency and predictability (and even of mere measurement) are more challenging. Broad capacity development efforts are thus needed to: (i) improve the quality, availability and reliability of trade-related data; (ii) enhance regulatory transparency; (iii) ensure policy coherence across various entities; and (iv) spur evidence-based debate on the strategic elements of trade policy. Advanced digital technologies may to some extent facilitate these institutional improvements and reduce the costs of compliance (for instance through the application of advanced analytics to quality control, the adoption of paperless trade, or remote container management techniques). However, in most LDCs these gains are likely to be partially offset by the fixed costs of the technologies themselves and the related need for skill upgrading and awareness raising among the business community. In the same vein, as shown by the relative success in the implementation of the Trade Facilitation Agreement and related SDT, upfront investments should be made to raise awareness among LDC constituencies about the technicalities, usefulness and strategic content of the various ISMs (chapter 4).

Third, *adequate policy space continues to be necessary* if LDCs are to foster structural transformation and break their dependence on primary products. As already recognized in the WTO's Doha Round, existing SDT measures (for LDCs and other developing countries alike) need an overhauling, but the Monitoring Mechanism has produced few concrete results so far (UNCTAD, 2016a, 2020b). At the very minimum, existing flexibilities in relation to the obligations of the TRIPS agreement should

> **Technology transfer should feature in the design and implementation of investment promotion regimes for LDCs**

be renewed beyond 2021, and LDCs should be reassured, for example through related "peace clauses" – that they will not be subjected to litigation, whether under the WTO or under bilateral trade/investment agreements, for policies adopted in response to the COVID-19 pandemic.[22]

Fourth, *stronger mechanisms to foster meaningful technology transfer by private firms are badly needed* to give concrete form to the obligations under Article 66.2 of the TRIPS agreement. Besides, the issue of technology transfer should feature prominently in the design and implementation of investment promotion regimes for LDCs, referred to in target 17.5 of the Sustainable Development Goals. Concrete steps in this direction could potentially include:

- Explicitly linking the use of public development finance through private sector instruments to genuine and documented practices on fostering technology transfer (such as joint ventures, creation of R&D facilities in LDCs, partnership with local research institutions, and the like);
- Paying greater attention to voluntary/mandatory technology transfer measures in the context of sustainability standards, corporate social responsibility (CSR) and responsible business conduct;
- Promoting the diffusion of open source software and digital products; and
- Creating a unified framework for the voluntary sharing of green technologies specifications and related intellectual property information, and building on the innovative business models applied in the health sector through the Tech Access Partnership (launched as part of the responses to the COVID-19 pandemic) and the Medicines Patent Pool.[23]

Fifth, without dismissing the urgent need for multilateral efforts to promote meaningful technology transfer to LDCs, *there is an ample scope to strengthen regional and South-South mechanisms for technological cooperation*. In the wake of the COVID-19 pandemic, this potential has surfaced visibly in health-related areas, but it could extend far beyond that, to other areas such as green technologies, industrial and digital cooperation. In this respect, the establishment of R&D consortiums, regional centres of excellence, cooperation frameworks for tertiary education are but examples of initiatives that could provide LDCs with additional opportunities to benefit from resource pooling and knowledge diffusion.

A final consideration to be borne in mind with respect to the forthcoming deliberation on LDC graduation is that it is imperative at the current juncture that these decisions take due account of the severity of the ongoing global recession and the seriousness of the socioeconomic impacts it is having. Looking forward, the priority should be to minimize long-term damage and renew international support to resilience building among LDCs. Simultaneously, emphasis on tailoring support to graduating countries should not come at the expense of diverting attention from the non-graduating LDCs, whose needs are even greater. Rather, the international community should seize the occasion to strengthen existing ISMs and make them more appropriate to a gradually more homogeneous category.

---

[22] This would be consistent with article 24 of the Rules and Procedures Governing the Settlement of Disputes, according to which WTO members "shall exercise due restraint in raising matters" involving LDCs and give particular consideration to their special situation".

[23] More information on the Tech Access Partnership and the Medicines Patent pool are available at the following hyperlinks respectively: https://techaccesspartnership.org/ and https://medicinespatentpool.org/.

References

Abu Hatab A, Cavinato MER, Lindemer A and Lagerkvist C-J (2019). Urban sprawl, food security and agricultural systems in developing countries: A systematic review of the literature. *Cities*. 94129–142.

AfDB (2020). African Development Bank launches record breaking $3 billion "Fight COVID-19" Social Bond. Available at https://www.afdb.org/en/news-and-events/press-releases/african-development-bank-launches-record-breaking-3-billion-fight-covid-19-social-bond-34982 (accessed 17 July 2020).

AfterAccess (2018). Understanding the gender gap in the Global South. DIRSI, LIRNEasia, Research ICT Africa. AfterAccess.

AGOA info (2018). Presidential Proclamation regarding Rwanda's AGOA eligibility. Available at https://agoa.info/news/article/15493-presidential-proclamation-regarding-rwanda.html (accessed 22 July 2020).

Agricultural Transformation Consultation Team (2019). APO Agricultural Transformation Framework. Asian Productivity Organization. Tokyo. (accessed 9 June 2020).

Akileswaran K and Hutchinson G (2019). Adapting to the 4IR: Africa's development in the age of automation. Tony Blair Institute for Global Change. London. (accessed 29 April 2020).

Akter S et al. (2017). Women's empowerment and gender equity in agriculture: A different perspective from Southeast Asia. *Food Policy*. 69270–279.

Ali D, Bowen DE, Deininger K and Duponchel M (2016). Investigating the gender gap in agriculture productivity: Evidence from Uganda. *World Development*. 87152–170.

Allen DT (2019). Farmers are using AI to spot pests and catch diseases. Business Insider. Available at https://www.businessinsider.com/farmers-artificial-intelligence-in-agriculture-catch-disease-pests?r=US&IR=T (accessed 10 June 2020).

AMFG (2019). AM Around the World: How Mature is 3D Printing in the Asia-Pacific Region? Available at https://amfg.ai/2019/11/20/am-around-the-world-how-mature-is-3d-printing-in-the-asia-pacific-region/ (accessed 27 August 2020).

Aminetzah D, Katz J and Mannion P (2020). How innovations in food sustainability can help feed the world responsibly. *McKinsey Quarterly*.

Andreoni A and Anzolin G (2019). A revolution in the making? Challenges and opportunities of digital production technologies for developing countries. Working Paper No. 7/2019. UNIDO. Vienna.

Arnaudo D (2019). Bridging the Deepest Digital Divides: A History and Survey of Digital Media in Myanmar. In: Punathambekar A, and Mohan S, eds. *Global Digital Cultures: Perspectives from South Asia*. University of Michigan Press. Ann Arbor.

Ashford LS (2007). Africa's Youthful Population: Risk or Opportunity? Available at http://www.brac.net/sites/default/files/glm/AfricaYouth.pdf.

AUC (2020). Africa CDC receives third donation of medical supplies from Jack Ma Foundation, co-hosts global MediXChange webinar on COVID-19. Available at https://africacdc.org/news/africa-cdc-receives-third-donation-of-medical-supplies-from-jack-ma-foundation-co-hosts-global-medixchange-webinar-on-covid-19/ (accessed 17 July 2020).

Aung LL (2020). Report on the economic, social and environmental consequences of COVID-19 on Myanmar and their implications for graduation from LDC status. United Nations Conference on Trade and Development (UNCTAD). Geneva.

Aung TT, Paul R and McPherson P (2020). "All my dreams are shattered": Coronavirus crushes Asia's garment industry. Reuters. Available at https://www.reuters.com/article/us-health-coronavirus-garment-idUSKBN22U34V (accessed 20 May 2020).

Aye TM (2018). 4 Agri-Tech Game Changers That are Transforming Myanmar's Agriculture Industry. ProspectsASEAN. Available at https://www.prospectsasean.com/agri-tech-game-changers-trasforming-myanmar-agriculture-industry/ (accessed 14 July 2020).

Bacha EL (1990). A three-gap model of foreign transfers and the GDP growth rate in developing countries. *Journal of Development Economics*. 32(2):279–296.

Bah EM (2011). Structural Transformation Paths Across Countries. *Emerging Markets Finance & Trade*. 475–19.

Baker L and Sovacool BK (2017). The political economy of technological capabilities and global production networks in South Africa's wind and solar photovoltaic (PV) industries. *Political Geography*. 601–12.

Baldwin R (2016). *The great convergence: Information technology and the new globalization*. Belknap Press. Cambridge (MA).

Baldwin R and Evenett S, eds. (2020). *COVID-19 and Trade Policy: Why Turning Inward Won't Work*. Centre for Economic Policy Research (CEPR). London.

Baldwin R and Robert-Nicoud F (2014). Trade-in-goods and trade-in-tasks: An integrating framework. *Journal of International Economics*. 92(1):51–62.

Baldwin R and Weder di Mauro B, eds. (2020a). *Mitigating the COVID Economic Crisis: Act Fast and Do Whatever It Takes*. Centre for Economic Policy Research (CEPR). London.

Baldwin R and Weder di Mauro B, eds. (2020b). *Economics in the Time of COVID-19: A New EBook*.

REFERENCES

Centre for Economic Policy Research (CEPR). London.

Banga K and te Velde DW (2018). Digitalisation and the future of manufacturing in Africa. Supporting Economic Transformation (SET). ODI. London.

Baraniuk C (2018). The crop-spraying drones that go where tractors can't. BBC News. Available at https://www.bbc.com/news/business-45020853 (accessed 14 July 2020).

Barefoot K, Curtis D, Jolliff W, Nicholson JR and Omohundro R (2018). Defining and Measuring the Digital Economy. Working Paper No. 2018–4. Bureau of Economic Analysis, United States Department of Commerce. Washington D.C.

Bärenfänger R, Otto B and Gizanis D (2015). Business and Data Management Capabilities for the Digital Economy. White Paper No. V1.0. Competence Center Corporate Data Quality (CDQ AG). Geneva, Switzerland.

Behrman J, Quisumbing A and Peterman A (2011). A Review of Empirical Evidence on Gender Differences in Non-land Agricultural Inputs, Technology, and Services in Developing Countries. ESA Working Paper No. 11–11. Food and Agriculture Organization of the United Nations.

Bell M and Pavitt K (1993). Technological Accumulation and Industrial Growth: Contrasts Between Developed and Developing Countries. *Industrial and Corporate Change*. 2(2):157–210.

BenYishay A, Jones M, Kondylis F and Mobarak AM (2020). Gender gaps in technology diffusion. *Journal of Development Economics*. 143(C):

Bernasconi-Osterwalder N, Brewin S and Maina N (2020). Protecting Against Investor–State Claims Amidst COVID-19: A call to action for governments. International Institute for Sustainable Development. (accessed 24 July 2020).

Beverelli C, Fiorini M and Hoekman B (2017). Services trade policy and manufacturing productivity: The role of institutions. *Journal of International Economics*. 104166–182.

Biggs T, Shah M and Srivastava P (1995). Technological Capabilities and Learning in African Enterprises. World Bank Technical Paper No. 288. World Bank. Washington D.C.

Bloomberg J (2018). Digitization, Digitalization, And Digital Transformation: Confuse Them At Your Peril. *Forbes*. Available at https://www.forbes.com/sites/jasonbloomberg/2018/04/29/digitization-digitalization-and-digital-transformation-confuse-them-at-your-peril/ (accessed 15 July 2020).

Bloomberg.com (2020). Tech Startups Are Flooding Kenya With Apps Offering High-Interest Loans. 12 February.

Bosio E, Jolevski F, Lemoine J and Ramalho R (2020). Survival of firms in developing economies during economic crisis. In: Djankov S, and Panizza U, eds. *COVID in Developing Economies*. Centre for Economic Policy Research (CEPR). London: 157–174.

Bradley C, Hirt M, Hudson S, Northcote N and Smit S (2020). The great acceleration. Strategy & Corporate Finance Practice. McKinsey & Company.

Bresnahan T (2010). General Purpose Technologies. In: Hall B H, and Rosenberg N, eds. *Handbook of the Economics of Innovation*. Elsevier. Amsterdam: 761–791.

Brianna Craft, Stella Gama and Thinley Namgyel (2017). Least Developed Countries' experiences with the UNFCCC technology mechanism. IIED Issue Paper. International Institute of Environment and Development (IIED). London. (accessed 24 July 2020).

Briguglio L, Cordina G, Farrugia N and Vella S (2008). Economic Vulnerability and Resilience: Concepts and Measurements. Research Paper No. 2008/55. United Nations University – World Institute for Development Economics Research (UNU-WIDER). Helsinki.

Brooks DH (2007). Industrial and Competition Policy: Conflict or Complementarity? Asian Development Bank. http://hdl.handle.net/11540/4061.

BuddeComm (2020). Myanmar begins to see increased competition in the fibre broadband Segment. GlobeNewswire. Available at http://www.globenewswire.com/news-release/2020/02/12/1983781/0/en/Myanmar-begins-to-see-increased-competition-in-the-fibre-broadband-Segment.html (accessed 6 July 2020).

Bughin J, LaBerge L and Mellbye A (2017). The case for digital reinvention. *McKinsey Quarterly*.

Cabeza Gutés M (1996). The concept of weak sustainability. *Ecological Economics*. 17(3):147–156.

Calderón C and Servén L (2010). Infrastructure and Economic Development in Sub-Saharan Africa. *Journal of African Economies*. 19(suppl_1):i13–i87, Oxford Academic.

Castellacci F (2011). Closing the Technology Gap? *Review of Development Economics*. 15(1):180–197.

Cayeux J, Dagorn J-C and Pascal P (2017). An analysis of the challenges facing the food system in Haiti. Papaye Peasant Movement (MPP) and Action Against Hunger. New York.

CDP (2020). Outcome of the comprehensive review of the LDC criteria. United Nations – Committee for Development Policy. New York.

CDP and UN DESA (2018). *Handbook on the Least Developed Country Category: Inclusion, Graduation* and *Special Support Measures*. United Nations. New York.

CDP and UN DESA (2020). Report on the twenty-second session (24–27 February 2020) – Economic and Social Council. Nr. E/2020/33. Available at https://undocs.org/en/E/2020/33.

Chandra A and McNamara KE (2018). Climate-Smart Agriculture in Southeast Asia. *Resilience*. Elsevier: 165–179.

Chandran N (2019). Growing pains: Southeast Asian farmers need cheaper agritech. Aljazeera. https://www.aljazeera.com/ajimpact/growing-pains-southeast-asian-farmers-cheaper-agritech-191227085148352.html. (accessed 9 June 2020).

Chang H-J and Andreoni A (2020). Industrial Policy in the 21st Century. *Development and Change*. 51(2):324–351.

Chenery HB and Bruno M (1962). Development Alternatives in an Open Economy: The Case of Israel. *The Economic Journal*. 72(285):79–103.

Chew R et al. (2020). Deep Neural Networks and Transfer Learning for Food Crop Identification in UAV Images. *Drones*. 4(1):7.

Cimoli M, Dosi G and Stiglitz JE (2009). *Industrial Policy and Development*. Oxford University Press.

Cirera X and Maloney WF (2017). *The Innovation Paradox: Developing-Country Capabilities and the Unrealized Promise of Technological Catch-Up*. World Bank. Washington (DC).

Cohen B (2006). Urbanization in developing countries: Current trends, future projections, and key challenges for sustainability. *Technology in Society*. Sustainable Cities. 28(1):63–80.

Crespi G, Fernandez-Arias E and Stein E, eds. (2014). *Rethinking Productive Development Sound Policies and Institutions for Economic Transformation*. Palgrave Macmillan. Basingstoke.

CTA (2019). The Digitalisation of African Agriculture Report, 2018–2019. The Technical Centre for Agricultural and Rural Cooperation (CTA). AJ Wageningen.

Day GS (2011). Closing the Marketing Capabilities Gap. *Journal of Marketing*. 75(4):183–195.

De Clercq M, Vats A and Biel A (2018). Agriculture 4.0 – The Future of Farming Technology. The World Government Summit. Dubai, United Arab Emirates. (accessed 8 June 2020).

Deloitte (2017). From Interpretation to prediction: Unleashing the Value of the Industrial Internet of Things. Deloitte China. Shanghai. (accessed 12 June 2020).

Deloitte (2020). The fourth industrial revolution: At the intersection of readiness and responsibility. Deloitte Insights. (accessed 26 May 2020).

Dennis C and Stahley K (2012). Universal Primary Education in Tanzania: The Role of School Expenses and Opportunity Costs. *Evans School Review*. 2(1).

Devanesan J (2020). How agritech solutions are shaping Myanmar's digital economy. Tech Wire Asia. Available at https://techwireasia.com/2020/06/how-agritech-solutions-are-shaping-myanmars-digital-economy/ (accessed 14 July 2020).

Development Initiatives (2020). Coronavirus and aid data: What the latest DAC data tell us. Briefing. Development Initiatives. Bristol.

Diyamett B and Mutambla M (2014). Foreign direct investment and local technological capabilities in least developed countries: some evidence from the Tanzanian manufacturing sector. *African Journal of Science, Technology, Innovation and Development*. 6(5):401–414.

Djankov S and Kiechel A-L (2020). The IMF and the World Bank can do more. In: Djankov S, and Panizza U, eds. *COVID in Developing Economies*. Centre for Economic Policy Research (CEPR). London: 374–385.

Djankov S and Panizza U, eds. (2020). *COVID in Developing Economies*. Centre for Economic Policy Research (CEPR). London.

Donald A, Lawin G and Rouanet L (2020). Reducing the Agricultural Gender Gap in Côte d'Ivoire : How has it Changed? Gender Innovation Lab. World Bank. Washington D.C.

Duval Y, Utoktham C and Kravchenko A (2018). Impact of implementation of digital trade facilitation on trade costs. ARTNeT Working Paper Series No. 174. Asia-Pacific Research and Training Network on Trade (ARTNeT). Bangkok.

Edquist C and Johnson B (1997). Institutions and organizations in systems of innovation. In: Edquist C, ed. *Systems of Innovation: Technologies, Institutions and Organizations*. Routledge. London and New York: 41–63.

EIU and UNDP (2018). Development 4.0: Opportunities and Challenges for Accelerating Progress towards the Sustainable Development Goals in Asia and the Pacific. Economist Intelligence Unit (EIU) and United Nations Development Programme (UNDP). New York. (accessed 15 May 2020).

Erkoc TE (2012). Estimation Methodology of Economic Efficiency: Stochastic Frontier Analysis vs Data Envelopment Analysis. *International Journal of Academic Research in Economics and Management Sciences*. 1(1):23.

REFERENCES

European Commission (2017). Industry 4.0 in agriculture: Focus on IoT aspects. Digital Transformation Monitor. European Commission. Brussels. (accessed 10 June 2020).

European Commission (2018a). Drones in agriculture. Digital Transformation Monitor. Internal Market, Industry, Entrepreneurship and SMEs, European Commission. Brussels.

European Commission (2018b). The application of the Union competition rules to the agricultural sector. Report from the Commission to the European Parliament and the Council No. COM(2018) 706 final. European Commission. Brussels.

European Commission (2020). Commission decides to partially withdraw Cambodia's preferential access to the EU market. European Commission -Trade news. Available at https://trade.ec.europa.eu/doclib/press/index.cfm?id=2113 (accessed 22 July 2020).

EY Global (2017). How digital agriculture and big data will help to feed a growing world. Available at https://www.ey.com/en_gl/advisory/how-digital-agriculture-and-big-data-will-help-to-feed-a-growing-world (accessed 8 June 2020).

Ezrachi A and Stucke ME (2016). *Virtual Competition. The Promise and Perils of the Algorithm-Driven Economy*. Harvard University Press. Cambridge, Massachusetts.

Fagerberg J and Verspagen B (2020). Technological revolutions, structural change & catching-up. Woking Paper No. 2020–012. United Nations University – Maastricht Economic and Social Research Institute on Innovation and Technology (UNU-MERIT). Maastricht. (accessed 31 March 2020).

FAO (2005). *Modernizing National Agricultural Extension Systems. A Practical Guide for Policy-Makers of Developing Countries*. Food and Agriculture Organization of the United Nations (FAO). Rome.

FAO (2009). Feeding the World in 2050. World Summit on Food Security, Rome 16–18 November 2009. Food and Agriculture Organization of the United Nations (FAO). Rome.

FAO (2011a). *Save and Grow: A Policymaker's Guide to the Sustainable Intensification of Smallholder Crop Production*. Food and Agriculture Organization of the United Nations (FAO). Rome.

FAO. (2011b). *Women in Agriculture: Closing the Gender Gap for Development*. The state of food and agriculture, No. 2010/11. (FAO). Rome.

FAO (2017). *The Future of Food and Agriculture – Trends and Challenges*. Food and Agriculture Organization of the United Nations (FAO). Rome.

FAO (2018a). *Future of Food and Agriculture 2018 – Alternative Pathways to 2050*. Food and Agriculture Organization of the United Nations. Rome.

FAO (2018b). *Our World Is Urbanizing Is Food on Your Agenda?* Food and Agriculture Organization of the United Nations (FAO). Rome.

FAO (2018c). *E-Agriculture in Action: Drones for Agriculture*. Food and Agriculture Organization of the United Nations (FAO). Bangkok.

FAO, IFAD, UNICEF, WFP and WHO (2019). *The State of Food Security and Nutrition in the World 2019. Safeguarding against Economic Slowdowns and Downturns*. Food and Agriculture Organization of the United Nations (FAO). Rome.

Feindouno S and Goujon M (2016). The retrospective economic vulnerability index, 2015 update. Working Paper No. 147. Fondation pour les études et recherches sur le développement international (Ferdi). Clermont-Ferrand.

Fetter R, Fuller A, Porcaro J and Sinai C (2020). You can't fight pandemics without power—electric power. Future Development, Brookings Institution. Available at https://www.brookings.edu/blog/future-development/2020/06/05/you-cant-fight-pandemics-without-power-electric-power/ (accessed 8 June 2020).

Foresight (2013). Future of manufacturing: a new era of opportunity and challenge for the UK. Project Report. The Government Office for Science. London. (accessed 26 May 2020).

Frey C and Osborne M (2013). The Future of Employment: How Susceptible Are Jobs to Computerisation? *Oxford Martin*. 114.

Friede M et al. (2011). WHO initiative to increase global and equitable access to influenza vaccine in the event of a pandemic: Supporting developing country production capacity through technology transfer. *Vaccine*. 29(Supplement 1): A2–A7.

Fuglie KO, Gautam M, Goyal A and Maloney WF (2020). *Harvesting Prosperity: Technology and Productivity Growth in Agriculture*. World Bank. Washington D.C.

Gadzala A (2018). 3D Printing: Shaping Africa's Future. Issue Brief. , Africa Center. Washington (DC) (accessed 11 June 2020).

Gagnon JE (2007). Productive Capacity, Product Varieties, and the Elasticities Approach to the Trade Balance. *Review of International Economics*. 15(4):639–659.

Garcia E (2014). The Need to Address Noncognitive Skills in the Education Policy Agenda. EPI Briefing Paper No. 386. Economic Policy Institute. Washington D.C. (accessed 26 July 2020).

Gauri P (2019). How the 5th Industrial Revolution Brings the Focus Back to Humanity. Thrive Global. Available at https://thriveglobal.in/stories/how-the-5th-industrial-revolution-brings-the-focus-back-to-humanity/ (accessed 26 May 2020).

Gebreeyesus M and Mohnen P (2011). Innovation performance and embeddedness in networks: evidence from the Ethiopian footwear cluster. MERIT Working Papers No. 2011–043. United Nations University – Maastricht Economic and Social Research Institute on Innovation and Technology (MERIT). (accessed 11 June 2020).

Gerszon Mahler D, Christoph Lakner, Castaneda Aguilar A and Wu H (2020). The impact of COVID-19 (Coronavirus) on global poverty: Why sub-Saharan Africa might be the region hardest hit. Available at https://blogs.worldbank.org/opendata/impact-covid-19-coronavirus-global-poverty-why-sub-saharan-africa-might-be-region-hardest (accessed 24 April 2020).

Gezgin E, Huang X, Samal P and Silva I (2017). Digital transformation: Raising supply-chain performance to new levels. McKinsey & Company.

Giri R, Quayyum SN and Yin R (2019). *Understanding Export Diversification: Key Drivers and Policy Implications*. International Monetary Fund. Washington (DC).

Glover D, Sumberg J, Ton G, Andersson J and Badstue L (2019). Rethinking technological change in smallholder agriculture. *Outlook on Agriculture*. 48(3):169–180.

Gökce Dessemond E (2019). Restoring competition in "'winner-took-all'" digital platform markets. UNCTAD Research Paper No. 40. UNCTAD. Geneva.

Grant Thornton (2018). 2018 CFO Insights on New Technologies. Survey Report. Grant Thornton.

Grow Asia (2019). *Driving AgriTech Adoption: Insights from Southeast Asia's Farmers*. Grow Asia Partnership Ltd. Singapore.

Grubler A (2012). Energy transitions research: Insights and cautionary tales. *Energy Policy*. 508–16.

GSMA (2016). *Agricultural Value-Added Services (Agri VAS) Toolkit 2.0*. GSMA. London.

GSMA (2020a). Mobile Gender Gap Report 2020. GSMA. London.

GSMA (2020b). Digital credit scoring for farmers: Opportunities for agritech companies in Myanmar. GSMA. London.

Guillaumont P (2009). *Caught in a Trap: Identifying the Least Developed Countries*. Economica. Paris.

Guillaumont P (2011). The concept of structural economic vulnerability and its relevance for the identification of the least developed countries and other purposes (Nature, measurement, and evolution). CDP Background Paper No. 12. United Nations publication. Sales No. ST/ESA/2011/CDP/12, New York (NY).

Guo X, Li G-R, McAleer M and Wong W-K (2018). Specification Testing of Production in a Stochastic Frontier Model. *Sustainability*. 10(9):3082.

Hagemann H, Landesmann M and Scazzieri R (2003). Introduction. In: Hagemann H,, Landesmann M, and Scazzieri R, eds. *The Economics of Structural Change*. Elgar. Cheltenham (UK) and Northampton (MA): xi–xlii.

Haldin-Herrgard T (2000). Difficulties in diffusion of tacit knowledge in organizations. *Journal of Intellectual Capital*. 1(4):357–365.

Hallward-Driemeier M and Nayyar G (2017). *Trouble in the Making?: The Future of Manufacturing-Led Development*. The World Bank.

Hausmann R and Chauvin J (2015). Moving to the Adjacent Possible: Discovering Paths for Export Diversification in Rwanda. CID Working Papers No. 294. Center for International Development at Harvard University. (accessed 10 October 2019).

Hausmann R and Panizza U (2003). On the determinants of Original Sin: an empirical investigation. *Journal of International Money and Finance*. Regional and International Implications of the Financial Instability in Latin America. 22(7):957–990.

Hausmann R and Rodrik D (2003). Economic development as self-discovery. *Journal of Development Economics*. 14th Inter-American Seminar on Economics. 72(2):603–633.

Helal Uddin Ahmed (2019). Pharmaceutical sector flourishing. The Financial Express. Available at https://www.thefinancialexpress.com.bd/views/pharmaceutical-sector-flourishing-1574867109 (accessed 24 July 2020).

Hendrix CS and Salehyan I (2012). Climate change, rainfall, and social conflict in Africa. *Journal of Peace Research*. 49(1):35–50.

Hofmann B, Shim I and Shin HS (2020). Original sin redux and policy responses in emerging market economies during the COVID-19 pandemic. In: Djankov S, and Panizza U, eds. *COVID in Developing Economies*. Centre for Economic Policy Research (CEPR). London: 353–361.

Htun P and Bock P (2017). Mobilizing Myanmar: A Smartphone Revolution Connects The Poor With Economic Opportunity. Myanmar FSP Framework Assessment and Feasibility Study. Partners Asia. Oakland (CA).

Hulten CR and Isaksson A (2007). Why Development Levels Differ: The Sources of Differential Economic Growth in a Panel of High and Low Income Countries. NBER Working Paper No. 13469. National Bureau of Economic Research (NBER). (accessed 22 April 2020).

REFERENCES

Huyer S (2016). Closing the gender gap in agriculture. *Gender Technology and Development*. 20(2):105–116.

Hyndman RJ, King ML, Pitrun I and Billah B (2005). Local linear forecasts using cubic smoothing splines. *Australian and New Zealand Journal of Statistics*. 47(1):87–99.

Iiyama M et al. (2018). Addressing the paradox – the divergence between smallholders' preference and actual adoption of agricultural innovations. *International Journal of Agricultural Sustainability*. 16(6):472–485.

ILO (2020a). Protecting migrant workers during the COVID-19 pandemic: Recommendations for Policymakers and Constituents. Policy Brief. International Labour Organization (ILO). Geneva.

ILO (2020b). ILO Monitor: COVID-19 and the world of work. Third edition April. Available at https://www.ilo.org/wcmsp5/groups/public/@dgreports/@dcomm/documents/briefingnote/wcms_743146.pdf (accessed 30 April 2020).

IMF (2017). Review of the Debt Sustainability Framework for Low Income Countries: Proposed Reforms. IMF Policy Paper. International Monetary Fund (IMF). Washington D.C. (accessed 16 October 2020).

IMF (2020a). *World Economic Outlook: The Great Lockdown (Chapter 1)*. International Monetary Fund (IMF). Washington D.C.

IMF (2020b). Six Charts Show How COVID-19 Is an Unprecedented Threat to Development in Sub-Saharan Africa. IMF. Available at https://www.imf.org/en/News/Articles/2020/04/13/na0413202-six-charts-show-how-covid-19-is-an-unprecedented-threat-to (accessed 17 July 2020).

IMF (2020c). *World Economic Outlook Update – June 2020*. International Monetary Fund (IMF). Washington (DC).

International Finance (2019). Technology uptake drives African logistics innovation. Logistics Magazine. https://internationalfinance.com/technology-uptake-drives-african-logistics-innovation/. (accessed 26 October 2020).

International Rescue Committee (2020). COVID-19 in humanitarian crises: a double emergency. International Rescue Committee. London.

Islam SN and Iversen K (2018). From "Structural Change" to "Transformative Change": Rationale and Implications. DESA Working Paper No. 155. Department of Economic and Social Affairs.

ITC (2018). What sells in e-commerce: New evidence from Asian LDCs. International Trade Centre (ITC). Geneva. (accessed 26 October 2020).

ITU (2019). *Measuring digital development: facts and figures 2019*. International Telecommunications Union (ITU). Geneva.

ITU (2020). *Measuring Digital Development: ICT Price Trends 2019*. International Telecommunication Union (ITU). Geneva, Switzerland.

Izmestiev A and Klingebiel S (2020). International (development) cooperation in a post-COVID-19 world: a new way of interaction or super-accelerator? Blog from the Development Policy Centre. Available at https://devpolicy.org/international-development-cooperation-in-a-post-covid-19-world-a-new-way-of-interaction-or-super-accelerator-20200501-1/ (accessed 17 July 2020).

de Jesus A (2019). Drones for Agriculture - Current Applications. Business Intelligence and Analytics. Emerj Artificial Intelligence Research. Woburn, MA. (accessed 9 July 2020).

John C, Ekpenyong EJ and Nworu CC (2019). Imputation of Missing Values in Economic and Financial Time Series Data Using Five Principal Component Analysis (PCA) Approaches. *Central Bank of Nigeria Journal of Applied Statistics*. (Vol. 10 No. 1):51–73.

Johnson O (2019). Digital Transformation of Africa: Hype or Reality? *2019 Annual Adebayo Adedeji Lecture*. United Nations Economic Commission for Africa (ECA). Palmeraie Palace Hotel, Marrakech.

Jones JW et al. (2017). Toward a new generation of agricultural system data, models, and knowledge products: State of agricultural systems science. *Agricultural Systems*. 15(5): 269–288.

de Jong RM and Sakarya N (2015). The Econometrics of the Hodrick-Prescott Filter. *The Review of Economics and Statistics*. 98(2):310–317.

Juma C (2015). Infrastructure for innovation. *New African Magazine*. https://newafricanmagazine.com/11031/. (accessed 12 June 2020).

Juma C (2017). Leapfrogging Progress. The Breakthrough Institute No. 7. https://thebreakthrough.org/journal/issue-7/leapfrogging-progress. (accessed 7 May 2020).

Kabir M and Salim R (2010). Can Gravity Model Explain BIMSTEC's Trade? *Journal of Economic Integration*. 25144–166.

Kalirajan KP and Salim RA (1997). Economic Reforms and Productive Capacity Realisation in Bangladesh: an Empirical Analysis. *Journal of Industrial Economics*. 45(4):387–403.

Kamasak R (2017). The contribution of tangible and intangible resources, and capabilities to a firm's profitability and market performance. *European Journal of Management and Business Economics*. 26(2):252–275.

Kerr S and England A (2020). 'They want us to leave' — foreign workers under pressure in the Gulf. Financial Times. Available at https://www.ft.com/content/77c2d7db-0ade-4665-9cb8-c82b72c2da66.

Khaltarkhuu BE and Sun T (2014). World Bank Data Blog. Available at https://blogs.worldbank.org/opendata/data-show-rise-domestic-credit-developing-countries (accessed 11 June 2020).

Kilonzi F and Kanai CK (2020). Electronic Cargo Tracking System and Its Effects on Revenue Realization in East Africa Member Countries. *International Journal of Scientific and Research Publications (IJSRP)*. 10(1):633–639.

Kim T, Ko W and Kim J (2019). Analysis and Impact Evaluation of Missing Data Imputation in Day-ahead PV Generation Forecasting. *Applied Sciences*. 9(1):204.

Klerkx L, Jakku E and Labarthe P (2019). A review of social science on digital agriculture, smart farming and agriculture 4.0: New contributions and a future research agenda. *NJAS – Wageningen Journal of Life Sciences*. 90–91100315.

Knabke T and Olbrich S (2018). Building novel capabilities to enable business intelligence agility: results from a quantitative study. *Information Systems and e-Business Management*. 16(3):493–546.

Knoblauch AM et al. (2019). Bi-directional drones to strengthen healthcare provision: experiences and lessons from Madagascar, Malawi and Senegal. *BMJ Global Health*. 4(4):e001541.

Kopf D (2018). Stop obsessing about GDP growth—GDP per capita is far more important. Quartz. Available at https://qz.com/1194634/the-world-bank-wont-stop-reporting-gdp-instead-of-gdp-per-capita-and-it-is-driving-me-crazy/ (accessed 17 June 2020).

Kose MA, Nagle P, Ohnsorge F and Sugawara N, eds. (2020). *Global Waves of Debt: Causes and Consequences*. The World Bank. Washington D.C.

Krishnan A, Banga K and Feyertag J (2020). AG-Platforms in East Africa: National and regional policy gaps. SET Supporting Economic Transformation. ODI and EIF. London. (accessed 6 August 2020).

Kumbhakar SC and Lovell CAK (2000). *Stochastic Frontier Analysis*. Cambridge University Press. Cambridge.

Kumbhakar SC and Tsionas EG (2011). Some Recent Developments in Efficiency Measurement in Stochastic Frontier Models. *Journal of Probability and Statistics*. 20111–25.

Kumbhakar SC, Wang H-J and Horncastle AP (2015). *A Practitioner's Guide to Stochastic Frontier Analysis Using Stata*. Cambridge University Press. Cambridge.

Laborde D, Martin W and Vos R (2020). Poverty and food insecurity could grow dramatically as COVID-19 spreads. IFPRI. Available at https://www.ifpri.org/blog/poverty-and-food-insecurity-could-grow-dramatically-covid-19-spreads (accessed 30 April 2020).

Lall S (1992). Technological capabilities and industrialization. *World Development*. 20(2):165–186.

Lange G-M, Wodon Q and Carey K, eds. (2018). *The Changing Wealth of Nations 2018: Building a Sustainable Future*. World Bank. Washington (DC).

Lawder D and Shalal A (2020a). IMF's Georgieva says world in recession, countries must "go big" on spending. Reuters. Available at https://www.reuters.com/article/us-health-coronavirus-imf-idUSKBN21E25S (accessed 15 July 2020).

Le Nestour A and Moscoviz L (2020). Five Findings from a New Phone Survey in Senegal. Center for Global Development. Available at https://www.cgdev.org/blog/five-findings-new-phone-survey-senegal (accessed 20 May 2020).

Llewellyn RS and Brown B (2020). Predicting Adoption of Innovations by Farmers: What is Different in Smallholder Agriculture? *Applied Economic Perspectives and Policy*. 42(1):100–112.

Mach KJ et al. (2019). Climate as a risk factor for armed conflict. *Nature*. 571(7764):193–197.

Maclean R and Marks S (2020). 10 African Countries Have No Ventilators. That's Only Part of the Problem. The New York Times. Available at https://www.nytimes.com/2020/04/18/world/africa/africa-coronavirus-ventilators.html (accessed 28 July 2020).

Mahmud F (2020). Bangladesh scientists create $3 kit. Can it help detect COVID-19? Aljazeera. Available at https://www.aljazeera.com/news/2020/03/bangladesh-scientists-create-3-kit-detect-covid-19-200323035631025.html (accessed 15 June 2020).

Makles A (2012). Stata Tip 110: How to Get the Optimal K-Means Cluster Solution. *The Stata Journal*. 12(2):347–351.

Manhas K (2019). Why the agtech boom isn't your typical tech disruption. *World Economic Forum, Global Agenda*.

Manyika J et al. (2013). Lions go digital: The Internet's transformative potential in Africa. Mckinsey & Company. (accessed 19 May 2020).

Marx B, Stoker T and Suri T (2013). The Economics of Slums in the Developing World. *Journal of Economic Perspectives*. 27(4):187–210.

REFERENCES

Massinga Loembé M et al. (2020). COVID-19 in Africa: the spread and response. *Nature Medicine*. 26(7): 999–1003.

McMillan M, Rodrik D and Sepúlveda C, eds. (2017). *Structural change, fundamentals, and growth: A framework and case studies*. International Food Policy Research Institute (IFPRI). Washington (DC).

McMillan MS and Rodrik D (2011). Globalization, structural change and productivity growth. NBER Working Paper No. 17143. National Bureau of Economic Research (NBER). Cambridge (MA). (accessed 26 October 2014).

Mekasha K (2015). Technology Adoption of Ethiopian Manufacturing firms: the Case of Textile and Leather Sector. Addis Ababa University. Available at http://etd.aau.edu.et/handle/123456789/8300 (accessed 29 July 2020).

Mensah J (2019). Sustainable development: Meaning, history, principles, pillars, and implications for human action: Literature review. *Cogent Social Sciences*. 5(1):1653531, Casadevall S R, ed, Cogent OA.

Merriott D (2016). Factors associated with the farmer suicide crisis in India. *Journal of Epidemiology and Global Health*. 6(4):217.

Mikalef P, Pappas IO, Krogstie J and Giannakos M (2018). Big data analytics capabilities: a systematic literature review and research agenda. *Information Systems and e-Business Management*. 16(3):547–578.

Miroudot S (2017). The Servicification of Global Value Chains: Evidence and Policy Implications. Presented at the UNCTAD Multi-year Expert Meeting on Trade, Services and Development, Geneva, 18–20 July 2017. Geneva. Available at https://unctad.org/meetings/en/Presentation/c1mem5_2017_124_S3_Miroudot_2.pdf.

Mittal S (2016). Role of Mobile-phone enabled Climate Information Services in gender-inclusive agriculture. *Gender, Technology and Development*. 20(2):200–217.

Mkandawire T (2011). Running while others walk: Knowledge and the challenge of Africa's development. *Africa Development*. 361–36.

Monga C and Lin JY (2019). Introduction: Structural transformation – Overcoming the cruse of destiny. In: Monga C, and Lin J Y, eds. *The Oxford Handbook of Structural Transformation*. Oxford University Press. Oxford: 1–32.

Moser CM and Barrett CB (2003). The disappointing adoption dynamics of a yield-increasing, low external-input technology: the case of SRI in Madagascar. *Agricultural Systems*. 76(3):1085–1100.

Moyo M-J and Lozansky T (2020). Working with Africa's apparel makers to produce personal protective equipment. World Bank Blogs. Available at https://blogs.worldbank.org/nasikiliza/working-africas-apparel-makers-produce-personal-protective-equipment (accessed 16 June 2020).

Mukasa AN (2018). Technology adoption and risk exposure among smallholder farmers: Panel data evidence from Tanzania and Uganda. *World Development*. 105: 299–309.

Mulla D and Khosla R (2015). Historical Evolution and Recent Advances in Precision Farming. In: Lal R, and Stewart B, eds. *Soil-Specific Farming*. CRC Press. Boca Raton, London and New York: 1–36.

Munnik J and Chen A (2020). Alcohol ban has South African distilleries pivoting to a new product. CNN. Available at https://www.cnn.com/2020/04/21/africa/south-africa-alcohol-ban-gin-distilleries-hand-sanitzer-spc-intl/index.html (accessed 16 June 2020).

Murray U, Gebremedhin Z, Brychkova G and Spillane C (2016). Smallholder Farmers and Climate Smart Agriculture: Technology and Labor-productivity Constraints amongst Women Smallholders in Malawi. *Gender, Technology and Development*. 20(2): 117–148.

Nadvi K and Schmitz H (1994). Industrial Clusters in Less Developed Countries: Review of Experiences and Research Agenda. Discussion Paper No. 339. Institute of Development Studies. Brighton, England.

National Research Council (1997). *Precision Agriculture in the 21st Century: Geospatial and Information Technologies in Crop Management*. National Academy of Sciences Press. Washington, DC.

Nayyar G, Vargas Da Cruz MJ and Zhu L (2018). Does Premature Deindustrialization Matter? The Role of Manufacturing versus Services in Development. Policy Research Working Paper No. WPS8596. The World Bank, 1–28. (accessed 16 June 2020).

Nazim Uddin Bhuiyan, Abdul Hakim and Fakhrul Alam (2019). Competitiveness and Global Prospects of Pharmaceutical Industry of Bangladesh : An Overview. *The Cost and Management*. 47(5):10–22.

Nebe C and Jalloh A-B (2020). Coronavirus pandemic driving tech solutions in sub-Saharan Africa. Deutsche Welle. Available at https://www.dw.com/en/coronavirus-pandemic-driving-tech-solutions-in-sub-saharan-africa/a-53175841 (accessed 28 July 2020).

Nkamleu GB (2011). Extensification versus intensification: Revisiting the role of land in African agricultural growth. *African Economic Conference*. United Nations Economic Commission for Africa.

Nordhaus WD (2002). Productivity Growth and the New Economy. *Brookings Papers on Economic Activity*. 2002(2):211–244.

Nuclear Threat Initiative, Johns Hopkins Center for Health Security and The Economist Intelligence Unit (2019). Global Health Security Index: building collective action and accountability. Nuclear Threat Initiative.

Obisesan A (2014). Gender differences in technology adoption and welfare impact among Nigerian Farming households. MPRA Paper No. 58920.

OECD (1978). Recommendation on Terms and Conditions of Aid. Available at http://www.oecd.org/dac/stats/31426776.pdf.

OECD (2016). *New Industrial Policies – OECD Science, Technology and Innovation Outlook 2016*. OECD. Paris.

OECD (2018). *Tax Challenges Arising from Digitalisation – Interim Report 2018: Inclusive Framework on BEPS*. OECD/G20 base erosion and profit shifting project. OECD. Paris.

OECD (2019a). Productivity Growth in the Digital Age. OECD. Paris.

OECD (2019b). *Climate Finance Provided and Mobilised by Developed Countries in 2013–17*. OECD.

OECD (2020a). Aid by DAC members increases in 2019 with more aid to the poorest countries. Available at https://www.oecd.org/dac/financing-sustainable-development/development-finance-data/ODA-2019-detailed-summary.pdf.

OECD (2020b). A systemic resilience approach to dealing with Covid-19 and future shocks. New Approaches to Economic Challenges (NAEC). Organisation for Economic Co-operation and Development (OECD). Paris. (accessed 10 June 2020).

OECD-DAC (2020). COVID-19 Global Pandemic – Joint Statement by the Development Assistance Committee of the Organisation for Economic Co-operation and Development. Tackling Coronavirus (COVID-19) – Contributing to a Global Effort. Development Assistance Committee of the Organisation for Economic Co-operation and Development (OECD-DAC). Paris.

Okereke C and Nielsen K (2020). The problem with predicting coronavirus apocalypse in Africa. Aljazeera. Available at https://www.aljazeera.com/indepth/opinion/problem-predicting-coronavirus-apocalypse-africa-200505103847843.html.

Oqubay A and Lin JY, eds. (2020). *The Oxford Handbook of Industrial Hubs and Economic Development*. Oxford Handbooks. Oxford University Press. Oxford, New York.

Osakwe PN and Kilolo J-M (2018). What drives export diversification? New evidence from a panel of developing countries. *UNCTAD Research Paper*.

Oseni G, Corral P, Goldstein M and Winters P (2015). Explaining Gender Differentials in Agricultural Production in Nigeria. *Agricultural Economics*. 46(3):281–462.

Palmer D, Nguyen Phillips A, Kiron D and Buckley N (2017). Achieving Digital Maturity. MIT Sloan Management Review No. 59180. MIT Sloan and Deloitte. Boston, MA. (accessed 2 July 2020).

Palmer D, Phillips A-N, Kiron D and Buckley N (2018). Coming of age digitally: Learning, leadership and legacy. MIT Sloan Management Review No. 59480. MIT Sloan and Deloitte Insights. Massachusetts.

Pappas IO, Mikalef P, Giannakos MN, Krogstie J and Lekakos G (2018). Big data and business analytics ecosystems: paving the way towards digital transformation and sustainable societies. *Information Systems and e-Business Management*. 16(3):479–491.

Peters K et al. (2020). Climate change, conflict and fragility: an evidence review and recommendations for research and action. Overseas Development Institute (ODI). London. (accessed 14 June 2020).

PwC (2017). Winning in mature markets. PricewaterhouseCoopers (PwC). Singapore.

Ray DK et al. (2019). Climate change has likely already affected global food production. *PLOS ONE*. 14(5):e0217148.

Reuters (2020b). "All my dreams are shattered": coronavirus crushes Asia's garment industry. 19 May.

Rodrik D (2011). *The Globalization Paradox: Democracy and the Future of the World Economy*. Norton. New York.

Rodrik D (2016). Premature deindustrialization. *Journal of Economic Growth*. 21(1):1–33.

Rodrik D (2018). New technologies, global value chains, and the developing economies. *Pathways for Prosperity Commission Background Paper Series; no. 1*. University of Oxford, Pathways for Prosperity Commission.

Roest J and Konijnendijk V (2018). Smartphones Are Common in Myanmar: Is Digital Finance Far Behind? CGAP. Available at https://www.cgap.org/blog/smartphones-are-common-myanmar-digital-finance-far-behind (accessed 6 July 2020).

Roland Berger (2019). Farming 4.0: How precision agriculture might save the world. Precision farming improves farmer livelihoods and ensures sustainable food production. Roland Berger Focus. Roland Berger. Frankfurt.

Røttingen J-A and Chamas C (2012). A New Deal for Global Health R&D? The Recommendations of the Consultative Expert Working Group on Research and Development (CEWG). *PLoS Medicine*. 9(5).

Saiz-Rubio V and Rovira-Más F (2020). From Smart Farming towards Agriculture 5.0: A Review on Crop Data Management. *Agronomy*. 10(2):207.

Sako M and Zylberberg E (2019). Supplier strategy in global value chains: shaping governance and profiting from upgrading. *Socio-Economic Review*. 17(3):687–707.

Sapsford R, Tsourapas G, Abbott P and Teti A (2019). Corruption, Trust, Inclusion and Cohesion in North Africa and the Middle East. *Applied Research in Quality of Life*. 14(1): 1–21.

Savić D (2019). From Digitization, Through Digitalization, to Digital Transformation. *Medford*. 43(1): 36–39.

Scarpetta S, Bassanini A, Pilat D and Schreyer P (2000). Economic Growth In The OECD Area: Recent Trends At The Aggregate And Sectoral Level. *SSRN Electronic Journal*. http://dx.doi.org/10.2139/ssrn.241568.

Schmidhuber J and Meyer S (2014). Has the Treadmill Changed Direction? WTO Negotiations in the Light of a Potential New Global Agricultural Market Environment. Overview Paper. E15Initiative. International Centre for Trade and Sustainable Development (ICTSD) and World Economic Forum. Geneva.

Schumpeter JA (1926). *The Theory of Economic Development: An Inquiry into Profits, Capital, Credit, Interest, and the Business Cycle*. Transaction Publishers. New Brunswick (NJ) and London.

Shah S, Soriano CB and Coutroubis AD (2017). Is big data for everyone? the challenges of big data adoption in SMEs. *2017 IEEE International Conference on Industrial Engineering and Engineering Management (IEEM)*. IEEE. Singapore: 803–807.

Sher D (2019). Five Footwear Industry Leaders That Use 3D Printing for Production Today: AM is clearly the way to go at adidas, Nike, New Balance, Reebok and Under Armor. Available at https://www.smartechanalysis.com/blog/five-footwear-industry-companies-use-3d-printing-today/ (accessed 5 May 2020)

Singh KM, Kumari P, Ahmad N and Shekhar D (2019). Role of women in agriculture: Technology-led, gender sensitive policy options. MPRA Paper No. 98070. University Library of Munich, Germany.

SmarTech (2019). SmarTech Issues New Report Projecting Footwear AM and 3D Printed Footwear Will Generate $6.5 Billion Yearly Revenues by 2029. News article. SmarTech Analysis. Crozet, VA. (accessed 5 May 2020).

Sodano V and Verneau F (2014). Competition Policy and Food Sector in the European Union. *Journal of International Food & Agribusiness Marketing*. 26(3):155–172.

Sorbe S, Gal P and Millot V (2018). Can productivity still grow in service-based economies? Literature overview and preliminary evidence from OECD countries. Economics Department Working Papers No. 1531. Organisation for Economic Co-operation and Development (OECD). Paris.

Sovacool BK, Tan-Mullins M, Ockwell D and Newell P (2017). Political economy, poverty, and polycentrism in the Global Environment Facility's Least Developed Countries Fund (LDCF) for Climate Change Adaptation. *Third World Quarterly*. 38(6): 1249–1271.

Sparling N (2018). Impact Terra Raises $3m to Support Smallholder Farmers in Myanmar. AgFunder. https://agfundernews.com/impact-terra-social-enterprise-myanmar-seed.html. (accessed 14 July 2020).

Streatfield PK and Karar ZA (2008). Population Challenges for Bangladesh in the Coming Decades. *Journal of Health, Population, and Nutrition*. 26(3): 261.

Sumner A, Hoy C and Ortiz-Juarez E (2020). Estimates of the impact of COVID-19 on global poverty. WIDER Working Paper No. 43/2020. United Nations University – World Institute for Development Economic Research (UNU-WIDER). Helsinki. (accessed 24 April 2020).

Sumner A, Ortiz-Juarez E and Hoy C (2020). Precarity and the pandemic: COVID-19 and poverty incidence, intensity, and severity in developing countries. WIDER Working Paper No. 77. United Nations University – World Institute for Development Economic Research (UNU-WIDER). Helsinki. (accessed 12 June 2020).

Surmeier A (2020). Dynamic capability building and social upgrading in tourism – Potentials and limits of sustainability standards. *Journal of Sustainable Tourism*. 28(10):1498–1518.

Sustainable Infrastructure Partnership et al. (2020). Investing in sustainable and resilient infrastructure – "Principles for recovery." United Nations Environment Programme. Available at https://www.greengrowthknowledge.org/sites/default/files/downloads/resource/SustainableInfrastructure-PrinciplesforRecovery.pdf.

Talavera JM et al. (2017). Review of IoT applications in agro-industrial and environmental fields. *Computers and Electronics in Agriculture*. 142283–297.

Tantalaki N, Souravlas S and Roumeliotis M (2019). Data-Driven Decision Making in Precision Agriculture: The Rise of Big Data in Agricultural Systems. *Journal of Agricultural & Food Information*. 20(4):344–380.

Thirlwall AP (1979). The balance of payments constraint as an explanation of the international growth rate differences. *PSL Quarterly Review*. 32(128):.

Thu HL (2020). This tech startup is improving yields for farmers in Myanmar. TechInAsia. Available at https://

www.techinasia.com/village-link-yields-farmers (accessed 14 July 2020).

Thum-Thysen A, Voigt P, Bilbao-Osorio B, Maier C and Ognyanova D (2017). Unlocking Investment in Intangible Assets. European Economy Discussion Papers No. 047. European Commission. Brussels.

TRALAC (2018). Tanzania, Uganda survive as Rwanda is removed from Agoa beneficiaries list. TRALAC – Trade Law Centre. Available at https://www.tralac.org/news/article/12904-tanzania-uganda-survive-as-rwanda-is-removed-from-agoa-beneficiaries-list.html (accessed 22 July 2020).

Travaly Y, Mare A and Kunda E (2020). Learning from the best: Evaluating COVID-19 responses and what Africa can learn. Next Einstein Forum. Kigali, Rwanda.

Tregenna F (2015). Deindustrialisation, structural change and sustainable economic growth. UNU-MERIT Working Paper No. 2015–032. United Nations University – Maastricht Economic and Social Research Institute on Innovation and Technology (UNU-MERIT). Maastricht. (accessed 18 August 2015).

Truman E (2020). The G-20 must wake up to the COVID-19 crisis. PIIE – Realtime Economic Issues Watch. Available at https://www.piie.com/blogs/realtime-economic-issues-watch/g-20-must-wake-covid-19-crisis (accessed 15 July 2020).

Tsan M, Totapally S, Hailu M and Addom BK (2019). The Digitalisation of African Agriculture Report 2018–2019. Technical Centre for Agricultural and Rural Cooperation (CTA) and Dalberg Advisors. Wageningen. (accessed 13 July 2020).

Udry C (2010). The economics of agriculture in Africa: Notes toward a research program. *African Journal of Agricultural and Resource Economics*. 5(1).

UN (2020). Policy Brief: The Impact of COVID-19 on Food Security and Nutrition. United Nations (UN). New York.

UN DESA (2019). *World Population Prospects 2019*. United Nations Department of Economic and Social Affairs (UN DESA), Population Division. New York.

UN DESA (2020). COVID-19 pandemic deals a huge blow to the manufacturing exports from LDCs. Policy Brief No. 71. United Nations Department of Economic and Social Affairs (UNDESA). New York. (accessed 26 May 2020).

UN WOMEN (2019). The gender gap in agricultural productivity in Sub-Saharan Africa: Causes, costs and solutions. Policy Brief No. 11. United Nations Entity for Gender Equality and the Empowerment of Women (UN Women).

UN Women (2020). As COVID-19 exposes the fault lines of gender equality, a strong focus on violence against women at the UN General Assembly. Available at https://www.unwomen.org/en/news/stories/2020/9/press-release-focus-on-violence-against-women-at-the-un-general-assembly.

UNCTAD (forthcoming). *UNCTAD's Productive Capacities Index: The Methodological Approach and Results*. United Nations Conference on Trade and Development (UNCTAD). Geneva.

UNCTAD (1999). Policies and non-fiscal measures for upgrading SME clusters - an assessment. Trade and Development Board Commission on Enterprise, Business Facilitation and Development Fourth Session Geneva, 19-23 July 1999 Item 3 of the provisional agenda No. TD/B/COM.3/22. UNCTAD. Geneva.

UNCTAD (2006). *The Least Developed Countries Report 2006: Developing Productive Capacities*. United Nations publication. Sales No. E.06.II.D.9. New York and Geneva.

UNCTAD (2007). *The Least Developed Countries Report 2007: Knowledge, Technological Learning and Innovation for Development*. United Nations publication. Sales No. E.07.II.D.8. New York and Geneva.

UNCTAD (2009). *The Least Developed Countries Report 2009: The State and Development Governance*. United Nations publication. Sales No. E.09.II.D.9. New York and Geneva.

UNCTAD (2010). *The Least Developed Countries Report 2010: Towards a New International Development Architecture for LDCs*. United Nations publication. Sales No. E.10.II.D.5. New York and Geneva.

UNCTAD (2012). *Economic Development in Africa Report 2012: Structural Transformation and Sustainable Development in Africa*. United Nations publication. Sales No. E.12.II.D.10. New York and Geneva.

UNCTAD (2013a). *The Least Developed Countries Report 2013: Growth with Employment for Inclusive and Sustainable Development*. United Nations publication. Sales No. E.13.II.D.1. New York and Geneva.

UNCTAD (2013b). *Trade and Environment Review 2013: Make Agriculture Truly Sustainable Now for Food Security in a Changing Climate*. United Nations. New York and Geneva.

UNCTAD (2014). *The Least Developed Countries Report 2014: Growth with Structural Transformation – A Post-2015 Development Agenda*. United Nations publication. Sales No. E.14.II.D.7. New York and Geneva.

UNCTAD (2015a). *The Least Developed Countries Report 2015: Transforming Rural Economies*. United Nations publication. Sales No. E.15.II.D.7. New York and Geneva.

REFERENCES

UNCTAD (2015b). *The Least Developed Countries Report 2015: Transforming Rural Economies*. United Nations publication. Sales No. E.15.II.D.7. New York and Geneva.

UNCTAD (2015c). *Making Trade Work for Least Developed Countries: A Handbook on Mainstreaming Trade*. Trade and Poverty Paper Series, No. 5. Geneva.

UNCTAD (2015d). *Trade and Development Report 2015: Making the International Financial Architecture Work for Development*. United Nations publication. Sales No. E.15.II.D.4. New York and Geneva.

UNCTAD (2016a). *The Least Developed Countries Report 2016: The Path to Graduation and Beyond: Making the Most of the Process*. United Nations publication. Sales No. E.16.II.D.9. New York and Geneva.

UNCTAD (2016b). *Trade and Development Report 2016: Structural Transformation for Inclusive and Sustained Growth*. United Nations publication. Sales No. E.16.II.D.5. New York and Geneva.

UNCTAD (2016c). *Economic Development in Africa Report 2016: Debt Dynamics and Development Finance in Africa*. United Nations publication. Sales No. E.16.II.D.3. New York and Geneva.

UNCTAD (2016d). Trade misinvoicing in primary commodities in developing countries: The cases of Chile, Côte d'Ivoire, Nigeria, South Africa and Zambia. United Nations Conference on Trade and Development (UNCTAD). New York and Geneva.

UNCTAD (2016e). Nairobi Maafikiano – From decision to action: Moving towards an inclusive and equitable global economic environment for trade and development. No. TD/519/Add.2. United Nations Conference on Trade and Development (UNCTAD). New York and Geneva.

UNCTAD (2017a). *The Least Developed Countries Report 2017: Transformational Energy Access*. The least developed countries report, No. 2017. United Nations publication. Sales No. E.17.II.D.6. New York and Geneva.

UNCTAD (2017b). Activities carried out in the implementation of the Programme of Action for the Least Developed Countries for the Decade 2011–2020: Sixth progress report. Available at https://unctad.org/meetings/en/SessionalDocuments/tdb64d7_en.pdf.

UNCTAD (2017c). *The Least Developed Countries Report 2017: Transformational Energy Access*. The least developed countries report, No. 2017. United Nations publication. Sales No. E.17.II.D.6. New York and Geneva.

UNCTAD (2017d). Information Economy Report 2017: Digitalization, trade and development. United Nations publication. Sales No. E.17.II.D.8, Geneva.

UNCTAD (2017e). *Trade and Development Report 2017: Beyond Austerity: Towards A Global New Deal*. United Nations publication. Sales No. E.17.II.D.5. New York and Geneva.

UNCTAD (2018a). *The Least Developed Countries Report 2018: Entrepreneurship for Structural Transformation: Beyond Business as Usual*. United Nations publication. Sales No. E.18.II.D.6. New York and Geneva.

UNCTAD (2018b). Selected sustainable development trends in the least developed countries. United Nations Conference on Trade and Development (UNCTAD). Geneva.

UNCTAD (2018c). *Achieving the Sustainable Development Goals in the Least Developed Countries: A Compendium of Policy Options*. UNCTAD. New York and Geneva.

UNCTAD (2018d). *Trade and Development Report 2018: Power, Platforms and the Free Trade Delusion*. United Nations publication. Sales No. E.18.II.D.7. New York and Geneva.

UNCTAD (2018e). Financing for development: Debt and debt sustainability and interrelated systemic issues. TD/B/EFD/2/2. Available at https://unctad.org/meetings/en/SessionalDocuments/tdb_efd2d2_en.pdf.

UNCTAD (2018f). Handbook on Duty-Free Quota-Free market access and rules of origin for the Least Developed Countries. United Nations Conference on Trade and Development (UNCTAD). New York and Geneva.

UNCTAD (2018g). *World Investment Report 2018: Investment and New Industrial Policies*. United Nations Conference on Trade and Development (UNCTAD). United Nations publication. Sales No. E.18.II.D.4. New York and Geneva.

UNCTAD (2019a). Selected sustainable development trends in the least developed countries. United Nations Conference on Trade and Development (UNCTAD). Geneva.

UNCTAD (2019b). *The Least Developed Countries Report 2019: The Present and Future of External Development Finance – Old Dependence, New Challenges*. United Nations publication. Sales No. E.20.II.D.2. New York and Geneva.

UNCTAD (2019c). Activities carried out in the implementation of the Programme of Action for the Least Developed Countries for the Decade 2011–2020. Available at https://unctad.org/meetings/en/SessionalDocuments/tdb66d2_en.pdf.

UNCTAD (2019d). *Digital Economy Report 2019: Value Creation and Capture : Implications for Developing Countries*. United Nations publication. Sales No. E.19.II.D.17. New York and Geneva.

UNCTAD (2019e). UNCTAD Rapid eTrade Readiness Assessments of Least Developed Countries: Policy Impact and Way Forward. No. UNCTAD/DTL/STICT/2019/7. United Nations Conference on Trade and Development (UNCTAD). Geneva.

UNCTAD (2019f). Competition issues in the digital economy. Trade and Development Board Trade and Development Commission Intergovernmental Group of Experts on Competition Law and Policy, Eighteenth session Geneva, 10–12 July 2019 No. TD/B/C.I/CLP/54. UNCTAD. Geneva.

UNCTAD (2019g). *Economic Development in Africa Report 2019: Made in Africa – Rules of Origin for Enhanced Intra-African Trade*. United Nations publication. Sales No. E.19.II.D.7. New York and Geneva.

UNCTAD (2019h). *Commodities and Development Report 2019: Commodity Dependence, Climate Change and the Paris Agreement*. United Nations publication. Sales No. E.19.II.D.18. New York and Geneva.

UNCTAD (2019i). *World Investment Report 2019: Special Economic Zones*. United Nations publication. Sales No. E.19.II.D.12. New York and Geneva.

UNCTAD (2019j). *Trade and Development Report 2019: Financing A Global Green New Deal*. United Nations publication. Sales No. E.19.II.D.15. New York and Geneva.

UNCTAD (2020a). *World Investment Report 2020: International Production beyond the Pandemic*. United Nations publication. Sales No. E.20.II.D.23. New York and Geneva.

UNCTAD (2020b). *Trade and Development Repot 2020: From Global Pandemic to Prosperity for All: Avoiding Another Lost Decade*. United Nations publication. Sales No. E.20.II.D.30. New York and Geneva.

UNCTAD (2020c). The Covid-19 Shock to Developing Countries: Towards a "whatever it takes" programme for the two-thirds of the world's population being left behind. United Nations Conference on Trade and Development (UNCTAD). Geneva.

UNCTAD (2020d). *Building and Utilizing Productive Capacities in Africa and the Least Developed Countries – A Holistic and Practical Guide*. UNCTAD. Geneva.

UNCTAD (2020e). Ethiopia Science, Technology and Innovation Policy Review. Science, Technology and Innovation Policy Review. UNCTAD. Geneva. (accessed 9 June 2020).

UNCTAD (2020f). Estimates of Global E-Commerce 2018. UNCTAD Technical Notes on ICT for Development No. 15. UNCTAD. Geneva.

UNCTAD (2020g). *Economic Development in Africa Report 2020: Tackling Illicit Financial Flows for Sustainable Development in Africa*. United Nations publication. Sales No. E.20.II.D.21. New York and Geneva.

UNCTAD (2020h). The coronavirus shock: a story of another global crisis foretold. United Nations Conference on Trade and Development (UNCTAD). Geneva.

UNCTAD (2020i). South-South Cooperation at the time of Covid-19: building solidarity among developing countries. United Nations Conference on Trade and Development (UNCTAD). Geneva.

UNCTAD (2020j). From the Great Lockdown to the Great Meltdown: Developing Country Debt in the Time of Covid-19. United Nations Conference on Trade and Development (UNCTAD). Geneva.

UNCTAD (2020k). The COVID-19 crisis: Accentuating the need to bridge digital divides. Digital Economy Update No. UNCTAD/DTL/INF/2020/1. (UNCTAD). Geneva.

UNCTAD (2020l). Ugandan e-commerce platforms power recovery from COVID-19 crisis. Available at https://unctad.org/news/ugandan-e-commerce-platforms-power-recovery-covid-19-crisis (accessed 27 October 2020).

UNCTAD and FAO (2017). *Commodities and Development Report 2017: Commodity Markets, Economic Growth and Development*. Commodities and development report, No. 2017. United Nations. New York Geneva.

UNCTAD, OECD and WTO (2020). UNCTAD-OECD-WTO Report on G20 Trade and Investment Measures (23rd Report, Joint Summary) June. Available at https://unctad.org/en/PublicationsLibrary/unctad_oecd2020d23_summary_en.pdf.

UNCTAD and World Bank (2018). *The Unseen Impact of Non-Tariff Measures: Insights from a New Database*. United Nations publication. Sales No. UNCTAD/DITC/TAB/2018/2. Geneva.

UNECA (2015). *Economic Report on Africa 2015: Industrializing through Trade*. United Nations Economic Commission for Africa. Addis Ababa.

UNECA (2019). *Economic Report on Africa 2019: Fiscal Policy for Financing Sustainable Development in Africa*. United Nations Economic Commission for Africa. Addis Ababa.

UNECA (2020). COVID-19: Lockdown exit strategies for Africa | United Nations Economic Commission for Africa. United Nations Economic Commission for Africa (UNECA). Addis Ababa, Ethiopia. (accessed 20 May 2020).

UNECE (2020). Trade Facilitation White Paper on Smart Containers. Real-time Smart Container data for supply chain excellence. White Paper No. ECE/

REFERENCES

TRADE/446. United Nations Economic Commission for Europe (UNECE). Geneva.

Ungar M (2018). Systemic resilience: principles and processes for a science of change in contexts of adversity. *Ecology and Society*. 23(4) https://doi.org/10.5751/ES-10385-230434.

UNHCR (2019). Global Trends 2018: Forced Displacement in 2018. Global Trends. United Nations High Commissioner for Refugees (UNHCR). (accessed 29 May 2020).

UNIDO (2013). *Industrial Development Report 2013: Sustaining Employment Growth: The Role of Manufacturing and Structural Change*. United Nations publication. Sales No. E.13.II.B.46. Vienna.

UNIDO (2018). *UNIDO Competitive Industrial Performance Report 2018*. United Nations Industrial Development Organization (UNIDO). Vienna.

UNIDO (2019a). *Industrial Development Report 2020: Industrializing in the Digital Age*. United Nations Industrial Development Organization (UNIDO). Vienna.

UNIDO (2019b). Absorbing Advanced Digital Production Technologies to Foster Industrialization Evidence from Case Studies in Developing Countries. Background document prepared for the Industrial Development Report 2020. United Nations Industrial Development Organization (UNIDO). Vienna.

United Nations (2001). Programme of Action for the Least Developed Countries – Adopted by the Third United Nations Conference on the Least Developed Countries in Brussels on 20 May 2001. United Nations publication. Sales No. A/CONF.191/11, New York (NY).

United Nations (2011). Programme of Action for the Least Developed Countries for the Decade 2011–2020. No. A/CONF.219/3/Rev.1. United Nations publication. Sales No. A/CONF.219/3/Rev.1, Istanbul.

United Nations (2015a). Paris Agreement. United Nations. Paris.

United Nations (2015b). Resolution adopted by the General Assembly on 3 June 2015: 69/283. Sendai Framework for Disaster Risk Reduction 2015–2030. No. A/RES/69/283. United Nations. Sendai.

United Nations (2015c). Transforming our world: the 2030 Agenda for Sustainable Development. No. A/RES/70/1. United Nations. New York (NY).

United Nations (2019). Climate change and poverty. Report of the Special Rapporteur on extreme poverty and human rights No. A/HRC/41/39. United Nations. New York. (accessed 12 June 2019).

United Nations (2020a). *Financing for Sustainable Development Report 2020*. United Nations, United Nations Inter-Agency Task Force on Financing for Development (UNIATFFD). New York.

United Nations (2020b). The parlous state of poverty eradication. Report of the Special Rapporteur on extreme poverty and human rights No. A/HRC/44/40. United Nations. New York. (accessed 12 June 2019).

UN-OHRLLS (2017). The Africa Regional Report on Improving Transit Cooperation, Trade and Trade Facilitation for the benefit of the landlocked developing countries. Current status and policy implications. UN-OHRLLS. New York.

USAID (2015). Supporting Digital Financial Services in Myanmar: Assessment of the potential for digital financial services in agriculture value chains. US Agency for International Development (USAID). Washington D.C.

Uzoamaka JN, Olagunju KO, Njuguna-Mungai E and Mausch K (2019). Is there any gender gap in the production of legumes in Malawi? Evidence from the Oaxaca–Blinder decomposition model. *Review of Agricultural, Food and Environmental Studies*. 10069–92.

Valensisi G (2020). COVID-19 and global poverty: Are LDCs being left behind? *The European Journal of Development Research*. https://doi.org/10.10/s41287-020-00314-8.

Van Reenen J (2019). Where Will Future Jobs and Growth Come From? Presented at the LSE Public Lectures and Events. London. Available at https://www.lse.ac.uk/Events/2019/05/20190522t1830vOT/Where-Will-Future-Jobs-and-Growth-Come-From.aspx (accessed 1 September 2020).

Vandycke N (2012). Transformation through infrastructure. The World Bank. Washington D.C. (accessed 12 June 2020).

Venter I (2020). Clothing, textile industry in project to produce face masks locally. Available at https://www.engineeringnews.co.za/article/clothing-textile-industry-in-project-to-produce-face-masks-locally-2020-03-31 (accessed 16 June 2020).

Vercillo S, Weis T and Luginaah I (2020). A bitter pill: smallholder responses to the new green revolution prescriptions in northern Ghana. *International Journal of Sustainable Development & World Ecology*. 1–11.

Vos R, Martin W and Laborde D (2020). How much will global poverty increase because of COVID-19? IFPRI. Available at https://www.ifpri.org/blog/how-much-will-global-poverty-increase-because-covid-19 (accessed 30 April 2020).

de Vries GJ, Timmer MP and de Vries K (2015). Structural transformation in Africa: Static gains, dynamic losses. *Journal of Development Studies*. GGDC Research Memorandum. 1–15.

Wade R (2004). *Governing the Market: Economic Theory and the Role of Government in East Asian Industrialization*. Princeton University Press. Princeton (NJ) and Oxford (UK).

WEF (2017). Supply Chain and Transport Briefing. World Economic Forum (WEF). Geneva. (accessed 1 April 2020).

Whitfield L, Staritz C, Melese AT and Azizi S (2020). Technological Capabilities, Upgrading, and Value Capture in Global Value Chains: Local Apparel and Floriculture Firms in Sub-Saharan Africa. *Economic Geography*. 96(3):195–218.

WHO (2019). Children: reducing mortality. World Health Organization (WHO). Available at https://www.who.int/news-room/fact-sheets/detail/children-reducing-mortality (accessed 25 May 2020).

Wijeweera A, Villano R and Dollery B (2010). Economic Growth and FDI Inflows: A Stochastic Frontier Analysis. *The Journal of Developing Areas*. 43(2):143–158.

WIPO (2017). *Global Innovation Index 2017: Innovation Feeding the World*. World Intellectual Property Organization (WIPO). Geneva.

Wolfert S, Ge L, Verdouw C and Bogaardt M-J (2017). Big Data in Smart Farming – A review. *Agricultural Systems*. 15(3): 69–80.

Woolcock M, Easterly W and Ritzen J (2000). *On Good Politicians and Bad Policies: Social Cohesion, Institutions, and Growth*. Policy Research Working Papers. The World Bank.

World Bank (2011). *More and Better Jobs in South Asia*. World Bank. Washington (DC).

World Bank (2020a). Combined Project Information Documents/Integrated Safeguards Datasheet (PID/ISDS). Myanmar Food and Agriculture System Project (P164448) No. PIDISDSA25232. World Bank. Washington (DC).

World Bank (2020b). COVID-19 crisis through a migration lens. Migration and Development Brief No. 32. World Bank. Washington (DC).

World Bank (2020c). *Global Economic Prospects, June 2020*. World Bank. Washington (DC).

World Economic Forum (2016). The Future of Jobs Employment, Skills and Workforce Strategy for the Fourth Industrial Revolution. Global Challenge Insight Report. World Economic Forum. Davos.

Worldwide Governance Indicators (2020). Worldwide Governance Indicators. Available at https://info.worldbank.org/governance/wgi/ (accessed 29 May 2020).

WTO (2019). Market access for products and services of export interest to Least Developed Countries. No. WT/COMTD/LDC/W/67. World Trade Organisation (WTO), Sub-Committee on Least Developed Countries. Geneva, Switzerland.

WTTC (2020). Travel & tourism recovery scenarios 2020 and economic impact from COVID-19. Research Note. World Travel and Tourism Council, London.

Xu H, Guo H, Zhang J and Dang A (2018). Facilitating dynamic marketing capabilities development for domestic and foreign firms in an emerging economy. *Journal of Business Research*. 86141–152.

Yigezu YA et al. (2018). Enhancing adoption of agricultural technologies requiring high initial investment among smallholders. *Technological Forecasting and Social Change*. 134199–206.

Yonah IB, Mourice SK, Tumbo SD, Mbilinyi BP and Dempewolf J (2018). Unmanned aerial vehicle-based remote sensing in monitoring smallholder, heterogeneous crop fields in Tanzania. *International Journal of Remote Sensing*. 39(15–16):5453–5471.

Zhao C et al. (2017). Temperature increase reduces global yields of major crops in four independent estimates. *Proceedings of the National Academy of Sciences*. 114(35):9326–9331.

Zhu P (2019). Five Visible and Invisible Forces Behind Digital Innovation. Innovation Management. Available at https://innovationmanagement.se/2019/03/20/five-visible-and-invisible-forces-behind-digital-innovation/ (accessed 26 July 2020).